Jens Gulden

Methodical Support
for Model-Driven
Software Engineering
with Enterprise Models

Logos Verlag Berlin

λογος

Bibliografische Information der Deutschen Nationalbibliothek

Die Deutsche Nationalbibliothek verzeichnet diese Publikation in der
Deutschen Nationalbibliografie; detaillierte bibliografische Daten sind
im Internet über http://dnb.d-nb.de abrufbar.

ISBN 978-3-8325-3536-0

Logos Verlag Berlin GmbH
Comeniushof, Gubener Str. 47,
D-10243 Berlin

Tel.:   +49 (0)30 / 42 85 10 90
Fax: +49 (0)30 / 42 85 10 92
http://www.logos-verlag.de

Abstract

A central research goal in information systems science is to achieve a close alignment between business processes, structures of organizations, and the functionality offered by enterprise information systems (EISs), which are used to support the work of organizations. Traditionally, there is a methodical gap between describing organizational incidents and software functionality, because organizations and software systems are understood and constructed with different terminology and on different levels of abstractions, typically also by differently educated groups of people.

In enterprise models (EMs), dedicated modeling language elements are used to express knowledge about processes in organizations, e. g., about who is responsible for performing actions, what resources are involved, and what strategic goals are intended to be realized by organizational means. The work at hand shows, how EISs can be created based on this knowledge, which serve as supporting software for performing these tasks.

Software development traditionally has to face a distinction between people who work with software, and people who create software. With the use of EMs, a chance opens up to closer involve the users of software systems into the process of developing and configuring the software. Building software from enterprise models is desirable, because once a dedicated relationship between enterprise models and software functionality has been established by a development method, involved users and responsible stakeholders can adapt the software according to their business needs, without having to deal with programming or technical details. This increases efficiency both in developing and operating the software, because software functionality is derived from requirements implicitly stated in EMs. Such a development procedure also promises to more efficiently adapt EIS to dynamic changes in organizations and their environment. Trust in the developed software system is also increased by involving users and responsible stakeholders into specifying the resulting software functionality.

The following research work elaborates a software development method to create EISs from EMs. The method is designed as a generic framework to work with any enterprise modeling language, and to generate software for any target system platforms, after appropriate configuration. Fundamental challenges in methodically transforming conceptual models to implementation artifacts, are faced by involving auxiliary models into the software creation process, and splitting up the transformation procedure into multiple dedicated phases. Using this approach, the abstraction gap between conceptual enterprise models and technical implementation artifacts gets systematically bridged by introduced methodical concepts, in order to perform an ontological turn from the bird's-eye-view description perspective of enterprise models, to an internal system perspective describing technical details of a software system.

The elaborated method provides means for efficiently guiding modelers and software developers through the software engineering process. It can be configured at multiple points, to choose the degree of automation on a continuum between a manually supervised development process with methodically scheduled manual development steps, and a zerocoding 100% code generation approach.

To clarify the theoretically introduced concepts, prototypical implementation examples are included in the present work. They demonstrate how to configure the method with model-transformations, validity checks, and domain-specific modeling languages, and serve as initial example cases for enterprise model driven software development using the *Software Engineering with Enterprise Models (SEEM)* method.

Zusammenfassung auf Deutsch

Ein zentrales Forschungsziel der Wirtschaftsinformatik ist es, einen Abgleich zwischen den Geschäftsprozessen und Strukturen von Organisationen, und der Funktionalität von Unternehmensinformationssystemen (Enterprise Information Systems, EIS), zu erreichen, mit denen die Arbeit von Organisationen unterstützt wird. Traditionell besteht eine methodische Kluft zwischen der Beschreibung organisationaler Gegebenheiten und der Funktionalität von Software, denn Organisationen und Softwaresysteme werden mit verschiedener Terminologie und auf verschiedenen Abstraktionsebenen beschrieben und konstruiert, und dies typischerweise von verschieden ausgebildeten Personengruppen.

In Unternehmensmodellen werden dedizierte Sprachmittel genutzt, um Wissen über Prozesse in Organisationen zu modellieren, zum Beispiel über handelnde und verantwortliche Akteure, eingesetzte Ressourcen, oder strategische Ziele, die durch organisatorische Mittel erreicht werden sollen. Die vorliegende Arbeit zeigt, wie basierend auf diesem Wissen EIS entwickelt werden können, die als unterstützende Software zur Ausführung dieser Aufgaben dienen.

Softwareentwicklung sieht sich traditionell mit einer Trennung zwischen Personen, die mit Software arbeiten, und Personen, die Software erstellen, konfrontiert. Unter Nutzung von Unternehmensmodellen eröffnet sich eine Chance, Benutzer enger in den Prozess der Entwicklung und Konfiguration von Software einzubinden. Es ist wünschenswert, Unternehmensmodelle zur Softwareentwicklung methodisch heranzuziehen, denn sobald eine nachvollziehbare Beziehung zwischen Unternehmensmodellen und Software-Funktionalität mit Hilfe einer Entwicklungsmethode etabliert ist, können beteiligte Nutzer die Software selbst entsprechend ihrer Bedürfnisse mittels Unternehmensmodellierung anpassen, ohne mit Programmierung oder technischen Details umgehen zu müssen. Das erhöht die Effizienz sowohl bei der Entwicklung als auch Anwendung der Software, denn die Software-Funktionalität wird aus Anforderungen abgeleitet, die implizit in Unternehmensmodellen erfasst sind. Eine solche Entwicklungsmethode verspricht außerdem, EIS an dynamische Veränderungen in Organisationen und deren Umgebung effizienter und kostengünstiger anpassen zu können. Außerdem wird das Vertrauen in die entwickelte Software wird durch Einbeziehung von Nutzern in die Anforderungsspezifikaton gestärkt, wenn Anwender und Leitungsverantwortliche in der Lage sind, die Funktionalität der Software in eigener Verantwortung zu gestalten.

Die nachfolgend dargestellten Forschungen erarbeiten eine Software Entwicklungsmethode zur Erstellung von EIS aus Unternehmensmodellen. Die Methode ist als generischer Rahmen entworfen und kann prinzipiell mit jeder Unternehmensmodellierungssprache verwendet werden, und für jede Zielarchitektur Software erstellen, nach entsprechender Konfiguration. Grundsätzliche Herausforderungen, die sich beim methodischen Übergang von konzeptionellen Modellen zu Implementierungsartefakten stellen, werden durch die Einführung von ergänzenden Zusatzmodellen in den Software-Entwicklungsprozess, sowie die Aufteilung des Transformationsverfahrens in mehrere dedizierte Phasen, angegangen. Mit diesem Ansatz wird die Abstraktionslücke zwischen konzeptionellen Unternehmensmodellen und Implementierungsartefakten durch methodische Konzepte systematisch überbrückt, um die Beschreibungsperspektive von der Vogelperspektive der Un-

3

ternehmensmodellierung hin zur internen Systemsicht auf Details eines Softwaresystems ontologisch zu drehen.

Die erarbeitete Methode erlaubt es, Software-Architekten und -Entwickler effizient durch den Entwicklungsprozess zu leiten. Sie kann an verschiedenen Stellen konfiguriert werden, um den Automationsgrad auf einem Kontinuum zwischen einem manuell beaufsichtigten Entwicklungsprozess mit methodisch vorgesehenen manuellen Entwicklungsschritten, oder einem "zero-coding" Entwicklungsansatz mit 100% Code-Generierung, auszuwählen.

Zur Veranschaulichung der theoretisch eingeführten Konzepte enthält die vorliegende Arbeit prototypische Implementierungsbeispiele. Sie demonstrieren die Konfiguration der Methode mit Modelltransformationen, Modellvalidierungen und domänenspezifischen Modellierungssprachen, und dienen als erste Anwendungsbeispiele für Unternehmensmodell-getriebenen Softwareentwicklung mit der *Software Engineering with Enterprise Models (SEEM)* Methode.

Contents

III A Domain-Specific Method for Model-Driven Software Engineering with Enterprise Models

List of Figures

List of Tables

List of Listings

Acronyms

API application programming interface

BLOB binary large object

BPEL Business Process Execution Language

BPM business process model

BPML business process modeling language

BPMN Business Process Modeling Notation

CIM computation independent model

CNC computer numerical control

CORBA Common Objects Request Broker Architecture

COTS commercial off-the-shelf

DBMS database management system

DDL data definition language

DSM domain-specific modeling

DSML domain-specific modeling language

DSSE domain-specific software engineering

EA enterprise architecture

EBNF Enhanced Backus-Naur Form

EEM extracted enterprise model

EIS enterprise information system

EM enterprise model

EMDSE enterprise model-driven software engineering

EME enterprise modeling environment

EMF Eclipse Modeling Framework

EML enterprise modeling language

EPC event-driven process chain

ESB enterprise service bus

GMF Graphical Modeling Framework

GPML general purpose modeling language

GUI graphical user interface

HTTP Hyper-Text Transfer Protocol

IDE integrated development environment

IP Internet Protocol

ISS information systems science

IT information technology

JSP Java Server Pages

MDA Model-Driven Architecture

MDD model-driven development

MDSE model-driven software engineering

MEMO Multi-Perspective Enterprise Modeling

MML MEMO Meta-Modeling Language

MWE Modeling Workflow Engine

OMG Object Management Group

ORB object request broker

OSGi Open Services Gateway initiative

P2P peer-to-peer

PAIS process-aware information system

PCSEE process-centered software engineering environment

PIM platform independent model

PPC production planning and control

PSM platform specific model

RBAC role-based access control

RUP Rational Unified Process

SAM Strategic Alignment Model

SEEM Software Engineering with Enterprise Models

SOA service oriented architecture

SOAP Simple Object Access Protocol

SQL Structured Query Language

UML Unified Modeling Language

URI uniform resource identifier

WfM workflow model

WfMS workflow management system

WSDL Web Services Description Language

WWW World Wide Web

XMI XML Metadata Interchange

XML Extensible Markup Language

XPDL XML Process Definition Language

XSD XML Schema Definition

XSLT Extensible Stylesheet Language Transformations

Abbreviations

e. g.   for example

etc.   et cetera

i. e.   that means

Printing conventions

Some conventions apply to the character style used for printing text:

Method-specific terms appear in sans-serif font. These are, e. g., technical terms, or names of components of the described method.

`Formal identifiers` are written in monospace font. These are, e. g., names of model elements or program code declarations.

"Inline citations", written in double-quotation marks, mark citations from other authors, in cases where they appear together with a citation reference in square braces.

"Phrases in natural language" are also written in double-quotation marks, they refer to natural language semantics which is not reflected by formal model elements, and appear without a reference to a citation source.

PERSON NAMES, PRODUCT NAMES or other named components with a non-technical identifier are written in small capitals.

Highlighted wordings are emphasized by an italic font setting.

Matrix of Contents

	Analysis	Design	Implementation
Meta²	1 Aligning organizational goals and technological infrastructure with model-driven software development 1.1 The vision: software made in a way everyone can understand 1.2 Describing organizations with enterprise models 1.3 Enterprise information systems for supporting organizational tasks 1.4 Business–IT alignment with methodical support 1.5 Domain-specific software engineering approaches 1.6 Deriving requirements towards enterprise information systems from enterprise models 1.7 Structure of this work 2 An overview example: Online web-shop	6 Method constituents 6.1 Overview 6.2 Models and modeling languages 6.3 Model transformations 6.4 Validity checks 6.5 Domain APIs for EIS	9 Example implementation strategies 9.1 Implementation strategies for process-members 9.2 Implementation strategies for actors 9.3 Resource implementation strategies
Meta	3 Concepts and terminology 3.1 Modeling languages, meta-models and model instances 3.2 Model transformations 3.3 Validity checks 3.4 Business process models and workflow models 3.5 Resources and information objects 3.6 Perceived type-instance blurring 4 Requirements towards an enterprise model driven engineering approach for enterprise information systems	7 Applying the method 7.1 Applying the method to enterprise information system development 7.2 Configuring the method to be used with a specific enterprise modeling language 7.3 Configuring the method for specific target architectures	10 Example scenario of a BPEL-orchestrated SOA target application architecture 10.1 Application scenario in the food supply chain domain 10.2 Domain-specific language for supply chain modeling 10.3 A distributed service oriented architecture (SOA) 10.4 Implementation strategy meta-model for a SOA platform 10.5 Executable BPEL workflow 10.6 Overall implemented example 11 MEMO enterprise models for developing JSP web applications 11.1 Adapting the MEMO enterprise modeling method 11.2 Configuring a JSP web-application target architecture
Instance	5 Enterprise models for model-driven software engineering 5.1 Organization theory concepts in enterprise modeling languages 5.2 Model-driven software engineering as an act of interpretation 5.3 Related research and existing approaches 5.4 Deficiencies of existing approaches and contributions by the proposed method	8 Design of a prototypical enterprise information system 8.1 General architectural design considerations 8.2 User interface sketch 8.3 Abstract domain API	12 Code generation and tooling support 12.1 Deriving executable artifacts 12.2 Code generation templates 12.3 Requirements towards tooling support 12.4 Enterprise modeling with the MEMOCENTERNG platform 12.5 Tooling on top of the ECLIPSE MODELING FRAMEWORK (EMF) 13 Evaluation 14 Remaining Work

Table 1: Matrix of contents

Part I

Motivation

I've been doing research for years
I've been practicing my ass off

Alanis Morissette, "Eight Easy Steps" from the album "So-Called Chaos", 2004

1 Aligning organizational goals and technological infrastructure with model-driven software development

1.1 The vision: software made in a way everyone can understand

An organization is a system of people with individual and shared goals, who perform actions with commonly shared resources, in an environment shaped by mutually established rules and traditions.

Taking part in an organization, as well as managing and steering the organization, requires the involved actors to have knowledge about tasks, responsibilities, resources and rules they deal with as part of their contribution to the overall organization. Everybody involved in an organization needs an appropriate degree of information about themselves being embedded in the organizational environment they act in. They also need to have knowledge about tasks and responsibilities of other participants in the organization, in order to efficiently interact with them. Every actor in an organization has a notion of the action system he or she is embedded in, as a very basic fundamental prerequisite to successfully be a part of the organization. An action system is an organization with its tasks, actors, resources and rules. Human actors take part in this organizational system, as well as automatic components and immaterial rules and goals.

Knowledge about an organization typically gets communicated in terms of processes performed by the organization, including information about the human actors carrying out individual tasks and actions, machinery and software that are required to perform these actions, resources that are involved, and rules and regulations that are obeyed when performing these action steps. Descriptions of these kinds have traditionally been communicated by diagram drawings or in text documents. They make use of conceptualizations around organizational roles, responsibilities, rules, tasks and resources. Economics and management sciences have formed to professionally handle these terms, and to use them for descriptive and prescriptive reflections on organizations. From these research areas, methods and theories have evolved about how to successfully structure organizations, formulate strategic goals, and set up efficient processes. The terminology behind this research thus provides an elaborated framework of concepts to express and handle knowledge about organizational structure and behavior.

25

Members of an organization use these commonly understood concepts, to create descriptions of organizational incidents and circumstances. They can do this with the help of enterprise modeling languages (EMLs), which typically provide graphical means for expressing knowledge about organizations with concepts originating from the professional terminology. As a result, a set of interrelated enterprise models is created. Given suitable methodical support, this set of models can automatically be consulted to configure and create software, which provides automatic support for carrying out the modeled processes in the organization.

If such a method can be provided, which allows to derive software from the knowledge in enterprise models, a new level of methodical software development can be reached, allowing everybody to configure his or her own EISs without programming, just by specifying desired tasks through visual domain-specific models, with a set of human-understandable, domain-specific concepts.

The upcoming research work suggests a software development method, which allows for exploiting the knowledge contained in enterprise models, to develop EISs for supporting organizational tasks and modeled processes of the organization. Depending on its configuration, the method can either fully automatically support the creation of EISs from enterprise models, or can provide systematic guidance in performing manual development steps throughout the development process. The research results achieved will contribute to a deeper understanding of how prospective users of software systems can be involved in software engineering, and are one step forward towards creating software in a way everyone can understand [Kro07].

1.2   Describing organizations with enterprise models

Business enterprises and other kinds of organizations are socio-technical systems, which are subject to various external and internal influences. A socio-technical system consists of human actors and technical constituents. The technical constituents, e. g., information systems, form the infrastructure on which the collaborative actions are performed by humans. The human actors typically do not only pursue the organization's goals, but additionally have individual goals and responsibilities, which they try to accomplish. Due to a multitude of dependencies among human actors and information systems, the qualitative complexity of an organization increases exponentially in relation to its quantitative scale. This means, while an organization develops and matures, it continuously becomes more difficult to oversee the relation between its intended goals on the one hand, and the actual implementation of operations that are performed to achieve these goals on the other hand.

To align the structure and behavior of a continuously maturing organization with its strategic goals, cognitive support is required to gain insight into the current situation of an organization, as well as into possible future constellations. Due to the high degree of interdependency and meshed complexity, such means cannot be provided by generic instruments of communication, e. g., by using linear natural language. Instead, an instrument to cope with these tasks is required to provide the required semantic expressiveness for knowledge explication. Such support is available through the use of enterprise models (EMs) [Fra94, Gro04, Rol00].

Enterprise models contain knowledge about the business processes performed in an organization, the actors and resources involved, organizational and operational responsibilities, and other aspects of how an enterprise works. When sensefully put together, these different aspects, also called perspectives or dimensions of an organization, provide a comprehensive multi-perspective view on an organization. This entire view cannot be achieved by a single type of model with a single modeling language, because the interwoven aspects of structure, dynamics, rules, etc., are too complex to be expressed without clean methodical distinction from other perspectives. As a consequence, multiple kinds of models are used to capture knowledge about the interrelated different perspective, and most enterprise modeling methods and enterprise architecture (EA) approaches suggest the use of multiple interrelated modeling languages to form a whole set of EMs. This general approach dates back to first enterprise modeling and EA methods, beginning with the ZACHMAN FRAMEWORK [Zac87], it characterizes the TOGAF standard [Gro04], and shapes products like the ARIS TOOLSET [Sch02b], the newly standardized ARCHIMATE [Lan09], and MULTI-PERSPECTIVE ENTERPRISE MODELING (MEMO) [Fra12].

Advanced enterprise modeling methods use interrelated multiple perspectives by incorporating multiple diagram types, which are internally related on the level of language design to allow sharing of identical concepts in multiple perspectives. This is vital to ensure semantic integrity among multiple perspectives, since referenced concepts from other perspectives are ensured to be further explicated in their own designated perspective. By incorporating knowledge from multiple perspectives of an enterprise, EMs contain a set of relevant facts not only about the organization as a socio-technical action system itself, but also about the desired functionality of software used for supporting the enterprise.

EMs are typically created and maintained by people who are familiar with the organization in focus, e. g., by employees or members of the organization, managers, or by external analysts, who have previously examined parts of the organization. These involved people, each one representing one view on specific requirements expressed in EMs, are the stakeholders in the modeling process.

Enterprise models are typically composed of graphical symbols on a visual diagram plane. To achieve an appropriate level of abstraction and understandability, enterprise modeling languages (EMLs) can be designed as domain-specific languages, which provide designated language concepts that facilitate modeling strategic goals, organizational structure, and operational behavior of organizations. The graphical symbols and the terminology that make up an EML are intended to allow involved stakeholders to gain a sufficient understanding of their area of interest represented in the enterprise models. This is especially relevant for those stakeholders with no formal sciences background, which is usually the majority of people in an organization. For this reason, it is recommended to use visual symbols that show well-known metaphors, and to label the model element types using a familiar terminology from the organization's environment.

EMs, as understood in the context of this work, are used for describing parts of organizations on an abstract level. Such descriptions cover relevant goals and missions of an organization, as well as its structural composition and processes that are performed to achieve the goals [SS05, Fra12]. Typically, an organization is not modeled entirely, but only those aspects are documented via models, which are subject to further planning, analysis, or software development. The term "enterprise" is understood as a synonym for "organization" in this work, there is no additional semantics attached to "enterprise" in comparison to "organization". Using the word "enterprise" neither implies any relationship to a commercially oriented organization, nor does it state anything about the size and complexity of the organization in question.

Some notions of enterprise models also include technical software models into the set of different perspectives, arguing that supporting software components are part of an enterprise in a way comparable to resources, processes, etc., and, as a consequence, they should be modeled as part of the set of enterprise models using traditional software system modeling techniques, such as the Unified Modeling Language (UML) [BJR99]. From such a point of view, a set of enterprise models consists of organization models, as well as of technical system models, which are both subsumed under the notion of enterprise models. The term "enterprise model", as used throughout this work, however, more closely denotes the notion of organization models, and does not cover technical system models. Instead, from the point of view of the work at hand, those software systems supporting an organization's work should not be modeled using traditional modeling techniques, they should rather be described in terms of implementation decisions explicitly related to the conceptual elements of the enterprise models, which is one of the main methodical proposals introduced by this work, the Software Engineering with Enterprise Models (SEEM) method.

To edit EMs, software tools are required, which make the contents of EMs accessible to users. While for pure documentation and communication purposes, a drawing editor would be sufficient, the full range of methodical value of enterprise modeling can only be gained, if dedicated model editors are used, which internally represent the formal semantics of the models, not only their graphical appearance in the diagram [GF10]. Once internal representations of the formal model semantics are available, i. e., the elements of enterprise models and their relationships are stored as a data structure in an object-graph, and not only as arbitrary graphical objects on a diagram plane, enterprise models are accessible to queries, analyses, and all kinds of automatic processing. This opportunity spans a bridge from a human-understandable description of an organization, to a systematic interpretation of this description for interfacing with technology.

Creating enterprise models with domain-specific languages fosters the separation of concerns between on the one hand incorporating general principles of the modeled domain on the language level, and on the other hand creating model instances that accurately describe a subject's perceived reality about real world constellations of concrete enterprises. The tasks of creating and editing model instances can be best performed by the stakeholders who are themselves involved in the organization. The upstream task of language design, however, is a genuine academic challenge to be carried out carefully with support of scientific research. This separation of concerns makes the use of enterprise modeling methods efficient and attractive for practical use. Modelers can rely on previously elaborated domain-specific languages, so the responsibility for ensuring semantic integrity and understandability among different groups of stakeholders is shifted to the process of language creation, making the use of individual models more efficient and less prone to errors.When models of enterprises and organizations are to applied with methodical support in a way understandable for all stakeholders, the use of elaborate domain-specific enterprise modeling languages thus is a first choice approach.

The range of possible uses of enterprise models is broad, once a coherent set of models from interrelated perspectives is available and maintained using domain-specific languages. Besides serving as means for communication, enterprise models can be utilized to develop information systems, which supply the described organization's tasks, e. g., by deriving executable workflow descriptions from business process models [ODvdA+09, RM06]. They can furthermore be used reflectively as tools to access information about operative systems and organizational entities represented in the models [FS09]. When applied in such a manner, enterprise models are no longer used for capturing knowledge from different perspectives to make it commonly accessible for diverse stakeholders, but they now serve as a repository of knowledge from which different stakeholders with their individual concerns can extract modeled facts and relate operational information to them.

1.3   Enterprise information systems for supporting organizational tasks

Enterprise information systems (EISs) are software systems for supporting the work of organizations, more precisely, supporting people in an organization to carry our their working tasks, in interaction with other people, and with automatic systems. EISs provide multiple variants of functionality, one of which is to guide human users through a sequence of working steps in regularly repeated business processes. In order to achieve this, the system must know about the user's role in the organization, the business processes he or she is involved in, and the resources that are used when performing individual steps in the processes. This also incorporates knowledge about collaboration relationships among multiple actors in commonly performed business processes, the order in which individual working steps are performed, and conditions under which parts of a business process are performed or skipped [Wes07]. Users access an EIS via front-end applications, typically in a distributed and shared environment. These front-end applications inform the user about which processes are to be performed, and which process-steps are to be taken next. E. g., a front-end application may display a "to-do" list to the user, indicating the steps of action that the user is expected to work on next. Once a working step is performed, the user notifies the system about completing the task, and in turn gets informed about possible subsequent working steps. If decisions are required to determine the following working steps, which cannot automatically be taken, the user is asked by the EIS to enter the appropriate decision interactively.

Besides guiding through sequences of working steps, an EIS typically contains support functionality for performing the individual working steps directly with the help of the EIS front-end application, or integrated applications invoked by the EIS. One typical example of such functionality is to provide access to information resources that are shared among multiple members of an organization [FC08]. To access these resources, an EIS can integrate viewers and editors for information objects, and can handle authenticated access to these information objects. When invoking external applications as part of the supportive work coordination, a vast amount of integration options exist with respect to achieving data integration, functional integration, process integration, propagation of security rights, and several other organizational and technological aspects of enterprise application integration [RMB01, Ver96].

A third building block of an EIS's functionality is the coordination of automatic processing steps where possible and desired. Automatic processing might either be performed by including automatic functionality directly in the EIS application, or by invoking external software components. The EIS bridges between human working steps and automatic processing, passing human input to automatic components, and re-injecting the results of automatic processing into the user's workflow. Automatic processing may influence, which further working steps are to be performed, or may result in information objects, which are subject to further handling by human actors or software components.

In addition to these core features, EISs may offer organization-specific features which are uniquely linked to the specific goals and competitive advantages of an organization. See Sect. 4 for a detailed analysis of requirements towards an EIS.

Traditional business conceptualizations regard EISs as a kind of information technology (IT) resources that are involved when performing specific processes [FC08]. However, this conceptualization does not allow for understanding EISs as a kind of formal representation of parts of the organization itself. Since EISs are actively acting automatic entities inside the organization, these entities necessarily encapsulate formal knowledge about the organizational action system and the process contexts they are applied in. In this sense, EISs are more than production resources to foster efficient process execution. They both reflect and shape the processes they are involved in. As linguistic constructions, they are derived from human perceptions of the world [Fra11d], which in turn have repercussions on the perceived reality once they are available as implemented technical artifacts.

As a consequence, in descriptions of an organization's action system, there is an internal connection between the action system described, and EISs that occur as part of these descriptions. Whenever an EIS is incorporated in the description of an organization's action system, it can be inherently assumed that the EIS contains formal internal descriptions of selected aspects of the action system, too, since otherwise the software could not successfully contribute to the processes it is intended to support.

EISs necessarily need to represent knowledge about the processes in an organization, and about how human actors and automatic components interact. In this respect, EISs are software representations of organizational structure and processes, like EMs are human readable representations of the same objects of interest. This connection makes it attractive to reason about a software development approach which interconnects both EMs and EISs, as it is carried out in this work, and justifies the assumption that it is possible to derive formal software system descriptions from organization models using a defined engineering method.

The development method to be elaborated has the purpose to bridge the business conceptualizations, as they are provided through enterprise models, to a formal description of a system's inner perspective given in technical software terms. Both kinds of descriptions are formulated in diverse languages and terminologies, one using business-related concepts to describe an action system from an outer organizational perspective, the other focusing on technical means for structuring a software system from its inner technical perspective. Still, on the description level, both modes represent alternative ways to express knowledge about those aspects, which are supported by EISs. The 'double-nature' of both description approaches, with their divergent terminology and concepts, is depicted in Fig. 1.

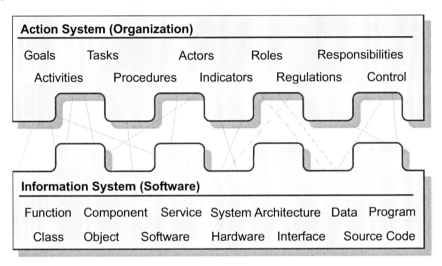

Figure 1: Action system and information system as interwoven human-task-technology system (according to ULRICH FRANK)

The software systems integrated by an EIS may be components of different kinds, e. g., back-end accounting systems, bookings systems or database management applications. Individual front-end workplace applications may also be integrated, such as office applications to present and edit information in documents. Even machine control software such as software for computation independent model (CIM) [Ver96, Wal92] may be subject to integration by a comprehensive EIS in a production industry context.

By integrating software components in a way specific to the processes of an organization, EISs form compound software systems of higher complexity and specificity than generic software tools potentially can. Having access to such a system might turn out to be a relevant competitive advantage for an organization.

From the perspective of a human user, an EIS provides access points for the individual to interact with the organization. To be able to provide this functionality, EISs expose front-end functionality to users, while at the same time they include back-end functionality to represent process knowledge, and to interoperate with other applications. Interaction with an EIS offers means for a user to integrate with the organization, and make himself or herself a part of the whole. Consequentially, EISs can have a fundamental social gluing function to constitute the organization.

An efficient EIS makes work for human users faster and less prone to errors. It thus also enlarges the circle of potential actors in the organization, since it allows to integrate actors into complex processes, who do not have the ability to oversee their interaction with the overall organizational interrelationships in its entirety.

Since EIS unfold their effectiveness only when specifically adapted to the organization they are used in, EISs cannot be offered from stock, and be generically sold and deployed. In order to acquire an EIS, the organization must take the decision to invest in the development of a specifically tailored EIS, and continuously consider re-investments to adapt the system to changes in the organization's processes and structure.

Whether to use an EIS or not cannot be decided individually by the users of the system, since the functionality of an EIS may cover multiple parts of an organization [FC08]. This means that the introduction of an EIS and the decision about developing an EIS, are inherent managerial tasks and require appropriate authority and discretionary power to decide about the investment.

Generic single-user software applications for performing working tasks, such as word processors and spreadsheets [XSS+04], provide functionality not bound to any specifics of organizational tasks and goals. A number of other software solutions are available as commercial off-the-shelf (COTS) applications [PW09, RMB01], which can be used to support collaborative tasks on the basis of generic functionality. Among these components are, e. g., e-mail applications, shared folders to exchange files, group calendars, wikis, etc. These tools provide generic functionality for editing merely unstructured documents in diverse usage contexts [LHM90]. This is the reason why office software applications can be produced from stock, and be offered in high volumes by a few number of vendors. When part of an overall EIS architecture as integrated applications for performing individual working steps, these applications conceptually appear as subcomponents of the EIS.

EISs denote software systems, which are used to support organizational tasks, e. g., scheduling of working steps for humans, managing information object access, invoking automatic processing components, or providing access to generic software components for organizational tasks. EISs, as they are understood in the course of this work, unfold their added value by encapsulating functionality that is specific to a particular organization. Their purpose is to provide only a limited set of functionality, which specifically supports users to perform tasks and processes in the organization they are part of.

1.4 Business–IT alignment with methodical support

One central research goal in information systems science is to achieve an alignment between conceptualized EMs and the EISs that are used to support their execution [GH09, HV93, LPW+09]. It is a cardinal management task to synchronize ideas about how an organization should operate, with the real circumstances under which the organization runs. With the use of IT systems as supporting units in organizations, this task also covers the behavior of software, and it becomes a managerial task to make sure that software systems in organizations operate in alignment with their business purpose [GH09]. From this constellation, a dilemma arises in managing organizations. On the one hand, it is an inherent managerial task to align the ideas and conceptualizations of strategic goals with the real actions going on in an organization. On the other hand, once software gets involved, a high degree of technical expertise is required to understand the operation of software, or even to develop software according to intended managerial conceptualizations.

The approach described here contributes to solving this problem, by specifying a dedicated software engineering method, which focuses on giving support for performing the transformation from conceptual enterprise models to technical implementation artifacts. The method combines existing conceptualizations and technological components, and gains an added value in flexibility and efficiency by offering an integrated and automated engineering procedure. Its central innovation lies in pre-structuring the process of transforming domain-specific enterprise descriptions to technical artifacts into multiple dedicated methodical phases.

This is achieved by separating the task of interpreting conceptual knowledge in input enterprise models, from the tasks of taking architectural design decisions based on the interpreted concepts, and finally generating software artifacts according to the design decision. These tasks are performed in subsequent methodical steps, and supported by automatic model transformations. Human design decisions are incorporated where required, and human software engineers are guided through the development process by tooling support. As interfacing concept between the two tasks of interpreting input models, and generating artifact output, the notion of "implementation strategies" is used, which get associated with conceptual elements of the input enterprise models using a mapping model.

Implementation strategies represent formalized descriptions of technical design decisions about how to control the code generation procedure. Which implementation strategies to apply for which conceptual notion, can either be decided by software architects during a development process, or automatic rules can be formulated beforehand, which allow an automatic association of implementation strategies with enterprise model concepts. After all required implementation strategies are specified and referenced from the mapping model, code generation templates will transform the chosen implementation strategies to software artifacts.

The implementation strategy pattern provides an abstraction over technological artifacts, while not being concerned with the actual implementation of these artifacts. This way, it provides an adequate abstraction to serve the purpose of a linking concept between interpreted domain-specific concepts in enterprise models on the one hand, and design-decisions for their technical realizations on the other hand. This allows the SEEM method to explicate an ontological turn from organizational descriptions to technical system specifications via dedicated modeling concepts, instead of hard-coding the decisions about how domain-concepts are interpreted and mapped, in a monolithic model transformation.

The combined use of a mapping model, implementation strategies, and the corresponding model transformations, provide dedicated methodical abstractions for coping with the method's requirements to bridge abstraction gaps between conceptual enterprise model specifications, and EIS implementations (see Sect. 4). Creating such a method is a genuine task of method engineering [BLW96, JJM09]. To have such a method at hand promises a benefit both in cost-efficient development of reliable EISs, as well as supporting the alignment between business requirements and information technology.

1.5 Domain-specific software engineering approaches

Domain-specific software engineering (DSSE) is a methodical approach to develop software on a higher level of abstraction, than with traditional development techniques, e. g., than with object-oriented modeling [KT08]. Older development methods make use of modeling as a way of abstracting from textual constructs in programming languages, which, e. g., is a done by the Model-Driven Architecture (MDA) [Obj03] approach combined with UML [BJR99], to visually express technical constructs of a software system. DSSE accounts for creating domain-specific modeling languages (DSMLs) as part of the overall software engineering procedure [Fra10], and then using these languages to create models which can be consulted for software artifact generation later on. By applying a DSML, models consulted for software engineering can reach a significantly higher degree of semantic richness, because the underlying language constructs of the modeling language do not refer to technical constructs of a target system only, but allow to describe the solution to a specific problem in adequate terms that structure the solution space.

Different characteristics of design approaches towards DSMLs can be classified into multiple categories, based on "domain expert's or developer's concepts", as well as on the "generation output", on "the look and feel of the system" to build, and on the "variability space" of the solution domain [LKT04]. A DSML may carry one or more of these characteristics, which allows to classify concrete DSMLs into distinct categories, depending on whether the characteristics are met or not. EMLs can be understood as DSML falling into the category of languages, which are exclusively designed based on domain expert's or developer's conceptualizations.

A comprehensive DSSE method comes with two major methodical components, which are a domain application programming interface (API), and code generation transformations. Code generation transformations bind together the abstract concepts in the DSMLs with the functionality provided by the domain API, by creating artifacts from domain-specific models, e. g. program code, which can be deployed on top of the domain API to form a complete software system. Code generation transformations provide the "glue" between domain-specific models and their technical implementation, they perform a formal interpretation of the meaning of the domain-specific model's semantics, to translate them into constructs of the technical software domain forming a running system.

These general methodical notions known from DSSE approaches can also be applied to EMLs, because EMLs are a specific kind of DSMLs. To provide a fruitful development method, however, concrete methodical decisions have to be taken in advance, in order to make the conceptual knowledge represented in EMLs efficiently applicable in a specialized DSSE procedure for enterprise model-driven software engineering (EMDSE).

1.6 Deriving requirements towards enterprise information systems from enterprise models

EMs are stated in terms of describing an organization from a high-level perspective, and the organization is presented as the primary subject matter. The terminology used in EMs covers concepts of actions, responsibilities, resources, goals, etc., which are all abstract enough to carry meaning independent from any concrete organizational or technological mode of realization. Both the organizational realization, as well as any possible technical implementation of the concepts, need to be operationalized by interpretation procedures, to derive applicable knowledge from the conceptual models.

When software development is put into focus, it becomes possible to derive a number of facts from EMs, which provide a solid fundament to methodically guide a software development process for these applications.

Among the requirements towards EISs that can be derived from EMs are

- the actions required to be performed in available business processes, i. e., the functions offered by the application

- the set of data resources and electronic documents the application will deal with by its functions

- relationships to other software components to be interfaced to

- user authorization information, derived from conceptually modeled roles and responsibilities

- task scheduling and physical resource allocation constraints

- user communication relationships and available information channels

Possibly, also meta-information about the software can be derived, such as strategic milestones for the software development process, or long term version management plans based on priorizations from strategic enterprise modeling perspectives.

To gain this knowledge from EMs, a procedure is required which allows for changing the focus on the primary subject matter in enterprise models from the *organization* as primary object of interest to the *software* as described object. Such a procedure resembles an ontological turn in the way the knowledge is looked at, from an outer perspective on the organic action system of an enterprise, to a formal perspective on internal software system components. A procedure of this kind is suggested in this work. The ontological turn will be accomplished by a multi-phase model transformation, and a methodically guided way to enrich the knowledge derived from EMs, with technical detail knowledge expressed using dedicated modeling constructs. The method can be configured along a continuum between a fully automatized procedure, using elaborate automatic transformations, or a methodically guided manual development process, combining manual develoment steps and software-supported automatized steps.

1.7 Structure of this work

The work at hand is structured into five main parts. Part I gives an overview on the role of EISs in organizations and introduces underlying questions of aligning business goals with technology in Sect. 1. A typical use case of the method is presented as an illustrative example in Sect. 2.

Part II lays out the fundamentals of the presented research work, starting in Sect. 3 with introducing underlying terminology and related scientific work. Essential requirements towards the method and its outcome are elaborated in Sect. 4, and an introduction into the methodological components, which are consulted to form the engineering method, is given in Sect. 5.

Part III elaborates the entire engineering method for model-driven development of enterprise information systems from enterprise models. The fundamental conceptual building blocks, which make up the methodical elements of the method, are presented in detail in Sect. 6. Dynamic aspects of the method are covered in Sect. 7, where methodical procedures of how to apply the method are illustrated.

In Part IV, prototypical example implementations are shown as an additional way of describing and clarifying the method. Sect. 8 contains general considerations about the architecture and implementation of enterprise information systems, and develops a domain API to formalize the design decisions taken for the creation of EIS. Concrete implementation strategies for conceptual enterprise model elements are suggested in Sect. 9. A comprehensive example of developing a supply-chain monitoring application in a service oriented architecture (SOA) environment is shown in Sect. 10, and more detailed information about the introductory example is made available in Sect. 11. The procedure for generating executable software system artifacts, and the tooling support that has prototypically been implemented to demonstrate the use of the method, are shown in Sect. 12.

Part V summarizes and evaluates the presented approach in Sect. 13, and Sect. 14 provides indications of further research work left for future considerations.

2 An overview example: Online web-shop

As an example, consider the business process model shown in Fig. 2, which has been created using the MEMO Control Flow [Fra11b] language. It represents a typical online order process, in which an internet user `Customer` places an order via a web page, and an employee of the `Shipping Department` of an organization is responsible for carrying out this order, and sending the requested goods to the customer.

The model shows that an order process is initiated, when a customer enters the web shop. As a first step, the customer browses through the product catalog and selects products to order. This step is modeled as a semi-automatic process-step indicated by the symbol of a human operating a computer, which means that it is performed as an interaction between a human user and a software system. By explicitly referencing the `Web Browser` resource, the model states by convention that this process-step is to be performed using a web-application front-end.

The business process model shows the order process only with relevant details from a business perspective. For example, it explicates alternatives in the flow of control and thus indicates, at which points decisions are to be taken. The model also explicitly names the information resources `Product List` and `Order`, as well as an existing information system which is described by its name `Storage Management IS` as to be used for managing the physical goods storage. Roles of responsible actors are referenced by each process-step with human interaction.

The roles and resources referenced from the business process model have been specified in separate organization and resource models. The organization model is shown in Fig. 3. The resource model simply lists the available resource types, without specifying further details. The allocations of resources, meaning the specifications of which resources are involved in which process-steps, are depicted in Fig. 4.

The technical architecture of the example application to be generated is shown in Fig. 5. It represents a Java Server Pages (JSP) [Ber03] application environment, with a central set of HTTP-accessible services realizing required coordination functionality, and client applications accessing the central set of services via a remote network connection. The central coordination service provides functionality to persist the states of running processes in one central place. This includes information about process-steps waiting to be performed, assigned actors responsible for performing process-steps, process instance variables, or synchronization points in process instances waiting to be reached. The example service API (see Appendix 6.5) provides this functionality as a set of JAVA classes. Alternative architectural conceptualizations might choose to put more responsibility into a central coordination node. This may include process coordination by using a central workflow processing engine, e. g., a Business Process Execution Language (BPEL) interpreter (see Sect. 10). The example implementation at hand realizes process coordination in a decentral way, by letting each actor's clients individually decide about further processing steps, assigning them to different actors where necessary.

To fully understand the meaning of the business process model (BPM) shown in Fig. 2, a number of assumptions are required to be known, which are not detailed out in the

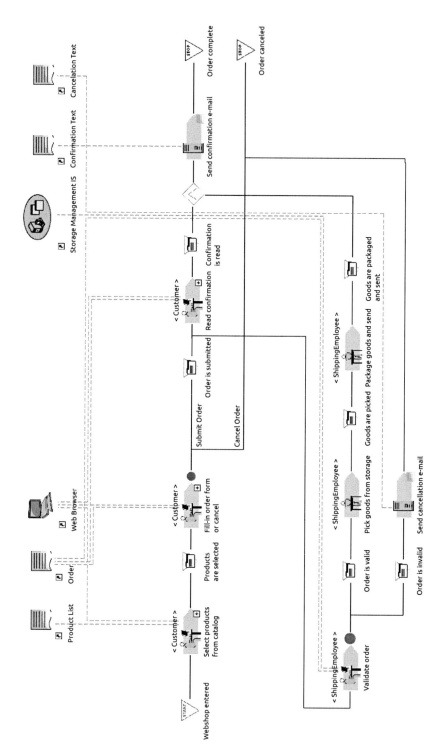

Figure 2: Business process model of an online order process

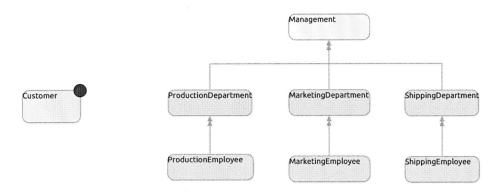

Figure 3: Organization model according to the example process

model. It is inherent to human understanding that perceived information gets enframed by the backgrounds and experiences of the recipient [Hum48]. As a consequence, on the conceptual business process level, it is very natural to leave out detail information, in order to make the model better understandable and efficiently perceivable.

However, to explicate all necessary knowledge needed to gain an automatically executable description of the process depicted in Fig. 2, some assumptions have to be made, to gain more precise semantics from the conceptual models. Some of these assumptions are:

- There is one single information resource Product Catalog which exists prior to starting the process. The name of the process-step "Browse product catalog and select products" indicates that this information resource is accessed in a read-only way. Domain-specific knowledge makes clear to a human user of the model that a catalog is typically subdivided into multiple entries. Making these entries readable via a graphical user interface (GUI) is the central task of this process-step.

- Order, although modeled with the same modeling construct as Product Catalog, does not represent a single information resource instance, but a type of information resource of which multiple instances can exist. This is clear to a human recipient with basic domain-specific knowledge, knowing that a commercial enterprise would typically deal with multiple orders over time. The name of the process-step "Place order or cancel" makes clear to a human recipient that a new instance of one order information object is to be created in this step.

- When semi-automatic process-steps, i. e. process-steps in which human users interact with software, reference to information objects, it can be assumed that the user will be presented a kind of electronic document as an interface to the desired information. The document may be editable or read-only, depending on the purpose of the process-step.

- Involving a Web Browser in a semi-automatic process-step can intuitively be interpreted in a way that a web-based front-end application is used to perform this process-step.

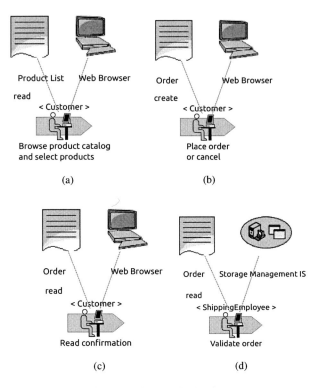

Figure 4: Allocation models according to the business process-steps and resources

- The role Customer, in combination with a web-based front-end application, gives the idea that the product catalog is publicly accessible via the internet. Otherwise, an explicit login step could have been modeled. The order process is thus publicly accessible for customers.

- The role ShippingEmployee will be filled by one concrete employee of the shipping department of the modeled company. One particular employee will be determined and will be responsible for processing the order in all subsequent steps of the same process instance. Since the role ShippingEmployee is used multiple times, it is reasonable to assume that during execution of the same process instance it will be the same employee who performs subsequent process-steps.

- The decision whether to submit an order or to cancel the order process is understood as a decision taken by the actor performing in the semi-automatic process-step "Place order or cancel".

- The decision whether a submitted order is valid or invalid, as a result of the semi-automatic process-step "Validate order", is also assumed to be taken by a human performing this process-step. The software component used in this process-step can thus be expected to offer user interface components to input the decision.

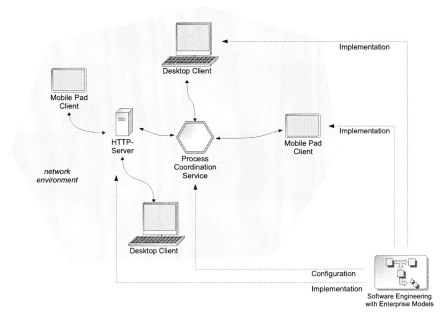

Figure 5: Architecture of a Java Server Pages (JSP) based application as generation target for the example

It is natural to human cognition that details are left out when communicating and symbolizing knowledge. As a consequence, there are still a large number of ambiguities and missing details in the model. Although providing suitable means for communication and gaining a common understanding about business processes among human stakeholders, the business process model intentionally does not give hints on all detail information that would be required to provide software support for the actors involved in the process. Because of this, a development method now is applied, which formalizes the interpretation of the conceptual model based on the above assumptions, to bridge from the conceptual business process level description to an executable implementation.

Applying the method The SEEM method presented in this work allows to augment the business process model with the required detail information for implementation, in a structured an repeatable manner. The method keeps the layers of abstraction separate, which either describe the conceptual business perspective with an intentionally blurred semantics, or describe implementation concepts that technically realize a software system. Intermediating concepts are provided by the method, which serve to explicate connections between both layers.

The first step to apply the method, is to convert the enterprise models to a compact representation which contains all extracted enterprise model concepts in a single non-graphical model. This step serves to get an internal representation of the enterprise models for easier further processing of the method. To perform this step, a horizontal model-to-model transformation is run, which converts the enterprise models to the internal representation.

The software architect gets informed by an automatic validity check, if the original enterprise models do not contain sufficient information to unambiguously create the extracted representation. In this case, the original enterprise models are revisited, and the transformation is run again, until the validity check succeeds.

After this step, the software architect selects implementation strategy modeling languages, which reflect possible implementation options on the desired target platforms. Subsequently, an initializing model-to-model transformation is run to create both an initial mapping model, and initial implementation strategy models. The according model-transformations, and the respective implementation strategy meta-models, have been developed earlier, as part of the adaptation of the method to the desired target architecture.

The generated mapping model is a non-graphical model structure as shown in Fig. 6, which binds concepts from the original enterprise models to modeled implementation strategies in a formal notation. When the transformation is run, the mapping model is initialized with a list of mapping entries, each one binding a concept from the extracted enterprise model to one or more implementation strategies listed in the implementation strategy model, or in multiple implementation strategy models, if artifacts for more than one platform are generated simultaneously.

The transformation also analyzes the enterprise models' semantics, to initialize the implementation strategy model with automatically suggested implementation strategies, and associate them to enterprise model concepts in the corresponding mapping model entries. Depending on the degree of automation, which is reflected by the effort put into developing platform-specific implementation strategy model initialization transformations, a 100% code generation approach can be strived for, which means to automatically create a fully populated mapping model containing all implementation strategy references required to successfully run the code generation step. Alternatively, if the effort for creating such elaborate transformation exceeds the one for manually making architectural decisions about how to represent enterprise model concepts via implementation artifacts, the mapping model transformation can be restricted to create a model with yet to be completed mapping model entries, in which references to associated implementation strategies are manually created by software architects and developers.

Remaining manual development tasks after initializing the mapping model, and its accompanied implementation strategy models, cover the detail specification of data types for information objects used throughout the business process, as well as creating GUI representations of these information objects, typically realized via form-views on the modeled data. The example uses XML Schema Definition (XSD) as data type specification mechanism for information objects, and XFORMS [Dub03] as technology to specify editable forms and other views for Extensible Markup Language (XML) data. Besides these technical specifications, a collection of product data with related images in a database needs to be created, and, in case of the chosen JSP web application target architecture, manual development work is additionally remaining for creating the visual web-site layout.

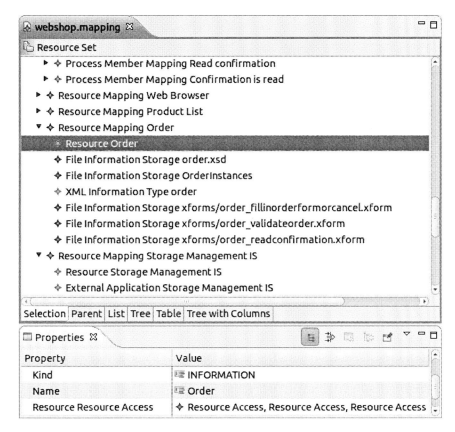

Figure 6: Mapping model with links to elements from the conceptual model and the implementation strategy model

After manually refining the initial mappings, the software architect runs validity checks on the mapping model and the implementation strategy models. The steps of manual refining and running validity checks are then iterated until the validity checks pass without complaints.

Subsequently, all information for creating a running software system is available in the combination of the extracted enterprise model (EEM) model, the mapping model, and the implementation strategy model. From these configurations, an executable software system is created by using a model-to-text code generation transformation, which takes these three models as input, and generates executable artifacts. An excerpt of the example's code generation templates in a surrounding editor application is shown in Fig. 7. The example code generation templates are written in the XPAND language (see Sect. 12).

Fig. 8 gives an impression of how the developed software presents itself via a graphical user interface.

```
main.xpt ⊠

«REM»
 *
 * Realization of implementation strategy 'Form'.
 *
«ENDREM»
«DEFINE implementation(ProcessMemberMapping pmm) FOR Form»
    «LET ! this.resourceAccessTargets.has() AS readOnly»
    <% deferred = true; // (don't go to next step, this step is blocked until form is submitted) %>
    <% out = headOut; %>
    <xf:model>
        <xf:instance><data xmlns=""><%=resources.get("«this.resourceAccessSources.first().name»")%></data>
        <xf:submission id="go" action="index.jsp?step=<%=step%>&amp;id=<%=processId%>" method="post"/>
        «IF readOnly»
            <xf:bind nodeset="//*" readonly="true()" />
        «ENDIF»
    </xf:model>
    <% out = bodyOut; %>
    <xf:group ref="/data">
        «REM» include xform from file «ENDREM»
        <%=context.readFile(request.getRealPath("/"), "«this.formDescription.name»")%>
    </xf:group>
    <div class="clear"> </div>
    «IF ! readOnly» «REM» if not read-only, output send-button «ENDREM»
    <xf:submit submission="go" class="buttonok" appearance="minimal"><xf:label class="buttonok"><img src=":
    «ENDIF»
    <% out = pageOut; %>
    «ENDLET»
«ENDDEFINE»
```

Figure 7: Code generation templates of the example project inside editor application

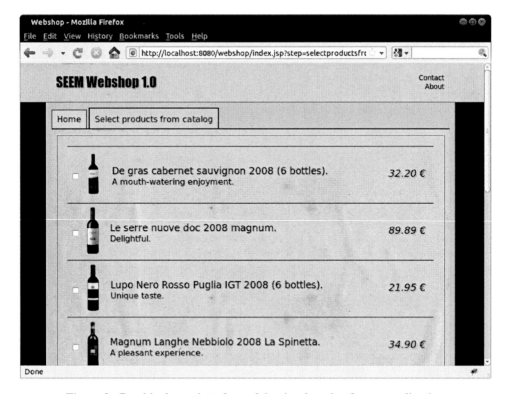

Figure 8: Graphical user interface of the developed software application

Part II

Approach

I come to you defences down
With the trust of a child

Peter Gabriel, "Red Rain" from the album "So", 1986

3   Concepts and terminology

Several key concepts and related terminology are used throughout the upcoming document. To introduce the underlying basics, and to form a list of prerequisite concepts for the method, these fundamental conceptualizations are sketched for introduction in the following.

3.1   Modeling languages, meta-models and model instances

Models in information systems science can be understood as semi-formal constructs, which allow to store and interchange knowledge, and serve as alternative means to human language or other means of expression, to utter facts about some perceived or constructed parts of reality. Models can generally be considered semi-formal, because they typically consist both of a syntactically strictly defined formal structure (which, stripped down to its mere syntax, could be called a data structure in computer science terms). Additionally, informal semantics can be expressed by using natural language labels and identifiers, as well as comments and annotations to model elements. If equipped with a graphical notation, applying visual patterns to model elements opens up a wide range of further means for expressing informal semantics.

For the purposes of the proposed method, the informal aspects of semantics stored in models will play a role when determining default values for formal elements in generated models.

Modeling languages   Syntax and formal semantics of models are specified via modeling languages. Every model is conforming to, or is "written in", an underlying modeling language. Models may also combine elements from multiple modeling languages, e. g., by referencing elements from other models, which are written in different modeling languages. If modeling languages provide a graphical notation, the syntax can be distinguished between an abstract syntax, which determines the formal structure in which model content is represented, and a concrete syntax, which consists of graphical notation elements that visually represent model elements.

Meta-models Modeling languages are semantic entities constructed by humans, which need their own means of expression to be specified. One way to specify a modeling language, is the construction of a meta-model [CSW08, Kle08], which expresses the available language elements, and the way they can be validly combined and interrelated throughout the use of the language. When applying a method, which makes use of multiple models in different modeling languages, and of model transformations describing relationships between these models, using meta-models to specify the involved modeling languages is an elegant way for specifying languages. When different meta-models are constructed using the same meta-modeling language [Fra08], they conform to an identifcal meta-meta-model, which allows to apply specialized model transformation languages for meta-models of that kind, and to reuse existing model tooling support.

Model instances In some contexts, the distinction between a model on the one hand, and a meta-model describing its modeling language on the other hand, remains clear without further need to mark the model as being an instance of its meta-model. However, sometimes the term model instance is used to explicitly denote the realized language artifact, not the language itself or its declaration. Being an instance of another model, is always relative to the use of the referenced other model as the language description of the instance. Because of this relative relationship, any meta-model can also occur in the role of a model instance, namely an instance of another meta-model (a meta-meta-model from the original point of view), which was used to specify the meta-modeling language the model conforms to. However, such confusion is not likely to occur in the course of the upcoming method description, because the developed method makes use of one level of model instances, and one cleanly separated meta-level.

To summarize the introduced terms, Fig. 9 visualizes the mentioned meta-meta-model, meta-model and model instance levels.

3.2   Model transformations

Formal relationships between models, in terms of how one model is semantically interpreted to influence the creation of another model or technical artifact, are described by model transformations. Model transformations take one or more models as input, and generate an output artifact, which is either another model, or a piece of technical artifact or any textual output generated throughout the transformation. Transformations, which output another model, are called model-to-model transformations, or m2m transformations. Transformations to general artifacts are referred to as model-to-text transformations, or m2t transformations.

The way how a model transformation operates, is declared via a model transformation specification. There are different approaches how to describe model transformation specifications. From a developer's point of view, model transformations are specified by programs in a specialized higher-order language, which allow to describe the desired transformation operations, in terms of querying information from the source models, and sub-

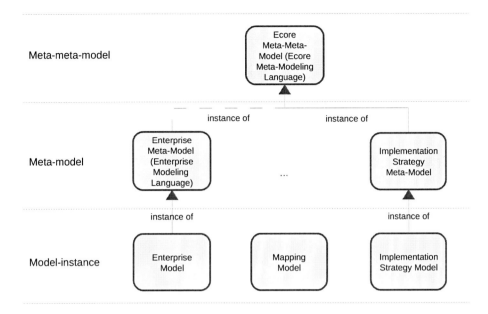

Figure 9: Meta-meta-model, meta-model, and model instance levels, with example model types used in the presented method

sequently control the output process of an artifact, more efficiently than general purpose programming languages can do. Several specific model transformation specification languages are available, e. g., QVC [Obj08], XTEND/XPAND [Eclc], or, in a wider sense considering Extensible Markup Language (XML) data structures as models, XSLT [Tid01] for transforming between XML formats. Specifications written in these languages provide sufficient information for a model transformation engine, i. e., an interpreter for the transformation specification, to execute the transformation. Every run of the transformation interpreter, with possibly different models as input, is called a model transformation instance. I. e., a model transformation instance comes into existence, when a model transformation specification is executed, and there can be any number of model transformation instances for one model transformation specification.

The specification of a model transformation generally consists of two complementary sides, which are typically declared using two different kinds of expression syntaxes in model transformation languages. The first logical step in performing a transformation is querying information from one or more source models, given as input to the transformation. For this purpose, multiple languages for describing model queries are available and may appear integrated as partial language for the query side in a complete model transformation language. To usefully operate on the queried data, the model transformation language also needs an output side, and means to control the generated output. This is typically realized by a template language with basic conditional and algorithmic expression features, which operates on the information queried from the source models, and outputs generated artifacts accordingly. Examples of model transformation specifications written in the XPAND language are provided in Appendices A.3.3 and A.4.3.

Since model transformations operate on input models and output models, which each may be formulated in a different modeling language, the specification of a transformation naturally has to be made with knowledge about the languages of all the involved models. This is required, because the specification of a transformation determines, which elements to query in the source models, and which elements to create in the target models or other output artifacts. Thus, there is a reference from each model transformation specification to the language descriptions (meta-models) of the models involved in the transformations.

It turns out that when referencing multiple modeling languages from one transformation specification, it is useful to have the language specifications formulated in a common meta-modeling language, according to a common meta-meta-model [Fra08]. Using the same meta-modeling language for all language specifications of involved models in a transformation, makes type relationships between elements in different languages easier to handle, and thus allows for easier binding between the query expressions in the model transformation language, and the subsequent output control expressions.

Model transformations, which output models or artifacts on the same semantic abstraction layer, as the source models are located on, are called horizontal transformations, while transformations, which convert between different levels of abstractions, are named vertical transformations. Horizontal model transformations represent the simpler class of transformations, because their task is mainly to re-structure the syntactic relationships between elements from different source modeling languages and target output languages, and to rename elements between different models. Vertical transformations typically transform models from a higher level of conceptual abstraction, to models which contain more concrete details about technological realization. In these transformations, semantic interpretation of the source models is performed, in order to grasp formalized facts expressed on a higher level of abstraction, which contain knowledge about the output on the lower level. To interpret content in an automatic transformation, hints based on analyzing identifier names, conventionalized model element constellations, or values in comment fields, etc., can be applied.

In Fig. 10, the relationships between modeling languages, model instances, model transformation specification languages, model transformation specifications and model transformation instances are schematically depicted.

Model transformations can create fully valid output artifacts, which are ready to be further processed, or to be deployed in a target environment. This class of transformations can be called total transformations. In contrast to total transformations, partial transformations create models as output, which are not immediately ready for further processing. Generated output from partial model transformations may still miss required values or references. These artifacts, which are typically models resulting from a partial model-to-model transformation (not artifacts from model-to-text transformations), require additional manual editing or other methodical means to be completed, before they can further be used.

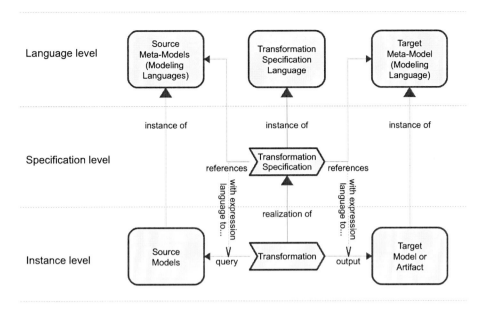

Figure 10: Relationships between modeling languages, model instances, model transformation specification languages, model transformation specifications and model transformations

A generic model-transformation-pattern Model transformations play an important role as methodical components in any model-driven development approach [KT08, Obj03]. They provide links between model instances that are used throughout a development process. At the same time, they contain formalized knowledge about the syntactic and semantic relationships between the modeling languages, in which the involved model instances are expressed. In order to describe the actions to be carried out by a model transformation, the transformation description must refer to language elements of both the input models, and output models, of the transformation. Transformation descriptions can be any programs that read in models, and output other models after some kind of processing. While such programs could in principle be written in any programming language, specialized languages are available, which provide dedicated programming constructs to perform model transformations, e. g., the XPAND language [Eclc], or QVT [Obj08].

The description of a model transformation provides formal operative semantics, which describes how two or more models interrelate. However, current model-driven software engineering (MDSE) approaches typically regard a model transformation as one monolithic mechanism, which performs the desired input-to-output mappings in one step [ZSZ11]. This point of view on model transformations reminds of the early days of software development, in which any architectural structuring of the internals of a software product was left over to the intuition of programmers, without providing architectural reflection about the relationships between the individual parts of the whole. It is thus one scientific goal, to reason about the internal structure of model transformations, and to identify architectural invariants that are common to all model transformations used for MDSE. Once common architectural features have been identified, they can be consulted to explicate a development method for creating model transformations, as part of an overall MDSE approach.

Having such a procedure at hand, methodical underpinnings for the challenge to get from conceptual descriptions (requirements) to executable systems are made available. By not merely treating model transformations as black boxes, which are functioning "somehow", but by taking care of their internal structure, the process of applying an MDSE method can be raised on a more elaborate methodical level. The Software Engineering with Enterprise Models (SEEM) approach developed in this work makes use of the identification of internal model transformation structures, by splitting the overall transformation process into multiple dedicated phases, which are easier to develop and to maintain individually, compared to a single monolithic transformation approach. These phases conform to the notion of a general model-transformation-pattern as shown in Fig. 11.

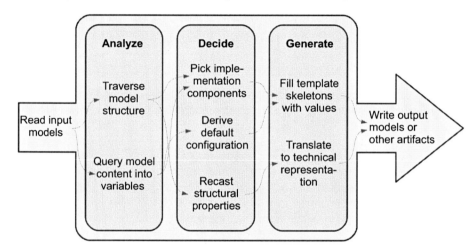

Figure 11: Model-transformation-pattern

The underlying idea of the general model-transformation-pattern is that any transformation procedure used in MDSE consists of applying the pattern of a) first analyzing the contents of the input models, b) then, based on this analysis, deciding how the structure of the resulting implementation artifacts is to be organized, and, c) finally outputting implementation artifacts based on structural decisions taken in b). The SEEM method makes use of three transformation phases, which are the adapter transformation (see Sect. 6.3.1), the mapping model initialization transformation (see Sect. 6.3.2), and the code generation transformation (see Sect. 6.3.3), to methodically reflect this general pattern, and to offer individually maintainable parts of the entire transformation description, instead of one monolithic transformation.

3.3 Validity checks

To determine, whether a model is complete or correct in a specified sense, validity checks can be applied. Validity checks, as understood in this work, perform tests on model instances for required values and available references. They may also perform semantic checks, i. e., query the content of a model and apply comparisons and other checks, to make sure that values supplied with a model are coherent for further processing. The terms "model checking" or "model validation" are sometimes synonymously used with "validity checking". To avoid misunderstandings concerning divergent uses of these terms in other disciplinary contexts, the work at hand exclusively speaks of validity checks.

Especially at points in the method, where incomplete models as results of partial model transformations have to be edited manually, validity checks are helpful to determine at which points a model still is considered incomplete. Based on this automatically derivable knowledge, methodical support can be provided, to efficiently guide software developers through a list of model elements which require further manual editing.

In the same way, as a model transformation instance resembles the execution of a model transformation specification performed by an interpreter engine, a validity check instance is the result of a validator's run, interpreting a validity check specification. A validity check specification contains of a list of boolean expressions, each one incorporating queries on the model, and describing formal rules that characterize a model's completeness or semantic validity. If any of the boolean expressions listed in the validity check specification results to `false`, the entire check has failed, and the model can be considered invalid or incomplete. Appendices A.3.1 and A.3.2 contain an example validity check specifications.

Boolean expressions that make up validity check specifications, are typically formulated in a model query language, which reads values from the validated models, and tests them against desired conditions. When applying model transformations and validity checks, it is recommended to use a validity check specification language, which makes use of the same query expression language as the model transformation language used in the same development project. Using the same query expression language makes it possible to share utility functions among model transformation specifications and validity check specifications. This way, complex queries can be reused both for validating models, as well as for querying model content to control a subsequent transformation process.

The validity check specification language used in the example projects in this work are written in the CHECK language. This language is part of the XPAND / XTEND language family contained in the Eclipse Modeling Framework (EMF), and uses expressions in the XTEND language to formulate boolean validity conditions for models. Shared queries can be modularized in extension files, which can be included both by validity check specifications in the CHECK language, as well as by model transformation specifications in the XTEND and XPAND languages.

3.4 Business process models and workflow models

There is a traditional distinction between models, which represent structural features of a system, and others, which incorporate knowledge about the dynamics of ongoing actions. Both aspects can be expressed with several different modeling languages. Static structure models for general purposes may be given as, e. g., entity-relationship models [Tha00], UML class diagrams [BJR99], or domain-specific system design languages, which focus on structure, e. g., the SAP Standardized Technical Architecture Modeling (SAP-TAM, [SAP07]) language.

Another ontological perspective is taken in by looking at the dynamics of a modeled system. Models, which capture information about actions and events in a system, belong to the class of process models. Such models typically express sequences of process-steps taken throughout a process, usually along alternative decision paths and parallel sequences. Process models may optionally also include the notion of events, which mark points with specific properties in the process sequences, e. g., a change in state of an entity, or a point at which specific knowledge about the process becomes available, e. g., "all following process-steps will be automatic".

There is an inherent link from process models to structure models, since any description of what happens, has to refer to entities, which either actively take part in the process, or are passively involved, e. g., by being manipulated or consumed in the process. This means that any process model necessarily has to reference structural elements. This is not the case vice-versa, since structure models indeed can be formulated without any explicit reference to process elements. However, structure models require at least implicit knowledge about processes that operate on the modeled structure, or a mechanism that works on it. Otherwise there would be no value in formulating structure models, they would be useless without anything to imagine that can happen according to the modeled structure.

The sequential relationship between individual process-steps, and optionally events, is typically expressed by a control flow relationship, which is often visualized in graphical process modeling languages as arrows or lines connecting individual process-step elements. Fig. 2 shows an example business process model, another example is given in Fig. 12 a). Both models are created with the business process modeling language integrated in the Multi-Perspective Enterprise Modeling (MEMO) enterprise modeling language family [Fra11c, Fra12].

Several traditional techniques to formulate general purpose process models are available, e. g., multiple variants of flow charts or structograms [NS73] or Petri nets [Dia10]. While these approaches focus on a conceptual description of processes, without a closer relationship to further applications of the process models, languages like the activity diagram language of the Unified Modeling Language (UML) [BJR99] provide a process modeling approach, which is prepared for linking process description constructs to object oriented structural software concepts.

A fine-grained distinction sometimes is required for differing between the notion of process types and process instances. Process models typically represent process types, i. e., they describe possible actions and events, which are to be realized by acting entities during process instantiation. To form a process instance, a process model has to be executed. While the process executes, realized indicators such as processing time, decisions taken to control the process flow, resources consumed, etc., can be documented in a log. This log can later serve to represent the process instance for ex-post reference. An actual process instance only exists during the time of its execution, due to the temporal nature of the issues expressed by process models.

The relationship between process type declarations and individual process instances is symbolized in Fig. 13. The figure shows how visual representations of process types can be enriched by information from process logs, to form an ex-post representation of individual process instances.

Business process models (BPMs) [Wes07] are process models with domain-specific semantics for expressing conceptual knowledge about processes in organizations. Applications of BPMs cover the description of work processes incorporating manual actions and human-made decisions, the interaction among humans, as well as the interaction with software systems or other machinery, and automatic steps. BPMs are used to express a high-level view on modeled process types without details on how individual process-steps are carried out. To provide this overview, and to link to other description perspectives, BPMs can contain references to entities such as persons, machinery or supplementary resources, which play a part in the modeled business process.

A high-level perspective is also taken in by workflow models (WfMs) [vdAvH04]. However, in contrast to BPMs, the aim of using workflow models is to provide a technical view on the automatically executable parts of business processes. As a consequence, a workflow model does not specifically relate to human actors or physical resources as BPMs do, these elements are missing compared to BPMs. Instead, WfMs are enriched with technical detail information about the invocation of software services.They are executable software artifacts on a high level of functional aggregation, used to orchestrate other software components which provide individual pieces of business functionality.

Fig. 12 a) shows an of a example conceptual business process model, as it can be used as input for the SEEM method, contrasted by Fig. 12 b), which contains a representation of a machine executable process derived from the conceptual model by means of the method. A larger number of elements in the executable model indicates that this model describes the process on a finer level of granularity and with different elements than the conceptual model. In the example, first an order message is sent from a retailer to a good's producer. After the order is confirmed, and the ordered good has been produced or released from stock, a transport instruction is sent to the logistician, who is responsible for transporting the goods. The generated Business Process Execution Language (BPEL) process is composed of a sequence of pairwise related receive and send operations, with optional plausibility security checks performed by a central coordination and execution platform, which runs the BPEL process. The exchange of documents is realized by transmitting XML-encoded EDIFACT [Ber94] messages via Simple Object Access Protocol (SOAP) calls to web-service operations. Several existing EDIFACT document types are consulted for implementing the electronic document communication, as it is modeled in the conceptual business process model. The ORDER type represents order documents, while ORDRSP is used for order confirmation. IFTMIN stands for "instruction for transport", which is a message type with semantics for configuring a transportation contract. RECADV finally realizes a document type for sending delivery confirmations.

As means of control, the coordination and execution platform monitors the electronic document exchange and performs validity checks on the exchanged information. In the example, this is done with regard to the IFTMIN message, which undergoes plausibility checks performed by the IFTMIN_AssetCheck service. Since ice cream is transported in the example case, this service may ensure that the transport instructions include the demand for keeping the temperature of the transported goods constantly below -4°C. In the generated BPEL process, the result of the IFTMIN_AssetCheck service is then processed by the subsequent if-block, and in case of an invalid transport instruction configuration, a corresponding mitigation process gets invoked. The remaining parts of the process implementation, which are not displayed in Fig. 12 b), handle the transport configuration and the exchange of the final RECADV confirmation document.

3.5   Resources and information objects

The range of conceptual language elements for expressing resources involved in process descriptions is typically narrow. Common business process languages offer generic resource concepts without further differentiation, e. g., the Business Process Modeling Notation (BPMN) only knows a plain general "Resource" concept. Some research activities aim at elaborating more differentiated resource description languages for specific domains [FHK+09]. These approaches, however, have not yet influenced widely used enterprise modeling techniques. Workflow-oriented modeling languages generally represent any resource by the technical concept of a variable carrying data.

The plain conceptualizations of the notion of resources on both the conceptual level, and the implementation level, may result from the fact that the notion of a resource is too general to be further differentiated by means of a general purpose modeling language on either level of abstraction. In fact, a resource can be virtually anything, the term "resource" belongs to the most overloaded terms in information systems science.

For the method proposed in this work, which serves to bridge between a conceptual process perspective, and an implementation view on processes, it makes sense to further differentiate between different notions of a resource. Resources in conceptual business process models may either be passive physical resources, which are goods, material, or physical documents, or active physical resources, such as information technology (IT)-equipment or machinery. In addition, conceptual BPMs can include resources with the notion of immaterial information resources, such as master data about products and related business partners, operative status information about a running processes, etc. [WMB+03] To interpret the meaning of resources in a conceptual BPM, it makes sense to distinguish any use of a general resource type by these fundamental categorizations.

In implementation-level models, such as workflow descriptions, a slightly different view on resources is taken in. By its very nature of describing a software system's operating steps, a workflow model does not need to reflect the notion of physical resources directly.

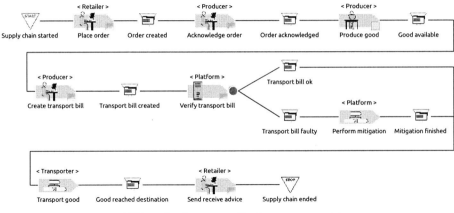

(a) Example of a conceptual business process model

(b) Example excerpt of an executable workflow model

Figure 12: Conceptual business process model versus implementation-oriented executable workflow model

Process type

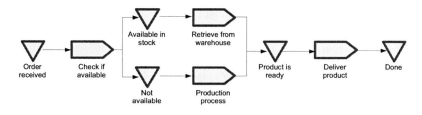

Process instances

Instance 1

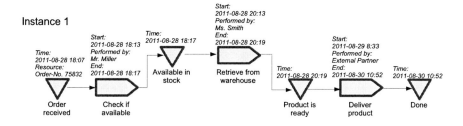

Instance 2

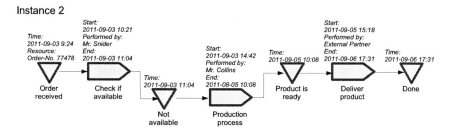

Instance 3

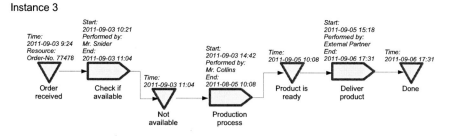

Figure 13: Relationship between process type declaration and process instances, with information from process logs for an ex-post representation of process instances

In software systems, any physical resource is indirectly represented by an information object, which describes the physical resource. A physical resource's description may consist of details about its location, size, weight, or other material properties. There is no way to directly cope with physical objects via software, which is why every reference to physical resources is indirectly wrapped into information objects on the implementation level. While with respect to this distinction, the notion of a physical resource becomes even less distinctive on the implementation level, than in the conceptual view, some additional generic structure can be applied to what an information resource is from an implementation perspective. Since for resources on the implementation level it is known that they are to be represented as information objects, generic features for describing information objects can be assumed as being part of the notion of information objects on the implementation level. Two of these features are a data type, which determines the information objects syntactical structure and possibly formal semantics, and a storage mechanism which provides means to represent the information persistently, if this is required by the process semantics. This more fine-grained notion of what a resource is on the implementation level will be exploited for formal specification in the course of the method elaboration.

3.6 Perceived type-instance blurring

Sometimes confusion appears about the distinction between the use of types and instances in enterprise models. In case of the dynamic perspective taken in by process models, there is a clean distinction between process types, which are declared by process models, and process instances, which come into existence by performing the processes, and which can ex-post be referenced and analyzed with the help of log data (see Sect. 3.4). Accordingly, process-step elements, events, and control-flow sequences are modeled on the type level, and are instantiated at process runtime. However, with regard to static model perspectives of enterprise models, the distinction between conceptually expressed types and instances is not always equally clear. Actor and resource concepts used in enterprise models sometimes appear not to fit into the type-instance dichotomy scheme. For the purpose of describing a software development method based on enterprise models, it thus needs to be examined, which impact this perceived ambiguity has on the requirements towards the engineering method.

The described constellation appears, e. g., when a model element representing an actor group describes both a type of an organizational group, as well as a typical singleton instance referring to a set of actors who form this group in a concrete organization. An actor group "accounting department", e. g., can be used in the context of referencing a functionally determined organizational unit, namely those parts of an organization which carry out accounting operations. In this sense, "accounting department" is a type of an organizational subsection, and in concrete organizations, concrete instances of this type of organizational department can exist. Such instances of the type "accounting department" may then be called "accounting department" again, since the singleton instance in a concrete organization needs no further distinguishing name to be uniquely identified.

On the conceptual enterprise modeling level, it is thus not necessary to rigidly distinguish between the notion of the type of an entity and an instance. This resembles the underlying natural language concepts of domain-specific enterprise modeling languages, because understanding natural language also is not bound to the formal type-instance dichotomy, which is a methodical tool of abstraction, not a natural property of entities. As a consequence, modeling concepts which represent entities in enterprise models may sometimes be used in either sense, without making explicit which level of abstraction, i. e., type-level or instance-level, is intended. In static perspectives of conceptual enterprise modeling, this distinction often is not necessary and can be blurred, since it is not required for understanding the organizational circumstances expressed by the model.

When referencing resources in business process models, again a conflict with the theoretical type-instance distinction appears to occur, e. g., when modeled resources are accessed multiple times from different process-steps inside the same process. During these accesses, a referenced resource may change its semantics from initially representing a resource type, to representing concrete resources as they will occur to be handled when the business process is carried out. This is the case when, e. g., a referenced resource model element initially represents a type of good to be ordered in a supply-chain process. An "order" process-step may validly reference this resource to represent the type of product ordered. During the further course of the process, when the ordered good is dispatched and transported to the purchaser who initially issued the order, the same resource model element that was used to represent a type of product when referenced from an "order" process-step, may now be validly referenced from a "receive good" process-step as a placeholder for the good instance that gets delivered to the issuer of the order as a result of the order process.

The above examples show that in enterprise models, a clear and formal distinction between types and instances is not necessarily needed or even intended. By blurring the borders between types and instances, and simply not applying the theoretical looking-glass of distinguishing concepts in a type-instance dichotomy, enterprise models gain an increased level of expressiveness and conceptual understandability for the purposes they are intended for. It is important to note that drawing a distinction between concepts on a type level, and concepts on an instance level, is only one possible theoretical perspective, which, in formal system descriptions, has proven to be useful to specify the semantics for formal concepts. However, there is nothing special in establishing semantics by using concepts beyond this formal distinction. The described blurring of the type-instance dichotomy thus is no deficiency of enterprise models, but a regular phenomenon in expressing conceptual semantics.

A software engineering method that facilitates the creation of software from enterprise models, consequentially has the task to translate the natural language semantics of enterprise models, in which types and instances may appear to be used interchangeably, to a system description, which disambiguates this blurring where required. Providing methodical means to specify this additional formal semantics avoids the above described theoretical problems that appear to exist with enterprise model semantics. The pseudo problem of a missing type-instance distinction in enterprise models becomes avoided, when a software development method provides means to explicitly disambiguiate the meaning of these elements with respect to the formally required type-instance distinction on the implementation level.

4 Requirements towards an enterprise model driven engineering approach for enterprise information systems

Valuable methodical support for enterprise information system (EIS) engineering has to meet a set of requirements, which both stem from the features an EIS is intended to support, and from demands towards the engineering method with regard to how software architects and developers are guided by the method in creating such a system. Both aspects are mutually interwoven, because the methodical procedure of how software functionality is created, also shapes the features of the resulting system.

EIS have been introduced as software systems, which are specifically tailored to support collaborative tasks in organizations (see Sect. 1.3). By their very purpose, these systems operate in a distributed environment, with multiple human and automatic actors interacting in processes and sharing information objects. To guide users through distributed collaborative processes, an EIS must be able to reference formalized process descriptions, it is thus inherently a "process-aware" information system [DvdAtH05]. EIS are central applications for users to access shared information resources in an organization, therefore they are also inherently "information aware" in the sense that they differentiate between different types of information resources and provide or invoke different viewers and editors for these information objects. Besides this, EISs interface to other applications, and are able to perform automatic process-steps. For interfacing with human users, EIS typically provide a graphical user interface (GUI).

Derived from the purposes an EIS is intended to serve, and from demands towards the shape of a methodical development procedure, a set of requirements can be stated which the implementation of an EIS is expected to fulfill. These requirements are now discussed in detail.

Requirement 1: **Provide effective and efficient methodical guidance**

One key task in software development is to handle the complexity of an entire system, by breaking it down into smaller manageable parts. To make an engineering method efficiently applicable and increase development productivity, this task should be explicitly supported by the methodical procedure. The use of a domain-specific modeling language is one approach in conquering complexity [Gro09a, KT08], because it allows to encapsulate complex semantics into abstract modeling concepts, which allows to divide modeled solution-spaces into different levels of abstraction.

In addition, methodical guidance can be provided through checking of the formal semantics of models used throughout the engineering process, especially by testing whether models are already completely specified for proceeding with subsequent methodical steps. If missing model elements can automatically be identified, or combinations of model elements can be detected as inconsistent, an automatic guiding mechanism can point software architects and developers to the corresponding places in model editors, and automatically generate a list of open to-do's to be performed on incomplete models. This list can lead architects and developers efficiently through a process of completing the models.

Any methodical procedure which guides in performing actions by providing conceptual reflection on how to perform them, and potentially with which tools to perform them, implicitly aims at an increase in effectiveness and efficiency. Effectiveness means that the correct use of the method will lead to a software system that fulfills the requirements specified. Projected onto the concrete task of providing a method for software engineering based on enterprise models, an effective method must succeed in providing solutions for formally interpreting the semantics of conceptual enterprise models, to translate them to technical implementation terms. This covers, e. g., the interpretation of business process models as workflow descriptions, the disambiguation of actor and resource specifications for technical purposes, and means for explicating the results of these interpretation steps in a way they become revisable and editable by human developers.

Aiming at efficiency denotes that the engineering process prospectively needs less development efforts than a generic or unspecific approach, or any other already known solution. This, of course, is a generic justification pattern for any purposefully performed engineering action, because it is unreasonable to perform an engineering process while a known alternative would lead to identical results with less efforts. Less efforts in software engineering can be understood as less time spent on developing, using less man power (which is important, because qualified software engineers are rare to find), and producing results which are less prone to errors, thus in turn cause lower maintenance cost.

Requirement 2: **Support various enterprise modeling languages**

The method to be developed should be configurable for using different enterprise modeling language families, with their associated enterprise modeling languages. This requirement stems from the research goal of constructing a generic methodical approach, independent from specific enterprise modeling methods. By including a configuration mechanism, which allows to plug-in any enterprise modeling languages (EMLs) and corresponding tools, it is made theoretically clear that the method can be applied independently from specifics in a concrete enterprise modeling approach.

Adaptability of arbitrary external enterprise models also supports the generic requirement for efficiency, because the method will be applicable with less effort if involved domain experts can continue using their familiar enterprise modeling tools, without possibly having to switch to another enterprise modeling approach.

Requirement 3: **Support distributed and heterogeneous architectures**

Actors interacting with an EIS, either human users or automatically acting machinery like software systems, must be considered to be locally distributed and physically placed remote to each other in an EIS environment. The engineering method should thus provide means to cope with the development of distributed software systems. Spatial distribution requires the overall EIS to operate concurrently with multiple front-ends which need to interact and coordinate their behavior. The system architecture thus must consider a mechanism to provide the coordination of a distributed system, which is typically solved either by introducing a central coordination component, or by consulting interaction protocols between individual front-end applications which provide common coordination without a central coordinating instance. Some processes in organizations include movement or transportation over large distances. In order to support these processes, an EIS should potentially be accessible through mobile front-end applications, too.

Technological components that are integrated through an EIS in a locally distributed environment can consist of heterogeneous system architectures, which make the components incompatible to each other. An EIS development approach must provide the flexibility to consult mechanisms for integrating heterogeneous software components, e. g., by incorporating object request broker (ORB) functionality into the software system created, which translates semantically integrated data between syntactically incompatible interfaces.

Besides dealing with semantic incompatibilities, the development method also has to take heterogeneous platform architectures into account, on top of which the developed software will run, e. g., different operating systems, hardware platforms, and programming languages. Due to the distributed and heterogeneous nature of EIS, the need arises to use a method which supports multiple of these target architectures at the same time. The method should thus support the development of software for target platforms, which were not yet specified by the time the method was conceptualized, and it should support the use of multiple different target platforms simultaneously in one development project.

Requirement 4:   Provide multi-user support

According to its distributed nature, an EIS must support multiple users, who operate in either the same or different concurrently running processes supported by the system.

For the engineering method, this means that functional components for user authentication and authorization must be made available. Since the system may also be used in parallel by multiple user simultaneously, multi-tasking and re-entrant behavior also need to be considered.

Requirement 5:   Enable process awareness

In order to provide functionality for supporting organizational business processes, the engineering method should make use of formalized knowledge about the processes supported by an EIS. This includes knowledge about which actor roles are involved in processes, which concrete users fulfill these roles, which resources are used, and at which points control flow is passed between different steps of actions from one user to a potentially other. From a user's point of view, an EIS front-end application should provide a comprehensive overview on the available process types and current process instances the user is involved in.

Knowledge about these organizational circumstances should be derived from enterprise models, to have a formalized basis for specifying the requirements towards the system to be developed.

Requirement 6:   Enable information awareness

Since information access is a relevant kind of action carried out by actors in an organization, one central feature for EISs is to offer access to available types of information objects in an organization, and to offer functionality for managing access to information object instances. In a collaborative environment, information objects may be shared among multiple users, or may be privately accessible by individuals.

To provide such functionality, several technical components must be accounted for by the EIS architecture, and consequentially by the engineering method that guides the process of implementing executable software on top of this architecture. At first, the development method must make use a type declaration system which allows to describe and differentiate different information object types.

As a second element, the method must either come with its own mechanism to persistently store instances of information objects and make them accessible by authorized users, or should allow to interface to components which are responsible for carrying out these data management tasks.

A third building block of providing information awareness is to include viewers and editors to allow users to access information objects and potentially edit them. Again, several options exist to realize such access, e. g., by internally providing editor software components as part of the EIS, or by referencing external viewers or editor applications. These options are to be explicated by the method.

Requirement 7:   Incorporate security aspects

Because an EIS is an important information backbone in an organization, data transmissions and technical communication using the system should be secured against interception and spoofing by means of security technologies [BFV$^+$11]. An implementation strategy meta-model should explicate security relevant functionality where possible.

Aspects of security may be considered indispensable features of distributed, multi-user systems in heterogeneous environments. To explicate this aspect separately, and point out its importance in an engineering method, is especially relevant for commercial, governmental or large-scale organizations, which can be expected to disclose severe vulnerabilities if using insecure EIS components.

Requirement 8:   Support the use of graphical user interfaces

To serve the purpose of efficiently supplementing human work, the functionality offered to users of an EIS should be accessible through intuitive front-ends with a GUI appropriate for the device used. The engineering method should support the development of GUI functionality on a level of abstraction, which closely follows the specifics of the conceptual domain and relieves developers from time-consuming manual development of GUIs, by automatically generating default GUI components where possible.

Requirement 9:   **Offer automatic processing capabilities**

EISs support carrying out processes in organizations. This also includes automatic processing steps to be taken into account by the engineering method. While supporting these is a very general requirement, because all pieces of software are intended to perform automatic actions in a general sense, there still are variants of architectural design decisions that come along with the realization of automatic processing steps.

Questions about realizing automatic processing steps cover the range of different programming mechanisms or languages, with which to formulate the desired automatic processing steps, as well as questions about which physical platform in a distributed environment should perform an automatic processing step, or which external component is responsible instead. The method should provide means for explicating these implementation design decisions.

Requirement 10:   **Allow for integration of external software components**

Interfacing between different software components is a general topic in building distributed, heterogeneous architectures [Ver96]. An EIS integrates external components to delegate functionality to.

Interfaces to external components can be established with a wide variety of remote invocation concepts and technologies, such as the use of Simple Object Access Protocol (SOAP)-based web-services, remote procedure calls, or wrapped command-line invocations to legacy systems. Options for explicitly choosing between these alternative implementation approaches should be offered by the method.

Requirement 11:   **Allow for integration of organization-specific functionality**

Depending on the usage scenario, EISs may provide a crucial added value for an organization by incorporating specific functionality supporting the organization's core competitive advantage. An example would be the integration of location-based geographic data via mobile devices for a logistic service company, which could, in combination with an appropriate routing mechanism, lead to significant competitive advantages in organizing the transportation of physical goods.

Generally, a method for EIS development should be open to integrate such organization specific functionality, to be able to reflect relevant competitive advantages of the organization in the EIS to be developed. The architecture of an EIS should be designed in a way which allows for general extensibility of its core functionality by specific features.

Requirement 12:   **Handle the abstraction gap between enterprise models and implementation descriptions**

A major theoretical issue when dealing with enterprise models on the one hand, and technical implementation descriptions, such as workflow models or source code, on the other hand, is the difference in the levels of abstraction [DvdA04]. A business process model

(BPM), e. g., is located on a conceptually higher degree of abstraction than executable workflow models or programs. Detail knowledge is left out, and an adequate blurring of concepts is performed. BPMs are intentionally imprecise, which allows them to offer information on a scale relevant to handle the modeled parts of an organization, while still remaining cognitively accessible for human modelers and model recipients (see Sect. 3.6).

The idea of being imprecise, however, is not compatible with technical implementation models, because in order to provide a machine-executable process description, the implementations need to be precise. A development method that leads from conceptual enterprise models to executable software thus needs to provide means to disambiguate knowledge expressed by conceptual models. The decisions about how concepts are disambiguated should be made explicit and persistent over time. This way, the design rationales are traceable at later points in time, and can be used as a basis for automatically generating executable technical components as part of a code-generation step in the development method.

Requirement 13: **Support performing the ontological turn from a bird's-eye-view perspective to an inner system perspective**

Enterprise models and implementation models show inherent incompatibilities, not only with regard to the level of conceptual abstraction of their elements' semantics, but concerning the ontological perspective they take in when describing systems. Enterprise models provide descriptions from a bird's-eye-view overview perspective on an organization. When creating and editing enterprise models, the modeling stakeholders look onto a described organization "from above". Except for the rules imposed by the abstract syntax of the modeling languages, there are no a-priori restrictions on what incidents can be modeled, and what content is expressed in the given domain of the modeling languages.

Implementation-level modeling strongly differs from handling this kind of semi-formal semantics. When modeling implementation technology, a technical system is described relative to an underlying technical architecture, which imposes structural and dynamic restrictions on the system to be implemented. On the implementation level, the execution of process-descriptions is not understood as a process flow which happens on its own through the actions of individually operating actors. Instead, the dynamics of a technical system implementation occur on the background of an execution mechanism, e. g., a workflow-model interpreter, which defines the operative semantics of a modeled process. To get from a conceptual overview perspective to a system view which is stated in terms relative to a given technical architecture, not only a different level of abstraction is required, but performing an ontological turn in the way how the descriptions are created. Methodical guidance should be provided by a development method to perform this turn of the ontological perspective.

Requirement 14: **Incorporate domain experts into the development process**

At an early stage in the engineering process, while creating conceptual enterprise models, domain experts without technical competencies should be able to participate in the conceptualization of requirements towards the software system. These domain experts may be prospective future users of the software system, managers, or external consultants.

Incorporating these groups of stakeholders at an early point in time into the development process, allows for capturing requirements towards the software system as early as possible, which reduces cost for performing later changes, and lowers the risk to put development efforts into functionality which later turns out to be useless. It also fosters the requirement for strengthening trust among stakeholders in the development process, since the experts can be sure that their expertise has a relevant influence on the following development process.

Requirement 15: **Strengthen trust among stakeholders**

EISs perform a linking role among members of an organization, and bind them together to constitute a socio-technical system. They provide an interface function between individual actors on the one hand, and the collective organization on the other hand. By operating an EIS, an individual member integrates into the organization, and shapes the organization by contributing and revising knowledge, or taking decisions that influence the organization in parts or as a whole. Such an environment requires mutual trust among the participants. Actors needs to trust that the information and collaboration processes made accessible by the system are authentic, and that his or her identity as part of the overall organization is authentically perceived by other participants. Resulting from these individual interests in authentically participating in the organization, all actors have an interest in the EIS to work according to a common understanding of the organization.

Using enterprise models commonly understood by all involved participants serves to establish an agreed notion about how the organization is intended to work, and how an according EIS should support the individual contributions of the involved stakeholders. They foster a common understanding of the desired EIS functionality, and thus provide the basis for mutual trust among all particpants involved, both at development time, and during the operative use of an EIS.

5 Enterprise models for model-driven software engineering

5.1 Organization theory concepts in enterprise modeling languages

The concepts and terminology used in enterprise models (EMs) to describe a socio-technical action system of human stakeholders and resources in an organization consist of a domain-specific set of terms adopted from organization theory [Daf09, PW09]. EMs in a narrow sense do not describe technical artifacts, they intentionally lack the terminology for characterizing details about objects in a technological domain. Some approaches integrate the notion of enterprise modeling with references to technical concepts specified by other modeling languages, e. g., by referencing Unified Modeling Language (UML)-like class diagrams [Fra02, Fra11c]. Others try to use the UML as modeling language for the conceptual enterprise modeling perspectives [Mar00, Rit07]. This way of integrating conceptual enterprise perspectives and technical views, however, does not provide a separation of concerns between conceptual action system modeling and technical software design, and is not followed in the upcoming research work. The notion of the term "enterprise model", as it is applied throughout the elaboration of the Software Engineering with Enterprise Models (SEEM) method, exclusively focuses on non-technical organizational descriptions. Any computation-specific or platform-specific information is separated in individual models and formulated at different stages of the development process by the responsible stakeholders.

Concepts from organization theory, which are involved in action system descriptions, typically reside in the semantic areas of actors, resources, interactions, business processes and strategy. The following subsections provide an overview on the meaning of these terms with respect to their use in an enterprise model driven software engineering method.

5.1.1 Actors

The notion of actors in an enterprise model resembles a generalization over people who are involved in performing processes in the organization. From a coarse overview perspective in enterprise models, an actor may be understood as either a role, which is to be fulfilled by concrete persons, a group of persons out of which one or more individuals are referenced, an individual person, or an automatic entity which actively operates during the execution of business processes in the organization.

A more fine-grained notion of the concept of an actor is given by business-related conceptualizations of organizational roles, positions, groups and individuals [Fra11a]. Roles are placeholders for specific sets of features, which can be associated with either groups or individuals [AG08]. These features can include access rights and further capabilities which mark a group or an individual as being suitable for performing some specific task in a business process. Individual persons can be member of one or more groups, and can fulfill any number of roles. Roles are considered to be fulfilled by a person if either a direct association between the person and the role exists, or the person is member of a group, the roles of which are transitively considered to be fulfilled by the individual group members.

For implementing a software system, it is relevant to know which detail semantics of the notion of an actor is intended. A software system needs to know whether specific process-steps are intended to be performed by individual persons in the organization, or whether suitable persons can be derived, e. g., by their membership to a specific group, or by having a certain role attached.

Some enterprise modeling languages provide this fine-grained set of concepts to describe the notion of actors as language concepts in their modeling languages. However, since these detail distinctions are not generally available with all enterprise modeling approaches, and because they may even be considered too detailed by responsible enterprise modelers and intentionally be left out on the conceptual modeling level, a software engineering method that bases on enterprise models should offer a mechanism to disambiguate the notion of actors in conceptual models. This allows to reflect the detail notions of roles, groups and concrete persons on the implementation level, and opens up the possibility to formally specify further interpretation options for project-specific settings.

5.1.2 Resources

The term "resource" covers a broad range of possible meaning in enterprise modeling. Any kind of physical entity can be considered a resource, if a relation to a process-step is to be explicated. Physical resources may be entities that help in performing a process-step, e. g., machinery or transportation devices, or may be transformed or consumed in the course of a process-step, such as raw material or lubricants. Covering the semantics of each of these concrete physical resource types in depth, would require to develop individual domain-specific modeling languages [Jun07]. Such a level of detail is, however, not required in most cases of enterprise modeling, which is why physical resources in most cases are merely modeled to exist, identified by a name with natural language semantics. Detail features of the individual physical resources are out of scope of enterprise modeling.

An important other kind of resources in organizations is information. Commonly shared information binds together multiple, possibly distributed, actors, and operationally controls and synchronizes different activities in an organization. There are multiple different shapes in which information can occur. It can be stored persistently as electronic or physical documents, or it can be temporarily generated and used during the execution of business processes [WMB+03]. On the conceptual level of enterprise modeling, occurrences of information are typically explicated using special kinds of resources. Enterprise modeling languages typically combine the notion of information types and concrete information objects, i. e., the same information resource modeling construct may be used to express individual existing information objects, groups of such objects, or information objects yet to be created (see Sect. 3.6). The context of using information resource modeling constructs is usually sufficient for understanding, in which way an information resource is meant to be used. An effective software engineering method that builds upon enterprise models, must take this into account and needs to provide a mechanism to disambiguate the notion of information resources, as it is intentionally blurred on the conceptual level, to concrete information type and storage specifications.

Software applications used in semi-automatic or automatic process-steps may also be modeled as resources involved in performing the process-step. If an enterprise modeling language does not contain an individual element for software, usually a general resource type is used to express software in a semi-formal way. On the conceptual level of business process models, there usually is no motivation to distinguish further concretions of software, e. g., whether the application is a traditional desktop application, or whether it is invoked as web service.

It is important to note that an EIS component itself does not have to be modeled explicitly as a software application. The existence of an EIS is inherent to the idea of automatically executing modeled business processes, so the EIS acts as an operative interpreting instance that manifests the semantics behind the business processes and is the default automatic actor if not otherwise modeled.

5.1.3 Interactions

Enterprise modeling languages may offer constructs for expressing interactions among entities of different kinds. These may serve to, e. g., explicate relationships among different actors, and specify potential communication channels by phone, e-mail or other means.

Modeling constructs for interaction may be restricted to the relationships among entities inside the organization, or may extend to external entities on different scales, such as customers and business partners, other organizations as grouped entities, or entire markets and market segments [Fra02].

5.1.4 Business processes

Business process modeling provides the central integrating perspective for enterprise modeling [Wes07, Fra11b]. Business process models refer to model elements from different perspectives on the enterprise, and relate them to the procedural view with regard to the process-steps which they play a part in. By looking at the procedures happening, these elements become presented in a configuration specific to the processes in focus, and contextualize knowledge about involved actors and resources, to form a complete description of an organization.

A set of basic element types is commonly used in business process modeling languages, with comparable semantics in most languages. One of these fundamental element types is the notion of a process-step. A process-step is any distinct describable action that is performed as part of a business process, either by human actors, machines, or as a software-supported interaction between both. Process-steps can be described on various levels of granularity. This means, a process-step may either describe a small step of action, e. g., automatically calculating a numerical value, or a coarse-grained composite action, e. g., writing a consultative e-mail to a customer and send it with the help of an e-mail client application. It is up to the conceptual modelers, which level of granularity to choose, and to decide whether a mix of multiple levels of granularity in a single BPM makes sense. When process-step actions are carried out, human actors may be incorporated, either as operatively performing personnel, or in supervising management capacities. Also, resources may be involved in performing process-steps, which either may cover physical resources, information resources, software resources or other process-specific resources. Business process modeling languages (BPMLs) typically offer language constructs to establish links from process-step descriptions to actor and resource descriptions, to express the various types of relationships that can exist among them. By modeling these assignments, BPMs gain a high degree of multi-dimensional integration, and become complex artifacts of knowledge expression.

Another basic type of model elements in BPMLs are events. Events indicate that something has happened or that some change of state has occurred. One sub-kind are start-events, which mark possible entry points into a business process, thus describe occurrences or conditions, under which an instance of a business process will be executed. Since various reasons for carrying out business processes are possible, the conceptual modeling construct of a start-event is specified via a wide range of informal semantics, which describe the actual meaning of the event in natural language.

Some BPMLs even enforce the use of event elements after every process-step, to explicitly model the state change that comes with the execution of a process-step. The description of events during a business process is thus typically related to the description of process-steps, and the semantics of each non-start event is tightly bound to its surrounding process-steps. In the most simple case, an event modeled in the course of a business process, only denotes that the previous process-step has ended. There is no additional semantics attached to events of this kind. Events with richer semantics may directly refer to possible outcomes of previous process-steps, e. g., they may model different possible decisions taken during the process-step, or results calculated. Depending on these outcomes of previous process-step, the business process may continue with different alternative procedures.

To describe the control flow of a business process, i. e., the logical order in which process-steps, events and other elements are expected to occur, BPMLs typically provide the language construct of a sequence between elements. A sequence in this sense represents the direct link between two elements in the business process. It if often graphically visualized in diagrammatic BPMLs as a directed arrow symbol. The term "sequence" does not refer to a sequential chain of multiple interlinked elements in the context of this work, such a pattern would rather be referred to as a sub-process.

Besides the three basic element types of process-steps, events and sequences, BPMLs may also offer language constructs to model additional features of the process control flow, e. g., the begin and end of parallely executed sub-processes, or the notion of interrupting events which may occur during the execution of a process or sub-process at an arbitrary time. Modelers responsible for conceptually expressing BPMs will have to make trade-offs between complexity and understandability of their models, when they apply these concepts.

Further advanced BPML conceptualizations suggest additional ways of enriching BPMs with enterprise specific semantics, e. g., by relating performance indicators and corresponding metrics to process model elements [SFHK11]. These developments show that the potential of applying enterprise modeling techniques has only yet begun to be productively exploited, and that a variety of further developments in the field of conceptual enterprise modeling can be expected in the future.

5.1.5 Strategy

The overall motivations for forming an organization are dependent on its strategic goals and purposes. There may be manifold reasons why an organization is formed or forms itself. One typical major reason for commercial enterprises is the gain of economic win. Although most commercial organizations share this major goal in the long run, they differ strongly in further breaking down this coarse-grained major goal into intermediate and subsumed sub-goals.

Strategic goals and purposes are long-term properties of a company, which are considered to remain stable over time [Win02]. They represent the main drivers for an organization's activities and its positioning in the social and economic environment. As a consequence, the structure and weighing of goals, and the explication of means which serve to reach them, play an important role for the conceptual understanding of enterprise models. Enterprise modeling languages typically offer modeling constructs to semi-formally explicate strategic goals and sub-goals [Köh12], interrelations among goals, e. g., refinement, enforcement, or substitution, and relations to the business processes, actors and resources, which serve as means to fulfill the goals.

Other kinds of concepts that are associated with the strategic level of enterprise modeling are the ability to express value chains [Fra12] or portfolios. This kind of knowledge provides an integrating roof under which the individual business process models and multiple partial structural models are integrated to form a comprehensive common whole. For software engineering purposes, there is no primary interest to relate to these conceptual strategic elements, although potentially the knowledge derived from this semantic area can also be incorporated for methodical support, e. g., to prioritize which modeled business processes are to be implemented first, or how a version management for future releases should be planned.

5.2 Model-driven software engineering as an act of interpretation

5.2.1 Conceptual vagueness in domain-specific modeling languages and models

A domain-specific software engineering approach describes how to utilize knowledge in domain-specific models to generate software from them. Such an approach provides a defined procedure to link from abstract conceptual descriptions of a domain to formal technical descriptions of a software system. This process cannot be performed as a syntactic horizontal transformation from one language to the other, because the ontological perspectives of both realms of description, the described reality covered by the domain-specific models on the one hand, and technical descriptions of implementation components of the software on the other hand, are typically orthogonal to each other, and reside on different levels of terminological abstraction. When enterprise models are consulted as conceptual models, the underlying concepts of a domain description are based on organization theoretical notions of roles, responsibilities, flows, metrics etc. Descriptions of software systems, on the contrary, operate with terminology determined by underlying execution paradigms and platform application programming interfaces (APIs) of running software, which in case of object-oriented system design are, e. g., components, interfaces, classes, methods, types etc. Getting from one realm of description to the other is not merely an act of translating between two languages. Instead, it consists of a semantic interpretation of one realm on the background of the other, to understand the semantics of the conceptual domain, and design a formal system with this understanding in mind.

Interpreting and understanding statements about a conceptual domain requires knowledge about the context in which conceptual descriptions have been stated, and about the intentions that have motivated modelers to create the descriptions. Conceptual models can only be understood with this background knowledge in mind, because the abstractions of the domain concepts, reflected as modeling language elements and model instance elements, can only serve to point out relevant distinctions to a domain expert, they are not intended to explicate and transfer all additional knowledge required to understand the modeled concept in total. This would not even be possible, because any natural or formal language description has to make a cut in going into details at some point, and presuppose culturally and socio-biologically acquired background knowledge on the recipient's side [Put88]. In other words, to understand something already implies to have understood other things about the context and intentions, which are not explicated. If this was not the case, meaning could not successfully be communicated by verbal statements, models, pictures, etc., because every utterance would have to transport knowledge about the entire context and intentions with it, which would make communication ineffectively complex.

For human understanding, it is the natural mode of thinking to involve background knowledge and contextual information as tacit knowledge [Bau99], which enables the understanding of further explications. For this reason, in conceptual modeling, it is reasonable and efficient to exclude detail information and knowledge that can be presupposed by expert modelers from the language elements and, as a consequence, from model instances. Conceptual models are intended to concentrate on expresssing those facts, which describe the unique and relevant aspects of the circumstances in focus. Conceptual vagueness on this level of abstraction is intended.

While conceptual vagueness increases the efficiency and effectiveness of conceptual modeling performed by human stakeholders, it stands in conflict with the automatic processing of the conceptual models for further use in a software engineering procedure. Automatic processing of content in conceptual models requires data processing techniques, which operate on semi-formal, and possibly incomplete data. This can be achieved by applying hints for extracting knowledge from models, and by offering a set of default values to be used when incomplete information is met.

5.2.2 Incorporating semi-formal interpretation transformations into model-driven software engineering with domain-specific models

Domain-specific modeling aims at supporting the interpretation of conceptual models and the resulting creation of technical system descriptions by automatic or semi-automatic model transformations and code generation techniques. In a traditional domain-specific software engineering (DSSE) approach [KT08], the interpretation of the conceptual semantics in domain-specific models is included as within the artifact generation templates, and, as a consequence, artifact generation templates for a conceptual domain-specific modeling language (DSML) do not only realize a simple structural mapping from model elements to artifacts components. Instead, their implementation incorporates domain related decisions about how to interpret model content in the input models, and at the same time, how to output software artifacts based on these decisions.

To successfully bridge the gap from the conceptual description realm to deployable artifacts, model-to-model transformations and artifact generation templates used in DSSE need to be able to perform semantic interpretation. This is an important difference to artifact generation procedures based on general purpose modeling languages (GPMLs), which intentionally keep the modeling language free from specific semantics. The SEEM method explicitly focuses on this interpretation task, and encapsulates it in a separate methodical step with dedicated model elements that allow to formally express the decisions taken throughout the process of semantic interpretation.

5.3 Related research and existing approaches

The SEEM method touches multiple research questions in the field of business process modeling, information technology (IT)-business alignment, and model-based software development. It partially overlaps with existing methodical approaches in model-driven software engineering (MDSE), and there are software products available, which claim to offer functionality for executing business process models. To relate the SEEM method to these existing approaches, representatives of related work are discussed in the following sections.

5.3.1 Model-driven architecture (MDA)

In its general notion, the term model-driven development (MDD), synonymously called model-driven software engineering (MDSE), refers to a kind software development method, which uses models to create software by means of transformation procedures from models to executable artifacts. Typically, model-driven development methods describe a procedure in which the stages of system conceptualization, system design, and system implementation, use their specific modeling languages, to provide the semantic expressiveness required to express design decisions on the corresponding stage. In this general sense, the proposed SEEM method is a model-driven development method, too.

Development methods, which consult models for expressing design decisions in a software development process, but do not come with a continuous chain of model transformations for creating executable artifacts from the models, can generally be subsumed under the term Model-Driven Architecture (MDA). MDA approaches use models as means of semi-formal communication among software architects and developers. Design decisions may be expressed with equal modeling constructs as in an MDD approach, however, the realization of these decisions is performed with traditional manual implementation techniques.

The general MDD and MDA conceptualizations form two poles of a continuum, between which any mixture of the approaches can be realized. For example, an MDA procedure may be enriched with a set of supplementary model transformations, which partially realize a formal transformation relationship between models and artifacts, but still plan for manual development work to be part of the artifact generation process.

Speaking about MDD and MDA in a general notion does not specify whether domain-specific modeling languages are used, or so-called general purpose modeling languages. In a narrower sense, the term MDA is a trademark label of a software development method issued by the Object Management Group (OMG) organization [Obj03]. This method describes options for possible realizations of a model-driven development procedure, and suggests to use general-purpose modeling languages of the UML.

CIM, PIM, and PSM models in MDD   The process of spanning the bridge from conceptual models to implemented artifacts in MDA is conceptualized in three stages along the phases analysis, design and implementation, with each stage having models of an associated type as its central objects of interest. During the development process, the level of conceptual abstraction is lowered from stage to stage by transforming a model from a higher conceptual abstraction level, to a model on a lower level of abstraction.

Models for capturing analysis conceptualizations, describing the problem space of a system to be developed, are called computation independent models (CIMs) in the context of MDA, because they are expected to describe requirements towards the system independent from any technical implementation. Models that carry information about the system design are named platform independent models (PIMs), as they conceptualize architectural options for technically realizing the desired system, without, however, specifying implementation details. The latter are finally captured for the implementation phase in platform specific models (PSMs), which reflect technical components of the system to be developed.

Although the individual models are associated with different levels of abstraction, and, as a consequence, describe different concepts and objects of interest, the OMG's MDA approach suggests to use the same general purpose modeling languages (GPMLs) as languages for describing concepts on each of the three stages.

The UML as standard modeling language for MDA and MDD   The OMG's MDA and MDD approaches are intended to complement the UML modeling language specification with a procedural framework in which the use of the UML as part of a software development process is methodically described. As a consequence, the model types offered by the UML are used in any stage of the methods. Using the UML languages on the implementation level to express PSMs is useful, because the modeling constructs offered by the UML typically are generalized abstractions over software technical artifacts, e. g., class diagrams mostly contain elements which can directly be mapped onto the constructs of object-oriented programming languages. This supporting argument for using the UML still holds true for PIM models, which also describe formal system structures, for which the UML can be said to be an appropriate choice of modeling language.

However, making use of the UML language family to conceptually represent the knowledge in CIMs, i. e., in models, which intentionally exclude the technical perspective from there modeled objectives, appears to be one methodical deficiency of the overall MDA conceptualization. If the aim of a model is to explicitly describe knowledge beyond technical and formal system structures, the language means for performing this description should not directly reflect these constructs.

While MDA specifies model types and transformations between them, it does not aim at fully relying on automatic transformations from CIM to PIM, PSM, and finally to executable artifacts. Over time, efforts for maturing MDA to an approach which resembles a full MDD engineering method, using entirely automated model transformation procedures, have not led to a successful outcome [Obj03]. The use of the general purpose UML languages has turned out to be too inflexible to capture all knowledge required for a fully automated transformation procedure. Consequently, the MDA approach typically plans all involved models to be edited manually and enriched with additional implementation specific artifacts, e. g., program code.

In MDA, models are used to help structuring the development process, and to express relevant design decisions in a semi-formal way for better cognitive grasping by the involved developers. However, MDA does not necessarily provide a substantial shift in increasing development efficiency, because the approach cannot guarantee that the methodical means for expressing CIMs are sufficient to capture relevant requirements and desired features of the prospective software system. Depending on the problem space, MDA might be helpful, but the method itself does not provide means to estimate, to which extent the use of GPMLs is efficient for a given requirements scenario.

It thus turns out that the modeling languages for expressing the conceptual and computation-independent models are a central weak point in the overall approach. This weak point has been one motivating momentum for an alternative development method conceptualization, which suggests the use of problem-adequate modeling languages to engage conceptual models as starting points for software development processes, as it is done by the SEEM method.

5.3.2 Rational Unified Process (RUP)

To complement the set of modeling languages introduced by the UML with procedural advice on how to apply these languages in a software development project, the authors who created the UML originally elaborated a method called Unified Process in parallel to the UML, which was later renamed to Rational Unified Process (RUP) [Kru03, Rat01, SK08].

The name "Rational" refers to the software company, which originally offered the method as a commercial product.

The RUP is actually a method framework, which does not describe concrete procedural steps for developing software, but imposes a structure on software development projects to be filled with technical development procedures. This is achieved by combining two traditional means for structuring methods, which are methodical perspectives, and methodical steps. Perspectives and steps are structured in an orthogonal way, forming a two-dimensional framework, in which each perspective is to be considered specifically in each step.

The RUP combines several concepts of object-oriented software planning, design and implementation in one joined framework [Kru03]. As part of multiple perspectives in each project phase, the method incorporates the notions of both business modeling, which resembles a general idea of conceptual domain knowledge specification by enterprise modeling, and requirements specification, followed by the traditional methodical steps analysis, design, implementation, test and deployment, and administrative perspectives. The RUP does not incorporate a methodical link for systematically interconnecting business modeling with requirements engineering. Nor does it provide means for systematically relating implementation-level design-decisions with the rationales behind conceptual elements appearing in the business models. Both aspects are regarded as separate methodical means, and interlinking between them is left to development work throughout the phases of the method.

The RUP has a much wider and more general focus than the SEEM method. It provides a generic project handling framework including aspects of project management and infrastructure planning, into which the SEEM method could be interwoven as methodical procedure for software development. In this case, SEEM would fill-in traditional notions of business modeling and requirements engineering, and blur the distinctions between both of them internally in the RUP framework, while still leaving the entire method applicable. Further ideas on integrating SEEM into the RUP shall not be discussed at this point.

5.3.3 Domain-specific software engineering

In its basic form, a domain-specific software engineering (DSSE) method requires three components to be made available prior to applying the method for software generation [KT08]. At first, a domain-specific modeling language is to be developed which provides means to express knowledge about a domain in a terminology that is well-known to domain experts. The language must be developed together with appropriate tooling support in form of a model editor, which allows to create and manipulate model instance in that language. This editor typically is a diagram editor, which uses graphical facilities to represent model concepts visually.

The second methodical component required for DSSE is a domain API, which provides abstractions of both conceptual features of the application to be developed, and technical features of the operating system and underlying device platform on which the generated application is intended to be run [KT08]. These abstractions may come in the form of abstract specifications, such as object-oriented interfaces or abstract classes, or as a set of project-specific API functions, which provide callable building-block functionality of the system to be developed.

The building-blocks provided by the API are invoked and used by program code that gets generated in the course of applying the domain-specific model-driven development method. This is done using code generation templates [CE00], which are the third kind of methodical components to be created before the method can entirely be applied. Code generation templates are programmed artifacts, which combine at least two semantically orthogonal kinds of program code: an "outer" set of template language constructs, which gets interpreted by a corresponding template language interpreter, and a set of "inner" target language fragments, which are wrapped into the template language constructs, and are assembled to complete program code artifacts according to the statements of the wrapping template language at build time.

To develop code generation templates, a higher level of software engineering expertise than for usual programming tasks is required, because code generation templates intentionally mix a meta-level of outer template language statements, and a concrete level of target programming language artifacts. Creating code generation templates requires a developer to be able to invent and apply programming patterns, which combine both levels of abstraction. Traditional development using a single programming language demands from a developer to be able to anticipate the behavior of a language's execution mechanism at runtime, based on the program code as it is written and readable. To make a code generation mechanism output executable program code, however, a developer has to imagine the resulting behavior from program code, which does not exist as a static artifact yet, but will itself be the result of an execution mechanism run at build time.

A well-designed API, which provides suitable abstractions for the application and the platform, can help reducing the complexity and thus the effort in creating code generation templates. There is a design trade-off between realizing functionality in the API, or implementing it via fragments in the code generation templates. Code generation templates and the API will thus most likely have to be iteratively developed, with experiences in creating one set of components influencing the other. Consequently, if software developers are available, who are capable of developing both kinds of components simultaneously, a significant increase in development efficiency can be anticipated.

The proposed SEEM method borrows some fundamental principles from domain-specific modeling (DSM), while it also enhances traditional DSSE approaches with new solutions. Concepts common with DSSE are the notion of the separation between a domain-specific model on a high abstraction level, and implementation artifacts on a lower abstraction level, which get derived by a defined transformation procedure from the higher level abstraction model. In combination with this general approach, the notion of a target architecture is important in DSSE for defining the transformation procedure [KT08].

The SEEM method also takes the notion of target architectures into account. As an enhancement to DSSE, it offers fine-grained methodical means by which the characteristics of target architectures are specified. This is done by incorporating the creation of implementation strategy meta-models for each target architecture in a development project, and the instantiation of implementation strategy model instances, which describe concrete target architecture components and functionality that is to be used in a later artifact generation process (see Sect. 6.2.3). This approach allows to separate the description of conceptual domain-specifics in the source DSML model on the one hand, and the specification of details about the technical target architecture domain in implementation strategy models on the other hand. Both types of models get interwoven by the mapping model. In combination, they provide sufficient information to run an artifact generation procedure as the final development step in the method.

This proposed approach solves the perceived phenomenon of different kinds of conceptual and technical domains described in the same domain-specific model, as it can often be discovered in DSSE projects [LKT04]. In traditional DSSE projects, which are typically restricted to using a single DSML, knowledge about the conceptual domain, and details about the technical implementation domain, as a consequence get mixed together in single domain-specific model instance. Relying on separate implementation strategy models providing information about the technical target architecture domain as orthogonal domain-specific models, allows to keep the conceptual domain models free from any implementation details. For the very purpose of the SEEM method, the enterprise modeling language must be expected to contain conceptual domain knowledge only, to allow to incorporate non-technical domain experts in early phases of the software development project (see Req. 14), and to be able to use any existing enterprise modeling tools and methods as the entry point into the method (see Req. 2). In this sense, the enterprise modeling languages used in SEEM resemble the first sub-type of DSML identified by [LKT04], which are DSMLs exclusively based on domain expert's concepts, without any implementation details incorporated.

The original DSSE approach considers a single domain-specific model as sufficient basis for a development procedure, as long as the corresponding modeling language makes sure to offer all required expressive means to capture knowledge required to generate the entire target software system as desired. This approach comes with the fundamental drawback of forcing all kinds of information required to build software into a single model, with a single underlying, project-specific modeling language. As a consequence, the DSML used for these purposes cannot offer a clean separation of abstraction layers, because it is required to mix concepts from multiple perspectives and abstraction levels into one language. Realizing such a mixture, the language does not distinguish between conceptual domain knowledge on the one hand, and technically related knowledge about the implementation domain on the other hand. The potential for reusing at least some aspects of either of the two domains is low using this approach, because domain-specific conceptual aspects and technical aspects are interwoven in a single language with respect to a concrete development project, which is less likely to be repeatedly useful for other development tasks than distinct conceptualization of the organizational domain and the technical domain.

As a more structured alternative to using a single monolithic transformation for bridging from conceptual models to implementation models, abstractions over the knowledge that is incorporated in a single transformation can be made and collected in auxiliary models, which hold information about how elements from the conceptual models are mapped to implementation-relevant knowledge. If such auxiliary models are applied, several design decisions and implementation contingencies about the software to be developed can be cleanly explicated by the use of models instead of weaving them into transformation specification source code.

5.3.4 Enterprise architecture

Research activities around formal and semi-formal descriptions of organizations and enterprises have been undertaken since the second half of the 1980s, beginning with [Zac87]. They have evolved as the conceptual foundations, which today underly enterprise modeling activities.

Unlike enterprise modeling, enterprise architecture is primarily located on a conceptual, business-oriented level, and it does not cover aspects, such as, development of formal languages, modeling tool development, or automatized model analysis [Gro04, Lan09, LPW+09]. The originators of enterprise architecture did not envision to use enterprise architecture description artifacts as the requirements foundations for software engineering projects. However, enterprise architecture (EA) and enterprise model (EM) share a common understanding of description perspectives and concepts to describe organizational structure as well as an organization's activities.

EA is primarily looking at the business side, discussing means for strategic planning, operative control, and for governing organizations to establish structure and rules for corporate behavior. EA research aims at providing managerial tools and guidelines to support shaping an organization in the desired ways.

From an EA perspective, EM provides a bundle of methodical means to guide the tasks of EA. EM enhances the methodical range by formal language construction and machine-supported model-editing via software model editors.

5.3.5 Business process model execution

From a theoretical point of view, a number of research questions are addressed when enterprise models are consulted for deriving executable software, especially when business process models are to be interpreted as executable workflow models.

In [ODvdA+09], a method is suggested to convert models in the Business Process Modeling Notation (BPMN) to executable Business Process Execution Language (BPEL) work flows. Other process modeling languages are not looked at, neither are other enterprise perspectives, such as organization models. The method is limited to generate BPEL models, which are to be manually revised by software developers. The SEEM method has a wider focus and aims at integrating multiple types of enterprise models on a methodological level. Since multiple input model types, and also diverse target architectures are supported by the SEEM method, the method may be configured to read in BPMN models, and generate BPEL, too. The implementation of the corresponding model transformations and code generation templates may in such a case be realized, e. g., based upon the work in [ODvdA+09].

Another approach for "bridging the gap between business models and workflow specifications" is discussed in [DvdA04]. The central idea of the proposed procedure is to methodically guide human modelers, i. e., domain stakeholders, architects and developers, through a process of human modeling actions to transform a given conceptual business process model to an executable workflow model. The methodical procedure is designed in a way to ensure that the resulting workflow model fulfills the criterion of the soundness meta-property. With respect to providing guidance for human developers, the SEEM method shares some fundamental goals of this approach, which are, however, realized using different concepts (see Sect. 6.4).

In [BBR11], an approach is suggested, which explicates relationships between conceptual elements in business process models, and workflow elements, through an individual type of model, called the Business-IT Mapping Model (BIMM). The suggested approach appears like a specialization of the SEEM method, since the general notion of an explicit mapping between business-level model concepts and implementation concepts using a mapping model is also a building block in SEEM. The approach in [BBR11], however, is not generalized to map to arbitrary variants of target architecture platforms expressed via implementation strategy meta-models, and the transformation procedure is not methodically separated into a dedicated initialization phase with a subsequent code generation phase.

Enterprise models comprise more than business process models only. This is taken into account by [ZSZ11], in which a general methodical approach is suggested for developing software from EMs. The approach uses a specifically adapted conceptual modeling language to capture enterprise knowledge. Additionally, several link types are introduced, instances of which can reference from elements of the conceptual model to elements of implementation-level modeling languages. Implementation-level elements are not further described by the proposed approach, it seems to be inherently assumed that existing modeling techniques for technical artifacts can directly be applied for this task. Since no further intermediating layer exists in the approach between enterprise model concepts and implementation, the method assumes a single-step transformation remaining to be developed for realizing a concrete development procedure. By using a specific set of modeling languages to capture conceptual knowledge, incorporating also a "requirements model" and a "concepts model", the approach relies on some specific prerequisies, which are not met by existing enterprise modeling language in use. This reduces the degree of reusability of existing enterprise models and enterprise modeling methods. The SEEM method, in contrast, allows the adaptation of diverse enterprise modeling languages to the method. It also uses dedicated modeling constructs to explicate relationships between enterprise model elements and associated implementation strategies, which in turn allows to split the overall transformation into multiple steps for reducing complexity.

An example of a concrete implementation of a transformation from an existing set of conceptual enterprise models to executable artifacts is presented in [Jun04]. The approach identifies syntactic similarities and differences between the Multi-Perspective Enterprise Modeling (MEMO) family of enterprise modeling languages and standardized workflow descriptions in the XML Process Definition Language (XPDL) language. Based on this examination, a set of auxiliary modeling languages is derived, to capture missing detail information not represented by MEMO constructs. A code generation procedure weaves together the information from the original conceptual models with the enhancing technical detail models, to generate executable XPDL.

One basic assumption, which is taken by [Jun04], is that every model element in conceptual models, especially the constructs describing business process models, can directly be associated with implementation-level concepts of the XPDL language ("Every process [. . .] will be mapped to exactly one activity", [Jun04] p. 41). While this assumption is a pragmatic restriction to keep the transformation procedure manageable, it does not take into account the different levels of abstraction between conceptual enterprise models and workflow implementations, which, among others, may come into notice by diverse degrees of granularity. In fact, it is a declared goal of conceptual business process modeling, to provide a less detailed and coarser grained view on processes than implemented workflows do. To cope with this fundamental difference between conceptual models and implementation models, a transformation procedure should provide means to change the level of granularity between input and output models, too. The approach suggests to perform refinements concerning the granularity of business process models on the conceptual level, by using a decomposition feature for individual process-steps. This resembles the manual modification of conceptual models to become as fine-grained as needed to a subsequent direct mapping to implementation steps.

Some research focuses on model-driven configuration of software, rather than model-driven software development [RMvdAR06, WHMN07, Zie10]. The fundamental requirements arising from transforming from a conceptual description layer to implementation-related artifacts, however, remain the same in this area of application, this is why the respective publications do not provide significant additional scientific value compared to publications about software development from the same groups of authors.

[MLZ08, RM06] discuss a number of conceptual mismatches between BPMN [Ini11] and BPEL [Men06, OAS07], which in the first place is BPMN's flow oriented process models, versus BPEL's block-oriented approach. A flow-oriented way of modeling processes makes use of interconnecting sequence elements between individual process-members (i. e., between process-steps and events, if applicable). Using a flow-oriented approach, alternative branches, e. g., are expressed by more than one outgoing sequence out of a process-member. Loops, e. g., are expressed by a circular structure of multiple sequences. In contrast to the flow approach, a block-oriented way of expressing sequence-flows makes use of specific language constructs, which determine, in what way inner elements of the block are executed. There are, e. g., `If`-blocks to express conditions, `While`-blocks to form loops, or `Flow`-blocks to indicate parallelism.

5.3.6 Analyses of business process models

For the purpose of semantically analyzing conceptual enterprise models, especially business process models, some fundamental research has been carried out about deriving specific meta-properties from given model instances. The term "meta-property" is used here to refer to a proposition which gives reflective information about a model instance. It is distinguished from the term "property", which refers to instance values and relationships specified in model instances. Deriving such meta-properties about processes and sub-processes would allow to perform an extensive automatic semantic analysis of enterprise models as part of the proposed SEEM method, when it comes to semantically analyzing the conceptual models, in order to derive default implementation strategies from them.

In [FFK+11, vDMvdA06] and others, the semantic property of soundness is discussed. For a process model to be sound, means to structurally ensure that any execution instance of that model will surely reach a termination event in the process model, i. e., every process runtime instance will surely stop after some time. When a process model is proven to be sound, it is ensured that no deadlocks can occur during runtime execution, and that no runtime instances can reach an endless loop. More generally, if focused on partial sub-processes of entire business processes, the soundness property can guarantee that a specific event inside an overall process model will be reached, after a specific previous sub-process has been executed. Detecting this property on input process model instances of the method may help to automatically decide which implementation strategy to use for the modeled constellation.

Additional meta-properties of process models, which can be derived via semantic analysis of model instances, are, e. g., reachability and executability, as they are discussed in [WHM08a, WHM08b]. In future elaborations of the method proposed here, this research may flow into the development of more fine-grained semantic analyses of conceptual enterprise models, in order to provide adequate means for automatically deriving suitable default implementation strategies associated to modeled business process-steps. In combination with these considerations, quantitative means for measuring structural properties of business process models [GL06] might also turn out to be effectively applicable.

Specific meta-properties, such as the possibility for conflicts of mutual exclusion, which is a generalization of the idea of deadlocks, are examined in [SSMB11]. For possible future enhancements, these approaches can be adapted as validation steps in the overall SEEM method.

A general notion of "forbidden behavior" is consulted in [SM06], to gain a theoretical grip on how correctness of process models can be defined. The proposed approach consists of a stricter notion of how to define correctness, compared to the notion of soundness, using a Petri-net-like intermediate language to represent process models originating from event-driven process chain (EPC) models. With the help of theoretically well-known Petri-net analysis techniques, aspects of validity in the original EPCs can be verified. Such an approach in a generalized form may be one candidate for semantically validating business processes in an early step of the SEEM method, if applied as implementation of the enterprise model validity check contained in the methodical procedure (see Sect. 6.4.1).

5.3.7 Incorporating actor and resource models into software engineering

BPMs form the most integrating perspective in enterprise modeling by giving insight into the executed procedures, and at the same time referencing resources, responsible actors, and possibly strategic considerations. Besides BPMs, dedicated modeling languages for resources and for organizational structure can provide additional information that may be incorporated into a model-driven software engineering procedure.

A generic resource meta-model to be used for describing resources in the context of an executable workflow is presented by [zM99]. The work is explicitly motivated by the need to complement workflow specifications with detailed formal descriptions of resources involved in the workflow, which also covers automatic resources, such as external applications or production planning and control (PPC) and computer numerical control (CNC) systems. One of the additions given to traditional simple resource models in [zM99] is the notion of roles for resources. For the dynamics of how to allocate resource instances to workflow steps at runtime, the article examines possible options in addition to the static meta-model.

Integrating different existing kinds of resource descriptions into a unified view is the main focus of [DDnHS99]. The idea behind the presented approach is to provide a common abstraction layer for different kinds of resources, which on the one hand provides a unified interface to reference any resource from workflow descriptions, on the other hand offers a common conceptual roof to build resource management systems. Resource management systems efficiently handle the allocation of resources from different sources during workflow runtime. The work presents a prototypical approach to develop such a system, and introduces a resource query language for standardized access to resources. The underlying resource model assumes a hierarchic structure among resources, introducing additional resource roles is also discussed by the article.

In [JC04], a lack of robust standards for integrating organizational perspectives apart from business processes into workflow applications is identified. It serves as the motivation to create an implementation-close contribution, which proposes a resource management framework specifically based on web-service technology. The environment architecture of the proposed approach is composed of a web service-based workflow execution engine (e. g., a BPEL interpreter) as the central execution component, which gets enhanced by a resource binding service, a work queue service for the organization, and a work queue service for individual agents.

Older foundations of work about the link between software and organizational structure models can be found in the area of role-based access control (RBAC) authorization [FKC07, SFK00]. Multi-user software systems, which make use of RBAC to determine access-rights to functionality, require configuration about available roles, relationships among roles (e. g., "includes" or "is part of" relationships), and user accounts with their association to roles. The information required to configure such systems can be derived from simple models that allow to specify entities of types role and user, and are capable of reflecting associated relationships among them.

5.3.8 Strategic models for software engineering

While some research has been carried out on deriving software from business process models, resource models, and organizational models, those model types of an enterprise modeling family, which allow for expressing long-term strategic goals and measures, have not yet been integrated into model-driven software development processes. Research about the relationship between conceptually modeled business goals on the one hand, and an IT oriented view on the other hand, is focused on deriving IT strategy planning and IT management guidance from business oriented strategy models [BAPC08, GPZ11]. Vice-versa, incorporating strategic IT concerns into business strategy modeling is also discussed by this research. The Strategic Alignment Model (SAM) [HV93] is one of the initiating conceptualizations for bringing business strategy and IT strategy together.

An integration between IT strategy conceptualizations and model-driven engineering techniques would in principle be possible, e. g., by using information about related strategic goals to prioritize access to functionality in the user interface presentation, or by deriving access-rights for the generated functionality, allowing only access to features on a level of strategic relevance, if a current user is authorized for that level.

5.3.9 Process-centered software engineering environments (PCSEEs)

Software products are available, which give support for making business process models machine executable. These products do not claim to solve the theoretical issues related to the mismatch of abstraction levels and viewpoints. Instead, they offer a set of pragmatic techniques to implement process-aware information systems (PAISs) from modeled business processes or workflows. These kinds of development environments constitute a class of process-centered software engineering environments (PCSEEs) [DvdAtH05, Gru02], which are specialized development tools that make use of process specifications to create software. Currently, three relevant products are available in the market, which are the ACTIVITI BPM PLATFORM, the JBPM package, and BONITA OPEN SOLUTION. These are individually looked at in the following paragraphs. All of these products are available under open-source licenses, the respective vendors make their businesses by offering consulting services as the commercial branch of their development activities.

Activiti BPM Platform ACTIVITI [Act, RvL11] is a framework for the JAVA programming language which allows to specify an implementation for BPMN process models in the JAVA programming language. It provides an API, which interfaces BPMN concepts with object-oriented JAVA elements, and a runtime execution interpreter for executing JAVA-implemented BPMN processes. ACTIVITY allows to embed this interpreter into regular JAVA programs, which makes it possible to use BPMN implementations the other way round, and invoke a BPMN-orchestrated piece of software as part of a JAVA program.

The ACTIVITI framework focuses on the reflection of BPMN concepts into a JAVA API, and on providing an interpreter engine to execute BPMN processes. Other facilities, such as a BPMN model editor, or an integrated development environment (IDE), in which manual development work takes place and from which ACTIVITI's components are invoked, are not part of the ACTIVITI solution. Resulting from this, ACTIVITI is not bound to a specific development environment, and can be used with multiple other applications and IDEs. Since currently, the ECLIPSE IDE [Eclb] is frequently used for many model-based engineering projects, one default environment for ACTIVITI is ECLIPSE, and there are plug-ins available which offer an integration of ACTIVITI into ECLIPSE.

A typical workflow when developing with ACTIVITI starts with editing a BPMN model from a conceptual point of view with a model editor, which stores the model in the standard Extensible Markup Language (XML) format for BPMN. Although this model will not initially contain details about its technical implementation, it has to be designed on a level of granularity, which allows for associating technical implementations with each process model element.

In a second step, technical implementations are configured, either by selecting pre-set functionality from the ACTIVITI API and set parameters as desired, or by providing custom-written JAVA classes. The classes to be developed implement interfaces or inherit from superclasses in the ACTIVITI API, which makes them accessible from ACTIVITI's BPMN process execution engine. E. g., a JAVA class, which implements a process activity as an automatically running JAVA fragment, will implement the API interface `org.activi-ti.engine.delegate.JavaDelegate`.

Before the BPMN model can be executed this way, information about which JAVA implementations are intended to reflect the BPMN elements, needs to be added to the BPMN model at development time. ACTIVITI suggests to add this information as detail annotations in the BPMN model, together with configuration parameters and other technical detail information for the implementation.

Finally, when JAVA implementations for the individual process-steps are available, and the BPMN model has been annotated with detail information about how to apply them for process execution, the annotated model can be interpreted by the ACTIVITI interpreter engine and executed as a program.

The ACTIVITI solution is specially focused on JAVA development, and requires manual coding in this language for most use-cases in practical environments. There is no conceptual way offered by ACTIVITY, which would allow to bridge the conceptual gap between BPMN process descriptions and technical software artifacts. Instead, ACTIVITI requires to create BPMN models on a fine-grained, low abstraction level, and already from a technical perspective, thinking in terms of web-service invocations and other technically determined distinctions. Hence, ACTIVITY cannot be categorized as a solution that operates on enterprise models in a conceptual sense to turn them to executable software.

jBPM In the same way as ACTIVITI, jBPM [JBo11] is a lightweight JAVA framework, which in its core consists of a BPMN execution engine, and a JAVA API for providing implementations for BPMN processes.

Around this set of core functionality, additional components have been created to supplement jBPM development. Among them are an ECLIPSE-based, as well as web-based, process model editor to edit BPMN 2.0 compatible BPMs. Further supplementary components are implementations for WS-HUMANTASK [Org10a] services.

The close relationship between jBPM and ACTIVITI results from common development roots in earlier versions of the jBPM project [Rüc11]. As a consequence, there a few principal differences between jBPM and ACTIVITI, which is why it is refrained from further describing jBPM.

Bonita Open Solution The software product BONITA OPEN SOLUTION [Bon, STH10] provides a development environment for process-driven software development. It is freely available as an Open Source Product. BONITA contains an integrated model editor for a derivate of the BPMN modeling language. Process models created with this editor are subsequently enriched with detail information about their implementation using a set of configuration dialogs offered by the BONITA development tools. BONITA provides a multitude of implementation options, which are, however, limited to the options offered by the BONITA environment. BONITA is primarily targeted to generate form-based web-applications. Besides these software development capabilities, the environment also supports process simulation and report generation tasks.

When developing with BONITA, BPMN models are enriched with proprietary additions to express fine-grained implementation-level semantics. E g., BONITA uses a more differentiated set of resources to represent IT system components. While this is a consequent approach to realize BONITA's development method, it breaks the standard compatibility to BPMN, making the modeling language effectively more complex than the BPMN standard intends, and requiring a proprietary model editor to make the additional model options accessible and editable for developers. This monolithic approach of integrating a proprietary process model editor requires additional learning efforts and causes switching costs, especially if a collection of process models already exists in another model format, which may not be possible to be reused.

BONITA does not conceptually distinguish between a business process description and a workflow model. From BONITA's perspective, both kinds of models are interchangeable and identically expressed in the BPMN modeling language. To use such models as a basis for further software development, the modeler already has to decide for the appropriate granularity and low level of abstraction to express process-steps appropriate to be interpreted as automatable work units. This means, BONITA requires BPMN merely to be used as a workflow language. BPMN models which express highly abstract conceptual business process descriptions will not be transformable to executable software using the BONITA approach.

The development approach realized by BONITA can be reconstructed in terms of the proposed SEEM method. Describing the BONITA approach with SEEM concepts, it uses a fixed process modeling language with links to other modeling perspectives such as a resource view. In combination, both form a specific set of enterprise modeling constructs. Since BONITA uses its own modeling language, there is no adapter transformation available to use an external editor, such as in SEEM (see Sect. 6.3.1). Mapping relationships from conceptual elements in the process model to implementation constructs, which in SEEM can be freely configured using implementation strategy meta-model constructs (see Sect. 6.2.3), are kept implicit in BONITA, however, come with a wide variety of configuration options to allow to choose different implementation variants. The form-oriented approach offered by Bonita resembles an application of the SEEM method, which primarily makes use of document-editing interaction with users, and uses form-based editors for information display and manipulation.

5.3.10 Self-referential enterprise information systems

Self-referential enterprise information systems are characterized by incorporating enterprise models, which describe the processes and business constellations the information system is meant to support, as editable business objects into the EIS itself [FS09]. One way to realize such a self-referential system is the use of enterprise models as user-interfaces to provide interaction mechanisms for invoking functional building blocks and business objects of the system.

The general architectural conceptualization of a self-referential EIS sees such a system as an enhanced EIS, combined with the functionality of an enterprise modeling environment (EME). An EME is a software application which allows for creating, editing and storing enterprise models, usually by offering multiple model editors, and management functionality to store and organize model artifacts. In such an environment, the functional features offered by the EIS are partially realized based on top of EME functionality, or parts of the EME are used as GUI for the EIS.

There are no implementations of self-referential EIS yet. The general architectural conceptualization of self-referential EISs, combined with the idea of innovative use-cases such a system allows to support, yet remain in a state of a scientific proposal for possible future research on EIS. The method developed in this work is specially suited to build self-referential EIS, because it already integrates the notion of EMs with EIS at design time and build time. Runtime integration of EME functionality, which also reflects EM concepts for its specific purposes, can be described with derived concepts. These could be made available in a configuration of the method that especially accounts for the development of self-referential EIS.

The architectural constellation of a self-referential EIS, understood as a combination of traditional EIS functionality together with an EME, is depicted in Fig. 14. To indicate the remaining research questions about how to conceptually interweave the EIS and the EMEs, the internal relationship between the two is indicated by a double-sided arrow labeled with "yet unexamined relationship".

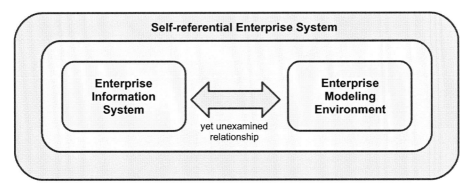

Figure 14: Basic architectural pattern of a self-referential enterprise system (according to [FS09])

5.4 Deficiencies of existing approaches and contributions by the proposed method

The sketched approaches for deriving executable software from enterprise models share some fundamental deficiencies, which are to be overcome by the SEEM method suggested in the work at hand.

One common problem induced with several of the existing approaches is the use of the same model artifact both for the representation of conceptual business-level concepts, as well as for architectural and implementation-level details. This affects all practical software products available for BPMN execution, such as ACTIVITI and BONITA. It is a wrong assumption that refining a model with technical details necessarily means to annotate existing conceptual models with that information in-place, i. e., using additional model elements in the same model. Regarding the fact that implementation technology is contingent and might be less stable over time than conceptually modeled knowledge, any dependency between enterprise modeling language constructs and implementation language constructs reduces maintainability over time. It also limits means to express different implementation-level design decisions for alternative target architectures, which may provide distinct technological realization options with different detail information required. Therefore, it is desirable that a method for enterprise model driven software engineering separates the conceptual business-level knowledge and the technical implementation details into separate languages, and provides means to loosely couple both levels of abstractions, without interfering the individual language definitions.

In those cases, where this separation is taken care of, and distinct model artifacts are methodically used to represent different levels of abstraction and viewpoints, new problems arise regarding the relationships between these models. This is, e. g., the case with the MDA approach, in which implementation models are created by model transformations from higher-level business-perspective models. In this constellation, the model transformations establish implicit dependencies among the different levels of abstraction, which are usually not back-traceable, after the implementation-level models have been created. As a consequence, changes that are made to either of the involved models may create inconsistencies among the different models. When re-running model transformations after changes to conceptual models have been done, typical problems of overwriting manual changes have to be conquered [Gul09].

Some approaches, such as [ODvdA+09, RMvdAR06], or the ACTIVITI and BONITA products, assume that a transformation at development time, or an interpretation at runtime, can be performed in one step. There is no internal structure suggested for the entire transformation or interpretation. Instead, it is assumed that conceptual source models as input are transformed by one monolithic step of transformation or interpretation to a deployable output. This assumption makes no use of the notion of a problem-adequate internal structure of the transformation, which consists of querying the input models, selecting suitable implementation building blocks that represent conceptually intended functionality, and outputting generated artifacts or triggering runtime execution.

Traditional DSSE approaches [Gro09a, KT08] suggest that any domain-specific software engineering project requires to design its own new domain-specific language and according model editor. This is necessary, because both the conceptual requirements, and project-specific technical realization options, have to be reflected simultaneously by the single DSML used by those asppoaches. As a consequence, cost for domain-specific software engineering projects always include the efforts for language and editor development, which may make up a high fraction of the overall project spendings, given the complexity of successful language design and the small number of experts available in this field. Users of a DSML need to be especially trained for each new language, since they cannot necessarily base their capabilities on earlier experiences. This is a relevant drawback not only in terms of cost and efficiency, but also with respect to the group of people who are able to utilize the domain-specific modeling language. Experts from other fields than software development will only be able to efficiently use modeling languages they are acquainted with. Reusing existing languages instead would not only lower development efforts and costs to create a new language. It would also reduce the workload required for stakeholders in conceptual modeling to learn and train the use of a new conceptual modeling language.

Most of the existing approaches are not aware of the fundamental conceptual problems, that have to be solved when offering a software engineering method which bases on enterprise models or other domain-specific types of models. The abstraction gap between conceptual models and technical artifacts are of fundamental ontological nature, and bridging this gap cannot be achieved with solutions located on the technological abstraction level or conceptual level separately. While some approaches identify this problem, none of them succeeds in incorporating solutions for bridging the abstraction gap on the methodological level, i. e., by shaping a proposed engineering procedure specifically with the goal in mind, to provide methodical means for letting humans do the necessary interpretation steps effectively and efficiently supported by methodical guidance.

While the SEEM method shares a number of fundamental concepts with approaches in the areas of DSSE, MDA and BPM execution, it delivers several scientific contributions, which address known problems associated with existing approaches.

Enterprise models offer a set of domain-specific language elements using a terminology familiar to domain experts, who are people with detail knowledge about the organization being modeled. The SEEM method allows to reuse existing enterprise modeling languages with an adapter transformation that interfaces to external EMLs. It also introduces additional models besides the domain models, which are intended to express how conceptual elements from enterprise models are to be associated with knowledge about implementation details. For expressing such associations, a mapping model is used, which allows to enrich elements from conceptual models with detail information about chosen implementation strategies, without modifying any constructs of the conceptual language. The model elements which are referenced as implementation specifications originate from implementation strategy models, which carry implementation detail descriptions that can be transformed to executable software artifacts by code generation or interpretation mechanisms.

The SEEM method resolves two relevant limitations imposed on other MDSE approaches. At first, SEEM does not use a single model transformations that directly transforms between models on different abstraction layers. Instead, in SEEM, a mapping model is initialized, together with at least one implementation strategy model instance. Elements from different levels of abstraction are linked to each other through references in the mapping model, making the relationships between conceptual elements and implementation strategies explicit and traceable. In other MDSE and DSSE approaches, these relationships are typically hidden in the execution logic of the model transformations, which transform models from one level of abstraction to another.

Another aspect of the described approach is the explicit use of implementation strategy models to reflect technical target architecture components. Such an explication of implementation strategy concepts in separate models outside the transformation templates, allows for reusing the implementation strategy meta-models as abstract descriptions of target architectures, and provides structuring means for separating concerns between model transformations and code generation templates. This gives an improved overview on the involved transformation templates and their functionality, which in turn leads to a more efficient and less error-prone software developing process (see Req. 1), also with implications on the ability to realize security-relevant functionality safely and certifiable as part of a reproducibly described engineering process (see Req. 7).

The problem of bridging the abstraction gap between conceptual enterprise models and implementation descriptions is addressed by explicating an internal structure of the model transformation from the conceptual models to executable artifacts. This way, the overall model transformation no longer remains seen as a monolithic black box, which "magically" outputs valid implementation artifacts. This kind of monolithic transformation would quickly become too complex to be efficiently maintained in development projects. Also, a single transformation necessarily has to mix interpretation functionality applied to the conceptual input models, with output functionality for generating software artifacts. This lack of separation of duties is overcome in the SEEM method by structuring the development process into multiple phases.

The SEEM method splits up the structure, on which the development procedure operates, into three distinct model types. These are the input enterprise models, the implementation strategy models containing implementation strategies about how to realize specific functionality on concrete systems, and the mapping model, which explicates relationships between the two earlier with dedicated mapping concepts. The process of transforming conceptual models to implementation artifacts is also divided into three separate phases. After the adapter transformation has been run to interface the conceptual input models to the method, the initialization transformation performs a semantic interpretation of the input enterprise models to generate a populated default implementation strategy model and corresponding default mapping model entries. Once these three models are available, and have undergone an optional manual review, the code generation transformation creates the corresponding software artifacts, which make up the final software system.

The method proposes a framework of implementation strategy types, covering questions about, e. g., how to implement process-steps, how to represent resources, or how to understand the notion of actors. While most of these questions have individually been addressed in existing research about how to make conceptual models implementable (see Sect. 5.3), the SEEM method unifies these approaches by making use of the dedicated abstraction of the implementation strategy mapping pattern.

Model validity checks are interwoven into the method, to provide additional guidance for human modelers and developers. This is done by automatically detecting locations in the involved models, which are underspecified or ambiguous. If such a case is detected by a validity check, the method falls back to an earlier step, and optionally points human modelers and developers to erroneous locations in the edited models. These steps iterate until the validity checks have passed. Including this automatic guidance of manual editing activities into the development procedure contributes to an increase in development efficiency enabled by the SEEM method.

Part III

A Domain-Specific Method for Model-Driven Software Engineering with Enterprise Models

All those signs I knew what they meant
Some things you can't invent
Some get made and some get sent

Coldplay, "Speed Of Sound" from the album "X&Y", 2005

6 Method constituents

The artifacts that are used throughout the method are briefly described in the following to introduce them before the procedural method description in Sect. 7.1. First, an overview is given in Sect. 6.1 to provide an understanding of each component's role as part of the overall method. Starting with Sect. 6.2, the involved artifacts are closer looked at. The following Sect. 7.1 will describe the procedures for using the introduced components.

6.1 Overview

Before the components of the method will be explained in detail, the method is described from a coarse overview perspective to give an understanding of the main architectural drivers that form the central principles behind the development method. With the relations among the major building blocks of the method in mind, the upcoming detailed descriptions will be easier to comprehend.

The method involves a set of modeling languages, model instances, model transformations, and validity checks. An external enterprise modeling language (EML) and corresponding tool is used to edit enterprise models.

6.1.1 Internal enterprise model representation language

The method uses an internal, simplified enterprise modeling language called extracted enterprise model (EEM), into which the input enterprise models get translated before applying further steps of the method. With the help of this intermediate enterprise model representation language, the method becomes adaptable to multiple enterprise modeling languages through one single model transformation which is executed initially when applying the method. All subsequent methodical steps remain independent from the original enterprise modeling languages used, since they exclusively operate on the internal EEM representation. The EEM representation language is fully introduced in Sect. 6.2.1.

6.1.2   Implementation strategies and mapping model

Implementation strategies represent possible options for creating output artifacts, which will be evaluated during the code generation step. This way, implementation strategies offer an additional abstraction layer for capturing design decisions, and decouple the code generation process from analyzing the conceptual input models. Implementation strategies will be thoroughly discussed in Sect. 6.2.3.

The purpose of the mapping model is to bind conceptual elements from enterprise models, represented in their EEM form, to implementation strategy descriptions. A mapping model consists of a list of mapping entries. Each mapping entry references one element from the conceptual input enterprise model, and one or more implementation strategy elements from an implementation strategy model. Together, both the conceptual semantics and the technical implementation description, provide sufficient information to control the subsequent step of automatic code generation for creating executable and deployable artifacts. The mapping model language will be explained in detail in Sect. 6.2.2.

6.1.3   Model transformations

Model transformations are used in different steps of the method, both for adapting the input enterprise modeling languages to the method, and for generating initial instances of the mapping model and referenced implementation strategy models. The model transformations used by the method are introduced in depth in Sect. 6.3.

6.1.4   Validity checks

Model validation rules are used to perform validity checks at specified points in the method. They can automatically collect valuable hints for software architects and developers, to determine at which points models have to be revisited and probably be completed or disambiguated manually. Validity checking steps as parts of the method are discussed thoroughly in Sect. 6.4.

6.1.5   APIs

General architectural features of an enterprise information system (EIS) are encapsulated by an application programming interface (API) which provides functions and data structures intended to be used by the generated artifacts. E. g., generated code may invoke function on objects provided by the domain API, or it may declare constructs which inherit from abstract super-constructs declared by the API.

A domain API which has prototypically been developed to demonstrate the use of this method is described in detail in Sect. 6.5.

6.1.6 Code generation templates

A set of code generation templates for creating source code and other implementation artifacts is finally fed with the configured mapping model and its mapping entries referencing both enterprise model elements as well as implementation strategy descriptions. With these conceptualizations at hand, the code generation templates have enough detail information to generate complete, executable or otherwise deployable artifacts. It is also possible to interpret this structure to execute it at runtime, which is an equivalent implementation option not further looked at throughout the remaining elaboration of the method.

Code generation templates are responsible for transforming implementation strategy descriptions, which typically reside on a level of implementation-independent, yet computation-dependent abstractions, into technical platform-dependent artifacts which rely on concrete technology to implement the desired functionality. The code generation templates thus are relating to concrete technologies, which are available on the respective target architectures. For each target architecture, code generation templates have to be developed individually.

Code generation templates are further discussed in Sect. 6.3.3.

6.1.7 Tooling support

Besides describing conceptual components of a method and giving insight into the procedural sequences which are performed to apply a method, a fully elaborated method also takes care about tooling support to provide software for applying the method.

Tooling support is consulted to provide model editors for manually editing model instances, to persistently store model instances throughout the application of the method, to invoke model transformation and validity checking engines, and to host a code generation template execution engine to finally output deployable artifacts.

A prototypical environment which supports these features is presented in Sect. 12.3.

6.1.8 Overview on the methodical procedure

A methodical description of how to apply the above components in a defined procedure is essential to the engineering method.

In its original form, the Software Engineering with Enterprise Models (SEEM) method is open to be used with any enterprise modeling language, and with any set of target platform architectures. Consequentially, to apply the method, it has to be tailored at two ends: the chosen enterprise modeling language has to be adapted at the input-side of the method by developing a suitable adapter transformation, and implementation strategy modeling languages, as well as code generation templates, have to be created for each target platform.

Details about these configuration procedures are described in Sect. 7.2 and Sect. 7.3. For the purposes of the subsequent overview description it can be assumed that the method has already been configured at both ends.

Provided the method has been prepared in this way, applying it for engineering an EIS can be structured into seven steps, with the possibility to iterate back to previous phases at specific points if preconditions for performing further steps are not met yet. The individual steps are:

1. Manually create and edit enterprise models

2. Automatically transform enterprise models to an internal representation for further processing

3. Automatically check for validity of the enterprise model representation, go back to phase 1 if the model is not considered complete yet

4. Automatically initialize a mapping model and corresponding implementation strategy models with reasonable default elements according to a semantic interpretation of the enterprise model representation

5. Optionally, manually review the initialized mapping model and implementation strategy models and replace defaults with more appropriate interpretations where necessary

6. Automatically check for validity of the mapping and implementation strategy models, go back to the previous phase if these models are not complete yet

7. Automatically generate application code or configuration files

Fig. 15 shows an overview on the steps that are performed when applying the method.

The fundamental purposes of the individual steps are described in detail in Sect. 7. They are now sketched to gain an initial understanding of the overall procedure.

Step 1: Create and edit enterprise models   The first task to enable starting the engineering procedure is the creation of enterprise models, which describe all relevant aspects of the modeled organization on a conceptual, computation- and platform-independent way. The task of creating enterprise models is usually performed by stakeholders involved in the modeled organization, or by external analysts. Software experts should accompany this group in order to guide the conceptual modeling process in a way that the models express relevant information exploitable for further processing.

Sect. 7.1.1 takes a close look at this initial step of applying the method.

Step 2: Transform enterprise models to a internal representation   The second step is to invoke an adapter model-to-model transformation which transforms the enterprise

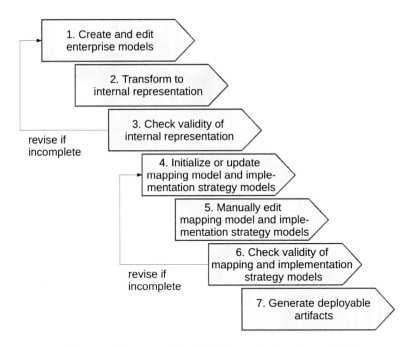

Figure 15: Steps performed when applying the method

models created using external modeling languages and tools. As a result of this transformation, the contents of the original enterprise models are expressed as a single model
artifact in an internal enterprise modeling language called EEM, which undergoes further
processing in the method.

The transformation and modeling languages involved in this step are explained in detail in
Sect. 7.1.2.

Step 3: Check validity of the enterprise model representation   The enterprise models
in their internal representation can automatically be checked for validity by invoking a
model checking script. This step supports an early detection of conceptual ambiguities or
incomplete specifications before implementation decisions are taken. It allows to iterate
back to step 1, if problems with the conceptual models are found.

The validity checking step is further explained in Sect. 7.1.3.

**Step 4:   Initialize or update the mapping model and the implementation strategy
models**   The mapping model is central to the method, it combines conceptual descriptions from the enterprise models with implementation strategy descriptions. When this
step is performed for the first time, it automatically initializes a new mapping model with
all entries that can automatically be derived from the enterprise model concepts. This
includes guessing possible default values for implementation strategies which match the

conceptual elements best. This step provides a major potential for increasing development efficiency, since it can take away uncreative, regularly repeated work from software architects and developers. If it is performed multiple times, in subsequent iterations an update is performed on existing mapping models which preserves existing entries.

The initialization procedure is discussed in detail in Sect. 7.1.4.

Step 5: Manually edit the mapping model and the implementation strategy models
After the automatic initialization, a phase of manual reviewing of the generated models is accounted for in the method. While for simple design decisions the automatic initialization procedure might have been able to select appropriate implementation strategies, complex functionality will have to be designed by software architects and developers.

Sect. 7.1.5 elucidates the details of this step.

Step 6: Check validity of the mapping model and the implementation strategy models   After the mapping model has both been automatically initialized, and optionally been manually edited, a validity check comparable to step 2 is applied, which tests whether the mapping model misses any specifications, or if some model elements are configured in an ambiguous way. In case one of these tests fails, the method iterates back to the previous step.

Details about the validity checking of the mapping model and its accompanied implementation strategy models are covered by Sect. 7.1.6.

Step 7: Generate deployable artifacts   Finally, code generation techniques as they are known from domain-specific software engineering (DSSE) approaches are applied to the set of models, which has been made available by the previous methodical steps. They output software artifacts to be deployed as running software. These artifacts may either be source code, or configuration components of any kind that describe a software system as desired.

Details on artifact generation are discussed in Sect. 7.1.7.

6.2   Models and modeling languages

When applying the method, three kinds of models are used to carry out the enterprise model driven software engineering procedure. These three kinds are enterprise models (EMs), a mapping model, and implementation strategy models. Other model types may be referenced as supplementary descriptions of technical artifacts, e. g., UML class diagrams, but these are not fundamental components of the method. One or more EMs artifacts serve as the starting point, from which a single EM representation called EEM will be derived as one single model artifact. The elements contained in the EEM will be referenced from entries in a mapping model, which associate elements from implementation strategy models with the referenced concept. The model types involved in this methodical setting are discussed in detail in the following subsections.

6.2.1 Enterprise models and their internal representation

EMs (see Sect. 1.2) are made available at the start of the EIS software engineering project by stakeholders of the modeled organization, or by external analysts who document their view on the organization with enterprise models. When creating enterprise models, these domain experts should be aided by software architects, who guide the use of enterprise modeling languages in a way the knowledge contained in the models can later efficiently be interpreted for software development. No technical details or implementation specific design decisions are taken by the software experts at this point yet, they only give advice in how to express conceptual knowledge with the existing language means, to reduce the need for disambiguation and detail specification activities in the subsequent software development process.

Enterprise models can be created with any EML for which semantic tooling support is available, for example ARCHIMATE [Lan09] using the CORPORATE MODELER SUITE [cL], the ARIS language [Sch02b] with the ARIS TOOLSET [Sof], or the MEMO language family [Fra12] supported by the MEMOCENTERNG application [GF10, Res]. Enterprise models can also be created using custom domain-specific conceptual modeling languages describing organizational circumstances and procedures. Demanding *semantic* tooling support means to use model editors which internally reflect the meta-concepts of the modeling language as elements out of which model instances are formed. The editors thus must not be limited to offer a graphical model representation for editing, but they need to contain knowledge about the structure of the applied modeling language, and are expected to internally store model representations in the abstract syntax format of the modeling language. When models are available in this format, they can further be processed, e. g., by model transformations.

Enterprise models may be stored as a single technical artifact, or as a collection of interrelated models, which each may be formulated in a different EML for different perspectives on an organization. For this reason, the terminology introduced with the method often speaks of enterprise models and enterprise modeling languages in plural, while single model artifacts may also be used.

To make use of various EMLs as conceptual source models for the engineering method, the method gets initially configured for accessing the information contained in the model instance artifacts of the chosen language. This is done via an adapter transformation, which is initially run to translate the original enterprise models into the EEM format, which is used for further processing. This way, any set of EMLs can be configured to work with the method, as soon as a corresponding adapter transformation is provided. After the EEM model representation is available, subsequent steps of the method can base on the same syntactic representation for enterprise models, and those automatic processing steps, which are subsequently performed, become reusable for different EML. Sect. 6.3.1 looks at the adapter transformation in detail, the overall configuration process to adapt enterprise modeling languages to the method is described in Sect. 7.2.

The EEM language offers a set of fundamental enterprise model element types, specifically tailored to reflect the conceptual information required for carrying out the software engineering method. The adapter transformation is responsible for creating model elements in this language and fill their attribute values with information derived from the original enterprise models. Models in the EEM format are not intended to be edited manually, neither by conceptual modeling stakeholders, nor by software architects or developers. Any changes to the conceptual models are made to the original enterprise models, and the EEM representation is automatically re-created when a new enterprise model version is available.

The language is specifically designed to formally provide all information required for the subsequent engineering process. This may lead to a situation where a detail concept is needed to be specified in the EEM model, although no corresponding language element in the source EMLs exists. In such cases, the semi-formal nature of enterprise models often allows to incorporate detail information via generic model elements, such as comment texts or key-value-tags associated with model elements. Using these model elements allows for specifying conceptual details, for which the original enterprise modeling language does not provide its own semantic constructs. Comment texts or tagged values can instead be used in the original enterprise modeling languages to encode any additional information. The adapter transformation is in charge for parsing this information and to propagate it to the corresponding model element in the EEM model representation. It is part of the configuration process for adapting a specific enterprise modeling language, to explicate the set of detail information entries and how their are included in the enterprise models. This is supposed to be done in an end-user documentation format, to allow all involved stakeholders, who take part in enterprise modeling activities, to understand the semi-formal extensions and to apply them where desired.

Since the EEM representation is derived via a horizontal model transformation, which performs a syntactic transformation from one enterprise modeling language to another, both kinds of models reside on the same level of abstraction and only differ in structure and labeling. Therefore, they are both referenced as "enterprise models" in the method description, where a distinction between original enterprise models and derived extracted representation is unnecessary.

The modeling language, in which the EEM representation is formulated, provides basic types for all fundamental enterprise modeling concepts. This includes process modeling concepts, elements to express organizational roles and actors with their structural interrelations, and resource modeling constructs with associated resource access explications. Although it includes all necessary constructs for further proceeding with a software engineering process, the language is kept as simple as possible, which reduces efforts for adapting enterprise modeling languages, and for further processing implementations. It only contains constructs to hold information required for the EIS engineering process.

For the same reason, the method does not specify a visual syntax for the EEM language. This is not necessary, because the model instances are not intended to be edited by humans. Interactive model editing and diagram visualization is only provided optionally on the tooling level for debugging purposes, see Sect. 12.3.

The EEM language is defined via a meta-model formulated in the MEMO Meta-Modeling Language (MML). This meta-modeling language is especially suited for expressing meta-models of conceptual domain-specific languages [Fra08]. Fig. 16 shows the entire EEM meta-model, individual components are focused subsequently.

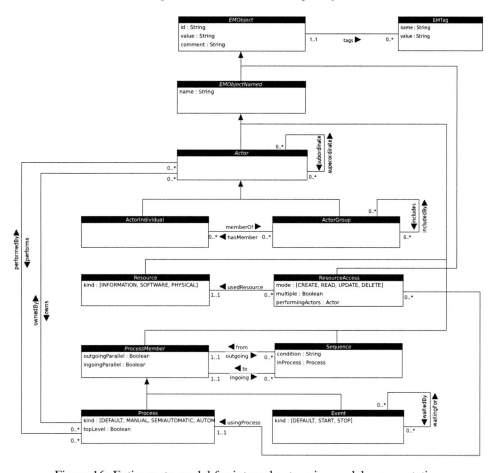

Figure 16: Entire meta-model for internal enterprise model representation

The language provides a core set of enterprise model element types as they can be found in most enterprise modeling languages. The concepts might be named differently in diverse languages, but the EEM language provides a generalization over multiple enterprise modeling languages to generally represent enterprise models in a stripped-down, simplified structure.

The meta-concepts of the EEM language are combined in a single meta-model, forming one modeling language which covers the relevant perspectives on an enterprise, including the process perspective, actor perspective with responsibilities and managerial authorities, as well as a resource perspective. Since all perspectives are integrated into one modeling language, a model instance in the EEM language is a single technical artifact, which is efficient to handle for further processing by model transformations as part of the method.

Classes `EMObject`, `EMObjectNamed`, and `EMTag` Elements of the EEM language are derived from two abstract superclasses `EMObject` and `EMObjectNamed`, which provide declarations for the attribute fields most model elements have in common. The name `EMObject` generally stands for "Enterprise Model Object". The MML declarations of these meta-classes are depicted in Fig. 17.

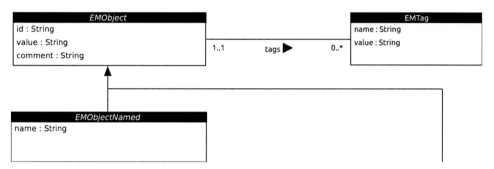

Figure 17: Abstract superclasses defining common attributes of elements

Attribute `id` (String) To reference model elements after re-generation of an EEM instance, an ID can be utilized which gets initialized by the adapter transformation with a unique string value that is dependent on the original enterprise model element and will be equal in subsequent transformations. This mechanism is currently not used by the prototype implementation of the adapter transformation, because the internal way of referencing model elements from other model instances (implemented by the Eclipse Modeling Framework (EMF), see Sect. 12.3) allows references to persist after re-generation of a referenced model, as long as no substantial changes had been made to its structure.

Attribute `value` (String) This attribute is used depending on the concrete subclass type for different purposes and explained together with the description of these classes, if applicable.

Attribute `comment` (String) The `comment` attribute is intended to copy any comment or description text that is attached to original enterprise model elements, for debugging and testing purposes if the EEM model is manually reviewed by a developer. This attribute has no dedicated function in the method.

Attribute `name` (String) Most model elements will be named, this is why the `name` attribute is incorporated. To still be able to declare meta-classes without names, this is done via the separate abstract superclass `EMObjectNamed`.

Class EMTag   References from class EMObject to class EMTag allow for attending tagged values to extend the language. As common to general tagging mechanisms, tags are composed of a name and value attribute pair, which both hold values of type string.

Actor perspective   To reflect the notion of roles and actors in the EEM language, a basic set of meta-classes to model actors and their relationships is part of the meta-model. The corresponding excerpts of the MML meta-class diagram are shown in Fig. 18.

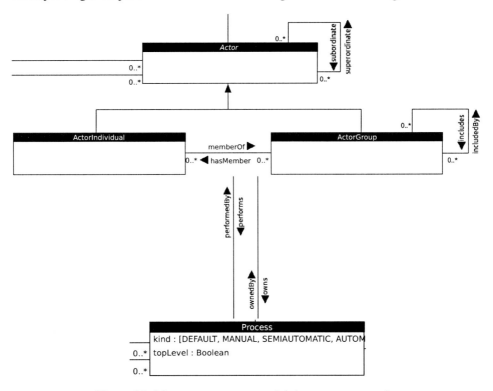

Figure 18: Meta-constructs to model the actor perspective

The abstract superclass Actor stands for any kind of actor, either a group role, an individual role, or a concrete user. Whether an actor represents an individual or a group, is further distinguished by the use of concrete subclasses of Actor, ActorIndividual or ActorGroup.

Whether a modeled actor is intended to represent an organizational role or to stand for a concrete person in the organization, is subject to further interpretation steps in the method. This distinction can be expressed by associating suitable implementation strategies to the conceptually modeled actors in the mapping model.

Relationship subordinate/superordinate   The subordinate/superordinate relationship expresses a hierarchy among actors. It uses many-to-many cardinalities, because any actor may in principle be subordinated to multiple other actors, while at the same time be superordinate to multiple others.

Relationship `memberOf/hasMember` The membership of an individual actor in an actor group is expressed by the `memberOf/hasMember` relationship. This relationship is again bidirectional and has many-to-many cardinalities, because in principle, any group can have multiple members, and every individual can be member of multiple groups.

Relationship `includes/includedBy` To express a containment relationship among groups, the `includes/includedBy` relationship is part of the meta-model. It allows to specify which group is part of another. The EEM validity check (see Sect. 6.4.1) should make sure that this transitive relationship is not populated with instances that form a circle.

Two more relationships interlink the actor perspective with the process perspective. They express which actors are involved in performing a process.

Relationship `performs/performedBy` By this relationship, a link between the process perspective and the actor perspective is expressed, which indicates which actors are operatively involved in performing a process-step. This relationship has many-to-many cardinalities, because any actor is potentially carrying out more than process-step, and there may be process-steps which require more than one actor to perform them, e. g., real-time communication among multiple actors.

Relationship `owns/ownedBy` In parallel to the `performs/performedBy` relationship, the `owns/ownedBy` relationship associates processes with actors, which hold managerial responsibilities for the process-step (process owners). Again, this is modeled as a many-to-many relationship, because any actor may generally hold managerial responsibility for more than one process-step, while in some cases one process-step might also be reasonably associated with more than one owning actors.

`Actor` types are referenced at one more point in a bidirectional relationship, as part of the ternary relationship `ResourceAccess`, which combines the actor perspective, the process perspective, and the resource perspective in describing which resources are incorporated in a process-step, and by whom.

Process perspective Meta-model constructs to reflect the process modeling perspective are displayed in Fig. 19. There are four meta-classes which make up the rudimentary set for describing processes. Class `ProcessMember` is the abstract superclass for both `Process` elements, as active procedural steps within the process model, and `Event` elements, which reflect state changes, externally triggered occurrences, etc. Processes may themselves be described as composed out of multiple sub-processes instead of being single atomistic process-steps.

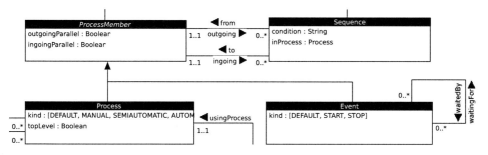

Figure 19: Meta-constructs to model the process perspective

Relationships `from/outgoing` *and* `to/ingoing`   All process-members are inter-connected via `Sequence` elements. One single sequence element specifies a flow in control from one process-member to another, associated via the references `from` and `to`. There may be multiple ingoing sequence elements per process-member, as well as multiple outgoing ones.

Attributes `ProcessMember.outgoingParallel` *and* `ProcessMember.ingoingParallel`   The modes of how to interpret the occurrence of multiple ingoing or outgoing sequences are controlled by the boolean attributes `outgoingParallel` and `ingoingParallel` of class `ProcessMember`. There are no explicit process elements to distinguish between parallel splits or alternative decisions. Instead, this semantics is expressed via the attribute `outgoingParallel` to the process-member from which multiple sequences go out. In cases where `outgoingParallel` is set to `true`, multiple outgoing sequence from a process-member are interpreted as a parallel split, while otherwise an alternative decision is realized. Alternative decisions typically are taken based on output information objects of the process-member from which the sequences go out.

Attribute `Sequence.condition`   In cases where multiple outgoing sequences are considered as alternative branches to be taken depending on a decision, the condition under which a sequence is followed may be attached as an expression string via the attribute `condition`. Although the actual implementation strategy for deciding which sequence to follow is determined by `ConditionImplementation` elements in the mapping model, the condition string given in the conceptual model can be used as hint for the initialization transformation which condition implementation to choose as default. In the conceptual model, the condition may be given as a formal condition term, or may consist of symbol values which indicate a decision taken in the previous process-steps, e. g., "yes", "no" or "canceled".

Attribute `Sequence.inProcess` *(Process)*   The complex attribute `inProcess` of a `Sequence` element points to a parent process element to which this sequence is associated. The same process-member may occur in multiple processes, because process-members in conceptual models describe types, which can be instantiated multiple times in one or multiple processes. Therefore, the sequences, which together make up the actual description of a process structure, are bound to specific parent processes and distinguish between multiple different process structures a process-member might occur in. Process members never have a parent process themselves, they are embedded into a parent process by connecting them either to the `from` attribute or to the `to` attribute of a sequence, which is indicated to be in the parent process by referencing it with its `inProcess` attribute.

Usually, the reference from `Sequence` to `Process` would be expressed as a relationship, not as a complex attribute, in the model. `inProcess` has been incorporated as a complex attribute instead for technical reasons, because by using a complex attribute, the other outgoing relationships of `Sequence` can automatically be detected as describing the end-points of an association class, which `Sequence` is modeled as. To provide a streamlined handling of the MML meta-model describing the EEM language by its corresponding model editor, `inProcess` is declared as an attribute.

Attribute `Process.kind` (Enumeration)   The attribute `kind` of meta-class `Process` allows to express different characteristics of process-steps, depending on whether on the conceptual level they are intended to be performed manually, semi-automatic with software support, or fully automatic.

Manual steps are marked with the attribute value MANUAL, and are typically performed by human actors without the help of the EIS, i. e., with a minimum of interaction between the user and the software system, only to indicate which tasks are to be done and which are completed.

Semi-automatic process-steps are marked with the attribute value SEMIAUTOMATIC and are the main kind of process-steps which gain support through the front-end applications of an EIS. They are typically implemented by software components that interactively moderate between the user and the EIS application, or by external applications invoked by the EIS.

Fully automatic conceptual process-steps refer to the invocation of any automatic, programmed functionality of a software system. This covers either the invocation of existing functionality in external systems, or newly developed functionality, which gets programmed as manual development work in the engineering process.

Attribute `Process.topLevel` (Boolean)   `Process` elements need not considered to be atomic, they can again be refined as process models, i. e., there are subprocesses described by `Sequence` elements which have the `Process` element set as their `inProcess` attribute.

Those `Process` elements which represent top-level processes, i. e., processes which themselves are not contained in any other process model, can explicitly be marked setting the `topLevel` attribute to `true`. Typically, those processes represent the granularity of entire business process models or single process diagrams derived from the original enterprise models.

Attribute `Event.kind` *(Enumeration)*   The `kind` attribute attached to the `Event` type allows to refine the semantics of events to express whether events are intended to be start events or stop events of a process. This semantics allows to better validate the structural embedding of events in a process, since start events can be validated to not have ingoing sequences, while stop events are constrained to have no outgoing sequences.

Relationship `waitedFor`/`waitedBy`   The reflexive bidirectional relationship `waitedFor`/`waitedBy`, which interlinks two instances of the `Event` type, allows to express dependencies among events. If two events are joined through this relationship, the event in waited-for direction can be interpreted as a trigger, while the event in waited-by direction is reacting on the trigger event and becomes active whenever a trigger becomes active, too. This mechanism can be used, e. g., to specify entry points into subprocesses, which can be invoked or triggered from multiple other events. Other semantic interpretation of the `waitedFor`/`waitedBy` relationship is possible by corresponding code generation templates.

Resource perspective   Resources are modeled by a meta-class named `Resource`. To model details on how a resource is accessed, an association class `ResourceAccess` is part of the language declaration. It connects the process perspective, the actor perspective, and the resource perspective in a ternary relationship. Due to its function of joining multiple perspectives, the meta-class `ResourceAccess` forms a semantically rich model concept from which detail information can be derived during the mapping model initialization transformation.

Both classes, their interrelationships, as well as their relationships to model elements of other perspectives, are assembled in Fig. 20.

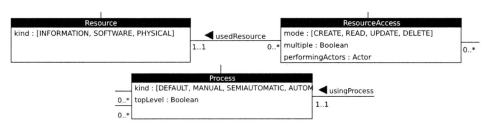

Figure 20: Meta-constructs to model the resource perspective

Attribute `Resource.kind` *(Enumeration)*   Using the `kind` attribute, different conceptual formings of resources are distinguished. The applicable values are `INFORMATION`, `SOFTWARE` and `PHYSICAL`.

While the `INFORMATION` kind specifically denotes information objects, and with `SOFTWARE` resources existing or yet-to-be-developed external software components are denoted, the category of `PHYSICAL` resources is kept very general and meant to cover all remaining resources. This is done according to the consideration that any generic physical resource cannot be treated other than being described by a document in the EIS, because an information system cannot do much more with physical entities. A natural language description, in turn, is flexible enough to cover all remaining formings of resources for the purpose of constructing the engineering method. If additional kinds seem appropriate for specific development projects, they can be added to the EEM meta-model with low effort by enhancing the list of available `kind` values in the enumeration.

Attribute `ResourceAccess.mode` *(Enumeration)*   The `mode` attribute belonging to the `ResourceAccess` type allows to express formal semantics on how a resource access is performed. This is done using the four basic "CRUD" function descriptions of storage access, `CREATE`, `READ`, `UPDATE` and `DELETE`, which may also be combined, if senseful (the `mode` attribute has a 1..n cardinality to possibly set multiple flags in parallel). Making this information available provides valuable conceptual semantics for selecting implementation strategies later. It is thus desirable to make this information available in the conceptual model, and if the original enterprise modeling languages do not provide identical means of expression, apply some hinting via comment text or tagged values to include this information on the conceptual level and make it accessible for an adapter transformation.

Attribute `ResourceAccess.multiple` *(Boolean)*   It can also be desirable to conceptually express whether a resource access is targeting a single entity of the accessed resource, or multiple ones. When accessing information resource instances, in some situations lists of multiple instances are intended to be accessed, instead of single entities, e. g., a product catalog consists of a list of product entries, but can conceptually be treated as a single resource. The `multiple` flag allows to express this intention.

6.2.2   Mapping model

The core purpose of the mapping model in combination with referenced implementation strategy patterns is to provide a mechanism for associating conceptual elements of EMs with implementation-specific details. This way, the mapping model and the implementation strategy patterns together offer a methodical approach to explicate the design decisions that go along with the ontological turn of first interpreting conceptual domain models, and then formulating technical implementation descriptions out of them. To fulfill this purpose, the mapping model language offers specific association classes, which allow for referencing enterprise model concepts on the one hand, and implementation strategies on the other hand.

The general pattern of such a mapping association is depicted in Fig. 21.

Implementation strategies may in some cases directly describe individual artifacts which later make up a deployable system. However, they may also refer to cross-cuttings aspects of the software system, and be consulted at diverse places in the code generation templates to query detail information about aspects of the EIS.

The mapping model thus serves to provide references to all required detail information about how to generate an EIS. This includes disambiguation and clarification of the enterprise model concepts, but also provides details on technical aspects, which are orthogonal to the domain concepts.

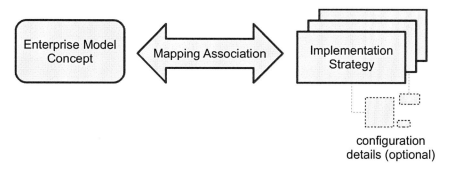

Figure 21: Pattern of a single mapping association

A mapping model instance is the container of two basic kinds of objects. At first, every mapping model owns a set of implementation strategy models, which are referenced via the `targetArchitectures` relationship and the `genericArchitecture` containment relationship. Each implementation strategy model holds a list of implementation strategy elements that can be chosen as associated implementation strategies for enterprise model concepts in mapping entries. One special implementation strategy model is always present in the mapping model, it holds generic implementation strategies which are assumed to be applicable to any target architecture. This generic implementation strategy model is referenced separately by the `genericArchitectureModel` containment reference as a singleton instance of class `GenericArchitectureModel`. It is not stored as a separate resource, but is an internal part of the mapping model.

The reference types from the mapping model to the implementation strategy models are displayed in Fig. 22 as an excerpt of the mapping meta-model. Since there will always be at least once concrete target architecture to output artifacts for, the `targetArchitectures` relationship is specified with a `1..*` cardinality, i. e., at least one implementation strategy model must be referenced from a separate model file.

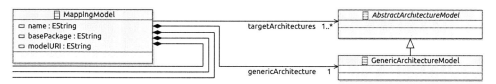

Figure 22: Excerpt of the mapping meta-model showing the use of implementation strategy models

The second central structure in the mapping model is a list of mapping entries, each one representing an association between an element in the enterprise model on the one hand,

and one or more associated implementation strategies from an implementation strategy model on the other hand. Mapping entries exist for four types of enterprise model elements, which are `ProcessMemberMappings`, `SequenceMappings`, `ActorMappings`, and `ResourceMappings`. The meta-classes for building up the mapping structures for these types of elements are displayed in Fig. 23. The `ProcessMapping` element in the meta-model serves as a container for `ProcessMemberMapping` and `SequenceMapping` entries, and does not reference any implementation strategy by itself.

In technical terms, a mapping entry is an association class, instances of which serve as a link between instances of the associated classes. In this case, the mapping entry association classes represent a one-to-many relationship between instances of `ProcessMember`, `Resource`, `Actor` and `Sequence` on the one side, and instances of concrete subclasses of `AbstractProcessMemberImplementation`, `AbstractResourceImplementation` or `AbstractActorImplementation`, as well as implementation strategies for sequences, on the other side.

The mapping meta-model contains abstract superclasses which act as placeholders for concrete implementation strategy types. They are referenced on the right-hand-side of mapping entries, representing the category of implementation strategies which fits to the type of the conceptual model element mapped on the left-hand-side.

Choosing an implementation strategy controls how a conceptual element will be technically realized in a software system. An implementation strategy description, specified by subclasses of the abstract meta-class `AbstractImplementation`, can be any kind of model element structure which can be evaluated to generate code fragments in the code generation phase. Implementation strategies specify domain concepts of a target system architecture in the sense of traditional domain-specific modeling (DSM) model concepts. They control the code generation process, and, if required, can themselves consist of diverse sub-elements with an internal structure.

When implementation strategy elements are referenced from a mapping model, they are first inserted into an implementation strategy model, and then referenced via a right-hand-side association from one or more mapping model entries. The structure of implementation strategy model instances is very simple. Implementation strategy model instances merely serve as lists of indivdual implementation strategy elements. Technically, these models are required to have a place where to persistently store implementation strategy model elements. Associating implementation strategy elements from mapping entries, without inserting them into a model first, would result in orphaned instances which could not be written to a permanent data storage when saving the models. This is the reason, why implementation strategy elements at least appear twice in the models, one time as children element inside an implementation strategy model with which they are persistently stored, and one or more times as referenced elements in mapping entries.

Most of the mapping entry meta-classes allow to associate multiple implementation strategies to one conceptual element. It is up the the code generation mechanism how to interpret these cases of multiple implementation strategies associated to one conceptual element. E. g., the meaning of multiple process-step implementation strategies associated to one conceptual process element could be understood as a linear sequence of implementation strategies, while a multitude of actor implementation strategies associated to one conceptual actor could be regarded as a set of alternative implementation options.

Kinds of mapping entries   Meta-classes which constitute the set of available mapping entry types are included in the mapping meta-model as subclasses of the common abstract mapping entry superclass `AbstractMapping`. There are four different types of mapping entries, according to the types of conceptual elements in the domain model they reference for mapping. These four types of mapping entries are

- `ProcessMemberMapping`, mapping between elements of type `ProcessMember` and `AbstractProcessMemberImplementation`

- `SequenceMapping`, mapping from one element of type `Sequence` to the three implementation strategy types `AbstractConditionImplementation`, `AbstractControlFlowImplementation` and `AbstractActorResolverImplementation`

- `ResourceMapping`, associating between `Resource` elements in the conceptual models and `AbstractResourceImplementation` implementation strategies

- and `ActorMapping`, which maps from `Actors` to `AbstractActorImplementation` elements

Process mapping entries   An instance of `ProcessMapping` is created for each business process model to be reflected. It contains `ProcessMemberMapping` entries and `SequenceMapping` entries, which bind elements from conceptual business process models (BPMs) to implementation strategies. While on a conceptual level, business process modeling languages (BPMLs) typically distinguish between process-step types and event types, for the mapping to implementation strategies this distinction can be blurred, and it can generally be spoken about associating process-members of any kind to process-member implementation strategies with the `ProcessMemberMapping` concept.

Sequences are direct connections between two process-members. They represent a possible single step in passing the control flow from one process-step to another during the execution of a process instance. To specify detail information about how a sequence is to be implemented, three orthogonal aspects are to be considered. These are

- the condition, under which the sequence in question is followed. Specifying conditions with sequences makes sense if more than one outgoing sequence from a process-member exists. In that case multiple outgoing sequences may represent alternative options for the control flow to be followed. If no condition is specified with a sequence, it is assumed that the sequence is always followed.

- an implementation strategy of how the passing of the control flow is realized. Multiple alternatives can be consulted depending on the underlying application architecture, which can be very contingent. Two possible modes of passing the control flow are, e. g., *a)* to internally invoke the next process-member implementation on the same front-end with the same user as operator, and, *b)* to notify a central process control flow manager that the control flow in the current process instance is to be passed to another front-end.

- an implementation strategy that specifies, which human user will be responsible for carrying out the next process-member, is the third aspect of passing the control flow, if human interaction is required at all for the next step. While the business process models typically name actor roles which are responsible for performing process-members, these roles need to be resolved at runtime to concrete human users, who fulfill the modeled actor roles. The according implementation strategy can specify, how actor roles are resolved to concrete persons.

The three aspects of specifying the implementation of passing the control flow, are formally expressed by three abstract types of implementation strategies, which are specified in the meta-model in Fig. 23. These types are `AbstractConditionImplementation`, `AbstractControlFlowImplementation`, and `AbstractActorResolverImplementation`, which are subclassed for concrete applications of the method by meta-classes that represent concrete implementation options.

A `SequenceMapping` element refers to instances of these three implementation strategies at the same time, unlike other mapping entries, which associate one type of conceptual element to exactly one type of implementation strategy. While the association to a condition implementations is optional, indicated by the `0..1`-cardinality of the reference to `AbstractConditionImplementation`, a concrete control flow implementation strategy is mandatory, which is specified by the `1`-cardinality of the reference to the condition implementation strategy. At least one procedure to resolve actor roles to concrete users is required to be specified. More than one concrete actor resolving strategy can also be associated, since the reference to the `AbstractConditionImplementation` instances is declared with a `1..*`-cardinality, which allows to chain together a set of alternative strategies than can subsequently be applied by an application to find suitable users.

Actor mapping entries   Actors occur in conceptual enterprise models in diverse shapes. E. g., enterprise models may use actors to denote groups of people, a specific position that is filled by a person, or actors may refer to concrete individual persons who fill a specific identifiable role in the organization. These diverse meanings attached to the notion of actors need to be disambiguated for the implementation of a software system. `AbstractActorImplementation` strategies serve to declare how actor types specified in conceptual models are represented by the software system.

For the implementation of a software system, typical techniques to implement concrete notions of actors can, e. g., be derived from the user management technology that is part of most operating systems. Provided appropriate concrete subclasses of `AbstractActorImplementation`, a binding from conceptual actors to the operating system concepts of user groups and user accounts can be described and be prepared for generative implementation.

There is a difference between the concepts of an `AbstractActorImplementation` strategy declared here, and an `AbstractActorResolverImplementation` strategy, which is part of the implementation specification for process sequences. `AbstractActorImplementation` strategies statically describe how actor concepts of the enterprise models are technically understood, and how they can be stored and managed as objects of the software system. `AbstractActorResolverImplementation` strategies, in contrast, describe how concrete persons are chosen, who conform to a given actor implementation. E. g., an actor resolver implementation will select a matching single user account that is member of a specific user group, if the actor to be resolved is specified by an `AbstractActorImplementation` to be a collective actor that is implemented by that user group.

Resource mapping entries   The structure of resource mapping entries is again simple. An instance of `ResourceMapping` refers to a conceptually modeled resource on the one side, and a corresponding instance of an implementation strategy description on the other side.   Resource implementation strategies are described by meta-classes, which inherit from the abstract superclass `AbstractResourceImplementation`.

Options for specifying concrete subclasses of `AbstractResourceImplementation` are discussed in Sect. 6.2.2.

Kinds of implementation strategies   Implementation strategies, as they are referenced by mapping model entries, are subdivided into several kinds, depending on what type of conceptual element they are intended to be related to.   Classifying the available implementation strategies is done by abstract superclasses, which group the implementation strategies according to their intended use.

The top abstract superclasses for implementation strategies of specific kinds, declared as sublcasses of the most general `AbstractImplementation` class, are

- `AbstractProcessMemberImplementation`

- `AbstractConditionImplementation`

- `AbstractControlFlowImplementation`

- `AbstractActorResolverImplementation`

- `AbstractResourceImplementation`

- `AbstractResourceAccessImplementation`

- `AbstractActorImplementation`

The root superclass of all implementation strategy types is `AbstractImplementation`. This concept is, however, too generic to specify any useful semantics, it only serves to group the inheriting implementation strategy types on the upper most level. Concrete semantics is carried by subclasses of `AbstractImplementation`, which categorize implementation strategies as intended for being associated with specific types in the domain model.

Throughout the meta-model, some abstract meta-classes exist as leaves of the inheritance hierarchy tree below `AbstractImplementation`. They are consistently named using the prefix `ArchitectureSpecific...`, and locate extension points in the model under which architecture-specific subclasses may be defined by separate meta-models. With the provided tooling support of the ECORE diagram editors, this is done by importing the extension point meta-class, or any other abstract meta-class in the inheritance hierarchy of implementation strategies, as shortcut elements into a new implementation strategy language. Once the meta-class has been imported to the new implementation strategy meta-model, implementation strategy language constructs can inherit from the imported concept, and become compatible to be used in combination with the mapping model language. The inheritance mechanism serves here to extend the mapping model language, and provides an interface for newly created language elements to the mapping model concepts.

Process member implementation strategies Implementation strategy types for process-steps are subclasses of `AbstractProcessMemberImplementation`, which makes them able to take part as associated implementation strategies in a `ProcessMemberMapping`. These strategies implement conceptual elements described in BPMs. They may represent implementations of fully automatic process-steps, semi-automatic steps which perform interaction with a human user, or support to guide entirely manual working steps. According to the variety of different process-step implementations, the `AbstractProcessMemberImplementation` concept is further structured by abstract subclasses which categorize the different kinds of process-member implementations. In the first place, there is a distinction between `AbstractProcessStepImplementation` and `AbstractEventImplementation`.

Although the model distinguishes between the meta-classes `AbstractProcessStepImplementation` and `AbstractEventImplementation`, the difference between the implementation of a process-step and the implementation of an event is not as relevant as the distinction between process-steps and events on the conceptual level. To generate deployable artifacts, both process-member types can have impact on code for workflow execution. All specialties of distinguishing between process-steps and events in the generated artifacts should thus be handled by the code generation templates, to remain fully flexible in realizing any possible implementation. As a consequence, on the level of the mapping model, the distinction between process-steps and events is rather blurred than further refined. Both concepts can equally be treated as process-members, and implementation strategies can be assigned interchangeably to both of the conceptual types.

The notion of an `AbstractProcessMemberImplementation` is further refined to reflect different fundamental kinds of process-steps. The additionally provided abstractions, which categorize process-step implementation strategy types into those which interact with human users, and those which perform automatic processing, are `AbstractInteractiveProcessStepImplementation` and `AbstractAutomaticProcessStepImplementation`.

Examples for concrete process-member implementation strategies are discussed in Sect. 9.1 and summarized in Fig. 42.

Manual process-steps implementation strategies Describing manual process-steps in conceptual business process models does not mean that there is no software representation on the EIS side for these steps. In fact, an EIS can support the execution of manual tasks in a comparable way as it supports semi-automatic tasks, by providing means to administrate which manual tasks are currently to be done, and in which process contexts they appear. There must also be an interactive component for a user to indicate when a manual task has been completed, and, optionally, with what result it was completed. All administrative task handling, and interactive communication with the user, is thus present in the same way as implementation strategies for semi-automatic tasks rely on them. From an implementation perspective, the `Manual` implementation strategy is thus treated identical as other interactive implementation strategies, by generating corresponding artifacts that provide the described user interaction component on a target architecture.

The resulting generated software component that implements a `Manual` implementation strategy may realize its own handling of manual tasks as part of an overall front-end API application that consists of generated source code. In an alternative architectural setting, the design decision may be taken to generate workflow descriptions as executable artifacts, which are to be executed by a workflow execution engine (workflow management system (WfMS)). In this case, existing specifications and implementing technologies exist, which can be made use of by the generated artifacts. For workflow engines, extensions exist which enhance the original set of Business Process Execution Language (BPEL) tasks by a standardized collection of workflow tasks that reflect manual tasks. This extended set of BPEL functionality is called BPEL4PEOPLE [Org10b]. Together with the WS-HUMANTASK specification proposed in parallel, it conceptually introduces a `People-Activity` task, and a set of concrete operations that implement manual working steps as web-services [RvdA07]. WfMS, which claim to conform to the BPEL4PEOPLE and WS-HUMANTASK standards, provide standard implementations of theses tasks, which can be referenced when specifying or generating workflow specifications.

If the mechanism for handling manual process-steps is to be implemented as internal functionality of an EIS front-end, its graphical user interface (GUI) representation can be realized, e. g., by a to-do list, which informs the user about what tasks are currently requested to be carried out manually [RDB+08]. The to-do list should offer interaction functionality that lets a user mark a completed human task step as finished after the step has been performed, to inform the EIS that this workflow step has been completed. Additionally, the to-do list can offer links to access documentation material that instructs the user in carrying out the task.

The concept of a to-do list can also be generalized to provide an entry point for the user to execute other semi-manual tasks which require user interaction. See Sect. 8.2.

Alternative options besides implementing the entire functionality as part of an EIS front-end GUI, or leaving the implementation to a WfMS, are possible. For example, if human tasks are relatively rare, and requests to perform them do not require immediate response, manual tasks management could be realized via an automatic e-mail notification system, which sends out requests for manual tasks to perform to a user, and gets notified about task completion by e-mail responses of the user.

Information access implementation strategies   To access information is fundamental in organizational environments, and, as a consequence, a task to be thoroughly supported by an EIS (see Req. 6: Enable information awareness).

Accessing information is typically expressed in conceptual enterprise models by specifying a relationship between a process-step and an information resource. On the conceptual level, such a compact way of expressing that information access takes place provides the desired degree of granularity and detail information.

For implementing a software component that provides information access to the user via a GUI, the semantics of what it means to access information needs to be refined. To access information can more precisely mean

- to edit one specific existing information object

- to edit multiple existing, possibly interrelated, information objects

- to pick information objects from a (possibly filtered or derived) list of information objects and optionally edit them

- to create a new information object of a specific document-type

- or, to create many information objects of a specific document-type

In addition, for every information object edited, the process of editing can either be regarded as a transient process that is only partially carried out and later to be continued, or as a final step of editing which completes an information object and makes it valid. A third mode of operation is editing information objects that are finalized after the editing process is finished, which means that the information object will not be available to further editing afterwards, only for viewing or reading its contents.

Given this complex set of variations, to formalize a complete notion of information access, additional parameters need to be specified in addition to conceptual relationships between information access process-steps and associated information resources. It needs to be specified

- which types of information objects are to be accessed

- which existing information object instances are to be accessed

- which existing information object instances are to be modified

- whether zero, one or more new object of these types are to be created during this editing process-step

- whether the user can pick one or more existing instances of these types to edit, and, if so, which filter should be applied to the list of existing instances of the types

- how a user interface looks like which presents the selected information objects in a useful combination

Since many of the specific semantics of information objects and their handling in a process context can generically be described and thus prepared for further implementation, the abstract superclass `AbstractInformationObjectAccessImplementation` is part of the mapping meta-model. It can be refined by concrete implementation strategies to denote which kind of information object is addressed on a concrete target architecture platform. Examples of such implementation strategies are displayed in Fig. 57.

Runtime parameters via named slots Accessing input and output resources is an implicit feature of a process-member implementation strategy. For software-implemented process-members, this means an implementation can expect some input information objects to be accessible from the current process runtime instance, and it can deliver zero or more output information objects as the result of its processing. The way how these input and output resources are accessed is modeled via the references `resourceAccessSources` and `resourceAccessTargets`, which both reference to instances of concrete subclasses of `AbstractResourceAccessImplementation`, which in case of accessing information objects can be further refined to `AbstractInformationObjectAccessImplementation`.

It is also desirable to access information object content at model design time to dynamically specify values of implementation strategy attributes. To do so, a mechanism can be provided which allows to access named slots as variables in mapping model parameters at model design time, and fill in the associated values at runtime. This is achieved by the convention of enclosing information object slot names in "#". Any fragment of an implementation strategy parameter value that appears inside # characters is intended to be interpreted at runtime as the name of an information object slot, the content of which is used to substitute the #-enclosed part with the actual slot content, using a string representation of the contained information object. E. g., to dynamically set the `address` attribute of the `WriteEMail` implementation strategy with a value derived from the slot `customerEmail`, the `WriteEMail`'s instance attribute `address` is set to the value `#customerEmail#`. References to runtime values may also be combined with constant value content, and there may be multiple references per attribute, as, e. g., a value of `Please remember #eventName# on #eventDate#` for the `subject` attribute. Fig. 24 shows an example of how runtime parameters are specified in a mapping model.

If required by a concrete engineering project, the mechanism which dereferences the values enclosed in # signs may be more complex than solely referencing named slots as string values. References may also consist of query language expressions, e. g., XPATH expressions, which retrieve values from structured XML data.

6.2.3 Implementation strategy models and corresponding modeling languages

More specific implementation strategies, which are not generically provided by the platform-independent implementation strategy elements of the mapping model language, require to be expressed in their own modeling language. Models in these languages serve as means for formally capturing design decisions a software architect makes when deciding how to implement a concept of an enterprise model for a concrete target architecture. Languages of this kind are called implementation strategy languages in the method, they get specified by implementation strategy meta-models.

An implementation strategy meta-model captures relevant technology related knowledge about the target platform for which software is to be developed. Implementation strategy meta-models are domain-specific models. The domain in question is the technical system, for which software is to be developed. The domain covered by implementation strategy meta-models is thus the technical domain of the target architecture, not the conceptual domain covered by enterprise models. For each target architecture platform the created software is intended to run on, e. g., web-application servers, mobile devices, or local desktop systems, an individual implementation strategy modeling language is required to be specified by an implementation strategy meta-model, which describes the technical features available on these platforms, including all parameters that are required to control an automated code generation process to generate executable artifacts.

Since the elements in an implementation strategy meta-model are subclasses of abstract superclasses specified in the mapping-model, elements from implementation strategy model instances are compatible with the mapping model structure. By providing inheritable abstract super-concepts, the mapping models becomes extensible by new implementation strategy languages which provide concrete types as subclasses of the abstract concepts.

There are two ways to provide concrete subclasses for these abstract superclasses. One option is to specify an implementation strategy modeling language, which contains language elements that directly inherit from the top-most abstract superclasses. These are, e. g., `AbstractProcessStepImplementation`, `AbstractResourceImplementation`, or `AbstractActorImplementation`. Another option is to subclass concepts from meta-model classes which are explicitly marked for being extension-points for implementation strategy meta-models. These are the abstract classes

- `ArchitectureSpecificProcessStepImplementation`
- `ArchitectureSpecificAutomaticProcessStepImplementation`
- `ArchitectureSpecificEventImplementation`
- `ArchitectureSpecificInformationStorage`
- `ArchitectureSpecificInformationObjectAccess`

118

- `ArchitectureSpecificSoftwareResource`

- `ArchitectureSpecificInformationType`

- `ArchitectureSpecificConditionImplementation`

- `ArchitectureSpecificControlFlowImplementation`

- `ArchitectureSpecificActorResolverImplementation`

- `ArchitectureSpecificActorImplementation`

- `ArchitectureSpecificResourceAccess`

- `ArchitectureSpecificSoftwareResourceAccess`

- `ArchitectureSpecificMenuItem`

- `ArchitectureSpecificAnswerOption`

- `ArchitectureSpecificUserInteraction`

These classes are marked in the diagram of the mapping meta-model as extension points, to indicate the concepts for which the mapping model is prepared to be extended by additional languages. Since most of these classes are directly inheriting from their top-most abstract superclasses, without adding their own attribute or method declarations, technically it does not make any difference whether classes in implementation strategy meta-models inherit from the extension point classes, or directly from the top-most abstract superclasses. However, using the extension point classes makes the purpose of extending the predefined set of generic implementation strategy types clearer.

6.3 Model transformations

During the application of the method, three model transformations are applied which sequentially support software architects and developers in performing an enterprise model-driven software engineering (EMDSE) process. The first one is an adapter transformation (introduced in Sect. 6.3.1), which serves to translate an external enterprise model artifact into an enterprise modeling language internally used for further processing.

The central transformation of the method is the mapping model initialization (described in Sect. 6.3.2), which creates a mapping model that associates concepts of the enterprise models with details about implementation strategies for creating software. The mapping model is automatically initialized with reasonable default values, to keep the amount of necessary manual editing activities for software architects and developers as low as possible.

A third transformation finally converts the technical descriptions given by modeled implementation strategies into executable software (see Sect. 6.3.3). One way to do this is to use code generation templates for outputting compilable and executable source code, alternative approaches are interpretation mechanisms, which apply execution semantics to models at runtime.

6.3.1 Adapter transformation for enterprise models

The first applied transformation serves to convert enterprise models, which are edited with an external model editor, to an internal representation. It serves as an adapter transformation for plugging-in different external enterprise modeling languages and editing tools, and make them identically usable in the subsequent steps of the method. This allows for reusing existing model transformations and validity checking rules where possible. The internal language to reflect enterprise models is called extracted enterprise model (EEM), which contains a set of basic enterprise modeling concepts in one compact modeling language. They reflect basic enterprise modeling concepts needed for further applying the software engineering method. The adapter transformation extracts the modeled semantics of these basic enterprise modeling concepts from the original enterprise models, and horizontally translates them into the EEM representation. The transformation outputs an EEM model file, and runs automatically without interaction.

The model which is generated as output of the adapter transformation is not intended to be edited in the course of the method. Any changes to the enterprise models are applied to the original models, and subsequently the adapter transformation is run to update the internal EEM representation. An immediate execution of the adapter transformation after changes are made to the enterprise models, while at the same time manual modifications of the internal representation are prevented, ensures that the internal representation and the original enterprise models are always in sync.

In simple cases, the internal representation and the external enterprise modeling language use semantically equal concepts. Transforming these concepts resembles a copying of the element's name and basic attributes to an identical modeling element in the output model. Besides this simple case, the adapter transformation has to cope with two kinds of mismatches: at first, there may be cases in which the internal representation demands a finer grained degree of semantics than provided by the original modeling language. One potentially place for this is the `mode` attribute attached to resource access relationships, which may hold the values `CREATE`, `READ`, `UPDATE` or `DELETE`. If an external enterprise modeling language does not provide means to specify these modes of access as additional semantics to resource accesses, the external enterprise model may be attached with comment notes or any other means of freely attached string values, which are then evaluated by the adapter transformation as informal hints to determine the formal EEM model content. When the adapter transformation is created, the use of informal information encoding via string values should carefully be documented in an end-user documentation, which describes the informal extensions to the enterprise modeling language required to make full use of the engineering method. An example of such a natural language description document is given in Appendix A.3.5.

The second kind of mismatch relates to the opposite case, when specific information from the external enterprise models is to be kept accessible in the internal representation, to later evaluate it in the mapping model or code generation transformations, but there are no corresponding modeling language constructs in the internal representation language. For these cases, the internal representation language allows to attach arbitrary key-value-pairs as tagged values to any model element in the internal EEM representation. Via storing of structured information in formatted strings, and later parsing these for evaluation in the mapping model initialization and code generation transformations, any kind of information can be encoded and passed on in the course of the method. In a very elaborate case, the format of a comment string with additional semantics may be specified via a formal language grammar, such as Enhanced Backus-Naur Form (EBNF) [MVM10].

An example model-to-model transformation that serves this purpose is listed in Appendix A.3.1.

6.3.2 Mapping model initialization transformation

The central model used in the proposed software engineering method is the mapping model. It explicates relationships between conceptual elements of the enterprise models on the conceptual side, and implementation strategies, which describe how to implement the corresponding concepts in a software system.

To create a mapping model, a list of mapping entries is initialized, each one referring to an enterprise model element with its "left-hand-side" mapping relationship. Subsequently, software architects and developers can decide which implementation strategies are suitable to reflect this conceptual element in a software system, and set the "right-hand-side" reference of the mapping entry accordingly. Deciding which implementation strategy to choose sometimes requires specific competencies and can only be performed by highly skilled software architects and developers. Other mapping operations, however, may simply need to repeatedly pick associated implementation strategies for specific kinds of conceptual elements. E. g., conceptual elements describing actors and actor groups can be expected to be repeatedly mapped to implementation strategies that realize the notion of an actor with the implementation concept of a user account or a user group of the underlying operating system. To create these mappings manually would impose a high workload on developers, with time-consuming repetitive tasks that unnecessarily bind experts' capacities.

To apply professional resources most efficiently, the proposed method accounts for an automatic initialization of the mapping model, with algorithmical steps that do not require human skills. These algorithmic steps are defined by the mapping model initialization transformation. Depending on the degree of automation strived for in a development project, initialization transformations can be created, which reach up to initializing the entire mapping model automatically. This degree is desired in cases when the method is configured to provide a 100% code generation automatic transformation procedure from enterprise models to executable artifacts.

The mapping model initialization transformation consists of two passes. First, it iterates over all elements in the enterprise models that are to be associated with implementation strategies, and creates a mapping model entry with a corresponding "left-hand-side" conceptual element reference for each of these elements. This automatic initialization creates a skeleton mapping model without references to implementation strategies yet. The basic structure of the mapping model now exists, and software architects and developers can optionally edit the model by manually picking suitable implementation strategies for each mapping entry.

As a second pass, the mapping model initialization transformation additionally guesses default implementation strategies depending on the enterprise model elements it meets during the initialization. This way, re-occurring design decisions can be automatized as part of the model transformation, and do not need to be performed manually multiple times. Since the mapping model is intended to be manually reviewed after the automatic initialization, the proposed defaults are not required to be perfectly precise. The algorithms that pick the defaults thus also are not required to be too complex, they may operate on simple hints and assume later human reviewing and correction, where required.

The two passes of the mapping model initialization transformation get implemented by two distinct model transformation descriptions. The first phase, which consists of creating a mapping entry for each conceptual element and setting the "left-hand-side" reference, can be performed independently from any aspired target architecture. The corresponding model transformation definition can thus generically be reused in any development project. The second transformation, however, needs knowledge about the target architecture for which default implementation strategies are to be guessed. It is thus developed separately, one transformation for each target architecture, and possibly specific to each development project.

Since in the second phase implementation strategy instances are generated, the model elements which represent these implementation strategies also need to be stored as part of a model instance. Therefore, the mapping model initialization transformation also creates one or more implementation strategy models, as instances of implementation strategy meta-models. As the result of the mapping model initialization transformation, there are thus at least two new files created, which are the mapping model instance itself, and one or more implementation strategy model instances holding those implementation strategy model elements which are referenced from the "right-hand-side" of the mapping model.

Selecting default implementation strategies is iteratively performed for each target architecture. The order in which the target architecture types are processed determines, which default selection will have priority. Each set of default guessing algorithms is implemented as separate model transformations, which can be executed in configurable sequence by the supporting tooling components (see Sect. 12.3).

In some cases, it will not be possible to determine reasonable defaults for an implementation strategy. No element will then be added to the mapping model entry, however, the mapping entry will remain part of the mapping model with an empty reference to an implementation strategy. When automatically checking the mapping model for completeness using validity constraints (see Sect. 6.4), locations in the model with missing references can automatically be detected, and developers can automatically be led through the remaining editing process of the mapping model.

When the second pass of the initialization transformation is run, it operates only on those mapping model entries that do not reference any implementation strategy yet. The transformation thus behaves idempotent when run multiple times, and does not modify any previously set entry. This allows to first edit entries manually, and preserve the chosen implementation strategies when the transformation is run. The initialization transformation can also be used for updating previously existing mapping models. In case of the update operation mode, the first steps of creating an empty mapping model and skeleton mapping entries will only be performed for enterprise model elements which are not mapped yet. Then, guessing default implementation strategies is performed for all mapping entries as described above, influencing only those mapping entries which have no implementation strategy set yet. The mapping model initialization transformation thus can be invoked in two modes of operation, which are

- the creation of a new mapping model with accompanied implementation strategy model instances

- or, the update of existing mapping models previously created, to incorporate yet unmapped new elements from enterprise models.

A prototypical mapping model initialization written in the XTEND language is listed in Appendix A.3.2. This transformation is accountable for creating the basic mapping model structure with a mapping entry for each referenced conceptual model element, and for selecting default implementation strategies. Appendices A.3.2 and A.4.2 contain listings of example model transformations, which select architecture-specific default implementation strategies for specific implementation targets. Example modeling workflow scripts for invoking the model transformations either in initialization mode, or in update mode, are also included in these Appendices.

6.3.3 Artifact generation and alternative approaches

Once all models created throughout the method are available and properly validated, a collection of formalized knowledge is available which contains all information required to derive a running software system from it. However, this knowledge is presented in a shape which is not executable by computers yet. Knowledge in the models first has to be mapped to a machine interpretable form.

One way to perform this mapping is to generate source code that realizes the modeled implementation strategies. To do so, a mechanism has to be specified which outputs source code that reflects the information in the models, e. g., by conditionally including fragments of source code depending on model content, or by reacting on model element attribute values and filling in variable parts of the source code with values derived from them.

The description of such a code generation procedure serves as an interface between non-executable model semantics, and technical execution semantics for a computer system. It offers a defined procedure, which deterministically maps model content to source code. The description of such a transformation procedure is provided by a set of code generation templates, or, more general artifact generation templates, because most languages for creating such generation procedures work with a template-based approach. In Appendices A.3.3 and A.4.3, examples of code generation templates are shown.

An alternative to performing an explicit artifact generation step is to interpret the models at runtime, using a mechanism that provides the implementations of model-described concepts through an interpreter program. Reading in the models, and acting according to their contents, is thus another way of defining technical execution semantics formally. This option to interpret models for execution, however, will not be examined in further detail. The method proposed here suggests to apply artifact generation techniques, because generation procedures at development time more cleanly separate between the language for describing the generation template, and the language in which the resulting software system will be created. This makes the development of code generation templates easier compared to writing a model interpreter. Other fundamental differences between code generation and interpretation, e. g., the ability to modify results of the transformation by editing the generated source code, will also not be discussed here, because making manual changes to generated source code artifacts is not considered a methodical step in the method elaborated here. There are approaches dealing with this question, which could be applied orthogonally [Gul09].

The approaches of generating artifacts at development time, and performing an interpretation at run time, can also be mixed. In this case, an interpretable model format is first generated from the models created throughout the methodical procedure, which is then suitable for run time interpretation by an interpreter engine.

Besides generating computer executable artifacts, code generation procedures can also be utilized to generate any other kind of artifact, computer or human readable. Among these are configuration files, which can be created depending on information given in the models, and also human-readable documentation, provided the model contents are enriched with documentation fragments. The variety of possible artifacts to generate, suggests to rather operate with the term "artifact generation" rather than "code generation", which both are applied synonymously throughout this work.

6.4 Validity checks

The proposed method guides software architects and developers through a sequence of model creation steps and model editing activities. While manual creation and editing of models is a creative and highly knowledge-dependent activity, automatic support for manual editing activities can be provided to some extent. At least, it can automatically be determined if a model needs further basic modeling activities, and, even more supportive for a developer, where in the model editing activities still are required. This allows for providing automatic wizards that lead developers through the sequence of editing affected locations in the models, until all formally determinable lacks are resolved.

To consider a model as "valid" means to consider all of its elements being complete and consistent. If all individual parts of the model recursively are considered valid, the model is considered valid in total. This assumes a notion of a model being a set of model elements which recursively are composed of elements again, which can safely be assumed, since the underlying architectural concepts which express models on the meta-meta level are built following this assumption.

For a single model element to be valid means that all of its attribute values and relationships carry reasonable values to allow the method to further continue without errors. Especially, an automatic check for validity in this sense should make sure that subsequent model transformations and code generation transformations can operate on the model without errors.

An automatic check for validity can be implemented by summing up the required conditions, under which each model element is considered complete and consistent. There are two options for formally specifying these conditions. The first option is to attach meta-information to attributes and relationships in the modeling language, which state whether values are required or optional, or to specify numerical cardinalities about the minimum and maximum number of elements referenced by a relationship instance. Most meta-modeling languages contain such features. Since most notions of validity are simply related to the question whether a value is available or not, the required meta-attribute, or a non-zero minimum cardinality, respectively, are simple but powerful techniques to specify the notion of validity of model elements.

The second option for specifying model validity is performed via traditional model-checking using explicitly formulated constraints written in a constraint language. Using checks for required attributes and non-zero cardinalities on relationships on the one hand, and explicit constraint-checking on the other hand, the models involved can to a useful extent be automatically checked for validity. Tooling support for the method provides automatic wizards, which indicate yet incomplete model elements and guide developers to the corresponding model-locations. The locations where to edit the model and fix a failed check can easily be determined due to the local character of the condition statements typically used in model checking languages.

The proposed method uses validity checks at two points in the methodical procedure. Validity checks are applied to the enterprise model representation in EEM format, and to the mapping model and its accompanied implementation strategy models. Both kinds of validity checks are discussed in the following subsections.

6.4.1 Validity check for enterprise models

After input enterprise models have been transformed to an EEM representation (see Sect. 6.3.1), a validity check is applied to the EEM model to make sure it can be processed by the subsequent operations of the method. Doing such a check at an early stage of the method increases the efficiency of applying the method, because it can avoid typical sources of errors in later stages of the method beforehand. E. g., the validity check can make sure that every conceptually modeled process-step is referencing at least one performing actor. Demanding this constellation from the conceptual models, allows for an unambiguous resolving of actor implementation strategies which describe the technical details about actor authentication and authorization.

In cases when incompleteness or ambiguities are detected, a list of problems is generated by the validity checking step, which gives a description on each detected problem in the enterprise model. The output of the validity check mechanism can be presented to modelers in terms of a to-do list which describes points of remaining work in the enterprise models. In a further elaboration of the method, it could also be the basis for a development supporting wizard, which guides software architects and developers step by step through yet unresolved issues about the enterprise model.

When issues are detected, modifications to resolve them are carried out on the original enterprise models. Afterwards, the adapter transformation is run again, and the enterprise model validity check is carried out on the internal representation of the enterprise models another time. This cycle is repeated until no more issues are detected by the enterprise model validity check. Unlike in typical cases with validity checks, not the checked model needs to be manually revisited in case the checking failed, but the original enterprise model is edited.

The internal enterprise model representation is not intended to be edited at all, it is re-generated after every version change of the enterprise models. Depending on the underlying tooling support, this conversion may happen transparently in the background whenever changes to the original enterprise models have been made. To locate the source elements of the detected issues, the proposed procedure could be enhanced by a tracing mechanism that is added to the adapter transformation. Such a tracing would keep a list of mappings from the original enterprise model elements to model elements in the internal representation, and would allow for implementing tooling support which automatically displays locations of detected validity issues in the original enterprise models.

Appendix A.3.1 shows a prototypical implementation of validity checks for EEM instances.

6.4.2   Validity check for the mapping model

The notion of validity of a mapping model is defined with regard to the operative semantics of a later code generation process or interpretation during runtime. A mapping model is considered "valid" in the sense of the method, if it contains enough and unambiguous information to perform code generation or interpretation. For the mapping model, this notion of validity is composed of two aspects. At first, a mapping model must contain mapping entries for all enterprise model elements that need to be associated to architecture-specific concepts. For example, every actor concept in the enterprise model must be associated to a corresponding actor implementation strategy, because otherwise all process-steps in which the actor is referenced remain underspecified for the implementation. The left-hand-side of the mapping will in most cases be set during the initialization transformation, except for optional mapping entries that are added manually. The right-hand-side of the mapping, i. e., the reference to an implementatiosn strategy, may, however, be left blank by the initialization transformation in cases when no reasonable default implementation strategy can be determined. It will thus regularly happen that a mapping model is not complete after initialization. Software architects and developers will revisit the default values chosen and will fill in the missing architectural concepts.

As a second aspect, each of the referenced implementation strategy descriptions from the referenced implementation strategy models has its own validity constraints, which specifically determine if code generation or interpretation of the described strategy can successfully be performed. During the check of the mapping model, these conditions are also validated, to form the second set of conditions which must hold true to be able to speak of a valid mapping model.

The implementation strategy model's attributes and child elements are intended to cover the semantic delta between what can automatically be derived from the conceptual enterprise models, and what is required to generate fully running software components. The attributes and child elements of implementation strategy descriptions can thus be expected to go into fine-grained detail. A high degree of interdependencies among detailed code generation configuration can be expected at this low abstraction level of concrete technology.

After the initialization transformation has been run, an implementation strategy model is usually still incomplete, unless the method has been configured to perform a 100% code generation transformation. The initialization transformation may create appropriate implementation strategy elements, but in some cases it may not be possible to initialize all attributes and further detail configuration with automatically derived values. For this reason, it is normal to assume that the mapping model validity check will initially fail when applied to a freshly initialized mapping model and its corresponding implementation strategy models.

In the course of the method, validity checks of the mapping model are applied to guide software architects to those model elements which need further specification and manual refinement. E. g., mapping entries for which no default implementation strategy could be determined automatically, will be detected by the validity check as being incomplete. The locations of these elements in the model are reported to the developers, which can possibly be done providing tooling support with a wizard to jump to error locations in the models.

Manual refinement of the auto-initialized mapping model, followed by a validity check to generate a list of the remaining to-dos, is iteratively repeated until the mapping model is considered valid, and the validity check passes without errors.

As part of the prototypical implementation of the method, example validity checks for mapping model instances are shown in Appendix A.3.2.

6.5 Domain APIs for EIS

If software is built on the source code level, by generating compilable or interpretable artifacts in a programming language, an additional point where to specify characteristics of the resulting system is a domain API. A domain API encapsulates conceptual features of the application, and technological specifics of its implementation on different platforms. In parallel to application characteristics modeled by implementation strategy models at development time, a domain API represents concepts of the application used at runtime, and it provides implementation building blocks as technological abstractions to be used by the components of the software system.

Domain APIs typically consist of multiple technological abstraction layers, ranging from a level of abstract interfaces that generically model the shape of the system to be developed, down to concrete implementation components that offer entry points for invoking implementation-specific functionality from generated artifacts. When developing software for multiple target architecture platforms simultaneously, for each target architecture, a concrete API is created to interface to the underlying platform. Abstract API specifications can potentially be reused on any target architecture. In parts they must be reused, in order to gain a set of common semantic concepts which allow multiple EIS components to interact in a distributed environment.

The design of a domain API can only take place after contingencies related to fundamental design decisions about a software system's architecture have been resolved. These design decisions determine, e. g., to build the system using generated source code in a programming language, or to use a centralized distributed client-server architecture. These decisions need to be taken with traditional software engineering expertise prior to conceptualizing a domain API. The domain API in turn reflects some of these decisions in terms of software artifacts.

Depending on the implementation technology used, the API may, e. g., be presented as a set of abstract and concrete classes in an object-oriented programming language, or may alternatively consist of a collection of services that are internally exposed to components of the EIS.

An example abstract domain API is shown in Sect. 8.3.

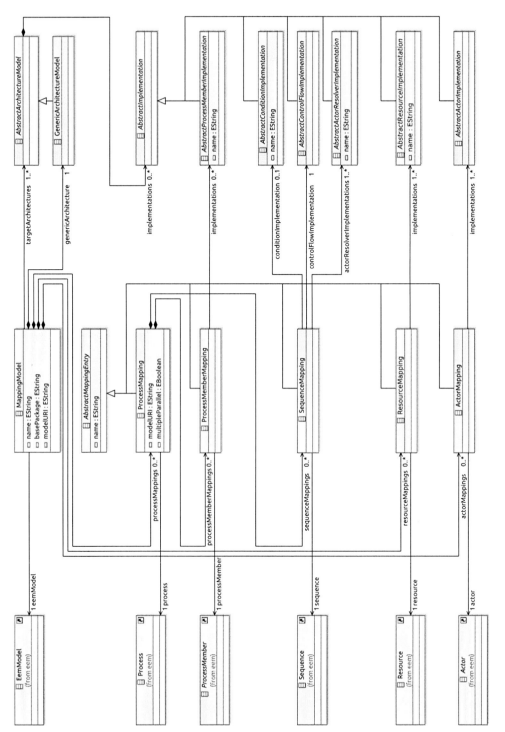

Figure 23: Entire meta-model specifying the core concepts of the mapping model language

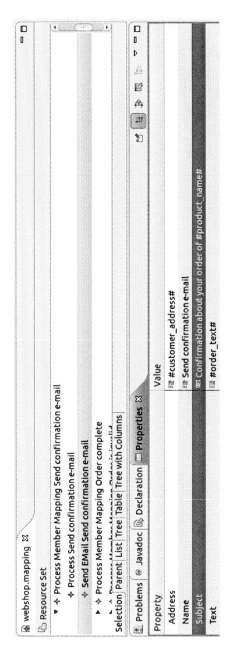

Figure 24: Implementation strategy specification in a mapping model editor, using dynamic parameter resolving

7 Applying the method

The overall methodical procedure contains of two optional configuration processes, which may have to be carried out once before the method is applied for software development.

In the first place, the method requires to be configured to use the EMLs with which the original enterprise models, that serve as input artifacts to the method, have been formulated. To perform this step of adaptation means to provide a suitable EM-to-EEM transformation which is first executed at the beginning of the procedure. Sect. 6.3.1 covers this in detail.

The overall methodical procedure, including the two optional configuration steps, is expressed as a business process model in Fig. 25. The individual parts of this comprehensive model are closer looked at in the following sections.

7.1 Applying the method to enterprise information system development

The fundamental steps of the method have already been sketched in an overview in Sect. 6.1.

Considering the method has already been configured for the desired EMs as input artifacts, and for target architectures as desired execution platforms to generate output artifacts for, the process of applying the method for EIS development consists of seven major steps, depicted from an overview perspective in Fig. 15, and in more detail by the business process model in Fig. 26.

To further describe the procedure, the overall process will be focused in detail excerpts in the following.

7.1.1 Step 1: Create and edit enterprise models

The origin of activities in a chain of engineering steps is the creation and maintenance of enterprise models. They are created and maintained by the involved stakeholders, i. e., members or employees of the organization or external analysts (see Sect. 1.2). For the purposes of software engineering, these stakeholders are accompanied by software experts who will help to guide conceptual modeling decisions in a way they become efficient for further processing the enterprise models in a tool-supported software engineering procedure.

Conventions that stem from the engineering process may determine the choice of appropriate enterprise model element types or attributes to express organizational knowledge in the enterprise models. E. g., using an Information resource type in an enterprise model to express the notion of an electronic document rather than a generic resource type, helps to efficiently apply hints for generating default implementation strategies for corresponding information objects and type descriptions.

It is important to notice that software experts, while they participate in enterprise modeling activities, do not append technical detail descriptions to enterprise models, nor do they elaborate architecture or implementation specific design decisions at this point yet. They guide the conceptual modeling decisions of how to express knowledge about organizations with enterprise models in a way that automatic model transformations, which are applied later, can use specific hints to suggest reasonable default implementation strategies for the modeled circumstances.

In the course of the method description here, enterprise modeling appears as a single initial step in the software engineering process. Of course, activities of enterprise modeling can be regarded in much more depth as complex negotiation processes among multiple stake-holders about complex abstractions. Enterprise modeling also is a continuous iterative activity for some organizations, reflecting continuous changes in dynamic environments. The elaborated method meets this concern by differentiating between an initial prepara-tion of the model instances used throughout the method, and an update procedure, which operates on existing models, and weaves in changes that have been made to the underlying enterprise models. For the purpose of describing the SEEM method, enterprise modeling activities are regarded as the initial methodical step for collecting the requirements for both the initialization, and the update procedures, of models used throughout the method.

Fig. 27 shows the excerpt of the overall process model which describes this initial step.

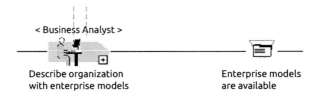

< Business Analyst >

Describe organization   Enterprise models
with enterprise models   are available

Figure 27: Create and edit enterprise models

7.1.2   Step 2: Transform enterprise models to a internal representation

The second step is automatically performed by a model-to-model transformation, which of course has to be developed by software engineers during the configuration of the method (see Sect. 7.3). To be able to adapt the method to multiple enterprise modeling languages, the contents of the enterprise models is transformed to an internal representation of those conceptual elements that will be used in the subsequent software engineering process. For this purpose, the method uses an internal enterprise modeling language called extracted enterprise model (EEM), which does not have a graphical representation, but represents all elements from the enterprise models which will undergo further processing by the method.

The EEM representation of the enterprise model is automatically derived as an injective projection from the original enterprise models to an EEM instance. Manual editing of the EEM instance is not intended by the method, model editors for the EEM language (see Sect. 12.3) are only provided for analysis purposes. Any changes that are intended to be made to the enterprise models are made in the original enterprise models using the available external model editors. To gain a consistent intermediate EEM representation after changes to the enterprise models have been made, the automatic transformation is re-run again.

7.1.3 Step 3: Check validity of the enterprise model representation

At this point in the method, it makes sense to check whether the provided information in the enterprise models is complete and unambiguous to be able to continue with the engineering procedure. A validity check is applied to detect missing information in the enterprise models, or to enforce disambiguations on the conceptual level.

The result of such a validity check is, in cases where defects are found, a to-do list referring to conceptual model elements, which still need modeling activities to be clarified. Such a to-do list provides an efficient mechanism to guide enterprise modelers through a sequence of modeling steps to solve explicitly located problems, which is a valuable automatic mechanism to foster efficiency in human enterprise modeling activities.

Since changes to the enterprise models are always carried out on the original enterprise models, not on the derived EEM instance, the transformation in step 2 has to be re-run after a revised version of the enterprise models is available. The method then carries on after this step.

The cycle of editing conceptual models, transforming them, and checking them, is modeled in the business process and displayed in an excerpt in Fig. 28.

7.1.4 Step 4: Initialize or update the mapping model and the implementation strategy models

For each enterprise model element, it is now to be decided if and how this concept is to be interpreted in terms of its relevance for implementing an EIS. This is done by filling the initially blank mapping model with mapping entries, each of which combines a conceptual enterprise model element with one or more corresponding implementation strategy descriptions.

Mapping entries either reference generic implementation strategies, which are included as language elements in the mapping model language, or they point to target architecture specific implementation strategies, which are defined as language elements in a separate implementation strategy meta-model.

In principle, all entries in a mapping model could be created and edited manually by software architects and developers. However, such an approach would require an excessive effort to manually decide for each implementation-relevant element in the enterprise models, even for regularly repeated constellations, which implementation strategy to apply, and with which detailed configuration this strategy is to be parametrized.

In order to meet the methodical requirement for efficient guidance (see Req. 1), the method accounts for an automatic initialization of mapping model entries. When initializing a new mapping model, an automatic model-to-model transformation creates a new mapping entry for each of the enterprise model concepts that are considered to be relevant for the EIS implementation. Besides purely initializing the mapping structure, the initialization transformation also guesses reasonable default implementation strategies from the enterprise model content. When a default implementation strategy is determined, its describing model element is added to the implementation strategy model of the target architecture platform the strategy is envisioned for, or to a generic implementation strategy model referenced by the mapping model which holds those implementation strategy descriptions that are not bound to any specific target architecture platform. Once an implementation strategy description is registered as a child element of an implementation strategy model, it can be referenced from any mapping entry in the mapping model.

Guessing of default values is done based on a set of configurable hints which allow to interpret the enterprise model semantics in a semi-formal way, e. g., based on matching name fragments against lists of keywords, which indicate to pick specific pre-configured implementation strategies. The proper use of these hints is one responsibility taken by software experts who take part in the conceptual modeling activities of the enterprise models.

The model-to-model transformation that is initially applied to create a new mapping model from scratch can also be executed in an update mode, which will only create mapping model entries which do not exist yet, and will only suggest default implementation strategies if no strategy is yet set in the mapping entry. This way, previously created defaults and manually edited implementation strategies remain untouched and stay associated with the existing enterprise model concepts which are unchanged. This update mechanism cannot ensure that previously picked implementation strategies remain consistent to the conceptual elements if the semantics of the conceptual elements is changed, e. g., by changing attribute values or by changing relationships the element has to other conceptual elements. However, the update mechanism does not overwrite previously edited entries, and thus allows for safe manual adaptation of the changes in a subsequent manual editing steps.

7.1.5   Step 5:   Manually edit the mapping model and the implementation strategy models

Since by the nature of algorithmic procedures, automatic programs can never fully reliably grasp the meaning of conceptual semantics, the default values assigned in step 4 can only be general suggestions based on hints. Automatic initialization and update of the mapping model can speed up development by preparing the required structure of the mapping model and by reducing development work of specifying implementation strategies for conceptual elements which could be derived automatically instead.

The automatic initialization can be expected to pick the right implementation strategy only in clean-room situations with enterprise models that have specifically been created according to the default hints, or in cases where the initialization or update transformation is specifically adapted as part of the development process, to shift development efforts from manual refinement work of the mapping to refinement of the automatic detection of reasonable defaults. Depending on the size of the enterprise models, and accordingly the mapping models, the decision to adapt the initialization or update transformation to project specific or organization specific needs may be a justified approach to increase development efficiency.

Manual editing activities are performed with the help of dedicated model editors for the mapping and architectures models, see Sect. 12.3. Fig. 29 shows the process of manually editing the mapping model in detail.

7.1.6 Step 6: Check validity of the mapping model and the implementation strategy models

After the mapping model has been initialized and manually revised, an automatic validity check can ensure that the mapping model is complete to undergo the next methodical steps. Therefore, the method comprises a validity checking step before implementation-specific artifacts are generated by code generation templates that take the mapping model and its referenced implementation strategy models as input.

The validity check contributes to an overall methodical engineering procedure which provides automatic means for guiding the working processes of software architects and developers (see Req. 1). It can automatically detect places in the models where manual work is necessarily required. If the validity check on the mapping model fails, the method iterates back to step 5, and software architects and developers are asked to fix the according model elements. Subsequently, the validity check is applied again, and the cycle is repeated as long as incomplete or inconsistent elements in the mapping model are found.

The cycle of initializing or updating a mapping model, manually revising it, and automatically checking its validity, is part of the overall methodical procedure displayed as an excerpt in Fig. 30.

7.1.7 Step 7: Generate deployable artifacts

Finally, when all of the above mentioned models are available, enough information is gathered which allows to generate software artifacts from the model using code generation techniques. These are usually realized using specialized template languages, this is why the term "code generation templates" is often used synonymously.

The resulting output of applying code generation techniques may be source code in a programming language, but also other artifacts which reside on the implementation level, e. g., configuration files to shape the behavior of existing software components, or deployable software descriptions on a higher level of abstraction, which are intended to be interpreted by corresponding execution components, e. g. workflow models interpreted by workflow management systems (WfMSs).

Helper artifacts may also be derived from the models, e. g., installation scripts to aid the deployment of generated software on the desired target platforms. With these mechanisms at hand, a code generation procedure becomes realizable which can automatically derive fully deployable artifacts from the models and does not require manual programming any more. Of course, in order to realize such a 100% code generation, sophisticated efforts have to be spent on the development of the code generation templates. The code generation templates become the place where architectural design decisions and technical knowledge are manifested. Besides the design of implementation strategy meta-models, the code generation templates belong to the central methodical artifacts on which manual development work is applied throughout the enterprise model driven software engineering procedure.

The code generation step as an excerpt of the last step in the method's business process model is shown in Fig. 31.

Run code generation and   Executable artifacts available
artifact creation

Figure 31: Generate deployable artifacts

7.2   Configuring the method to be used with a specific enterprise modeling language

To apply the engineering method, an EML has first to be chosen as the source modeling language to formulate conceptual, domain-specific EMs. Once the language has been selected, it has to be adapted to be used with the method. This section describes how this adaptation is performed.

The process-steps indicating the decision to use an EML, if it is not adapted to the method yet, are represented in Fig. 32. In case this decision is taken, the methodical steps shown in Fig. 33 are performed to realize the adaptation of an external EML to the method. Such EMLs can be any conceptual languages that provide a combination of process modeling languages and static organization structure languages, to be able to describe processes, actors and resources in an organization. These requirements may be met by a comprehensive set of EMLs [Fra02, SN00], or by an enhanced business process modeling language, e. g., BPML enriched by suitable hints to express basic actor and resource types.

Sect. 11.1 gives an example of adapting the MEMO EML to the method. The example model-to-model transformation, which serves as adapter transformation for the MEMO language family, is contained in Appendix A.3.1.

The individual steps for adapting enterprise modeling languages, as modeled in Fig. 33, are

1. Identify language concepts equivalent in EML and EEM

2. Implement transformation rules for equivalent language concepts

3. Formulate hints to express other EEM concepts in EML

4. Implement transformation rules for other language concepts via hints

These four steps are executed sequentially one after another. Two document artifacts come into play when adapting an EML, which are the

- Transformation rules from original enterprise models to extracted representation, and, optionally,

- Hints about how to express additional semantics in the original enterprise models

The transformation rules are given as an interpretable script, e. g., in the XTEND language (see Sect. 12.5.3). Hints for expressing additional semantics in the enterprise models are written in human language, because they are targeted to human modelers, who are responsible for creating and maintaining the enterprise models.

The four methodical steps for adapting an enterprise modeling language are described in the following.

7.2.1 Step 1: Identify language concepts equivalent in EML and EEM

The EEM language provides a core set of semantic concepts, which can be found in several different enterprise modeling languages with a comparable meaning, although probably differently named. The first step to take when adapting a new EML to the method, is to identify those concepts in the source EML, which can be mapped to elements of the EEM language by a merely syntactical renaming, with possibly minor semantic transformations.

As a result of this step, a software architect or a qualified modeling language engineer documents, which concepts in both languages can directly be mapped to each other without further semantic interpretation required.

7.2.2 Step 2: Implement transformation rules for equivalent language concepts

Since identifying of common mappable concepts in two different languages is considered an architectural task, which requires specific expertise on language engineering and meta-modeling for language definition, the proposed method separates between identifying mappable concepts, which is done in step 1, and implementing an executable model transformation that creates an EEM instance from source EML models.

This implementation performed in the second step is done by creating a suitable model-to-model transformation by qualified software developers, e. g., using the XTEND (see Sect. 12.5.3) language.

7.2.3 Step 3: Formulate hints to express other EEM concepts in EML

Assuming not all elements required to transform a complete EEM model can be mapped directly from concepts of the source EML, some concepts and entries remain, which cannot be directly derived by a syntactic transformation. To cover these cases, a software architect or modeling language designer specifies informal hints how to incorporate the required semantics in the source enterprise modeling language, using generic language constructs for attaching comments, such as, e. g., tagged values or description fields. A tagged value is a generic model element which carries a named value of a generic data type, typically a string value. A set of multiple tags attached to an element can be understood as a list of key-value-entries associated to this model element. With this modeling construct, any kind of additional information can informally be encoded as tagged values and be attached to model elements. In turn, the information can be evaluated by model transformation scripts and code generation templates, to guide the automatic interpretation process. The tagging approach is not a theoretically clean approach, especially because formal semantic integrity of string-encoded information cannot easily be verified, and the development process becomes more prone to errors. However, to include additional information into models, using tagged values may be the mechanism of choice when efforts for adapting a language on the meta-model layer are unreasonably high. In extreme cases, separate textual grammars can be specified [ANT, Ecld], which describe a syntax of encoded strings that can formally be checked.

An example of attaching a hint to a source EML is incorporating the notion of a read/write access-mode to a resource access. While the EEM requires such an access mode to be specified along with `ResourceAccess` elements, some source EMLs may not provide built-in means for specifying the notion of a resource access mode. In these languages, e. g., a resource access is simply modeled as a plain relationship between a process-step and a resource, without further formal attributes. If the source EML, however, provides a generic comment field on the relationship element, or if a tagged value to carry a mode-string can be applied to the expressed resource access, the hint to document would ask the conceptual modelers to apply a comment string "read" or "write" (and possibly additional modes) via these modeling constructs. The adapter transformation, in turn, will be extended by software developers to parse the string value in the comment field, or the tagged value, and detect the mode in this way, if appropriate string values "read" or "write" are found.

The hints are documented by the responsible software architect for two target audiences: the first one being the group of stakeholders responsible for creating and maintaining EMLs, who are in an ideal case supported by qualified conceptual modeling experts, and the second group being the software developers, who implement the use of the hints as part of the adapter transformation that creates the EEM instance in the following methodical step. Since end-users of the EML are targeted by the documentation, writing the documentation has to be carried out with special care regarding the use of a clear and simple language.

An example natural language documentation about how to apply hints in conceptual enterprise modeling languages is given in Sect. A.3.5. Fig. 34 shows an excerpt of an enterprise modeling environment, in which a Multi-Perspective Enterprise Modeling (MEMO) enterprise model is edited enriched with additional semantics using the hint text `CREATE` in a description field of a resource access model element.

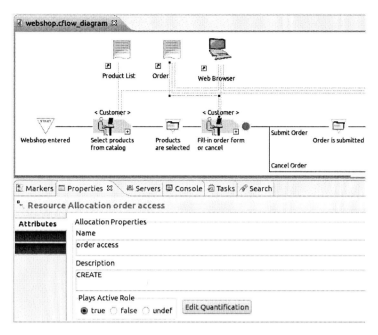

Figure 34: Enriching an enterprise model with additional semantics via a comment text hint

One case of insufficient matching between EML and EEM needs not to be taken care of, which is the mapping of those concepts available in the source EML, but not represented in the EEM language. Since the EEM language has intentionally been designed to include the set of concepts which is required to express model instances used for further proceeding with a software engineering process, any additional conceptual information is not required to be specified for the software development method, and can thus remain untransformed by the adaptation transformation.

7.2.4 Step 4: Implement transformation rules for other language concepts via hints

After the set of hints to complete the expressiveness of the source EML has been established, the model-to-model transformation initially implemented in the second step is enhanced to interpret the hints in the source models, and to project the derived information onto elements of the generated EEM instance. To do so, the transformation script may either use simple parsing techniques, such as comparing string-values, or searching for occurrences of specific patterns in strings. The transformation may also consult syntax parsers to read complex object structures encoded in strings, e. g., using XTEXT [Ecld] or ANTLR [ANT]. Provided the source model specifies all required concepts and hints, the resulting model output of the adapter transformation is a complete EEM model, which is ready to be successfully validated by the EEM validity check.

To show how to adapt the method to use a specific enterprise modeling language and its corresponding model editing tools, a prototypical adaptation of the modeling languages of the MEMO enterprise modeling method, and its tooling environment MEMOCEN-TERNG is demonstrated in Sect. 11.1.

7.3 Configuring the method for specific target architectures

For every new target architecture, a new implementation strategy meta-model is created, which captures the specifics of this architecture by declaring modeling language elements, instances of which describe concrete implementation approaches to realize the specific functionality of the architecture. A new implementation strategy model is created by initializing an empty meta-model, importing the abstract superclass `AbstractArchi-tectureModel` from the mapping meta-model, and creating a new meta-class named according to the target architecture as subclass of `AbstractArchitectureModel`. This class becomes the root model class for the new implementation strategy model, and inherits all required containment relationships to reference instances of implementation strategies of diverse kinds as child elements of the root model class. This way, implementation strategy model instances become containers for model element instances that describe specific implementation strategies for that architecture. These elements can in turn be imported into mapping model instances, and be referenced as associated implementation strategies from the mapping entries of the mapping model.

The detail processes of configuring the method to generate artifacts for a specific target architecture platform are shown in Fig. 35 and Fig. 36.

Fig. 35 denotes the methodical steps to decide to use a yet unadapted target architecture with the method. The procedure of developing the required method artifacts to allow the creation of deployable software components by the method is the detail process displayed in Fig. 36.

The procedure consists of 12 sequential steps, which are to:

1. Conceptualize a target architecture API

2. Implement the target architecture API

3. Meta-model architecture-specific process-step implementation strategy types

4. Meta-model architecture-specific event implementation strategy types

5. Meta-model architecture-specific actor implementation strategy types

6. Meta-model architecture-specific resource implementation strategy types

7. Meta-model architecture-specific information object implementation strategy types

8. Meta-model architecture-specific sequence implementation strategy types

9. Conceptualize hints at choosing default implementation strategies

10. Implement hints at choosing default implementation strategies

11. Implement code generation templates for generic implementation strategies

12. Implement code generation templates for architecture-specific implementation strategies

Steps 3 to 8 are performed by creating an implementation strategy meta-model that declares the available types of implementation strategies, which are specific to the target architecture in focus.

Several document artifacts are referenced, created or modified while the adaptation procedure is carried out. These artifacts are:

- The target architecture API description

- The implementation strategy meta-model representing characteristics of the target architecture

- A set of hints at choosing default implementation strategies

- A model-to-model transformation to initialize or update the mapping model

- Validity checking rules to test for completeness and consistency among architecture-specific elements in model instances

- Artifact generation templates to project architecture-specific model elements onto deployable artifacts

The 12 methodical steps to prepare the method for a specific target architecture are laid out in detail in the upcoming subsections. Along with their explanation, the use of document artifacts during these steps is further explained.

Examples for applying the upcoming steps are presented in Sections 10 and 11.2, where implementation strategy models for a BPEL-driven service oriented architecture (SOA) platform and a Java Server Pages (JSP) web-application platform, respectively, are developed. The resulting example implementation strategy meta-models are shown in Figures 62 and 68.

7.3.1 Step 1: Conceptualize a target architecture API

A target architecture API describes the characteristics of EIS software components in a distributed environment on a software technical level. It both provides abstract concepts, which are applicable on multiple concrete platforms with different technologies, and offers executable functionality per platform, which implements building blocks of the application functionality and is intended to be invoked by the generated artifacts of the EIS.

Some parts of a target architecture API are mandatory, they can optionally be integrated if specific functionality of a platform is intended to be used by the EIS. When this architecture-specific functionality is offered by an API, corresponding implementation strategy types are typically modeled in the implementation strategy meta-model in steps 3–9. These implementation strategy types are instantiated as parts of a mapping model, by which they are associated to conceptual elements of the EMs. The code generation templates responsible for generating artifacts on the target architecture in question, will react on these implementation strategies where specified, and will generate code that invokes the corresponding specific target architecture API functionality.

The result of modeling an API is a set of object-oriented models, e. g., in the Unified Modeling Language (UML) [BJR99], declaring technical building blocks and their interface operations, on top of which artifacts forming an EIS front-end will be generated. Conceptualizing an API is considered to be the typical task of a software architect, and is separated from the actual implementation of API functionality in the description of the method, covered by the next step.

7.3.2   Step 2: Implement the target architecture API

After the target architecture API has been conceptualized, concrete functionality offered by the interface operations needs to be implemented. The implementation is built using the available technology of the target architecture platform, including available programming languages and underlying system API functionality of the platform.

This methodical step resembles classical manual software development work, which can be performed as a part of the overall methodical procedure, e. g., using traditional object-oriented software development approaches [BD10, Sch02a].

7.3.3   Step 3: Meta-model architecture-specific process-step implementation strategy types

Some target architectures may allow for offering specific functionality to be used for supporting the execution of business processes with an EIS. This may refer to technical features, which are available on specific target architectures only, and thus have to be conceptualized separately as possible process-member implementation strategies in a separate target architecture specific implementation strategy meta-model.

New process-step implementation strategies are specified in an implementation strategy meta-model by importing the abstract superclass `ArchitectureSpecific-ProcessStepImplementation`, which is declared in the mapping model, into the implementation strategy meta-model, and subclassing it with the desired implementation strategy. This way, new process-step implementation strategies are declared compatible to the mapping model's mapping mechanism, and can be referenced from instances of class `ProcessMemberMapping` in the list of mapping entries in a mapping model. Alternatively, classes describing process-step implementation strategy types can also be inherited from any other abstract class in the meta-model, which is a subclass of `AbstractProcessMemberImplementation`, from the general abstract superclasses `AbstractProcessStepImplementation`, or from the upper-most

`AbstractProcessMemberImplementation`. The use of the `Architecture-SpecificProcessStepImplementation` extension point is encouraged, if an implementation strategy is to be explicitly marked as architecture-specific.

An example for an architecture-specific process-step implementation strategy is, e. g., functionality to invoke a phone-call as implementation of a conceptual process-step "call customer by phone". Such functionality can be realized on mobile phone devices, or specifically equipped hardware platforms which integrate a telephone or a headset for telephony. The corresponding implementation strategy meta-model would incorporate a process-member implementation strategy `InitiatePhoneCall`, the use of which as associated implementation strategy to a conceptual process-step "call customer by phone" would cause the code generation template to generate code which invokes the corresponding platform-specific functionality.

To keep the method efficiently applicable and support architects and developers in choosing reasonable implementation strategies, the mapping model initialization transformation (see Sect. 6.3.2) should be enhanced by target architecture-specific parts, which, in the case of the example, could detect name fragments including "phone", and would pick an instance of the `InitiatePhoneCall` strategy as default implementation strategy associated to the conceptual model element via a mapping entry in the mapping model.

7.3.4 Step 4: Meta-model architecture-specific event implementation strategy types

In the same way as architecture-specific implementation strategies for conceptual process-steps have been declared in the previous step, architecture-specific implementation strategies intended to describe concrete options to implement events in conceptual business process models can be specified. The mapping meta-model does not enforce a distinction between implementation strategies for process-steps and those for events, both are subsumed under the `AbstractProcessMemberImplementation` concept (see Sect. 6.2.2). However, for the methodical procedure of adapting target architectures, it makes sense to distinguish the steps of identifying process-step implementation strategies and event implementation strategies, since in order to establish a mapping from the conceptual models, the clear, orthogonal distinction between process-steps and events has of course to be kept to provide senseful operational semantics. As a consequence, the implementation strategy types that are designed in this step can be declared as subclasses under the mapping meta-model's class `ArchitectureSpecificEventImplementation`, which marks the implementation strategies explicitly as realizations of event interpretations for a specific platform. As with implementation strategy types for process-steps, implementation strategy types for events can be created in the implementation strategy meta-model, after the abstract superclass `ArchitectureSpecificEventImplementation` has been imported from the mapping meta-model to inherit from it.

There are two opposite directions in which the notion of an event can be underfed with an operationalized interpretation by software functionality. The first idea about what an "event" means as part of a software system is an external state change or occurrence of input. In this sense, a conceptually modeled event represents some external occurrence which is input into the software system as a trigger to cause further process execution.

Such understanding of an event implementation is suitable to be associated to conceptually modeled start-events, or to events in BPMs which cause process execution to wait until an external trigger is received. As a concrete example, such a notion of an event implementation would be given by an implementation strategy, which maps the choice of a drop-down menu item of an EIS front-end's main menu bar to a conceptual start-event of a process type, to cause a new instance of that process type to be spawned when a drop-down menu entry is chosen. Front-end platforms that provide concepts such as main menu bars and drop-down menus can offer such implementation strategies for events, others do not make use of these metaphors, but may provide other sorts of possible event implementation options.

A second interpretation of how an event, as it occurs in a conceptual BPM, is to be understood in terms of software functionality, is focused on events that occur during the execution of a process, not as start or end events. Most of these events are not modeled to block the control flow until an external state change is detected, but they passively represent individual stages reached during process instance execution. This understanding of event implementations does not regard an event to react on external state changes, but sees an event itself as the representation of an internal state change of the process control flow. Reasonable implementations of such events, if they are not ignored at all from the implementation perspective, behave like process-step implementations and perform some action in response to the control flow having reached the event, e. g., a logging operation. This is the reason why the mapping model does not enforce an orthogonal distinction between process-step implementation strategies, and event implementation strategies, because with this notion of event implementations in mind, implementation strategies for process-steps and implementation strategies for events become interchangeable.

7.3.5   Step 5: Meta-model architecture-specific actor implementation strategy types

The notion of actors is relevant to an EIS, because it is the very purpose of an EIS to support organizational cooperation among different actors. A proper reflection of actors in the organizational models, and in turn appropriate reflection by supporting software systems, is relevant, because the use of actors, and the conceptual differentiation between roles, groups, individuals, positions, committees, etc., are central design principles for organization management and forming [Daf09, HC06]. This can even have legal consequences for an organization, because there are steps of actions in an organization, which are only allowed to be carried out by specific actors, e. g., accessing security relevant or secret information, handling hazardous substances, or establishing legal contracts on behalf of the organization. Depending on the sensibility of tasks carried out in an organization, the importance of modeling "what" is done in an organization by use of BPMs, is superimposed by the relevance of "who" performs specific actions. Means for interpreting the operational semantics of actor types are thus carefully to be adapted to the method, with the context of project related requirements and target architectural specifics in mind.

A core understanding of what kinds of software technical information objects are to be used to represent actors in a software system, is described by the general user management model that underlies most operating systems. A general set of implementation strategies for actors, which allows for platform-independent specification of implementation strategies, can thus be offered by strategy types that map the conceptual actor types of groups, roles, positions, and individuals, to the technical objects of user-groups and user-accounts. In any distributed system environment, the interacting participants will need to be identified by something comparable to a user-account, and may optionally be categorized into groups, so this is a notion that is generic enough to be said to be architecture-independent. This general understanding is modeled as architecture-independent implementation strategies in Sect. 9.2.

Depending on project-specific needs and technical capabilities of an adapted target architecture, further notions of actors can be introduced. As an example, a typical web-application provides means to handle public anonymous actors accessing the application via the internet. Technically, this kind of actor is unique to web-applications exposed to the public internet. It requires specific handling for re-identifying users over time, e. g., by anonymous session IDs. An architecture-specific actor implementation strategy to be included in a web-application implementation strategy meta-model could thus be represented, e. g., by a class `WebSessionUser`, which inherits from the abstract super-class `ArchitectureSpecificActorImplementation` that has previously been imported into the implementation strategy meta-model to provide a link to the mapping meta-model. See Fig. 68.

If more fine-grained adaptations with respect to choosing a concrete individual actor from actors of the introduced type are required, the code generation templates that react on `AbstractActorResolverImplementations` as part of sequence implementations in processes, additionally need to be made aware of how to handle the new actor implementation strategy type (see Sect. 9.1.5). Actor mapping entries in mapping models allow to associate more than one actor implementation strategy to a conceptual actor element. This is possible to enable actor resolver implementation strategies to optionally pick from multiple alternative realization options when choosing a concrete individual for a given actor type.

7.3.6 Step 6: Meta-model architecture-specific resource implementation strategy types

Two fundamentally different kinds of resources are typically distinguished on the conceptual EML level, which are on the one hand physical resources representing material objects and machinery, and on the other hand intangible information and software resources.

The implementation of detail representations of physical resources is by nature independent from any target architecture of a software system, because physical resources cannot directly be represented in a software system, only indirectly via information objects that provide descriptions of the physical entities in question. However, to allow a project to specify detail informations about physical resources, the mapping meta-model contains the abstract meta-class `AbstractPhysicalResourceImplementation`, which can be imported in implementation strategy meta-models and be extended to provide custom physical resource descriptions in a meta-class inheriting from it.

For the realm of information and software resources, it can be expected that a concrete target architecture offers a variety of available technological components that may potentially be of interest to act as implementations for software resource concepts. The capabilities of these components can be modeled as meta-classes that inherit from the imported abstract meta-class `ArchitectureSpecificSoftwareResource`, which is one of the explicitly marked extension points of the mapping meta-model. Architecture-specific software resources may, e. g., be local applications or system services, for which implementation strategy descriptions with more specific semantics than the generic `ExternalApplication` meta-class are to be provided. The `ExternalApplication` implementation strategy is suggested as one architecture-independent software resource implementation strategy example, together with `WebService` and `CustomResource`, in Sect. 9.3. Another alternative to use architecture-specific software resource implementation strategy is to explicate specific API functionality existing on the target platform, either made available by the domain API that underlies the generated component on this architecture and has been developed in the course of the project, or by exposing system API functionality which is specifically available on this architecture.

Information resources are considered of special relevance in the context of EISs, their implementation is covered separately in the following section.

7.3.7 Step 7: Meta-model architecture-specific information resource implementation strategy types

Information resources are considered to be important kinds of resources from the perspective of an EIS. This is because information objects play constitutive parts in organizational forming and behavior, and by nature are entities handled by software systems. The mapping from conceptual information resources onto implementation concepts can be performed in a fine-grained, technology-driven manner, if different concrete technologies for describing data types and data storage mechanisms are available. Unlike the reflection of physical resources in an EIS, which in principle is limited to keeping a description about the physical resource as an electronic document, several technological options exist to describe information object types, to operate on information object instances, and to store information objects persistently, if desired.

Specifying implementation strategies for information resources means to provide disambiguation mechanisms for a number of detail questions which are intentionally not explicated on the conceptual enterprise modeling level. These concrete details refer in the first place to a distinction between the notion of information object types and information object instances, which on the conceptual level sometimes are used interchangeably, unaware of the difference on the implementation level (see Sect. 3.6). Implementation strategies also need to explicate whether individual information object entities are modeled by conceptual information resources, or if a set of multiple information objects is denoted. Since on the conceptual level storing and retrieving of information objects is often only assumed implicitly, i. e., not modeled at all, a technical realization also must take care of persistence mechanisms, a distinction of temporary and persistent information objects, and strategies for identifying information objects across multiple storage and retrieve steps.

The mapping meta-model declares the class `ResourceMapping`, which associates a conceptually specified resource to one or more resource implementation strategies. To implement a fully specified information resource, including information object type handling, information object instance processing, and persistent storage mechanisms, typically two kinds of implementation strategies are associated to a conceptually specified information resource. These are, at first, an implementation strategy that reflects a technology to specify a type system, and, secondly, a strategy describing mechanisms to store and retrieve information objects persistently.

Type system implementation Most concrete architectures provide mature technologies for describing and instantiating data types. Because of this, it can be expected that adapting architecture-specific information resource implementation strategies will be a common operation during the preparation for new development projects.

Type systems are mechanisms, which allow to describe data types using a schema of some kind, and optionally provide means to validate data instances with respect to conformance to a given schema. Examples are the XML Schema Definition (XSD) language, ECORE meta-models in the EMF environment, diverse type systems provided by middleware standards, e. g., the Common Objects Request Broker Architecture (CORBA), or type specification systems from programming languages. Implementation strategy descriptions are incorporated into the implementation strategy meta-model, by subclassing the imported abstract meta-class `ArchitectureSpecificInformationType` with meta-classes describing a specific type system technology.

To further explain the method, the XSD type specification mechanism will be used as an example technology to formulate implementation strategies for. This is done as part of a set of generic example implementation strategies, because it can be assumed that implementations of the XSD language and corresponding XML instance parsers are available for almost any front-end architecture platform. See Sect. 9.3.1 for the example implementation strategies.

Persistence implementation A full implementation of an information resource additionally requires information about how to store and retrieve persistent information objects, and how to identify them over multiple process instances over time. To give this information, architecture-specific ways of storing information objects can be specified via subclasses of the abstract meta-class `ArchitectureSpecificInformation-Storage`. If a specific information storage mechanism is restricted to be used with some information types only, the architecture-specific validity checking conditions for the mapping model should be adapted at this point, too, to test whether only valid combinations of information type implementation strategies, and information storage implementation strategies, have been used as references in a `ResourceMapping` entry.

Example implementation strategies for reading content from a uniform resource identifier (URI), writing and reading files on the front-end's file-system, or using an application-specific central storage service, are specified for further explanation of the method in Sect. 9.3.1.

7.3.8 Step 8: Meta-model architecture-specific sequence implementation strategy types

As part of the implementation of sequence concepts, i. e., direct steps of control flow passing from one process-member to another, three aspects of an implementation are specified in a `SequenceMapping` entry. These are the strategy of how to cause the control flow to be passed, the strategy to pick a new instance of an actor if a group of actors, or a role or a position not yet involved in the process, is requested to carry out the next process-step, and, as a third component, an optional condition to determine if the sequence step is to be carried out or not.

For all three implementation strategy types, abstract superclasses exist in the mapping meta-model as dedicated extension points, from which architecture-specific implementation strategy descriptions can be inherited as meta-classes in an implementation strategy meta-model. The abstract superclasses to interface to are `ArchitectureSpecificControlFlowImplementation`, `ArchitectureSpecificActorResolverImplementation` and `ArchitectureSpecificConditionImplementation`.

If the developed EIS consists of workflow descriptions executed by a WfMS, the corresponding control flow, actor resolver and condition implementation strategies may be specified to reflect concepts realized by the workflow description language and its execution mechanisms. This may apply, e. g., when workflow descriptions using the BPEL4PEOPLE or WS-HUMANTASK concepts are part of the implementation.

The semantics of concrete control flow implementations, implemented actor resolver strategies, and kinds of conditions, can be influenced by various kinds of factors determined both by domain-specific requirements, and technological constraints on the chosen target architecture platform. They can hardly be estimated from the abstract method engineering perspective. To provide further explanation of the method, generic example implementation strategies for sequence implementations are proposed in Sect. 9.1.5.

7.3.9 Step 9: Conceptualize hints at choosing default implementation strategies

The set of transformation rules and functions that are used to create an initial mapping model and implementation strategy model can be split into two categories: one part of the transformation functionality is independent from the target architecture and is used to query information from the enterprise model representation. This is the case with functions that are used to determine properties from the enterprise models, e. g., resolve responsible actors of a process-step, retrieve information about involved resources, etc. The second part uses the results of these query functions to output a default mapping model and default implementation strategy models, the latter being dependent on platform-specific target architectures. Consequently, when adapting the method to a new target architecture, the architecture-dependent part of the transformation rules is to be implemented with respect to the specifics of the implementation strategy language, or multiple languages, created in the first step.

One general kind of hint required to be available with every choice of an architecture-specific implementation strategy is to detect whether a concept is intended to be represented on that architecture at all. This can be detected in the integrating business process perspective, by determining for every process-member on which target architecture it will be implemented. Depending on the semantics of the process-member concept, there may also be multiple target architectures for one process-member, e. g., when collaborative process-steps or human-machine interactions are modeled.

Hints for determining on which target architecture a process-step is intended to be used can be derived from multiple information sources in the model. A first option is to base the default detection algorithm on actor types. If instances of architecture-specific actor types are declared as performing actors, e. g., `WebSessionUser`, the default detection algorithm may assume that the intended target architecture is the corresponding web-application architecture. Another option is to base the detection on resources attached to process-steps. If, e. g., a web-browser software resource is attached to a process-step, the default detection algorithm may be written to treat this as a mark to implement the process-step as part of a web-application front-end. Other means of using hints, e. g., based on model element names containing keyword-phrases, or comment-strings and tagged values (see Sect. 7.2.3), may alternatively be consulted.

The result of the architectural considerations taken in this step is a set of hints, which list means for expressing knowledge in conceptual enterprise models, for which no explicit conceptual language elements exist. Asking responsible stakeholders, who maintain the conceptual enterprise models, to model according to these hints, on the one hand limits their degrees of freedom to informally express knowledge in a way of their choice. On the other hand, rules about applying hints may offer guidelines of how to express specific constellations unambiguously, which even may increase efficiency of modeling, and foster intersubjective understanding of the model based on these supplementary guidelines.

Since both the conceptually modeling stakeholders, and the software developers, who formulate model transformation rules based on the elaborated hints, are the target audience of the elaborated hints in this step, the documentation of the design decisions taken in this step should be formulated in a way suitable both for end-users and technical experts.

7.3.10 Step 10: Implement hints at choosing default implementation strategies

This step of implementing the previously conceptualized set of hints is separately declared in the method, to indicate that at this point the work can be delegated from a software architect to an expert in applying model transformation languages. Technically, the implementation of algorithms for choosing architecture-specific default implementation strategies boils down to create model transformation rules that are additionally applied when the mapping model initialization or update transformation is run, together with a function to detect whether this target architecture is to be used to implement the conceptual element at all. This detection function and the model transformation rules are implemented according to the hint documentation, which has been created during the previous design step.

The procedure to detect default implementation strategies is to iterate over all existing mapping entries in the mapping model, grouped by the types of conceptual elements they reference on the conceptual side. In cases where no corresponding implementation strategy is mapped to a conceptual elements in a mapping entries, i. e., the `implementations` reference of the mapping entry instance is empty, a potential candidate for detecting a default implementation is found. Depending on the type of the conceptual element, i. e., separated for process-steps, events, actors, resources, etc., different hints can now be applied per target architecture to determine a reasonable default implementation strategy. If such a strategy can be detected, the model transformation causes an implementation strategy instance element to be created in the implementation strategy model instance, and sets a reference in the mapping entry's `implementations` reference to this newly created implementation strategy element instance. All changes are made in-place to the model instances during the transformation execution, afterwards the models are saved to their persistent storage.

The algorithm as described above is idempotent, i. e., running it a second time on the previously modified models does not cause any further changes. This is the case, because detection of default strategies is only performed for mapping entries with a yet empty `implementations` reference. In cases where a default strategy can be derived, it is added as member to the `implementations` reference, which in turn blocks detection of defaults on any further possible runs of the algorithm. In the other cases, where no default can be derived, the `implementations` reference remains empty, and also remains empty after further runs of the same detection algorithm. For empty `implementations` references, suitable implementation strategies have to be chosen manually, otherwise the subsequent validity check on the mapping model will not pass.

In addition to be stable towards applying the algorithm multiple times, and preserving previously created automatic associations to default strategies, the default detection mechanism is also stable towards manual entries that have been made in the mapping model, because no mapping entries, which already contain any strategy associated, are touched by the transformation. This way, later changes in the source EMs, with subsequent runs of the default detection mechanism to automatically update the mapping model, will preserve existing design decisions already explicated in the model, and will in some cases be able to automatically adapt changes in the conceptual models to corresponding mapping model entries. In those cases where changes in the conceptual models cannot automatically be adapted, the mechanism ensures that no damage is done to the existing mapping model, and allows to manually feed in the required adaptations.

Examples of architecture-specific parts of model transformations are provided in Appendices A.3.2 and A.4.2. They are implemented in the XTEND model transformation language.

7.3.11   Step 11: Implement code generation templates for generic implementation strategies

Code generation templates are used to create technical artifacts from the descriptions of implementation strategies, which are given by implementation strategy element instances in the implementation strategy models, referenced from the mapping model. When interpreted by a code generation script engine, source code or other technical artifacts are created as output, which may call domain API functions, individually implement functionality, or provide configuration options for shaping a software component's behavior. During the generation process, parameters specified in the implementation strategy element instances are queried, and are used to control the artifact output and the generated functionality accordingly.

The implementation strategy descriptions reside on the same level of semantic abstraction as the targeted output artifacts and parametrize the code generation process with knowledge about the platform-specific implementation. The model-to-text transformations that are to be developed thus mainly are horizontal transformations, serving to syntactically convert between the representations of implementation strategy descriptions in the implementation strategy models, and the executable or interpretable source code artifacts. In case of the templates to be developed, this means that most of the code representation for implementation strategies can straight-forwardly be created as pre-configured blocks of code, which are output to the target artifacts including variable parts filled with parameters derived from the implementation strategy model elements. While querying the implementation strategy descriptions is the main source of information for controlling the artifact generation process, the code generation templates can also resort to information additionally retrieved from the associating mapping model and the referenced conceptual models.

Code generation templates contain the entire knowledge about which concrete technology to use for implementing the desired functionality on the targeted architecture. The implementation may in some cases be supplemented by domain API functionality, which gets invoked at runtime by generated code. In other cases, the specification of the implementation strategy's functionality may be realized mainly by the generated code, keeping the domain API leaner and focused on architecture-specific features.

The method makes a distinction between generating artifacts for implementation strategy types that are generically included as parts of the mapping model without any reference to a specific target architecture, and other implementation strategy types, which originate from architecture-specific implementation strategy meta-models that are created as part of the individual engineering project. Generic implementation strategies previously exist, before a specific target architecture is chosen. Code generation template functionality for handling these implementation strategies may partially be reused from other target architecture adaptations, and may build upon general abstractions made available by the strategy type declarations. Code generation functionality for handling architecture-specific implementation strategies, in contrast, is typically developed in parallel to the specification of the corresponding architecture-specific implementation strategy meta-model. When both parts are developed at the same time, the specification of the implementation strategies can in turn be adjusted to specifics imposed by the technical realization. To put a light on these two different modes of developing code generation templates, the currently described step focuses on realizing generic implementation strategy types from previously existing implementation strategy meta-models, while the next and last methodical step covers those implementation strategy types, which are specifically modeled during the development project as part of adapting the method to a target architecture.

Examples for generic implementation strategies that can be expected to be implementable on multiple target architectures are the process-step implementation strategies `Message` and `Form`, as well as `Menu` and `Question`. Among others, these strategies can be expected to be used frequently for describing implementation options on multiple diverse architecture platforms.

7.3.12 Step 12: Implement code generation templates for architecture-specific implementation strategies

As a second step in developing code generation templates, and the last step of the overall sub-process of adapting a target architecture, those parts of functionality which are newly introduced by implementation strategy types in project-specific implementation strategy meta-models are dealt with. Separating this part of developing code generation functionality as an individual methodical step, allows to specifically iterate between the development of the implementation strategy meta-model on the one hand, i. e., the development of those language concepts which are later consulted to control the code generation mechanism, and, on the other hand, the development of the code generation templates, as well as an optional domain API in parallel. If the same group of developers is simultaneously working on these components, a significant gain in efficiency can be expected to be achieved. This can be assumed, because developing these artifacts extensively requires to take design decision that balance out functionality between the three of these components, and repeatedly requires to decide in which component to integrate a change, and which interdependencies to other components are to be obeyed.

Developing code generation templates requires a higher degree of programming skills than writing artifacts directly, because it not only requires to develop program fragments in the target programming language or other artifacts that describe functionality, but it also incorporates the use of a template language, which accesses model data, potentially processes it, and controls the output of artifact fragments. When creating code generation templates, the responsible software developers need to operate with at least two programming languages in parallel, and mix constructs from both languages into single code generation templates. This requires a higher degree of expertise than software development with traditional development approaches, and narrows down the range of available professionals who can perform these tasks.

An example set of code generation templates in the XPAND template language, and corresponding invocation scripts, are referenced in Appendices A.3.3 and A.4.3. The first set of templates generates artifacts for a web application platform, the second set generates artifacts for a BPEL-driven SOA environment as target architecture platform.

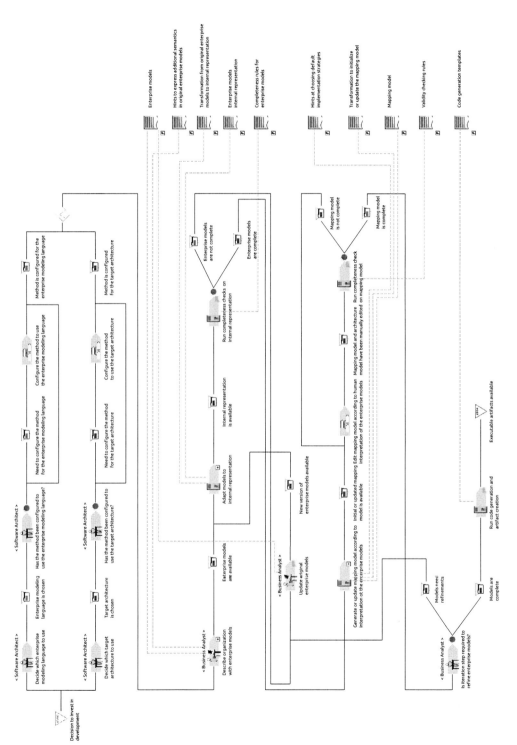

Figure 25: Overall methodical procedure

153

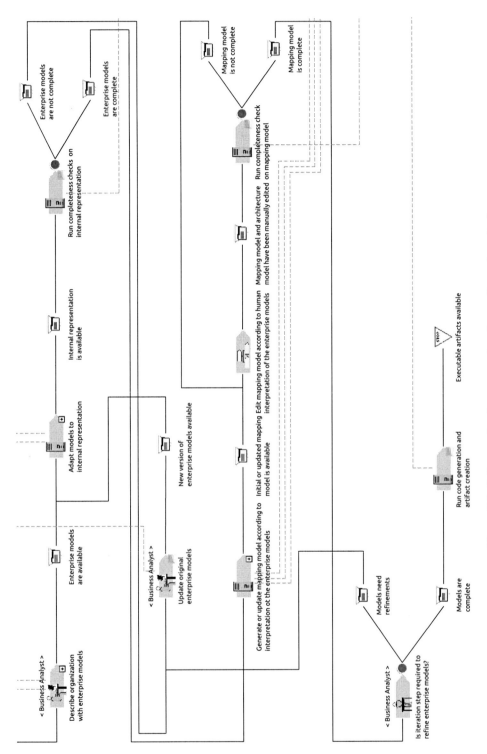

Figure 26: Software development using the configured method

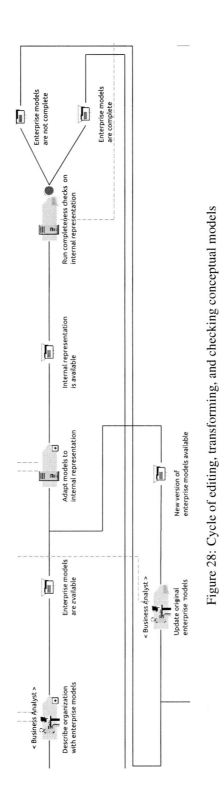

Figure 28: Cycle of editing, transforming, and checking conceptual models

155

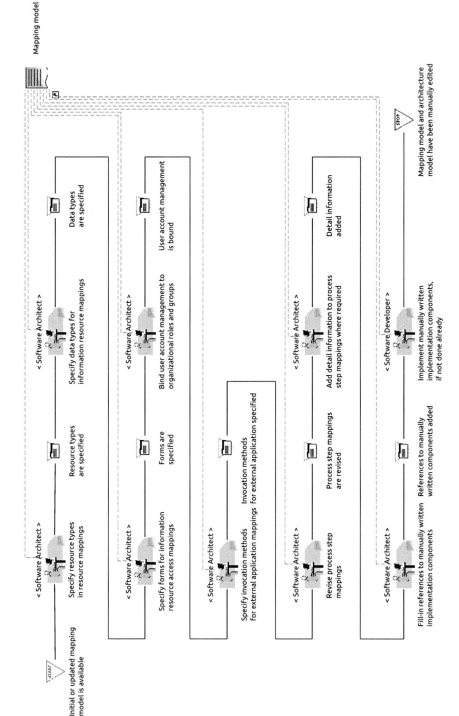

Figure 29: Process of manually editing the mapping model

156

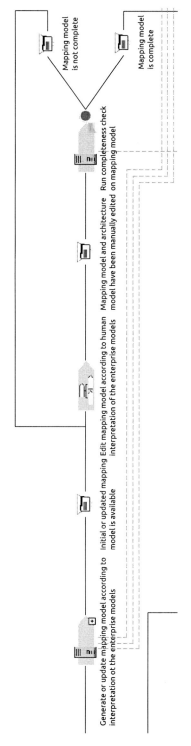

Figure 30: Cycle of initializing or updating a mapping model, manually revising it, and automatically checking its validity

Figure 32: Taking the decision to adapt the method to a set of enterprise modeling languages

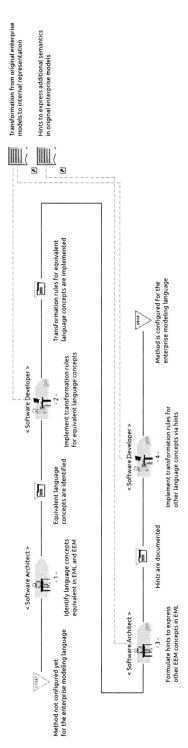

Figure 33: Sub-process to adapt the method to a set of enterprise modeling languages

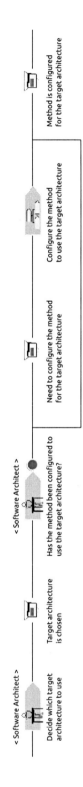

Figure 35: Taking the decision to adapt the method to a new target architecture

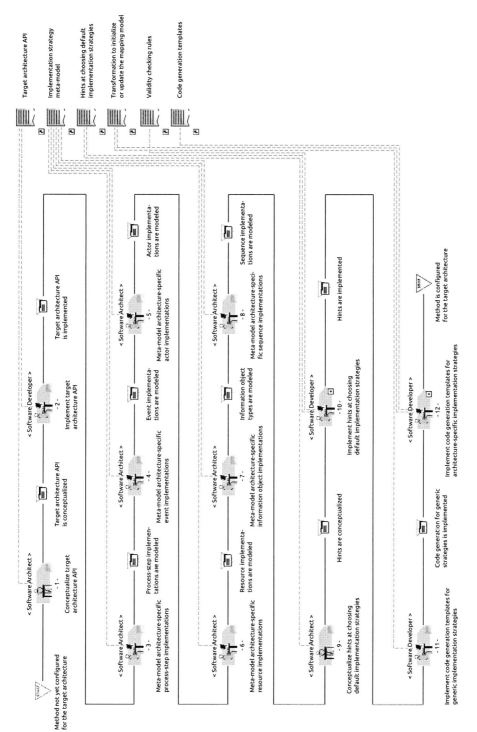

Figure 36: Sub-process to adapt the method to a new target architecture

161

8 Design of a prototypical enterprise information system

Up to now, the method components and their application have been described on a general abstract level, independent from any concrete enterprise modeling language (computation independent conceptualizations), independent from available implementation strategies (platform independent conceptualizations), and independent from specific technical details about the realization of the implementation strategies (platform specific conceptualizations). On each of these three layers, a wide variety of contingent realization options exist, with diverse alternatives of how to concretely specify conceptual elements and technological components in the context of applying the suggested method.

In a first step, general design considerations, as they have to be taken into account for any software engineering project independently of the applied engineering method, are made. Determining the design of the software system to be created resembles the design phase as described by several known software engineering process methods [DBLV09, SK08]. These design considerations both relate to platform independent aspects, and platform-specific implementation issues. Sect. 8.1 covers this initial conceptualization phase.

Platform-specific design decisions that are to be taken determine the way how functionality is realized and presented to a user on a specific front-end. While all kinds of front-ends can be assumed to provide computing capabilities as well as display technology to interface with a user via a graphical user interface (GUI), the front-ends may be restricted to be used with specific programming languages and application programming interfaces (APIs), and the available GUI metaphors may differ on diverse platforms. As a consequence, the design decisions must incorporate how to realize GUI components that offer functionality provided by implementation strategies in a platform-specific and architecture-bound way. Sect. 8.2 takes a closer look at the user interface conceptualization for an enterprise information system (EIS).

When the system design is specified, both for the entire distributed system, as well as for the individual front-end functionalities, a domain API is made available. This API provides common abstractions used throughout the EIS, e. g., interfaces and type declarations of shared objects, prepared to be used by multiple generated software artifacts on potentially different target architecture platforms. An abstract example domain API is presented in Sect. 8.3.

Concrete conceptualizations of exemplary implementation strategies, which form the building blocks of EIS functionality, will further be elaborated in Sect. 9.

The integration of computation independent concepts of enterprise modeling languages with the method finally is demonstrated in Sect. 11.1, where an existing external enterprise modeling language is adapted to the method.

8.1 General architectural design considerations

To prepare the development of code generation templates or any other execution mechanism for a running EIS, general design decisions need to be taken with regard to the target architecture on which the application is intended to be executed. These general decisions relate to questions of coordination in a distributed environment, control flow management, the possible use of a workflow execution engine, architectural options for data storage mechanisms, and responsibilities for automatic execution of algorithmic process-steps. These facets of general design consideration are discussed in the following.

8.1.1 Coordination in a distributed environment

One fundamental design decision with significant influence on the implementation components to be created in a development project, lies in the decision how to technicallly realize control over the process flow, i. e., how the overall software system coordinates in which order individual process-member implementations are to be executed. EISs are required to provide automatic mechanisms that control the execution of process-member implementations in the right order, according to the underlying business process model (BPM) descriptions (see Req. 5). Since it is also a main purpose of an EIS to at the same time provide a system which supports the integration of multiple distributed actors and multiple distributed software components (see Req. 3), a coordination mechanism must be available which binds together distributed components and allows to control the interaction work among them. Assuming that every actor is using at least one front-end application at a time to perform his or her work, there must be a facility which allows the coordination of these multiple front-ends on their client nodes, e. g., to notify about process-steps in which the client is to take part, or to pass over workflow control to a different client and an according user, if a change of an actor is intended in the business process model (see Req. 5).

The conceptualizations of either a central process flow control point of responsibility, or a decentralized architecture, form another continuum along which combined mechanisms in an actual implementation environment can be applied. A mixture of both approaches may, e. g., consist of a decentralized messaging system, in which client nodes autonomously communicate about passing control flow and associated data to each other, accompanied by a central observer component which keeps track of the overall process instance states, and may also hold responsible for providing long-term persistence services and locking or synchronizing functionality.

Centralized process flow control   One option to ensure that process-step implementations are executed in correct sequences, and that control flow is correctly passed between users and front-end, is the use of a separate control flow management entity, which actively knows about the modeled process structures, and tells front-ends to invoke the process-steps that are to be executed per user.

The traditional architecture to realize this coordination component is a client-server architecture [TvS03], which distinguishes between back-end and front-end roles. In practice, such a control flow component is typically realized using a dedicated process execution language interpreter deployed on a central process orchestration node, e. g., a Business Process Execution Language (BPEL) execution engine running on a single server.

Besides actively coordinating the process instance executions, the central back-end component can additionally keep track of monitoring the process instances that are currently being executed, and can be used to impose usage control mechanisms on the behavior of client instances [NS07, PHB06], which can be relevant in untrusted, security-demanding environments (see Req. 7).

The general pattern of a centralized client-server architecture, which incorporates multiple distributed physical machines in a network environment, is displayed in Fig. 37.

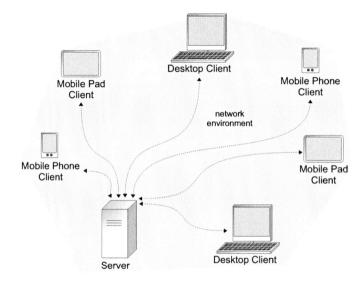

Figure 37: Distributed components in a client-server architecture

The prototypical example implementations of the method presented in this work both base on a client-server architecture.

De-centralized process flow control   An alternative to a centralized process control approach is letting every client implementation decide individually which next process-steps are to be executed. Instead of centralizing knowledge and control about the process execution, the latter option requires involved client implementations to have knowledge about a partial structure of the overall processes they are involved in, and they gain control on how to interface to other nodes during process execution.

A decentralized conceptualization incorporates distributed client nodes, which locally take the responsibility to invoke process-steps according to the modeled process descriptions, and pass the process control flow to each other autonomously when the control flow changes or splits to other clients. This system design pattern is also typically referenced as peer-to-peer (P2P) architecture [Ras97]. There are multiple theoretical options to realize such a coordination in a distributed setup without a central control instance, which can be implemented as control mechanisms, if the design option to implement the control mechanism individually for the project is chosen.

The decision whether to choose for a decentralized architecture may be influenced by necessary security considerations in untrusted or open environments (see Req. 7). When developing software with increased claims for security, the decentralized system style offers the inherent disadvantage of physically passing responsibility for executing parts of the executed process to individual client nodes in the distributed environment. If no accompanying monitoring and/or central message passing mechanisms are established in the system, this allows any client with malicious intent to manipulate the process control flow in undesired ways. The efforts for building and applying mechanisms to prevent such malicious use may exceed the efforts for operating centralized and better monitorable system architectures. As a consequence, a decentralized system architecture is less likely to be chosen as the underlying system pattern in security-sensitive environments than a central control flow approach.

The design decision, whether to use a central process flow control component, or apply a decentralized control flow architecture, also exhibits aspects with regard to the centralization or decentralization of data storage handling. This issue is discussed in the next subsection.

8.1.2 Realizing data storages

A mechanism for storing data is required by the EIS, in order to manage the use of information resources in a distributed environment and persistently spanning over multiple sessions of each user.

Diverse technical approaches exist for making data persistent, and make data accessible in a distributed environment. The most popular solution to this challenge is using a centralized relational database management system, which is accessed remotely by distributed clients [RG03]. Other approaches may support the use of differently structured data, e. g., XML databases [BDG+00]. In theory, also a distributed storage of data on diverse front-end devices can be imagined, together with a shared access protocol, which allows remote clients to access this persistent data without the use of any central controlling instance.

For the purpose of a prototypical implementation design, a central data storage service can be conceptualized that handles entire XML documents as persisted units on a central server. This way of storing data persistently implicates a number of unsolved deficiencies, e. g., synchronization problems if multiple concurrent accesses are not properly schedules, or the resource is not properly locked during potential modifications. These problems belong to a well-known set of theoretical core principles in computer science, with a variety of elaborated solution approaches, which is why they further remain undiscussed here.

The prototypical implementation suggests an `IInformationObjectStorageSer-vice` interface as part of the domain API, which describes a central persistent storage service. Its declaration is shown in Fig. 39.

8.1.3 Automatically executed process-steps

As with every distributed architecture, trade-offs occur where to locate the controlling components that determine the dynamic behavior of the running process instance. In an architecture with centralized back-end components and remote front-end clients, automatic processing steps can either be designed to be processed on back-end servers, or be executed on front-end devices. The extreme ends of this trade-off are known as either a strict "thin client" solution, where as much as possible processing logic is handled by centralized components, or a "fat client" approach by which front-end functionality is used to perform processing.

The example implementation puts its focus on demonstrating how multiple alternative platforms are integrated as one EIS. For this reason, the upcoming prototypical realization will put most automatic processing responsibility onto the clients, while the back-end server component remains a simple centralized control and storage mechanism keeping track of the process-steps executed on the clients.

8.2 User interface sketch

If an EIS is intended to provide human user access as part of the implemented processes, core parts of its functionality have to be exposed to human users by graphical user interface (GUI) components which provide access to the available functionality. As a raw sketch, Fig. 38 assembles multiple prototypically sketched GUI widgets to represent components in a GUI environment, as they are generally required in an EIS to perform human user interactions during software-supported business processes. Any concrete target architecture is expected to offer more ergonomic GUI concepts which will realize these abstract elements in a platform specific way.

Some target architectures, such as a service oriented architecture (SOA) orchestration environment running BPEL processes, may make use of extending standards such as the BPEL4PEOPLE human interaction extension to BPEL, which will cause interpretation engines implementing the BPEL4PEOPLE standard [Org10b] to render GUIs that will contain more detailed and concrete realizations of the abstract example given here. In Sect. 10, the option of choosing a BPEL execution environment as a target implementation architecture for the Software Engineering with Enterprise Models (SEEM) method is discussed in greater depth.

The abstract GUI components sketched in Fig. 38 represent human interaction access points for using core functionality of EISs, such as being notified about tasks to perform, choose tasks to perform, work on tasks in-place in the environment of the EIS front-end application, or spawn external applications to work on semi-automatic tasks as part of a workflow process. Tasks to be performed in-place may typically be related to viewing or editing form documents. Tasks performed with the help of external applications may cover editing of standard office-type electronic documents, e. g., MICROSOFT WORD® files.

A technically simple, but nevertheless important interaction feature of an EIS, is to inform human users about manual tasks to be performed, and to notify a central coordination system when the user marks a manual tasks as completed [RDB+08]. Handling the requirement interaction steps for performing human tasks may be implemented by a standard framework implementation, e. g., BPEL4PEOPLE [Org10b].

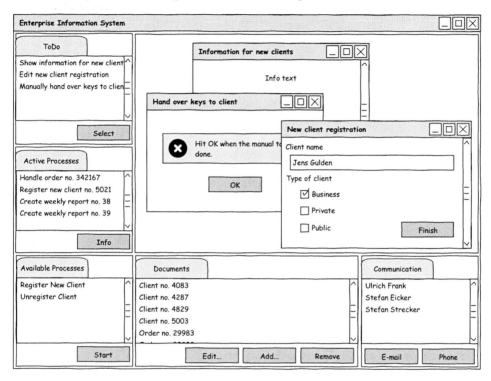

Figure 38: Schematic sketch of an abstract user interface with generic interaction functionality for an EIS front-end

The interaction components sketched in Fig. 38 get realized with a different visual look-and-feel by different kinds of implementations. However, the type of functionality that is made accessible to human-computer interaction by the individual parts of the GUI remains invariant with regard to different implementation technologies. To further describe the sketched GUI elements, their functionality is closer looked at in the following subsections.

8.2.1 Process instance management functionality

A first set of interaction options that are made accessible to a human user by the GUI in order to provide interaction with the EIS consists of means for accessing and managing the current process instances, in which the user is involved as a participating actor. Such a list is made available as a GUI component, which allows the user to select a running process-step instance and cause the front-end application to display all GUI components which are currently active to support the user in performing this process-step. The GUI element which is responsible for offering this functionality is displayed on the middle left-hand-side in the sketched application window in Fig. 38, placed in the box labeled "Active Processes". This box contains the list of process instances the user is currently involved in.

Depending on whether the overall system conceptualization allows for directly creating new process instances from the front-end, and given the current user is authorized to start new process instances this way, the GUI offers a list of process types which are available for the current user to be directly instantiated. This functionality is sketched in the lower part of the left-hand-side in Fig. 38, with the box labeled "Available Processes", showing those types of processes which the current user may directly instantiate. Selecting a process type and pushing the "Start" button initiates a new instance from the currently selected type entry. It depends on the business process conceptualizations that are realized by the EIS, whether a direct instantiation of processes makes sense, or does not need to be offered as front-end functionality.

8.2.2   Process-step editor functionality

The main middle area in the sketched application window in Fig. 38 hosts individual editor windows, which provide software functionality internally offered by the EIS to perform individual process-steps in-place with the EIS front-end application. If this support is not provided by an external application, the process-step front-end implementation opens a window in this main area.

Process-steps for viewing or editing electronic documents typically interact with the user by opening an editor window showing the document, and optionally allowing to edit it where required for performing the process-step. Since functionality for accessing and handling information is especially relevant in EIS (see Req. 6), the overall GUI provides additional points of access to information handling functionality, which are discussed in the following subsection.

8.2.3   Information access and document editing functionality

Document handling functionality is realized by displaying a list with currently accessed and edited document instances and available document types. Selecting an item from the list opens a corresponding GUI editor component which provides access to the document, or shows a newly created instance of a document type. The editor may either be a component internally available as part of the EIS front-end application, or an external editor which is associated to be responsible for handling the document instance in focus.

A GUI element, which offers the above described interaction functionality, is displayed in the lower-middle part in the sketched application window in Fig. 38. It is shown as a box labeled "Documents". The entries gathered in "Documents" provide access to existing documents, which may be grouped by their document types or by another business-related grouping criteria. The "Edit...", "Add..." and "Remove" buttons allow for directly performing actions on the document instances and types, which may in turn lead to events fired in running process instances, e. g., as "new document created" or "document deleted" business events.

8.2.4 Manual task handling functionality

During the execution of process instances, some process-steps are intentionally performed manually. These process-steps typically are expressed by corresponding model elements in the conceptual business process models, which mark them as "manual". Although these process model elements by nature of the manual tasks do not contain any formal semantics about the internal composition of the task to be performed, basic software support for guiding the execution of manual process-steps is offered by the EIS front-end. Software support for performing manual process tasks notifies the user when a manual task is to be performed, optionally provides additional links to instruction documents about how to perform the task, and allows to gain an overview on what manual tasks are currently to be performed.

After a manual task has been completed, the EIS provides means for the user to notify the system about the completion of the corresponding process-step. In cases where a result is achieved by the manual task, the EIS additionally offers input facilities for entering the achieved results of a manually performed process-step. This functionality is vital for the overall process control mechanism to work, because the execution of manual process-steps needs to be interfaced to the software system by at least allowing the system to notify the user about manual process-steps to be performed, and allow the user to respond by marking a manual process-step as completed when it is done. Optionally, return results or, in case of unsuccessful execution, problem documentation is supplied by the user.

In the GUI sketch in Fig. 38, the manually performed process-steps are listed in the "To Do" list box in the upper-left corner. It shows the currently performed process-steps, including manual ones.

In other concrete implementation environments, GUI interaction element for handling manual process-steps are provided by underlying standard implementations, e. g., interpreters of the BPEL4PEOPLE [Org10b] specification. These implementations will typically provide the core functionality sketched by the abstract GUI model discussed above, and add more standard specific and implementation dependent features to the GUI.

8.2.5 Decision functionality

During the execution of a process, there may be alternative branches to choose how to proceed with the process, or information may be required to parametrize further process-step instances to be used in the process. These decisions to control the process flow are interactively queried from the user via the GUI front-end. For example, at some point during the execution of a process, the user is presented a menu from which to choose further actions to take. Or, different modes for performing subsequent automatic or semi-automatic operation are offered interactively, to allow the user to determine in which way subsequent steps of action are performed.

Taking decisions resembles performing manual process-steps in the sense that the result of the decision is solely dependent on human responsibility, and cannot be calculated algorithmically. However, taking a decision about the subsequent process control flow typically does not impose any external activities. Thus, comparable to performing a manual process-step, the user remains operating the software system, and enters his or her decision via input GUI elements.

The abstract GUI model shown in Fig. 38 does not demonstrate specific GUI elements for entering decisions, since these may be realized by standard pop-up menus and input forms as they are available on most GUI-capable platforms. Like any other process-step to be performed, a decision to take may appear in the to-do list of tasks yet to be performed sketched in the upper-left corner of Fig. 38.

Depending on the process semantics, decisions may also be required to be taken immediately, in which case the EIS front-end prompts the user directly at the point in time when the decision result is required to continue with the process flow.

8.2.6 Communication functionality

Communication is vital to most distributed organizations, and support for communication, either internally among members of the organization, or externally with business partners and other associates, is one core axis along which the activities of an organization can be described and overseen. As a consequence, communication tasks play a central role in business process descriptions, and require functionality to foster communication as an integral component of an EIS.

An EIS typically provides access to individual communication facilities, e. g., an external e-mail client application. It also supports the user in overviewing his or her possible communication partners by giving a list of persons and institutions to contact. This list of contact persons can be context-sensitive, to show those contact partners with a higher priority, who are most likely to be contacted in the course of the currently performed process-step.

Communication often is an explicit part of the business processes that are supported by the EIS. Hence, the EIS's workflow control functionality and communication functionality are interwoven, to allow for initiating communication relationships as parts of running process instances, as well as to be able to treat communication activities as starting point triggers for spawning new process instances. For example, a new order process instance may be spawned when an e-mail arrives at a given e-mail address. As part of this newly started process instance, an employee of the dispatch department will be assigned to handle the order, make sure the goods are available for packaging, and finally send out an e-mail to the customer to notify him or her that the order has arrived. The first communication activity, receiving an order by e-mail, automatically starts a new process instance.

The second communication activity is initiated during the execution of the process, and the process execution engine automatically invokes an external e-mail client as the corresponding communication tool.

The abstract GUI model in Fig. 38 contains an area in the lower right part of the sketched application window, which contains a list of possible communication partners, with whom communication can be manually initiated from the EIS front-end, complementary to the automatic communication handling functionality provided by the EIS.

8.2.7 Project specific functionality

Besides generic features providing human-computer interaction facilities in an EIS, any individual development project may require to offer specific functionality, which reaches beyond the generic patterns of interaction with the EIS. Concrete EIS implementations will, in addition to what is shown in the generic sketch in Fig. 38, also incorporate means to access project specific functionality, which in the end reflect specifics of the organization supported by the EIS, and allows to accentuate competitive advantages within the EIS.

Since in principle no further assumptions can be made from a general method description perspective about the specific functionality to be realized in individual projects, the option for including specific GUI functionality can only be mentioned at this point, without preparing further methodical underpinning for this.

8.3 Abstract domain API

Resulting from the previous considerations about general architectural decisions and available end-user functionality in an EIS, a compact abstract domain API has been designed, which provides generic platform-independent interfaces as an object-oriented structural basis for a distributed EIS. This API is given as an example of how some of the fundamental concepts discussed in the method description can be realized in an object-oriented software system. Not every software development project using the SEEM method will make use of an own domain API, if, e. g., basic concepts for executing workflow steps are instead provided by an execution mechanism such as a workflow management system (WfMS).

Several fundamental design decisions are reflected by the example API, e. g., the decision to use a centrally controlled process management engine and a central information object storage system. The API formalizes these design decisions by providing abstract interfaces and classes to describe the system's architecture. It may additionally contain concrete and reusable implementations, which are invoked either from generated code or from a runtime interpreter.

The example API is displayed as a Unified Modeling Language (UML) class-diagram in Fig. 39.

The classes displayed in Fig. 39 are organized into two distinct packages, which express the architectural role of the components described by these interfaces. The first set of interfaces resides in package `application`. These interfaces provide the fundamental structure of implementation components running as part of distributed front-end applications. The second set of interfaces is organized in package `backend`, to describe the centralized server components that coordinate the workflow and manage persistent data storage.

The example domain API serves as technical means to clarify concepts of the described method. It is not applied in the prototypical implementations presented in Sect. 10 and Sect. 11.

8.3.1 Front-end API interfaces

The first set of interfaces model the front-end application functionality for EIS on an abstract level. They are displayed in Fig. 40 as an excerpt of Fig. 39.

Figure 40: Front-end API interfaces for distributed EIS applications

Interface IUserSession The `IUserSession` interface represents a session for an individual user per front-end application. There can be at most one session per front-end application, but a user may be logged into multiple sessions at once at different locations and on different front-end devices.

The notion of a `IUserSession` binds together the identification of a concrete user with his or her current status in working on process-steps. Every user is considered to be involved in zero or more process instances at the same time. Being involved in a process instance means for a user to have to work on at least one process-step that is part of this process instance. The `IUserSession` interface allows to query all those process-step instances which currently are requested to be performed by the user. Derived from these process-steps, the process instances in which the user is currently involved can be determined. A user is also considered to be involved in a process instance, if he or she has already performed a process-step from this process instance, and according to the process type model, another process-step from the same instance might follow later for the same user. As long as any other actor is involved in this process instance, i. e., the process instance has not reached a defined end event yet, a user remains involved in a process instance, if, by the structural declaration of the process, there is a chance that the user will have to perform another process-step from the same process instance.

To coordinate with other front-ends in the distributed environment, the `IUserSession` interface holds references to the central coordination components for process control flow and data persistence. It uses the `IProcessControlService` to query scheduled process-steps for the user, and to notify other front-ends of other users, if the control flow is to be continued at another place.

The `getUsername()` method of the interface allows to query, which user is authenticated as owner of this `IUserSession`. Implementations of process-steps may use this to get the current user name for further evaluation of access rights or other user-related information.

With the `getProcessControlService()` method, access to an instance of `IProcessControlService` is gained. An implementation of `IUserSession` should return a reference to a locally callable object of type `IProcessControlService`, which transparently interfaces to the underlying implementation of the central process control service, i. e., a local caller of methods on this instance will not notify that the implementation is actually accessed via a web-service call to a remote machine.

The `getInformationObjectStorage()` method provides access to the central remote information object storage. In the same way as the `getProcessControlService()` method, `getInformationObjectStorage()` returns a locally accessible object, whose methods transparently adapt to the remote web-service for information object storage.

`getScheduledProcessSteps()` returns a list of `IProcessStep` instances which are prepared to be performed by the user, but have not been started yet. Using this function will allow to build a to-do list in a front-end GUI, in which the user is able to pick which process-step to perform next.

Finally, using the `scheduleProcessStep(schedule)` method, a new process-step is requested to be performed by either the same user on the same front-end, or any other combination of user and logical location in the distributed environment. This method is typically called at the end of a `IProcessStep`'s `execute()` method from concrete implementations of `IProcessStep`, to pass the control flow on to process-member implementations, which are determined to follow as subsequent steps in the process.

In order to reference concepts from the `backend` package, the UML model of the domain API (see Fig. 39) contains a dependency relationship from class `IUserSession` to package `backend`. Interfaces from package `backend` are used via the methods `getProcessControlService()`, `getInformationObjectStorage()` and `scheduleProcessStep(schedule)`.

Interface `IUserProcess` The `IUserProcess` interface represents a process instance referenced from one `IUserSession`. Every process instance owns a unique identifier, which is global to all client front-ends participating in the process. It can be retrieved via the method `getProcessID()`. The `IUserSession` interface wraps around this global id to give each process instance a local identity, and provides additional local functionality attached to process instances.

A reference to the user session representation of type `IUserSession` is retrieved via the method `getSession()`. Every instance of `IUserProcess` belongs to exactly on parent `IUserSession`.

The `getInformationObject(key)` method retrieves an information object from a named memory slot that is locally associated to the `IUserProcess`. The inverse operation, putting an information object into a named slot, is realized by the method `setInformationObject(key, Object)`.

Interface `IProcessStep` With the `IProcessStep` interface, the most general representation of an executable software representation of a process-member is given. The core purpose of encapsulating executable functionality by instances of this concept is fulfilled by incorporating a "strategy" pattern (in the terminology of [GHJV94]) with the `execute()` method. The `execute()` method is invoked by the front-end application when an instance of the implemented process-step is scheduled to be performed and started as member of a running global process.

Implementations of the `IProcessStep` interface may apply a more fine-grained structuring to their internal execution. It is, e. g., possible to add a generic abstract class that implements `IProcessStep`, and refines the coarse notion of a single `execute()` method to a more detailed sequence of `prepareExecute()`, `doExecute()`, `cleanupExecute()`. Concrete implementations can then subclass this abstract superclass and override the individual methods where desired.

Besides providing the `execute()` method, the `IProcessStep` interface keeps a reference to the process instance, of which it is part, accessed via the `getProcess()` method.

A straight-forward notion of a life-cycle is attached to instances of `IProcessStep`. Via the `getState()` method, a state code is retrieved, which has the symbolic meaning defined in class `ProcessStepState` (see below). State handling is considered an affair of the managing application, i. e., a concrete implementation of `IUserSession`, which keeps track of scheduled process-steps, and their execution when requested by the user or the system.

As already noted in Sect. 9.1, on the implementation level, it appears useful to blur the distinction between conceptually expressed process-steps and events, which are, however, well-justified distinct concepts on the domain-specific level of enterprise models. Using only a single notion of process-step in the API allows for a generic and interchangeable application of `IProcessStep` implementations for both process-steps and events. This consideration stems from the idea that implemented representations of events will, if not trivial, have to perform some automatic actions in most cases anyway. Since this is also the generic notion behind process-steps, a distinction between process-step implementations and event implementations is not made in the API. This design decision is taken in parallel to the meta-modeling of the concepts in the mapping model, which declare all process-member implementation strategies as subclasses of the general abstract meta-class `AbstractProcessMemberImplementation` (see Sect. 9.1).

Class `ProcessStepState` The states that a process-step implementation instance goes through from being scheduled, to being started, executed and ended, are represented by the entries in class `ProcessStepState`. The meaning of the symbolic state identifiers are as follows:

- `WAITING` marks a process-step implementation instance as being scheduled to be performed on the local front-end

- `STARTED` indicates that an instance's `execute()` method has been invoked, and that the operation is still proceeding

- `FINISHED` denotes a state when the process-step has regularly finished

- and `CANCELED` marks a process-step as irregularly terminated in a technical sense, e. g., if a runtime error occurs on the level of the execution engine or underlying programming language

Note that the `FINISHED` and `CANCELED` states do not refer to any conceptual information about a successfully finished or unsuccessfully finished process-step in the sense of the business process model. If, on the business process level, process-steps may lead to different results in terms of regular completion versus cancellation, these outcomes and their influence on the subsequent process control flow should be modeled explicitly on the business process level.

8.3.2 Back-end API interfaces

The second group of interfaces modeled by the API describes the most basic back-end functionality, required by a distributed EIS architecture with centralized coordination components. Fig. 41 shows the back-end interfaces, which are further explained in the following, as an excerpt of Fig. 39.

Figure 41: Back-end API interfaces for a central coordination server for distributed EIS applications

Interface `IProcessControlService` The `IProcessControlService` interface describes a remotely accessible service for control flow coordination among multiple front-end clients. To provide this functionality, the service manages a list of process-step schedules, which are entries that request a specific user to perform a type of process-step as part of a running process instance.

Process-step schedules are requests from a previous user performing a previous process-step, to a new user to perform a new process-step. Both users may be the same, although in case of keeping the control flow associated to the same user, control flow passing may also be handled locally by the front-end client, independently from the central process control service back-end.

The currently sketched API expects front-end clients to regularly poll the information about requested process-step schedules from the central service. There is no notification mechanism that pushes information about newly added process-step schedules for a specific user to his or her running client application, which makes the service architecture for the process control service appear reasonably simple.

Using the `scheduleProcessStep(schedule)` operation, remote clients add a request to users on possibly other clients to execute a process-step. The detail structure of the passed `schedule` parameter is described further below.

To query the list of currently scheduled process-step requests for a given user, the `getProcessStepSchedules(username)` is to be invoked at least after every completion of a single process-step, to present an updated list of process-steps to perform to the user.

When a process-step has been performed on a front-end client, the client notifies the central control service about the step's completion by calling `removeProcessStepSchedule(processElementId)`.

To be able to instantiate process-steps on the client front-end, they must be uniquely related to one process instance which they belong to. To start a new process from one of the front-ends, the process control service must first be requested to generate a unique id for the new process instance, which will globally identify this process instance among all front-ends that will possibly get involved in performing process-steps as part of this process instance. The new process id is requested from the central service by calling `createNewProcess(type)`. All available types of process-step implementations are identified via a unique number, too. It is up to the code generation templates to mark every generated concrete process type implementation with an increasingly counting number, making each type uniquely identifiable.

Interface `IProcessStepSchedule` With the interface `IProcessStepSchedule`, requests for process-steps to be carried out are described and handled. The individual entries which describe the request are:

- `getProcessID()`: Returns the id of the process instance in which the process-step is intended to run.

- `getRequestingProcessElementID()`: Returns the id of the process-step from which the request is issued, i. e., the process-step that is the previous step in the logical control flow.

- `getRequestingUserName()`: Returns the user account identifier under which the previous process-step was executed.

- `getProcessStepTypeId()`: Returns the unique type identifier which marks an instantiable class that implements `IProcessStep`. The id is one-to-one mappable onto a class-name, pointing to the class that gets instantiated on the requested user's front-end when the process-step is scheduled for execution.

- `getUsername()`: Returns the user account name, for which the requested process-step is to be executed. The process-step will be scheduled for requested execution on that front-end platform, on which the user currently is logged in or will log in the next time.

- `getProcessScheduleID()`: If a process-step schedule is handled centrally by the process control service, it owns a unique id. The id allows for identifying the schedule entry for later removing it from the central list of scheduled process-steps, after the step has been executed on a front-end client. Process-step schedules, which are only used locally to pass the control flow among process-steps that are subsequently performed by the same user on the same front-end client, do not make use of this id.

- `getProcessStep()`: Front-end applications will create executable instances of process-step implementations as a reaction to requested process-step schedules. For each process-step schedule, there will be exactly one associated process-step implementation, i. e., an instance of a class that realizes interface `IProcessStep`. Implementations of the `IProcessStepSchedule` interface on the front-end keep a reference to this executable process-step instance, which is accessible via the `getProcessStep()` method.

Interface `IInformationObjectStorage` The `IInformationObjectStorage` interface describes another central service, which is responsible for realizing a common data storage and exchange mechanism for the distributed EIS. The service is kept simple and only declares the notion of loading and storing information objects. The kind of object is kept open by the interface, however, the interface is suggested with the implementation of a shared XML file base in mind, in which entire XML documents are stored.

The `loadInformationObject(username, type, location)` service method serves to retrieve an information object from a named location. In implementation terms, this may be thought of as retrieving an XML document from a file, which is stored on the central information object server. With the `saveInformationObject(username, information, location)` method, an information object is stored on the server.

This basic retrieve-and-store model is not suitable for productive use, since it ignores aspects of concurrent access to information objects. Also, working on the granularity level of entire documents makes some information access tasks unreasonable inefficient. However, the concept is rich enough to demonstrate the use of a central information object storage service in a distributed EIS environment.

To make this mechanism feasible for productive use in a shared environment, i. e., avoid loss of information and inconsistencies caused by uncoordinated concurrent access, the two access methods could be combined with at least a locking mechanism that prevents an information object from being used concurrently in two different process-steps at the same time. A more elaborate API for productive use in organizations should take this into account.

The domain API is one out of two mechanisms in the SEEM method, which formalize knowledge about a target architecture for which software is to be created. The second mechanism are implementation strategy types specified via an implementation strategy meta-model. Example implementation strategy types are elaborated in the following section.

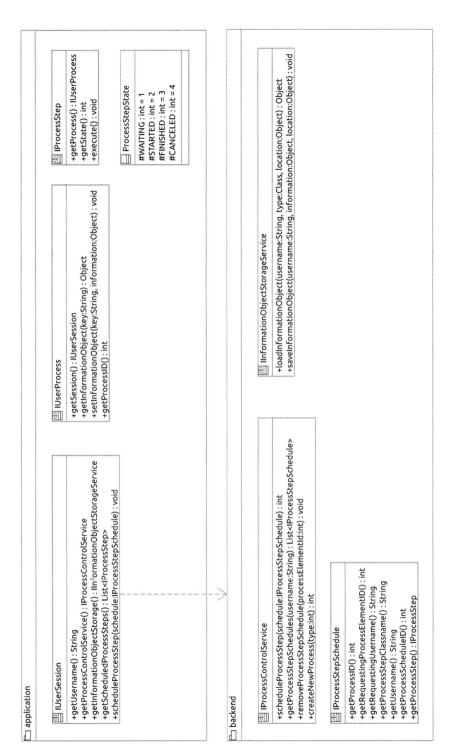

Figure 39: API interfaces to implement EIS functionality

179

9 Example implementation strategies

To deal with a variety of target platform architectures, the method supports two kinds of implementation strategy descriptions, which are on the one hand generic and platform-independent implementation strategies, which are applicable to all target architecture platforms, and, on the other hand, implementation strategies available on a specific architecture only, exclusively enabled by the use of specific underlying technology. The latter kind cannot be known in advance before the method has been configured for concrete target architecture platforms, and thus will have to be meta-modeled as part of the adaptation of the method for concrete target architecture platforms.

To exemplify the use of generic implementation strategies, the prototypical implementation suggests a number of platform-independent example implementation strategies which are considered to be useful for EIS development. They are integrated as language elements into the mapping model and are specified as concrete subclasses of the following abstract superclasses:

- `AbstractProcessMemberImplementation`
- `AbstractConditionImplementation`
- `AbstractControlFlowImplementation`
- `AbstractActorResolverImplementation`
- `AbstractActorImplementation`
- `AbstractResourceImplementation`
- `AbstractResourceAccessImplementation`
- `AbstractInformationTypeImplementation`
- `AbstractInformationStorageImplementation`

9.1 Implementation strategies for process-members

Meta-classes which make up the platform-independent implementation strategies for process-members of the mapping meta-model are displayed in Fig. 42 in ECORE notation. They are further discussed in the following sections.

9.1.1 Interactive process-steps

Subclasses of `AbstractInteractiveProcessStepImplementation` provide implementation components for semi-automatic process-steps, which perform interaction with the user on a front-end device. The following meta-classes are included in the mapping meta-model to exemplify types of interactive process-step implementation strategies.

- Form

- Message

- Menu

- Question

- WriteEMail

- VisitWebsite

- ManualWebServiceAccess

- ManualExternalApplicationAccess

- ManualTask

Fig. 43 and Fig. 44 show the meta-classes representing these implementation strategy types. They are described in the following.

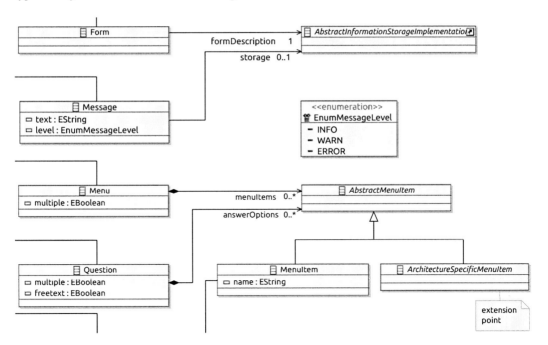

Figure 43: Meta-model excerpt specifying platform-independent user decision implementation strategies

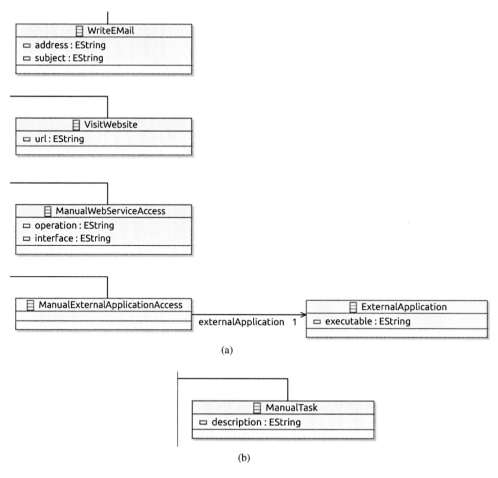

(a)

(b)

Figure 44: Meta-model excerpts specifying more platform-independent user interaction implementation strategies

Form Providing access to information objects is a central task for EISs (see Req. 6: Enable information awareness). The Form implementation strategy allows to describe such access on a generic level. The strategy gets realized through editor functionality presented on the user's front-end platform. The editor used by a Form strategy may allow to modify the information, or may display information for read-only documents only. See Sect. 9.3.1 and Sect. 9.3.4 for information access implementation strategies.

Content to present in a document is provided by a resource source access (see Sect. 9.3.1). Depending on the type of resource access, which may, e. g., be TextAccess or XML-Access, the document may use different GUI elements to make information objects of different types accessible.

In complex interaction scenarios, the Form implementation strategy can be combined with others and occur multiple times in different instantiations to implement one single conceptual process-step. In cases when this is done, the mapping model entry of the implemented process-step associates multiple implementation strategies to one conceptual process model element, to describe the implemented process-step in more fine-grained terms than the conceptual model.

Message A `Message` implementation strategy resembles a `Form` strategy, with the only difference that the information objects made accessible to the user are presented in a read-only mode. The user is intended to retrieve information from the information object, rather than editing it.

Menu The `Menu` implementation strategy describes a front-end component that provides a menu, from which the user is asked to choose an item. After an item is picked, the chosen item is remembered by the current process-step instance. It can later can be queried to, e. g., select the subsequent process control flow using `MenuItemChosen` condition implementation strategies mapped to outgoing sequences of the current process-member (see Sect. 9.1.5).

When associated with a start-event of a modeled process, the `Menu` implementation strategy carries the semantics of an asynchronously picked menu item, e. g., a global application menu in the menu bar of a front-end application. The evaluation of the picked item in the subsequent control flow happens similarly to the evaluation of results from `Menu` implementation strategies.

The menu items that are intended to be available in the set of options to choose from are specified via instances of `AbstractMenuItem`. This can either be a generic `MenuItem` instance, for which the code generation templates use a default menu type available on their target architecture, or may be provided by architecture specific subclasses of the extension point `ArchitectureSpecificMenuItem`.

Question With the `Question` implementation strategy, a generic notion of a specific type of interaction with the user can be described. A question is considered to be composed of the question text itself and, optionally, multiple answer options, which may describe possible options for the user's input. To express the notion of alternative answer options, the `AbstractMenuItem` class is used again here. An instance of the `Question` implementation strategy may simply ask for a free-text answer, indicated by the `freetext` attribute set to `true`, but it also may make use of any set of interaction widgets that reflect possible answer options.

WriteEMail Associating the `WriteEMail` implementation strategy to a process-step means to interpret the step as a human task to write an e-mail. To realize this strategy, the code generation templates can generate artifacts which, e. g., invoke the system's default e-mail browser on a user's front-end device.

VisitWebsite   When the `VisitWebsite` implementation strategy is applied, a process-step is implemented to guide a human user in opening a web browser and pointing to a specific address. This functionality can be realized by generated artifacts that open the system's default web browser.

ManualWebServiceAccess   The `ManualWebServiceAccess` implementation strategy leads to the invocation of a GUI for setting parameters of a specific web-service, invoke the service manually, and read the returned results.

ManualExternalApplicationAccess   With a `ManualExternalApplicationAccess` implementation strategy, the generated EIS is advised to invoke external software which then interacts with the user. Depending on possible interface mechanisms, the external software may return results to the EIS.

ManualTask   The `ManualTask` implementation strategy is a placeholder for a human task performed outside the software-supported functionality of the EIS. From an implementation perspective, the implementation strategy `ManualTask` appears as a special case of interactive process-step. While from a conceptual point of view there is a clear distinction between process-steps that are carried out interactively with the EIS, and manual process-steps, this distinction blurs when it comes to support each class of activities by software. Indeed, any kind of software support for tasks that are to be carried out manually, needs to interact at least on a minimal scale with the user, to show what manual task is to be performed, and to allow the user to tell the system that a manual task has been finished. At least this basic functionality must be available, otherwise the manual task would remain unsupported. According to these considerations, from an implementation point of view, support for manual process-steps is to be provided by an implementation strategy, which makes use of user interaction at the front-end, and thus resembles implementation strategies for realizing semi-automatic process-step conceptualizations.

9.1.2   Additional high-level process-member implementation strategies

Some of the interactive process-step implementation strategies are further categorized under the abstract superclass `AbstractProcessHighLevel`. These kinds of implementation strategies can be considered to represent comparably coarse-grained pieces of functionality of an application, typically represented by a main functional area of a front-end application, such as the user-account management. The example high-level implementation strategies included in the mapping meta-model are:

- `Welcome`

- `Login` and `Logout`

- `AdminAccounts`

- EditMyAccount

These implementation strategy types are modeled via the meta-classes shown in Fig. 45 and described subsequently.

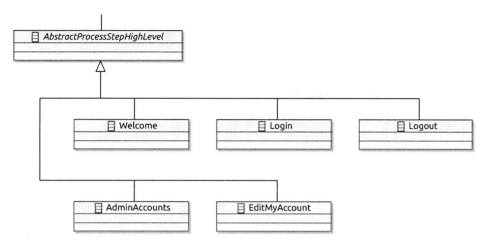

Figure 45: Meta-model excerpt specifying platform-independent high-level process-steps

Welcome   The Welcome implementation strategy realizes the notion of an introductory process-step, which shows an initial menu or piece of documentation to the user.

Login and Logout   With the Login and Logout strategies, process-members of the conceptual models can be declared to be interpreted as login or logout operations that are explicitly mentioned in the conceptual process model.

Unlike it may initially be assumed, associating these implementation strategies to conceptual process-members does not necessarily invoke the corresponding functionality of showing a login or logout prompt at the point when the process control flow reaches this element for a specific user. Instead, a Login implementation strategy, e. g., may also indicate that a login must be enforced earlier in the process, or that users generally have to authenticate before they operate the system. A Logout strategy can be interpreted by generated artifacts in a way that the user is forced to log out from the system at this point in the process.

AdminAccounts   The AdminAccounts implementation strategy stands for a whole block of functionality that is involved in creating and maintaining user accounts in a multi-user system (see Req. 4: Provide multi-user support). This functionality can be prepared to be realized by generated artifacts either by including its implementation in a runtime framework (maybe using existing external frameworks), which simply needs to be invoked as a whole by generated artifacts, or by including large parts of constant artifact descriptions for this functionality in the code generation templates.

EditMyAccount Comparable to the `AdminAccounts` implementation strategy, the `EditMyAccount` strategy describes the functional area of a multi-user application, which allows any user of the system to edit its own account's information entries. Again, this large piece of functionality can be prepared as an entire building block of functionality via a runtime framework, or as fixed code in the artifact generation templates.

9.1.3 Automatic process-steps

Implementation strategies, which subclass `AbstractAutomaticProcessStepImplementation`, are considered to run automatically without user interaction. Formulating implementation strategies for this purpose resembles in identifying different ways of invoking executable software components, e. g., a call to a web-service, or the execution of manually programmed code. In cases where the method is used for developing an integrated application architecture on top of a middleware platform, a possible technical realization of implementation strategies for automatic steps may also lie in configuring application connectors [RMB01, Ver96] provided together with the middleware solution. Examples for concrete implementation strategies of this kind are

- `Synchronizer`

- `SendEMail`

- `SendSMS`

- `Automatic`

- `CustomAutomatic`

Meta-classes for example implementation strategies of this type are displayed in Fig. 46. The meta-model contains an abstract extension point class `ArchitectureSpecificAutomaticProcessStepImplementation`, which provides a superclass to be inherited from when additional process-step implementation strategies are specified in an implementation strategy meta-model to reflect specific target-architecture features.

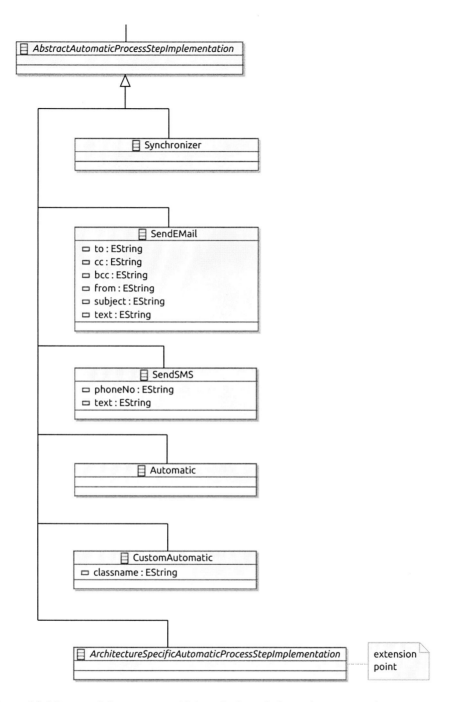

Figure 46: Meta-model excerpt specifying platform-independent automatic process-steps

Synchronizer   A `Synchronizer` is an example for a process-member implementation strategy which can describe both implementations for process-members, as well as for events. On either elements, this implementation strategy is to be understood as a rule on how to handle control flows that come from multiple different ingoing sequences. If a `Synchronizer` implementation strategy is attached to a process-member, the generated execution artifacts should take care for blocking the control flow at this point until control flow from all incoming branches, if they are active, has reached the synchronizer.

SendEMail   The `SendEMail` implementation strategy describes a functional building block for automatically sending e-mails by the EIS. This strategy is not to be confused with `WriteEMail`, which targets to invoke an interactive e-mail editor for the user. Code generation templates for this strategy can derive information about mail recipients, the sender name, the subject line, and, of course, the e-mail text with possible attachments, from named information object slots and information resources attached to the corresponding conceptual process-step. Further technical detail information, such as the mail-server address, login credentials, the protocol used, etc., can be specified to the code generation templates by conventional configuration files, which are global to the code generation process and list configuration values given as contents in the models.

SendSMS   Another communication channel is addresses by the `SendSMS` implementation strategy. It is intended to result in implementation artifacts which use appropriate messaging channels to propagate SMS text messages to mobile phone devices.

Automatic   The `Automatic` implementation strategy type provides a placeholder for declaring that the implementation of the associated conceptual process step lies exclusively in the responsibility of the code generation templates. This fallback strategy allows to apply traditional code generation techniques and to by-pass the SEEM method's notion of bridging between conceptual elements and implementation artifacts by the use of implementation strategies.

CustomAutomatic   With the `CustomAutomatic` implementation strategy, all varieties of automatic functionality can be woven into the EIS providing functionality via a JAVA class. The runtime domain API framework provides the interface `IProcessStep`, which allows to make functionality from custom-coded classes callable from the EIS. Any JAVA class accessible on the class-path, which implements the `IProcessStep` interface, can be specified through the meta-class `CustomAutomatic`'s attribute `classname`. Its `execute()` method will be invoked when the process control flow reaches the point to run the implementation of the process to which the `CustomAutomatic` strategy was associated. Automatic processing can the be performed by the JAVA code itself, or it interfaces to other components by manually developed code.

9.1.4 Event implementation strategies

Although the mapping model blurs the conceptual distinction between process-steps and events for implementation purposes, and allows to generally associate instances of `AbstractProcessMemberImplementation` to either `Process` or `Event` elements, some implementation strategies can be categorized to be primarily intended as technical realizations for events.

Those process-member implementation strategies for events are

- `EventResourceCRUD`

- `EMailReceived`

These classes, together with abstract classes below `AbstractEventImplementation`, are displayed in Fig. 47.

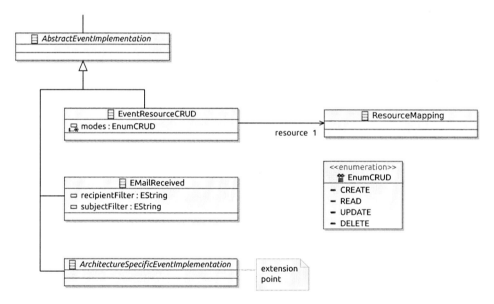

Figure 47: Meta-model excerpt specifying platform-independent event implementation strategies

EventResourceCRUD   The mapping suggests one realization of this notion by the class `EventResourceCRUD`, which, when associated to a conceptual start event of a process, could provide an implementation that triggers the execution of that process once a specific information object has been created, read, updated, or deleted.

EMailReceived   The `EMailReceived` implementation behaves according to its name and understands a start event of a process to be fired, when an e-mail is received on a mail server. The example meta-class contains two filter attributes, which, when set, may restrict the activity of the implementation to mails which contain the specified fragments in the recipient mails address (filtering mails sent to specific addresses), or to mails with specific text fragments in the subject line. In the same way as it has been suggested for the code generation of implementing artifacts for the `SendEMail` strategy, further details about the mail server configuration, i. e., the server address, used port and protocol, can be specified to the code generation templates by global configuration files.

Several other generic event implementation strategies can be thought of and might be added depending on development project needs, e. g., a strategy that reacts on arrival of e-mails.

9.1.5   Sequence implementation strategies

Sequences describe the dynamics among process-members in processes. They are responsible for connecting process-members, i. e., process-steps or events, so that these become declared as being elements in one or more process type declarations. Process-member elements in the extracted enterprise model (EEM) representation of BPMs are not bound to a specific process type, they can be referenced from any number of process types to be declared as a part of it. The process instance, in which a process-member type is instantiated, is instead determined by the the ingoing sequence which instantiates the process-member type. Sequences are declared relative to a specific process type, their parent process-member type set via a `Sequence`'s attribute `parent` in the EEM language. The structure of sequences, from which process-member types are referenced, for the process context in which instances of process-member types are instantiated.

Keeping the constitutive role of sequences for the process context in mind, it turns out that there are multiple dimensions to the interpretation of the notion of sequences between process-members, and for each of them an implementation strategy has to be provided. The conceptual notion of passing the control flow to another process-member, which is what sequences express in BPMs, has at least three orthogonal aspects that need to be refined for implementing a mechanism that automatically supplements process execution. These aspects are to be resolved independent from the actual execution mechanism that will control processes, may it be an interpreting workflow engine (WfMS), or distributed program code that handles passing of control flow explicitly.

From the conceptual BPM point of view, sequences may lead across boundaries of both spatial distribution between systems, and diverse actor responsibilities. To provide an implementation for sequence concepts, both aspects of either passing the control flow to a different machine in the distributed environment, and/or passing the control flow to another responsible role for performing the next process-step, meaning that probably a concrete user has to be determined at runtime who fills in the requested role. A third orthogonal dimension is the handling of conditions, under which sequence steps are taken or probably ignored.

The three dimensions of sequence implementations, control flow implementation strategies, condition implementation strategies, and actor resolver implementation strategies, are focused individually in the following.

Control flow implementation strategies   In a distributed environment, there are two principal options for how a control flow between two process-member implementations can be realized. Either the control flow points to a process-member which is to be executed locally on the same front-end and under the same actor role's responsibility, or the front-end platform changes on which the next process-member implementation is to be executed. In addition to this, a different actor role may be specified to continue interacting with the next process-member implementation.

Continuous   To specify details on how the control flow is to be implemented in the above described cases, two default strategies are included in the meta-model, which both inherit from the abstract superclass `AbstractControlFlowImplementation`. The `Continuous` control flow implementation strategy assumes a subsequent locally executed process-member implementation, for the same user in the same actor role, and on the same front-end target device. This kind of implementation strategy allows to combine process-steps into sequences, so they can automatically be executed. Together with condition implementation strategies (see below), complex descriptions of the dynamics between process-steps can be formally expressed, and be executed automatically by the created EIS.

ToDoList   In all other cases, in which the control flow either passes to another front-end, or another actor becomes responsible for performing, the `ToDoList` implementation strategy is used. Using this way of implementing control flow, the next performing user is determined using an actor resolving strategy (see below), and an entry is added in the user's to-do list on the desired target front-end. The process then stops until the user selects this entry again from the to-do list to be performed. More sophisticated implementations could incorporate notions of priorities or deadlines, by which the to-do list entry needs to be performed, or immediate execution on the remote front-end could be requested, at least as soon as the responsible user logs in.

The `ToDoList` implementation strategy can also optionally be applied if neither the front-end nor the user change. This usage resembles a deferred control flow, which offers the next process-step for execution in the user's to-do list, and waits for the user to decide when to continue the process.

Fig. 48 shows the meta-model's sub-structure which includes the control flow implementation strategy meta-classes.

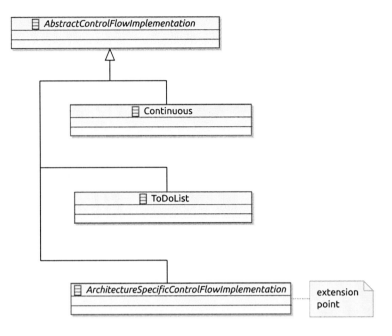

Figure 48: Meta-model specifying platform-independent control flow implementation strategies

Actor resolver implementation strategies In those cases, where a sequence's control flow is specified to continue with a process-member, for which a different actor or user is responsible than for the previous process-step, the way of how to change to another user must be described in detail. When an actor-role is associated to a process-step on the process type level, it is implicitly assumed that during the execution of the process, there will be a concrete person who fulfills the actor-role. For the implementation of an EIS, methodical means are required to specify implementation strategies of how to retrieve a concrete person, e. g., identified by a user-account, to fulfill a given actor role. Multiple options are possible here, which are expressed by concrete subclasses of the abstract superclass `AbstractActorResolverImplementation`. The model suggests the following strategies:

- `SameUser`

- `MatchingUser`

- `FixedUser`

- `ChooseUser`

These strategies are further described below, their declaration in the meta-model is visualized in Fig. 49.

192

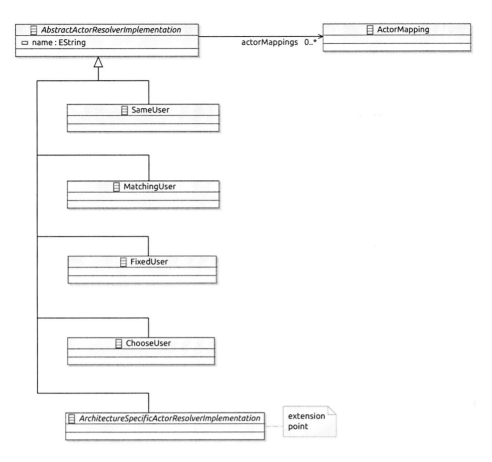

Figure 49: Meta-model excerpt specifying platform-independent implementation strategies for actor resolvers

SameUser The `SameUser` implementation strategy is the trivial strategy, which expresses that no change in user-to-actor assignments take place before continuing with the next process-step.

MatchingUser When the `MatchingUser` implementation strategy is applied, an algorithm picks a concrete user who fulfills the requested actor role. This may be done based on information derived from the organizational perspective of the underlying enterprise models given at modeling time, and from runtime information in user databases. Optionally, the applied algorithm may judge its decision based on current work load balances from the individual users, and may prefer to choose users who fulfill the requested role, who currently have less estimated workload to do. Depending on the engineering project, other more sophisticated implementation strategies may be developed.

FixedUser   The `FixedUser` strategy describes the simple case that a concrete person's user-account is invariantly associated to a conceptual actor roles. This may be applied for singleton actor-roles.

ChooseUser   As an alternative to automatic determination of a concrete user, a matching user may also be picked manually from a list of those known users who fulfill the requested actors role, or multiple roles, for the subsequent process-step. This implementation strategy is expressed by the `ChooseUser` meta-class. To implement this mode of actor resolving, an EIS front-end provides GUI components that let the current user choose the desired next user. More elaborate implementations may allow to specify, if someone else but the current user is in charge to take the decision who is to fulfill the requested actor role. An implementation for this could build upon information from advanced organization models included in the set of enterprise models, e. g., a 'responsible, accountable, consulted, informed' (RACI) matrix [BD09], which specifies stakeholder responsibilities. Such detail models may be consulted, for instance, to create mechanisms for delegating the choice to responsible actors in a higher management layer.

Condition implementation strategies   A third dimension of implementing sequences, which has to be underfed with an implementation description, is the handling of optional control flow branches, which may be constrained by conditions to be evaluated at runtime. The corresponding implementation strategies are expressed as subclasses of `Abstract-ConditionImplementation`, and may realize any kind of boolean function. Among the example condition implementations are tests for given answer options of previously asked questions, described by the meta-class `AnswerGiven`, or selected menu items in `Menu` processes, specified via instances of `MenuItemChosen`. Lower-level abstractions such as string value comparisons or manually provided code in the target architecture programming language are also available, using the meta-classes `ResultCompare` and `CustomCondition`, respectively. The meta-model also includes composite implementation strategies to express the boolean operators `AND`, `OR` and `NOT`.

The meta-classes for condition implementation strategies are shown in Fig. 50.

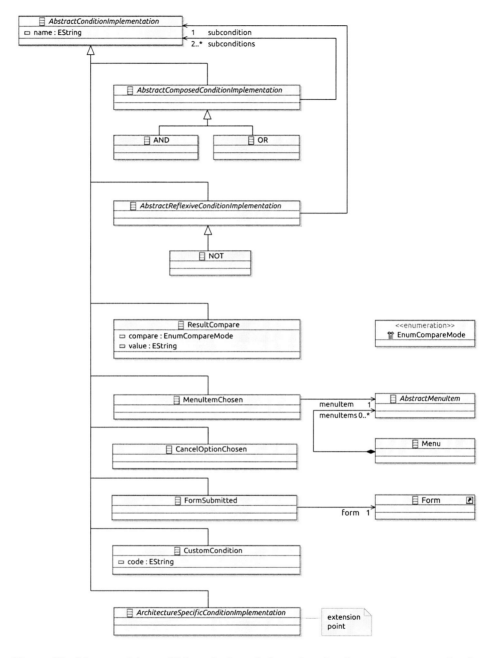

Figure 50: Meta-model specifying platform-independent implementation strategies for conditions

9.2 Implementation strategies for actors

In Sect. 6.2.2, strategies for picking a suitable concrete actor, when another actor role is requested by the business process description to continue performing a process, have been discussed. These strategies assume that a mechanism exists, which associates a list of concrete persons to actor roles they can fulfill. The details on how this list is determined per actor role are explicated using actor implementation strategies, specified by subclasses of the meta-class `AbstractActorImplementation`. The concrete subclasses of this class, as suggested by the meta-model, are based on a traditional user account management as it is realized by common operating systems or other infrastructural components, such as, e. g., database management systems. The idea is to explicate the notion of what an actor is by implementation constructs such as user accounts and user groups. In addition, two generic role implementations are included, one for anonymous users, i. e., everybody who is unauthenticated, and one for the role of an administrator, which is a traditional concept in multi-user systems that has unrestricted access to all functional areas of a software system.

According to this traditional notion of user identification, concrete strategies suggested by the meta-model are `Anonymous`, `UserGroup`, `UserAccount` and `Administrator`.

Fig. 51 shows example declarations in the meta-model for implementation strategies of this type, together with an extension point class for target-architecture specific extensions.

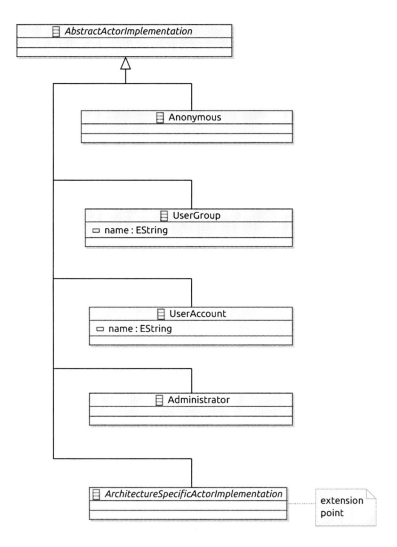

Figure 51: Meta-model excerpt specifying platform-independent implementation strategies for actors

9.3 Resource implementation strategies

Resource implementation strategies play a relevant role for EIS development. Especially information resources are relevant concepts to realize the functionality of an EIS, because it is one core task of EIS to provide efficient access to shared information resources of the organization (see Req. 6: Enable information awareness).

Another kind of resources relevant from an EIS implementation perspective, are software resources, which describe external software components to be integrated by the EIS. EISs are responsible for integrating heterogeneous system components to form a coherent and efficiently usable whole (see Req. 3: Support distributed and heterogeneous architectures), this is why access to external software components is a core area of functionality to EIS.

All other kinds of resources are initially subsumed under physical resources from the software system's perspective, which means that they do not have an representation in the software system, besides a human-readable description text. Refinements of this notion can be made depending on project specific needs of an organization. There may be kinds of resources specially suited for being reflected by software, used in organization-specific process-steps for which project-specific process implementation strategies are implemented. In this case, additional concrete resource implementations can be added to the meta-model as subclasses of either `AbstractResourceImplementation`, or be incorporated in a project-specific implementation strategy model by subclassing `ArchitectureSpecificResourceImplementation`. It is then up to the code generation templates and the project-specific process-step implementations to handle the software representation of this resource type accordingly.

To formally express the basic distinctions between the three initially provided kinds of resources, the meta-model includes the abstract superclasses

- `AbstractInformationResourceImplementation`

- `AbstractSoftwareResourceImplementation`

- `AbstractPhysicalResourceImplementation`

Concrete implementation strategies to realize these three kinds of resources are illustrated in the following.

9.3.1 Information resource implementation strategies

Concrete subclasses of `AbstractInformationResourceImplementation` express strategies that explain how conceptually specified information resources are reflected as data types and data storages in a software system. To give the required detail information, two kinds of implementation strategies are associated with an information resource, which cover both how to formally describe information objects types as data types, and how to persistently store information objects as data. The notion of an information object instance does not need to be explicated, it is implicitly and invariantly provided by the notion of data in the underlying execution mechanism that will run the EIS, may it be a high-level interpretation mechanism such as, e. g., a workflow engine, or a programming language with its execution model.

The first dimension of the implementation of an information resource is a formalized description of the information resource's type. Such descriptions are given by formal type description mechanisms, of which many have evolved in the history of software development, e. g., data types in object-oriented programming languages, database schema definition languages, or XML schema descriptions. Since there are several ways to explicate data types in software systems, a subclass of `AbstractInformationResourceImplementation` is `AbstractInformationTypeImplementation`, the concrete subclasses of which allow to specify data type descriptions in diverse implementation variants. The concrete implementation strategies for data types included in the mapping model are

A `ResourceMapping` entry can contain references to both kinds of implementation strategies via the multi-valued `implementations` association, which allows to specify both semantic dimensions of the type and the storage of an information resource.

Information type implementation strategies   Three information type implementation strategies are exemplified in the meta-model. This list of available strategies can, however, be extended with representations of any type-specification mechanism that exists in software developing, if additional type implementations are required in an engineering project.

The type implementation strategies initially suggested by the meta-model are `Text-InformationType`, `XMLInformationType` and `ExternalDocumentInformationType`. The text information type is used for unstructured string data.

XML types are specified by making use of the XML Schema type description language [vdV02]. The type description document of an XML Schema description, which itself is an XML information object, is reflexively referenced as XML information resource via the `schemaResource` association of the `XMLInformationType` meta-class. This way, it can either be specified inside the mapping model as a literal information object using an instance of `LiteralInformationObject`, or be included from an external file URI via a `FileInformationStorage` or a `URIInformationStorage`, as it is typically desired to access third-party XML schema declarations or type-descriptions from a central schema repository (see below on information storages).

Information resource types which are interpreted as instances of `ExternalDocument-InformationType`, are considered to be handled externally by other software components. From the EIS perspective, the artifacts storing to these information objects are binary large objects (BLOBs) with an unknown internal structure. Examples for information resources realized with such a type description are MICROSOFT WORD® documents. When using such documents as realizations of information resources, the WORD application is configured as an external editor application, which will be invoked by the corresponding `Form` or `Message` process-steps.

The hierarchy of meta-class below the abstract `AbstractInformationResource-Implementation` meta-class is displayed in Fig. 52.

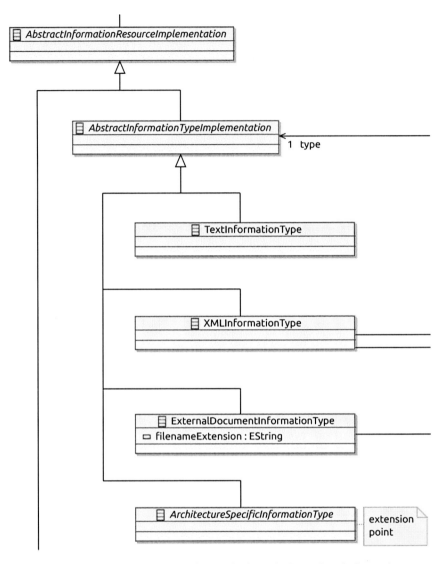

Figure 52: Meta-model excerpt specifying platform-independent information types

Information storage implementation strategies   There is a second aspect to the specification of implementation details about information resources, which declares the way how instances of data types are stored. There are diverse ways for software systems to make data persistent, the concrete subclasses of the `AbstractInformationStorageImplementation` represent alternative implementation options which get accordingly resolved by the code generation templates.

Examples of information storage implementation strategy types given in the mapping meta-model are

200

- `URIInformationStorage`

- `FileInformationStorage`

- and `LiteralInformationStorage`

The meta-classes describing possible information storage implementations are shown in Fig. 53.

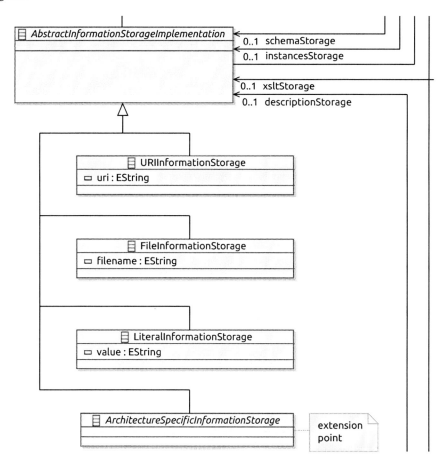

Figure 53: Meta-model excerpt specifying platform-independent information storage implementation strategies

URIInformationStorage   A `URIInformationStorage` is described via a uniform resource identifier (URI) string, which may locate an artifact resource on the internet, or through any locally resolvable access scheme. The `URIInformationStorage` strategy may provide read-only resources only, for which case the validity checking conditions of the mapping model may contain a rule to ensure resource source accesses only (see Sect. 9.3.4).

FileInformationStorage The `FileInformationStorage` implementation strategy advises the code generation templates to operate with artifacts stored on a local file system.

LiteralInformationStorage The `LiteralInformationStorage` implementation strategy represents not a regular persistent storage, but allows to incorporate literal information object values into the model. By their constant nature, this kind of storage can only be involved in read accesses, implemented by information source access implementation strategies as described below.

The list of available information storage implementation strategies can be extended by other technical means to make data persistent, e. g., by introducing the concept of a relational database, with corresponding resource access implementation strategies, such as SQL queries, and according data type implementation strategies, to express data in terms of table column definitions. The abstract implementation strategy concepts of the method are expressed on an abstraction level high enough to include either traditional database techniques, or prospectively new approaches for storing and retrieving data that are yet not available.

9.3.2 Software resource implementation strategies

Software resources in the conceptual enterprise models represent any kind of software system external to the EIS, and, since enterprise models are taking in a birds eye view on the entire organization, also the EIS itself may be represented as a software resource in enterprise models. Subclasses of `AbstractSoftwareResourceImplementation` allow to specify concrete implementation details about how to interpret conceptually specified software resources.

The meta-model comes with three example implementation strategies for external software resources. These are the concrete implementation strategy classes `ExternalApplication`, `WebService` and `CustomResource`.

ExternalApplication An `ExternalApplication` component is considered to be callable on the user's front-end system via a traditional shell command. The code generation templates take care to realize according invocation code.

WebService A `WebService` implementation strategy marks a conceptual software resource to be interpreted as a web-service. The mechanism for invoking web-services is standardized in the context of SOA technology frameworks, and the code generation templates can rely on existing web-service frameworks for implementing the actual service invocation behavior in an artifact.

CustomResource All other kinds of software resources are intended to be subsumed under the `CustomResource` meta-class. When resolving the implementation for instances of this implementation strategy type, the decision about which invocation mechanism to use is not stated in the mapping model, but is deferred to manually developed code, which either is invoked as wrapper to delegate to an external component, or implements desired functionality directly.

Instead of using a `CustomResource` implementation strategy, the meta-model may be extended by organization-specific software resource types, which explicitly describe additional external software types and corresponding invocation mechanisms.

A reflexive representation of the EIS is not required in the mapping model, which itself is already a description of the EIS in abstract technical terms. Consequently, resources which denote the EIS itself may remain without mapping entry, or may occur with an empty set of implementation strategies in the mapping model. Of course, the conceptual information of which process-members are explicitly modeled to access the EIS as a software resource is not lost this way, it remains included in the conceptual EEM enterprise model representation, and can be queried for semantic analysis when required.

The available implementation strategy types for interfacing with software components are shown in Fig. 54.

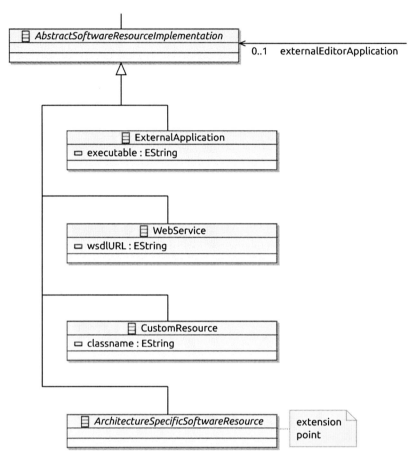

Figure 54: Meta-model excerpt specifying platform-independent software resource implementation strategies

9.3.3 Physical resource implementation strategies

For the abstract superclass `AbstractPhysicalResourceImplementation`, there is only one concrete example implementation strategy, which is `PhysicalResource-Description`. This meta-class is intentionally named to not end in "Implementation" but "Description", because the mapping model assumes that physical resources cannot be implemented at all by a software system, and that the only representation of a physical resource in an EIS can be given by a description. This description is modeled to be stored by a `AbstractInformationStorageImplementation`, which in turn allows to apply any information object type and appropriate storage mechanisms to hold the resource description, ranging from unstructured text strings stored internally by the EIS, over structured XML documents with corresponding form GUIs, to external document edited by external editor applications.

The meta-classes describing physical resource implementations in the explained sense are shown in Fig. 55.

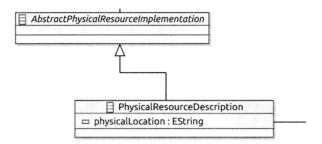

Figure 55: Meta-model excerpt specifying the physical resource implementation strategy

9.3.4 Resource access implementation strategies

Another aspect of providing the software implementation for resource handling in an EIS is concerned with accesses to resources. Strategies for realizing resource accesses are closely related to resource implementation strategies, and add additional orthogonal aspects to resource implementations regarding the dynamics, with which resource accesses are performed in a process.

The basic pattern of a resource access is performed, while a process-step is executed, which accesses that resource. It consists of a sequence of retrieve actions before the process-step is executed, and optionally a sequence of store actions after the process-step is executed. This general pattern of resource retrieve-and-store accesses around a single process-step can be observed even for manually performed process-steps with manual access to physical resources: before a process-step is executed, the required resources are retrieved (if they are not at hand already from previous process-steps), and after a process-step, possibly modified resources are brought back into place (or kept in reach for further process-steps to come). The sets of resources that are retrieved and stored by these accesses need not necessarily be the same, because some resource might not need to be stored back again, e. g., physical resources that are consumed by the process-step, or information resources that are only accessed for reading. Others may be created throughout the process-step, and be stored without having been retrieved beforehand.

The basic pattern of an AbstractProcessMemberImplementation strategy referencing any number of possible AbstractResourceAccessSourceImplementation, and any number of AbstractResourceAccessTargetImplementation strategies, is shown in Fig. 56.

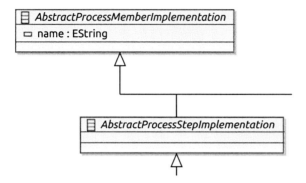

Figure 56: Meta-model excerpt showing the basic pattern of an AbstractProcess-MemberImplementation strategy referencing resource source and resource target accesses

The terminology of the meta-model speaks of "source accesses" when a resource is retrieved, and "target accesses" when a resource is stored. Corresponding abstract superclasses which express this distinction, and partially refine it for accesses on information resources, are

- AbstractResourceAccessImplementation

- AbstractResourceAccessSourceImplementation

- AbstractResourceAccessTargetImplementation

- AbstractInformationObjectAccessSourceImplementation

- AbstractInformationObjectAccessTargetImplementation

- AbstractStorableInformationObjectAccessImplementation

The meta-class AbstractResourceAccessImplementation is the top-most superclass to categorize its subclasses as specifying resource access implementation strategies. It carries no specific semantics besides this categorizing function. The other classes distinguish between source accesses and target accesses, and the last two refine this notion with regard to access to information object resources. Concrete subclasses can choose to implement either of the access directions, or provide an implementation strategy for both directions using multiple inheritance from both kind of abstract superclasses.

With the AbstractInformationObjectAccessImplementation meta-class, the notion of accessing an information object that can persistently be stored with the use of an AbstractInformationStorageImplementation strategy is expressed. The meta-model provides first sketches for concrete, genericially applicable, resource access implementation strategies. For text information resources, the meta-classes Text-Create, TextRetrieve, TextStore, and TextDelete are provided. Accesses

206

to XML information resources are described by the meta-classes `XMLAccess`, `XML-AccessById`, and `XMLTransformation`, which inherit from the refined abstract superclasses `AbstractXMLAccess`.

Implementation strategies for resource accesses to other types of information objects are not contained in the meta-model, except the generic `ExternalDocumentAccess` strategy, which combines the notion of a source access and target access by means of an external editor.

More elaborate implementation strategies, than the examples given here, could describe how information access is handled by a process-step with richer semantics. One way to semantically characterizing information access in greater depth, can be derived from distinctions of data access modes in information systems. These distinguish between four modes of data accesses in information systems [WMB$^+$03]:

- access to master data, which typically is not changed frequently, once created

- access to transaction data, e. g., the in- and out-flows of goods or money

- access to transfer data, which denotes technical data intermediately used to communicate between software components

- and, access to preliminary data, which, by the semantics of the process, only has a limited lifetime in the process

Depending on these characterizations, different concrete implementations for handling information objects represented as data can be chosen by code generation templates, when generating executable artifacts from the mapping model and its referenced models.

Fig. 57 shows the meta-classes that are involved in specifying storable information object access implementation strategies.

For completeness, the meta-model also mentions an abstract class `AbstractSoftwareResourceAccess`, which can be utilized to categorize implementation strategies for how to access software resources. However, no concrete subclasses expressing a notion of accessing software resources are included as examples. The notion of a software resource implementation is already closely connected to the way how the software resource is accessed, in terms of invoking executable functionality on an external (or manually developed internal) software component. With the refinements offered by the available software resource implementation strategies, the code generation templates thus already have enough information to create executable artifacts handling the software resource accesses. A more detailed specification of access to software resources does not need to be modeled.

It has already been argued that physical resources usually cannot be reflected through software other than by giving a description of the resource (see Sect. 9.3.3). Accordingly, access to physical resources does not require software implementation strategies, since the access happens outside the software system. However, to keep the method open to also refine a notion of access to physical resources if required, there are abstract superclasses, which act as extension points for possible enhancements of the mapping language with a more in-depth notion of physical resources. The categorizing abstract superclass marking physical resource accesses is `AbstractPhysicalResourceAccess`, the meta-class `ArchitectureSpecificPhysicalResourceAccess` provides an explicit extension point for these semantics.

To generally extend the notion of resource accesses with architecture specific implementation strategies, the generic extension point `ArchitectureSpecificResourceAccess` is finally also part of the meta-model.

Fig. 58 gives a comprehensive overview an all meta-classes involved in refining resource implementation strategies and resource access implementation strategies, as they have been presented in this section.

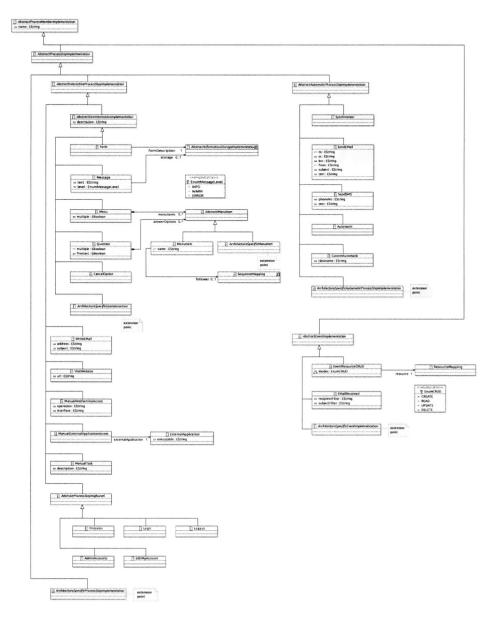

Figure 42: Entire meta-model specifying platform-independent implementation strategies for process-members

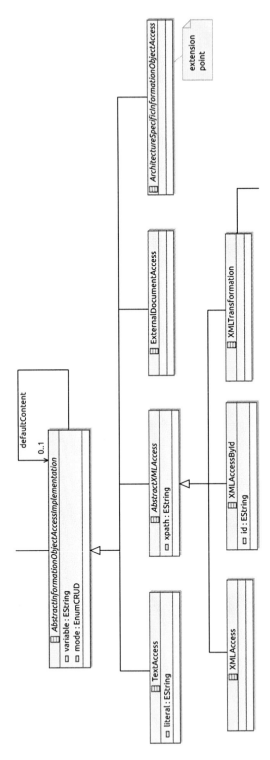

Figure 57: Meta-model excerpt specifying platform-independent storable information object access implementation strategies

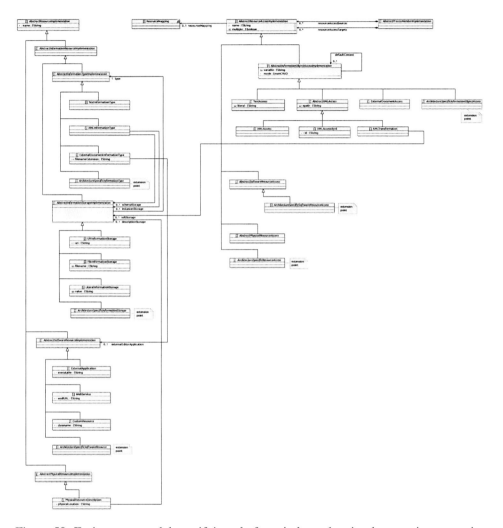

Figure 58: Entire meta-model specifying platform-independent implementation strategies for resources

Part IV

Applying the Method: Prototypical Design and Implementation

I can program a computer
Choose the perfect time
If you've got the inclination
I have got the crime

The Pet Shop Boys, "Opportunities (Let's Make Lots of Money)" from the album "Please", 1986

10 Example scenario of a BPEL-orchestrated SOA target application architecture

10.1 Application scenario in the food supply chain domain

The Software Engineering with Enterprise Models (SEEM) method has been applied to build a research prototype for the food industry domain.[*] This economic sector faces a high degree of complexity in size and dynamics, with a large number of market participants acting to a great extent independently. While the traded goods, food and aliments, involve an increased level of risks connected to health and other security issues, the goods and their distribution processes currently are mostly unprotected along the supply chain, and exposed to potential vulnerabilities, either by intended threats or unintended disasters. Risks in the food supply chain can potentially range from quality leaks and recipe manipulations, to disease infections or poisonings. To reduce the threats along the food supply chain, it is desirable to introduce mechanisms that allow for an IT-supported usage control and a more reliable risk management along the supply chain.

The process flow in current food supply chains typically evolves from an independent peer-to-peer communication, with each supply chain partner and their corresponding IT system communicating directly with each other using isolated systems. The communication covers document exchange between food retailers and food producers, dealing with order documents and subsequent confirmations, and document exchange between producers and logisticians, about the transport of produced goods. In current supply chain realizations, the electronic internet communication between the participants is not necessarily secured, and the overall flow of the supply chain process is not coordinated and controlled, because no joint overview on the overall supply chain process is available from any of the involved systems. The individual supply chain activities thus cannot be controlled for validity in

---

[*]The work presented in this section has partially flown into the project RESCUEIT, funded by the German Federal Ministry of Education and Research (Bundesministerium für Bildung und Forschung, BMBF) under support code no. 13N10963 – 13N10968. Associated consortium partners mentioned with their respective brands are REWE-INFORMATIONS-SYSTEME GMBH, SAP AG, EISBÄR EIS GMBH, and BAAM LOGISTIK.

the overall process flow, it is possible for an outside attacker, or for a malicious inside supply chain member, to manipulate supply chain processes in a way it cannot be noticed by any of the involved supply chain members or further parties. E. g., transport instructions may get manipulated to operate on wrong goods or to target deliveries to invalid locations. In the unsecured peer-to-peer setting, it cannot be ensured that transport instructions are consistent with order documents that have earlier been passed among other supply chain partners, and matching security requirements cannot be ensured in such an environment. Causes of these risks are either man-in-the-middle attacks, who may supervise unsecured communication and may manipulate interchanged documents, or intended or unintended misbehavior of supply chain member, e. g., failure of an involved IT-system.

These fundamental vulnerabilities of supply chain processes, as they are currently present in the food industry sector, can be overcome by taking in a comprehensive overview perspective on supply chains and the actions performed by the individual supply chain members during the execution of the supply chain process. Achieving a bird's-eye-view on all involved activities, acting entities and resources allows to perform checks for validity and consistency of exchanged documents and executed process activities along the overall supply chain system. If such a comprehensive overview in total is made available, security mechanisms can be established on the level of the entire distributed system landscape, which will not be limited to provide local security aspects for independent, isolated systems of the individual supply chain partners, but which introduce new security features for distributed systems, such as transparency and usage control [PHB06].

10.2 Domain-specific language for supply chain modeling

An approach to gain a comprehensive overview on an entire supply chain is to model the involved supply chain members, their actions, and the involved resources in a conceptual enterprise model. This model can subsequently be annotated with specifications of security requirements, which cover the entire distributed system as the object in focus to be secured. A suitable modeling language for creating a supply chain model can be composed of domain-specific model elements for expressing involved actors, action steps in the supply chain, and elements to express resources, physical as well as immaterial ones. Such a modeling language with corresponding model editor tooling support is available as a research prototype developed by one of the RESCUEIT project partners [MS11]. An example model of a food supply chain created with this model editor is shown in Fig. 59.

The model excerpt in Fig. 59 shows an abstraction of a food supply chain, in which a perishable dessert containing fresh eggs is ordered by a retailer, produced by a food manufacturer, and shipped by a logistician. Two of the involved parties are indicated in the model excerpt as vertical swimlanes.

As a security requirement towards the supply chain, the model indicates the demand for a signed document communication of the delivery contract, to ensure the authenticity of the delivery contract and to reduce the possibility of fraud delivery contracts issued by an unauthorized party. This security requirement is visualized in the model using a sym-

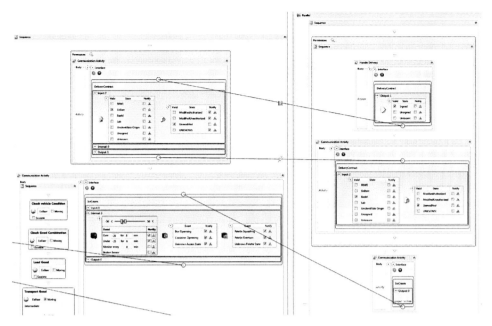

Figure 59: Excerpt of an example food supply chain model in a domain-specific modeling language (contributed to the RESCUEIT project by the project partner SAP AG)

bol, which shows a pencil signing a paper document. It appears both at the side of the sending and the receiving party of the delivery contract, together with graphical user interface (GUI) elements to further configure the demand for document signing. Using this graphical symbol, the modeling language represents the desired conceptual meaning of the security concept "signed electronic document" with a suitable metaphor from the domain's context.

As another example of a security requirement, a cooling vehicle is required for the transportation of the food, which is a relevant security constraint in the given example case of food containing fractions of fresh egg products. The security requirement demanding a cooled transportation is indicated by a thermometer symbol attached to the transport action in the lower-left communication activity model element, accompanied by a double slider to specify the allowed temperature range, and other GUI elements to configure further options of temperature monitoring.

Using this domain-specific modeling language, supply chains can be configured from a bird's-eye-view perspective by management staff without detail knowledge about the technical realization of the individual security demands. Once the conceptual demands towards the supply chain are captured in the model, it remains a methodical task to ensure the alignment between the modeled requirements on the one hand, and the real-world execution of the supply chain processes, which consists of electronic document exchange and physical goods transportation, on the other hand. Ensuring this alignment requires organizational and technological steps to be taken, the latter of which are looked closer at in the following.

10.3 A distributed service oriented architecture (SOA)

Bringing together the conceptual view of the supply chain model, and the actual supply chain process execution performed by multiple actors and their information technology (IT) systems, requires to introduce a monitoring and logging component as a new component in the supply chain systems architecture, which keeps track of the individual steps of action taken by the supply chain members and their IT systems. To keep introductory costs and acceptance barriers as low as possible, the existing peer-to-peer communication setup among the supply chain members is not to be changed in principle, and existing IT systems at each supply chain member's location remain operating with a minimum of configuration changes. This is achieved by interfacing existing individual IT systems to local enterprise service bus (ESB) components, which re-route existing communication through the additionally introduced monitoring and control component. This re-routing of communication traffic happens transparently to the involved supply chain member systems, the only changes in existing IT systems can be expected to be limited to modifying communication endpoints, i. e., the Internet Protocol (IP) addresses of communicating partner systems, which get changed to point to the local ESBs. With such a communication architecture, the overall supply chain process becomes monitorable and observable by the introduced monitoring component, with minimal invasive changes to the existing systems.

Besides enabling usage control, the use of multiple distributed ESBs also allows to selectively apply existing security technology to encrypt and obscure communication traffic among supply chain members, because distributed communication happens through the involved ESBs only, and can be enriched with additional layers of security independently from the supply chain members' legacy IT systems. Applying such security technology additionally lowers the risk of external intrusion into the supply chain process.

Fig. 60 shows the different architectural constellations without and with additional logging and monitoring component. Fig. 60 a) displays the original legacy situation, with the supply chain partners communicating directly in a peer-to-peer environment. In contrast to this setting, Fig. 60 b) pictures the situation after introducing the central logging and monitoring component. From the involved partners' isolated points of view, the change in setting up the communication relationships remains small, however, with the central logging and monitoring component introduced, there now exists an entity with sufficient knowledge to keep track of the overall process instance states.

10.4 Implementation strategy meta-model for a SOA platform

The target architecture of the example project, for which code is to be generated, is a service oriented architecture (SOA) [Erl06, Gro09b] environment, in which a Business Process Execution Language (BPEL) process is controlling the dynamics of the overall distributed software system. Each of the interoperating systems is accessible as a web-service. The according interfaces and operations during interactions can thus be described in terms of web-service specifications. The implementation strategy meta-model

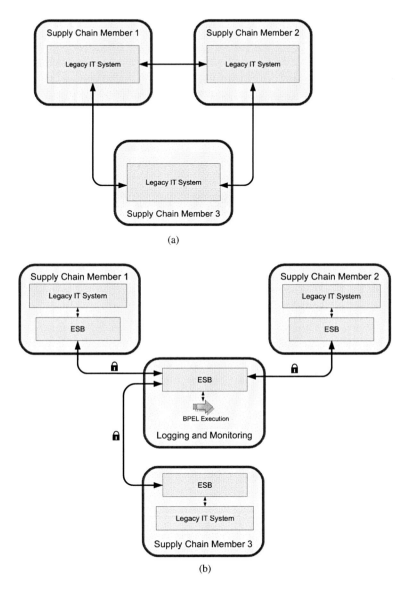

Figure 60: Conceptualizations of the distributed architecture, a) original peer-to-peer setting, b) using ESB proxies to securely interconnect existing legacy systems

offers concepts for describing web-service providers, the web-services they make accessible, and the operations that can be invoked on the web-services. These concepts are represented by the meta-classes `WebServiceProvider`, `WebService`, and `Web-ServiceOperation`. `WebServiceProvider` is integrated with the generic mapping meta-model by sub-classing the generic abstract type `ArchitectureSpecificActorImplementation`, `WebService` represents a specialiization of the generic `ArchitectureSpecificSoftwareResource` concept. One additional technical concept representing communication facilities of the SOA is the notion of a message queue for interchanging continuous data streams among involved partner systems. This concept is represented by the meta-class `MessageQueue`, which also is considered to integrate with the generic mapping meta-model as a sub-class of `ArchitectureSpecificSoftwareResource`.

These types belong to the technical domain of a distributed SOA environment, they are not conceptual elements on the same level as the language concepts used in enterprise modeling languages, which are used as the starting point of the SEEM method. Instead, these technical domain types can be described by an implementation strategy meta-model, which makes up a domain-specific language especially suited for describing the technical aspects of the SOA development project. Provided suitable tooling support, as e. g. available with the ECLIPSE Eclipse Modeling Framework (EMF) packages (see Sect. 12), this implementation strategy meta-model can automatically be converted into a model editor, which allows to create and edit implementation strategy model instances in the specific language described.

The set of previously described core concepts of the implementation strategy meta-model for a SOA platform with BPEL control is shown in Fig. 61.

Further classes in the meta-model describe specifics of the underlying technical infrastructure of a SOA and its application in the specifically desired use-case, which is primarily based on securing and monitoring electronic document communication, along with traditional input and event handling of a distributed SOA application. The technical elements which implement the electronic document monitoring together with monitoring of the ongoing supply chain process are reflected by the target architecture specific meta-types of process-step implementation strategies, defined by the meta-classes `CommunicationMonitoring`, `PhysicalStepMonitoring`, and `LogicalStepMonitoring`, which inherit from the abstract meta-class `ArchitectureSpecificProcessStepImplementation`.

To describe the connection between multiple process-steps in such an architecture, the meta-class `WaitForMessage` is included as a concrete sub-class of `ArchitectureSpecificControlFlowImplementation`. Using this control flow implementation, in contrast to the generic `Continuous` control flow implementation, will cause the implementation to receive input documents associated with the next process-step, before the process continues.

The implementation components for handling electronic document exchange, as well as the security handling mechanisms applied during electronic document communication, are expressed as target-architecture specific ways of performing information object accesses.

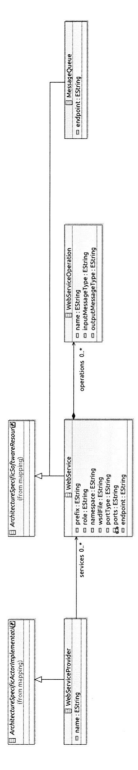

Figure 61: Core concepts of the implementation strategy meta-model for describing a SOA environment

This is why they are declared as sub-classes of the abstract meta-type `Architecture-SpecificInformationObjectAccess`. Implementation strategies for information object accesses, which represent electronic document exchange in a SOA, are declared by the meta-classes `ReceiveMessage` and `SendMessage`, which denote the actions performed by the controlling BPEL process to realize to orchestration among involved partner systems. On this concrete technical level, the focus rather lies on receiving and sending actions performed by the control process, not, as on the conceptual level, on sending and receiving actions carried out by involved business partners's systems. This is why the notions of sending and receiving appear to be inverse on the two levels of abstractions, comparing the conceptual model elements with the accordingly mapped entries of the `SOAarchitectureModel` implementation strategies.

In addition to performing operations of document exchange, the application of security techniques such as encryption and decryption of electronic documents, or the creation of digital signatures and their later verification, are part of the functionality provided by the coordinating control process. These parts of functionality are represented by the meta-classes `Encrypt`, `Decrypt`, `CreateSignature`, and `VerifySignature`, respectively. Finally, the `ProofAuthentication` implementation strategy type denotes the use of a credential based proof-protocol, to verify the validity of electronic documents received.

The entire notion of an implementation strategy meta-model for a SOA is represented by the container class `SOAArchitectureModel`. It serves to instantiate implementation strategy models of this specific kind, but also allows to contain any of the inherited generic architecture concepts provided by the generic mapping model and implementation strategy model conceptualizations given as prepared elements of the method (see Sect. 6.2.2).

In Fig. 62, the entire meta-model is shown. An example implementation strategy model instance in the language defined by this meta-model is shown in Fig. 63, as it is being edited with the automatically generated EMF tooling support.

10.5 Executable BPEL workflow

An excerpt of a visual representation of the executable BPEL workflow model, generated as output of the applied model transformations, is shown in Fig. 64. Appendix A.4.4 contains the entire source code of the generated BPEL workflow model.

In a SOA environment, an important role is played by interface declarations for web-services, which can be exchanged among web-service implementation platforms of different kinds. The interfaces are specified via Extensible Markup Language (XML) documents in the Web Services Description Language (WSDL), an interface specification given in the WSDL is typically called in short "a WSDL". WSDLs provide a uniform way to expose the technical specification for using web-service functionality remotely from any client on the internet.

The input and output interfaces of BPEL workflow processes typically are also described by WSDL interface declarations. This makes any BPEL process accessible in the same

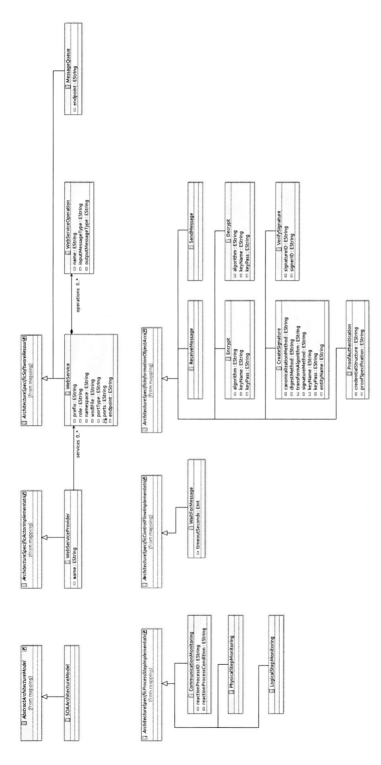

Figure 62: Entire implementation strategy meta-model for describing the example SOA target architecture

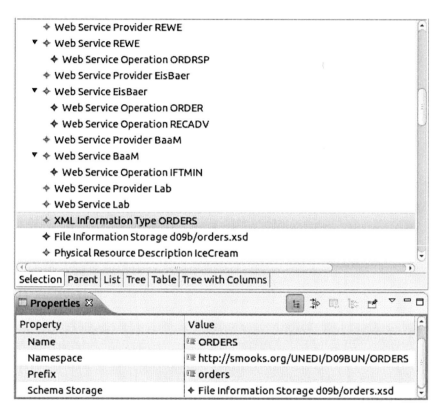

Figure 63: Example implementation strategy model instance in the language defined by the implementation strategy meta-model

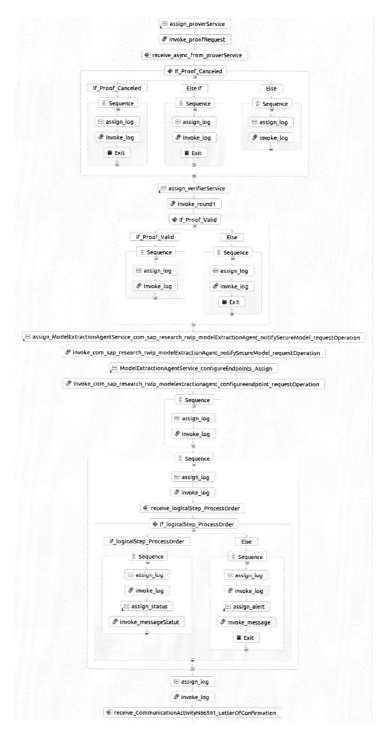

Figure 64: Excerpt of a visual representation of the generated executable BPEL workflow model

way as a web-service, which makes the concept of web-service and their interfaces be recursively addressable from BPEL processes.

To offer an entirely automatized software generation procedure, the code generation templates developed for the SOA target platform also take care for creating the corresponding WSDL interface description for the generated BPEL workflow model. In addition, required configuration files for deploying the BPEL model and its WSDL interface declaration, are output by the code generation templates of the configured method. A graphical representation of the generated WSDL is shown in Fig. 65, the corresponding XML artifact is included in Appendix A.4.4.

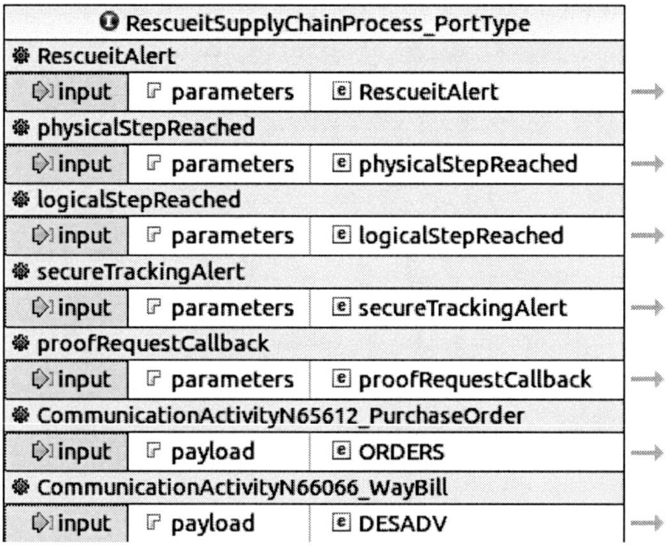

❶ RescueitSupplyChainProcess_PortType		
❀ RescueitAlert		
▷ input	⌐ parameters	e RescueitAlert
❀ physicalStepReached		
▷ input	⌐ parameters	e physicalStepReached
❀ logicalStepReached		
▷ input	⌐ parameters	e logicalStepReached
❀ secureTrackingAlert		
▷ input	⌐ parameters	e secureTrackingAlert
❀ proofRequestCallback		
▷ input	⌐ parameters	e proofRequestCallback
❀ CommunicationActivityN65612_PurchaseOrder		
▷ input	⌐ payload	e ORDERS
❀ CommunicationActivityN66066_WayBill		
▷ input	⌐ payload	e DESADV

Figure 65: Excerpt of a graphical model representation of the generated WSDL interface declaration for the BPEL process

By introducing the BPEL process execution component as an intermediary entity, which keeps track of the entire communication relationships along the supply chain, the supply chain process can become subject to both monitoring and usage control by an entity with enough knowledge to keep track of a process's overall state. Although the original peer-to-peer architecture of the earlier communication setup among the supply chain partners is intercepted by the central monitoring and control entity, from the supply chain partners' points of views, there is only a minor change in the communication setup, which consists of changing the technical end-point address of a targeted service from the originally addressed supply chain partner, to the process orchestration component.

The model transformations and models specified when applying the SEEM method represent a set of formal description means that define the relationships between the conceptually specified security requirements, which are stated from a non-technical business-oriented perspective, and the concrete technical realization as it is provided by the generated BPEL process, as executable output artifact of the method.

The SEEM method can be applied in a zero-coding manner, meaning that all components and program logic of the finished executable artifacts will be generated by the model transformations and artifact generation steps automatically, without further developer interaction. Of course, configuring the method in this way shifts development efforts into template configuration and generator development, requiring higher meta-programming competencies than straight-forward artifact development. For this reason, there may be cases in which a zero-coding approach is inefficient in terms of development efforts and costs.

In those cases, where a zero-coding approach can be provided, and the involved model transformations and generators can automatically be executed in sequence, which outputs executable artifacts without further developer interaction, the SEEM method offers a controlled, repeatedly applicable, and as a consequence, certifiable method to interlink the conceptual semantics from business perspective models to secure technical implementations. Having such a certifiable method at hand, fosters the acceptance of the created IT-system, and increases trust in the proper functionality of the systems. In addition, business perspective stakeholders with limited, yet basic knowledge about technical process implementations, can make use of BPEL visualization tools, to "read" the generated output artifacts and to punctually check the generated process for valid implementation. This trust on the side of the conceptual business stakeholder perspective is an inevitable prerequisite for a comprehensive security architecture.

10.6   Overall implemented example

The implemented method components, which realize a zero-coding transformation approach, are represented in Fig. 66. Numbers in the visualization indicate the procedural order, in which order model transformations are applied.

The first model involved is the conceptual supply chain model, which is serialized to a file in a straight-forward file format, as an XML language instance. The example supply chain model data file is included in Appendix A.4.4.

The adapter transformation converts the XML file to an EMF compatible model instance representation. The implemented adapter transformation for the example is included in Appendix A.4.1.

Via the initialization transformation, a mapping model as well as an implementation strategy model instance are created. The initialization transformation takes the extracted enterprise model (EEM) model as input, and outputs a mapping model, which establishes references between conceptual elements of the supply chain model on the one hand, and implementation strategies for the chosen concrete target architecture of a BPEL process orchestration engine in a SOA environment. Since the presented example realizes a zero-coding approach when it comes to generating the final executable artifacts, all mapping model references created are complete, and point to implementation strategies in the implementation strategy model that have been completely determined by the initialization transformation. The applied example initialization transformation scripts are reproduced in Appendices

A.3.2 and A.4.2. The initialization transformation also uses a simply structured external configuration file, from which technical parameters are transfered into the generated implementation strategy model. This configuration file is shown in Appendix A.3.3. An overall configuration file for specifying the base directory and project name is also reproduced in Appendix A.3.3.

From the set of models now available after the previous transformation steps, which are the conceptual supply chain model representation, the implementation strategy model instance describing concrete implementation components, and the mapping model binding both together, an executable BPEL artifact is generated by a model-to-text code generation transformation. The corresponding XPAND transformation description can be viewed in Appendix A.4.3. The resulting BPEL process in textual representation is included in Appendix A.4.4, it has already been introduced as a graphical excerpt in Fig. 64.

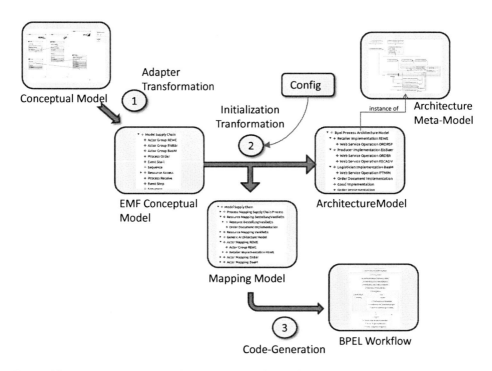

Figure 66: Overview on the implemented example method components and steps (according to [GBKK12])

To invoke the individual transformation steps, invocation scripts have been used for each transformation. These scripts can also be combined into one overall transformation script, which automatically runs the entire transformation sequence in one step to produce the desired output artifact in a zero-coding style. The scripts for individual transformation invocations, including optional checking steps between each transformation step, are included in Appendices A.3.1, A.3.2, and A.3.3. They are written in the Modeling Workflow Engine (MWE) language included in the EMF tooling components shipped with the ECLIPSE modeling tools (see Sect. 12.5). The combined transformation steps, which in a zero-coding approach can be executed automatically in one sequence, are invoked altogether by the combined `00-run-all.mwe` transformation, included in Appendix A.4.3. (The numbers in front of the script names ensure a sequential sorting when the files are displayed in a file-system view.)

11 MEMO enterprise models for developing JSP web applications

To present alternative adaptations of the method, besides the ones exemplified in the comprehensive BPEL generation example (see Sect. 10), this section gives further details on how the introductory web shop example in Sect. 2 has technically been realized. This example uses MEMO enterprise models as conceptual models describing the socio-technical environment of the software to be generated. The software, this time, is created as executable Java Server Pages (JSP) web application artifacts, which represent dynamic webpages running on a web-server in the internet. The application architecture resembles a traditional web-application environment, with web-server and web-client running on physically remote machines, communicating through the internet via the Hyper-Text Transfer Protocol (HTTP).

11.1 Adapting the MEMO enterprise modeling method

11.1.1 The MEMO language family as input enterprise modeling languages

The MEMO enterprise modeling method [Fra12] offers modeling perspectives for strategic goals and high-level actions, as well as for modeling organizational roles, resource entities and processes. These multiple perspectives are centrally integrated through the use of process control flow models. In process control flow models, process-steps get associated with responsible actors whose roles are defined in organization diagrams. Resources are modeled with a resource modeling language and can be allocated to process-steps, to express which resources are accessed in that specific process-step. The semantic integrity of these multiple perspectives on an organization is internally ensured by the language architecture. Fig. 67 shows an excerpt from the MEMO process control flow model in the introductory example (see Sect. 2), in which organizational roles and resources from other perspectives are referenced.

11.1.2 MEMOCENTERNG as editor application

Tooling support for creating and editing models of the MEMO language family is available via the MEMOCENTERNG [GF10, Res] software application.

The languages included in MEMOCENTERNG are the *Organization Diagram* language for modeling organizational structure [Fra11a], and the *Process Control Flow Language* [Fra11b], which allows to express semantically rich process model descriptions of business processes and other methodical procedures in organizations. The Process Control Flow language is enhanced by the *Process Decomposition Language* which is used for specifying static decomposition relationships among process-steps, i. e., expresses which process-steps are further described by more fine-grained process models. Finally, the *Strategy Diagram* and *Activity Diagram* languages for expressing strategy, goals and actions from a high-level strategic view are part of MEMOCENTERNG.

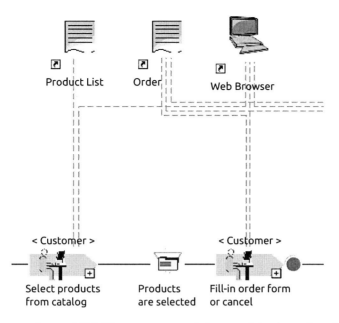

Figure 67: Excerpt from a MEMO process control flow model referencing elements from other perspectives

To model physical and non-tangible resources in business contexts, the *ResML* is included in the set of modeling languages, accompanied by the *Allocation Diagram* language which is responsible for expressing the mappings between process-steps and resources.

MEMOCENTERNG forms a comprehensive environment for enterprise modeling from multiple perspectives, store and manage interrelated models in a common environment, and further process models inside the same platform, since the platform is based on the Eclipse [CR08] environment which can additionally be enhanced by a multitude of third-party supplementary components for software development.

Fig. 69 shows an example process control flow model, and other models, being edited in MEMOCENTERNG.

11.1.3 Adapter transformation to configure the method for the MEMO language family

To adapt the method to the MEMO language family as input enterprise modeling languages, an adapter transformation (see Sect. 6.3.1) has to be created in order to use MEMO models as input and translate them to the intermediate EEM representation. Once this representation is available, the components and activities defined by the SEEM method can be applied to a conceptual model format known at development time of the method, which allows to make use of generic automation components that have been developed together with the SEEM method.

The MEMOCENTERNG implementation is also based on the ECLIPSE modeling tools. This allows to use the internal model transformation languages and tools integrated in the EMF packages to formulate the desired adapter transformation. In the example implementation, the XTEND [Eclc] language from the EMF tooling components is used.

MEMOCENTERNG stores models for different conceptual perspectives, i. e., the process perspective, the resource perspective, the organization structure perspective, etc., as individual model instances. For the adapter transformation to create a single comprehensive EEM model, it is thus necessary to use all individual input models as input to the transformation, while a single model instance is output as the transformation's result. The XTEND language supports to have multiple input models for model-to-model transformations.

Appendix A.3.1 shows the prototypical implementation of the model transformation that translates a set of interrelated MEMO enterprise models into an EEM representation. A script to invoke the transformation with multiple required input models is given in Appendix A.3.1

11.2   Configuring a JSP web-application target architecture

As an alternative example to the introduced BPEL generation target (see Sect. 10), details about generating a JSP web application are discussed in the following section. This target architecture has been used in the introductory example in Sect. 2, to prototypically realize the conceptually modeled functionality of a web-shop.

The initialization of JSP-platform-specific implementation strategies is performed by the script contained in Appendix A.3.2.

11.2.1   Example implementation strategy meta-model for a JSP web-application platform

The prototype implementation accounts for generating front-end functionality as web application. Web application usage scenarios can differ strongly from local application usage, especially because they can be performed by actors who are external to the organization and possibly are anonymous.

The meta-classes suggested by the web implementation strategy meta-model are shown in Fig. 68, and described in the following.

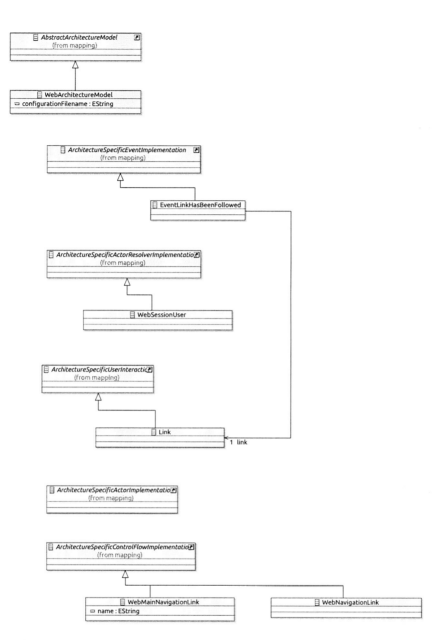

Figure 68: Example implementation strategy meta-model for a web application architecture

The `WebArchitectureModel` meta-class represents the entire web implementation strategy model as root element.

To enrich the set of available event implementation strategies, the `WebFormHasBeen-Submitted` meta-class has been included in the meta-model as a subclass of the mapping meta-model's abstract meta-class `ArchitectureSpecificEventImplementation`. It allows to describe that an enterprise information system (EIS) reacts on form input received from a web page. This implementation strategy may be applied both to start events, or to events in between process-steps, the code generation templates will distinguish these two cases and generate appropriate artifact representations.

To resolve concrete users that fulfill an actor role, the `WebSessionUser` meta-class is part of the meta-model. It subclasses the abstract meta-class `ArchitectureSpecificActorResolverImplementation` from the mapping meta-model, and thus allows to describe an additional actor resolver implementation strategy based on session ids. Session ids are a concept specifically available on the underlying technological platform of web-applications.

With the `HTMLForm` implementation strategy, an additional kind of information editor is introduced to the set of editors that can be used when `AbstractInformationAccessImplementation` process-member implementation strategies are implemented. The `HTMLForm` meta-class represents a kind of editor which is specific to underlying web application technology.

12 Code generation and tooling support

12.1 Deriving executable artifacts

With the method being adapted to an enterprise modeling language, appropriate implementation strategies being available for all targeted front-end architecture platforms, and a domain application programming interface (API) which formalizes rudimentary architecture design decisions at hand, all kinds of methodical artifacts to describe an executable software system are available. A final methodical component is required now to transform this description of a software system into actually running software. The mechanism, which achieves this, is rather complex than complicated, i. e., it has to deal with a large number of available model elements to derive an executable system from, but this transformation is primarily a horizontal transformation, which preserves the level of abstraction the model elements already reside on, and merely performs a syntactic translation from one technical artifact to another. This transformation can be named "horizontal", because the mapping model and its accompanied implementation strategy models contain language elements that explicitly describe implementation strategies. Executable artifacts derived from these models thus reside on the same low level of abstraction as the models, because the model elements intentionally carry knowledge about implementation details.

There are multiple alternative approaches to derive executable artifacts from models. One straight-forward idea is to interpret models at runtime, i. e., read the model content, and react accordingly by invoking implementation components depending on the model elements that are encountered during model analysis. Such an approach requires an interpreter to be developed, which knows about the operational semantics of the model elements and behaves accordingly. From a programming point of view, this means to write a program which at start-up reads in the model files, and then traverses the structure of the model elements, testing for the existence of specific model elements, acting accordingly, and evaluating element attributes to finally invoke a subcomponent which realizes the implementation of the modeled implementation strategy with the specified parameters. An advantage of this approach is the flexibility in reacting on changes in the models. Whenever a model has changed, the interpreter needs only to be restarted again, and can continue operating on the new model. However, with every change in the underlying modeling languages, the interpreter has to be adapted, too.

Although an interpretation mechanism as sketched is possible for runtime execution of models, it is not the commonly used mechanism to make models executable, because it is inflexible in reacting on changes in the modeling languages, and it encapsulates too much knowledge about the formal interpretation of model content in hard-coded program code.

Another approach for getting executable software from models is typically applied in domain-specific software engineering (DSSE) projects and can equally be applied to the method proposed here. The approach is based on transforming model content to software artifacts at development time, which creates an entire software system based on components that in principle could have been developed manually, too, but are results of automatic transformations from the models.

Software development projects, which apply artifact generation techniques to gain an executable software system, are called "generative" development approaches [CE00]. To demonstrate a prototypical engineering process, the generative approach is chosen in the following to transform the models created with the method to an executable software system.

12.2 Code generation templates

When talking of applying code generation templates in the context of this work, any use of a mechanism is denoted, which is capable of transforming models to technical artifacts that constitute the implementation of a software system. The term "code" originates from traditional uses in model-driven program code generation to output source code in a programming language, but code generation templates are also able to output textual artifacts of any other kind, e. g., configuration files or data representations. Code generation templates are applied using a model-to-text transformation engine, which both takes the code generation templates, and the models to be transformed, as input, and generates textual artifacts as output.

Language elements of a template language are used to query content from the input models, transform it, and optionally insert it in the generated output artifacts at desired places. Besides this, language constructs can conditionally decide based on model content whether to include fragments into the generated output artifact or not.

The interpretation mechanism of a model-to-text transformation invokes code generation templates by traversing the input models, and feeds instance data met during traversal as parameters to the templates. The model-to-text mechanism may provide constructs to associate specific model elements to specific template parts, so that different templates can be specified to be evaluated for different model elements.

While a code generation template is being evaluated, model content is reflected via variables in the template language, and can usually be queried and modified using programming language constructs of the template language. Different code generation template languages may provide different ranges of functionality to work with model content inside the template, but basic functionality for comparing values and conditionally include output fragments or not are included in any code generation template language.

When a code generation template has been identified by the model-to-text engine to be applicable to a model element, and variables internal to the template have been set to reflect the model element's content, the template gets evaluated linearly from top to bottom, copying all constant fragments of partial output artifacts to the generated output, insert values in the output at places where specified, and decide on conditional inclusion of output fragments depending on evaluated conditions. Using this mechanism, the semantics captured in model element instances in principle can be interpreted as any kind of technical artifact of a software system, by constructing the according code generation template that output the artifacts in question.

To be used in the method, individual code generation templates are created for each target architecture. The artifacts required to describe a deployable software system, are prospectively different on each unique target platform. This is why, in principle, every target architecture needs its own set of code generation templates, which all take the same combination of the mapping model and accompanied models, but create different artifacts, specific to the technical needs of the underlying implementation architecture. However, if parts of code generation for different target architectures turn out to contain common elements, most template languages provide abstraction mechanisms for reusing sub-templates in multiple contexts.

The prototypical implementation to demonstrate the method uses the XPAND code generation template language, for which a model-to-text engine and additional tooling support are available through the ECLIPSE modeling project components. See Sect. 12.5.5.

Example code generation templates, which generate JAVA and BPEL source code artifacts from the models in the examples, are included in Appendices A.3.3 and A.4.3.

12.3 Requirements towards tooling support

When applying the previously described method, a number of model artifacts are being operated on, either by manual editing activities using model editor software, or by automatic transformations that are performed by a model transformation engine. To efficiently apply the proposed method, tooling support must be made available to support manual editing activities and perform the automatic steps.

Tooling support is both required to implement automatic processing steps, e. g., model transformations or model checking steps, and in the form of model editors which enable software architects and developers to access and edit model content. The following section lists the requirements towards appropriate tooling support for the proposed method.

At first, a set of enterprise modeling languages is required, including a business process modeling language with interrelated organization modeling and resource modeling facilities. In addition, a meta-modeling language should be available to specify domain-specific modeling languages and to generate corresponding diagram editors or tree-node editors.To generate and modify models automatically, a mechanism to execute model-to-model transformations needs to be included in the tooling environment, as well as validity checking functionality, which is required to validate the formal semantic correctness of models. With the help of code generation functionality, models are transformed to textual artifacts, e. g., to source code or configuration files. Such functionality is expected to be part of the tooling support, too.

Finally, all components should be bound together in a common environment to make their functionality efficiently accessible to software architects and developers.

To offer implementations of the required tooling components, a software environment has been chosen which integrates technological building blocks for realizing the required functionality. The environment and the individual components are described in the following.

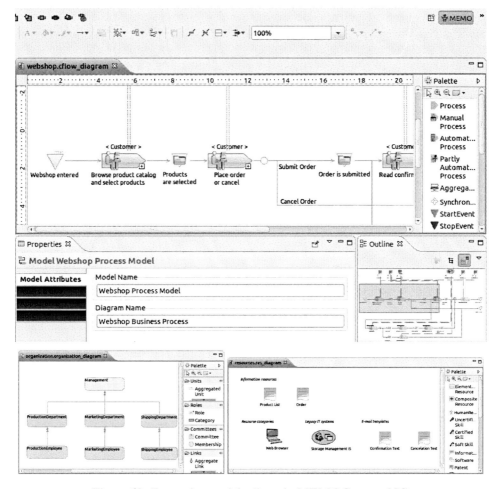

Figure 69: Enterprise model editors in MEMOCENTERNG

12.4 Enterprise modeling with the MEMOCENTERNG platform

The MEMO enterprise modeling languages with corresponding diagram editors provides a scientifically grounded approach for enterprise modeling [Fra94, Fra02, Fra11d, Fra12]. The languages are implemented as a set of diagram editors in the MEMOCENTERNG environment [GF10]. An example of a business process model edited with MEMOCENTERNG's control flow diagram editor is shown in Fig. 69. The language family also contains an organization modeling language for explicating organizational relationships and structure, as well as a resource modeling language. Excerpts of corresponding models, edited in MEMOCENTERNG, are also shown in Fig. 69.

12.5 Tooling on top of the ECLIPSE MODELING FRAMEWORK (EMF)

ECLIPSE is known to most software developers as an integrated development environment (IDE) for software development [CR08]. The underlying technology of the ECLIPSE PLATFORM [Eclb] implements a set of generic concepts for loosely coupling software components at runtime. This architecture is built upon the Open Services Gateway initiative (OSGi) component platform. The platform can flexibly be extended by plug-ins, so-called "bundles" in the OSGi/ECLIPSE terminology, which are loaded into the common platform at runtime. The use of this technology allows to combine functionality of different kinds, which are not a-priori conceptually interwoven but are aimed to be related to each other. Using this mechanism, the ECLIPSE PLATFORM allows to integrate tooling functionality in a single place, without requiring the components to be dependent on each other at design time, which makes development easier and independent from each other. This architecture has been utilized to integrate the above implementation technologies and offer tooling support in a single place.

One set of functionality especially related to handling models is provided by bundles from the Eclipse Modeling Framework (EMF) [Ecla]. Once these bundles are added to the ECLIPSE IDE, they provide functionality to define modeling languages, create editor components for models, allow users to interactively edit model instances, and provide mechanisms to serialize model instances to permanent storage, and load them back from there again.

The EMF includes an object-oriented general purpose modeling language (GPML) called ECORE [SBPM09], which is used throughout the framework as a modeling language for defining the types and their interrelations for other modeling languages. It is thus used as a meta-modeling language for specifying other, typically domain-specific, modeling languages, which then can be further processed by components of the EMF. Using these components, tooling support for realizing the methodical steps proposed by the SEEM method has been created, which is shown in the following.

12.5.1 Mapping model editor

An editor for mapping models is required by the method to allow manual adjustments of the default values generated as default implementation strategies, and to supply additional manual decisions where required.

Tooling support to edit mapping models is offered by a non-graphical tree-structure editor, which integrates into the ECLIPSE development environment and gets automatically derived from the meta-model specification of the mapping model language [Gro09a]. Only minor manual adjustments have been made to the `genmodel`, which is a component of the EMF mechanism to automatically generate model editors from meta-model specifications.

Detail attributes of model elements are displayed in a separate part of the GUI, which is the properties view. If active, the properties view is typically shown at the bottom-middle of the ECLIPSE window. Attributes are displayed there are a set of key-value pairs in a two-column table, with the name of the attribute in the left column, an the value of the attribute in the right. The value of the attribute can be edited, with corresponding GUI widgets according to the attribute's type.

The mapping model editor is able to supplement the main purpose of the mapping model, which is to bind together elements from multiple modeling languages, with adequate functionality. The editor achieves this by offering editor functionality for referenced languages as well, which means that besides providing functionality for editing the core mapping model entries, the mapping model editor also provides access to the referenced conceptual enterprise model representation elements on the one hand, and elements from implementation strategy models or generic implementation strategy model elements on the other hand.

Editor functionality for EEM representation elements, which are referenced towards one direction of each mapping entry, allows to browse these elements in detail, and also potentially to edit them, although manual modification of the EEM representation is not envisioned as a step in the methodical procedure.

Editing facilities for referenced implementation strategy model elements are also offered. This efficiently supplements the use of the method, since it allows to perform all manual editing activities of models, as they are conceptualized in step 5 of the method (see Sect. 7.1.5), to be performed in one place, implemented by the single mapping model editor component.

A screenshot of the mapping model editor in use is shown in Fig. 70.

12.5.2   Implementation strategy meta-modeling with ECORE

The platform underlying to MEMOCENTERNG is an ECLIPSE integrated development environment (IDE) with additionally plugged-in modeling extensions. As part of these extensions, the meta-modeling language ECORE [SBPM09] is provided by the core ECLIPSE MODELING FRAMEWORK (EMF, [Ecla]). It is used to declare modeling language specifications. The EMF supports the automatic creation of model editors out of modeling language specifications, which means that tooling support for ECORE-specified modeling languages is inherently available in the form of automatically generated editors. Further enhanced with the ECLIPSE GRAPHICAL MODELING FRAMEWORK (GMF, [SBPM09]), also generation facilities for graphical diagram editors are available.

As a convenient extension to the meta-modeling capabilities already provided by the ECLIPSE modeling frameworks, MEMOCENTERNG additionally contains the MEMO META MODELING LANGUAGE (MML, [Fra08]), which internally builds upon ECORE and the ECLIPSE modeling framework extensions. It simplifies the creation of conceptual domain-specific modeling languages with graphical diagram editors.

12.5.3   Model-to-model transformations with the XTEND language

A relevant feature for implementing the engineered method is the execution of model-to-model transformations. Creating and updating the mapping model with reasonable default

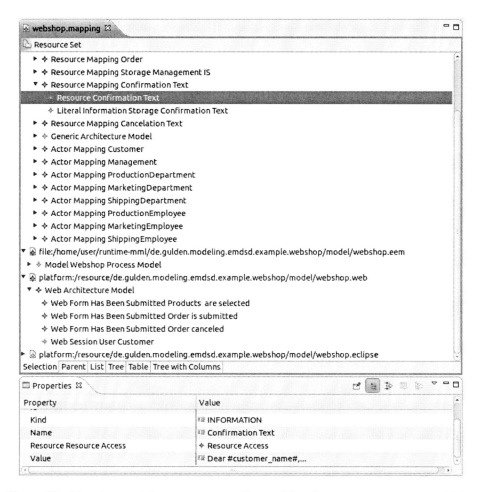

Figure 70: Mapping model tree structure editor, with references to separate model instances

values accelerates the development of prototypes and helps focusing the attention of software architects and developers on those design decisions, which cannot be taken automatically by deriving defaults. The model-to-model transformation from an enterprise model representation to an initial combination of a mapping model and implementation strategy models thus serves as a crucial methodical step in performing the shift from a conceptual business perspective to an implementation-level description.

To implement the required model-to-model transformations, the XTEND language has been chosen. XTEND has been developed especially for transforming model instances of ECORE meta-models. It provides programming language constructs which complement the structural meta-concepts of ECORE with corresponding dynamic semantics for accessing and modifying model instance content. The language is available as part of optional extensions to the EMF framework, and can be installed within each ECLIPSE environment. The fundamental principle of XTEND is to enhance the static structural declaration of a modeling modeling with dynamic functions that are available to be executed on instances of model elements, e. g., to query values, modify attributes, create new child elements, etc. The functions written in the XTEND language may be used in an object-oriented notation, which makes them appear as if they were object-oriented methods that can be invoked on instance of model elements during a model transformation or validity check run. The language follows a functional paradigm, which allows for compact language constructs to access model elements, e. g., multi-valued attributes and relationships are syntactically accessed in the same way as single-valued attributes, and the language provides implicit iteration over sets of multi-valued attributes or relationships, when values queries from multi-values attributes are further processed.

XTEND model transformations a executed by an interpretation engine, which gets configured with a an input model file, an output file, and a start transformation function to invoke.

Fig. 71 shows a part of an editor for XTEND scripts in the development environment. Example XTEND scripts, which have been developed as part of the prototypical implementation, are listed in Appendices A.3.1, A.3.2, and A.4.2.

12.5.4 Model-checking with the CHECK language

The CHECK language is a mechanism for specifying validity conditions (also called constraints) on model-instances. It uses boolean expressions from the XTEND language to specify validity conditions and is easy to learn and apply for developers who are already familiar with XTEND.

As part of the method to be engineered, the CHECK language provides a mechanism to find places in the model where manual editing activities are required by software architects or developers. Applying model checking thus serves a relevant function in providing guidance for architects and developers in their working processes, by pointing them to places where design considerations and implementation activities are required.

CHECK scripts that have been developed for the prototypical implementation of the method are listed in Appendices A.3.1 and A.3.2.

12.5.5 Code generation with XPAND templates

To create executable artifacts from the implementation-level descriptions that are provided by the mapping model and accompanied implementation strategy models, code generation facilities are consulted. Code generation serves to create source code in a programming language, or to output configuration files which control the behavior of higher-level execution engines, such as workflow engines or script interpreters. See Sect. 12.2 for a detailed introduction.

Fig. 71 shows the editor for XPAND templates, as it appears inside the common development environment, together with the editor for XTEND templates.

```
initMappingWeb.ext ☒

  * Throughout the transformation process, identity among model elements is
  * judged on String values of name or label attributes.
  */
WebArchitectureModel updateMapping(MappingModel this):
    this.targetArchitectures.typeSelect(WebArchitectureModel).has() ?
        (this.targetArchitectures.typeSelect(WebArchitectureModel).update(this)
        -> null) :
        (let newArchModel = new WebArchitectureModel:
        this.targetArchitectures.add(newArchModel.update(this)) ->
        newArchModel
        );
```

```
session.xpt ☒

import de.gulden.modeling.emdsd.api.impl.eclipse.AbstractEclipseProcessLogin;
import de.gulden.modeling.emdsd.api.impl.eclipse.AbstractEclipseProcessLogout;
import de.gulden.modeling.emdsd.api.impl.eclipse.ui.AbstractEclipseProcessEditor;
import org.eclipse.core.resources.ResourcesPlugin;
import org.osgi.framework.BundleActivator;
import org.osgi.framework.BundleContext;
import java.util.*;

public class «this.javaName()»Session extends AbstractEclipseSession {

    public «this.name.toFirstUpper()»Session() {
        super();
        this.setSessionName("«this.name»");
    }

    @Override
    public String getRuntimeProjectName() {
        return "«this.basePackage».runtime";
    }

    @Override
    protected String getImplementationModelRuntimeURI() {
        return "platform:/plugin/«this.basePackage»/model/«this.basePackage».im";
    }

    @Override
    protected String getPasswordPropertiesURI() {
        return "platform:/plugin/«this.basePackage»/passwords.properties";
```

Figure 71: Editors for XTEND and XPAND scripts in the development environment

241

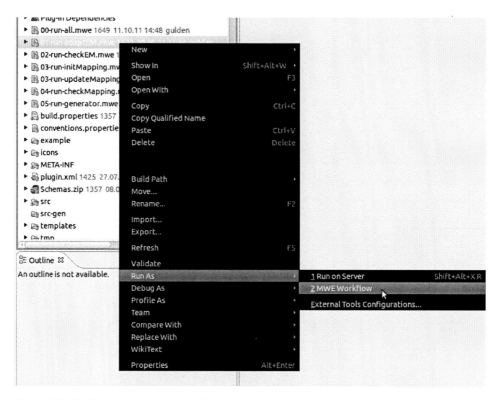

Figure 72: Built-in menu functionality in the ECLIPSE environment to invoke transformations and validity checks of the method

12.5.6 GUI components to invoke the transformation steps in the method

The on-board EMF components allow for an integration of the developed transformations into the ECLIPSE IDE, by wrapping them into MWE workflow scripts, which in turn can be invoked through the IDE's `Run As...` menu. This mechanism is depicted in a screenshot excerpt in Fig. 72.

An alternative way to invoke the transformations of a configured SEEM method, is to configure the ECLIPSE GUI to provide additional menu entries and toolbar buttons for invoking the transformation scripts. To offer directly visible toolbar buttons in the GUI, a set of pictorial symbols is to be selected for labeling the buttons, with each symbol representing the individual transformation steps in a distinguishable way. The transformations and validity checks to be symbolically represented are 1) the adapter transformation, 2) the enterprise model validity check, 3) the mapping model initialization, 4) the mapping model update, 5) the mapping model validity check, and, 6) the code generation. Six distinct, memorable symbols have been created to represent these steps. They are collected in Table 2 and are used as button labels in the GUI implementation.

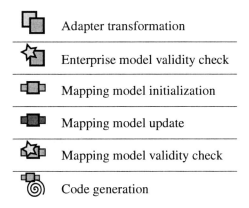

⊡	Adapter transformation
☆	Enterprise model validity check
⊡	Mapping model initialization
⊡	Mapping model update
☆	Mapping model validity check
◎	Code generation

Table 2: Button symbols representing the method's transformations and validity checks

Fig. 73 shows an excerpt of a screenshot, which contains the method-specific menu and the corresponding GUI toolbar with the specific buttons and symbols chosen above. Every menu entry and corresponding toolbar button is used to invoke one transformation step in the method.

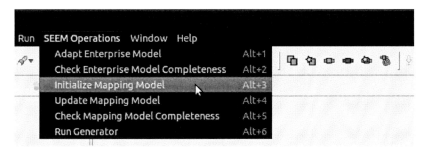

Figure 73: Menu and toolbar in the ECLIPSE environment to invoke transformations and validity checks in the method

12.5.7   EEM model editor for test purposes

Although the method does not require to manually edit enterprise models in their EEM representation (EEM models are automatically transformed from original enterprise models, see Sect. 7.1.2), the set of tooling components also includes both a tree-based editor for EEM models, as well as a diagram editor with a simple graphical notation. Both editors have been automatically generated by a one-click editor generation feature from the MEMO Meta-Modeling Language (MML) editor. Screenshots of the editors are displayed in Fig. 74.

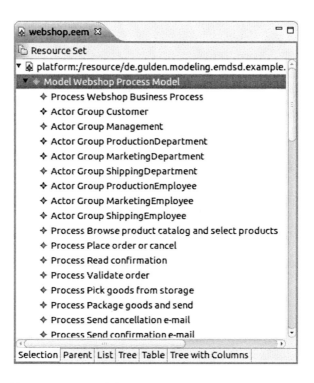

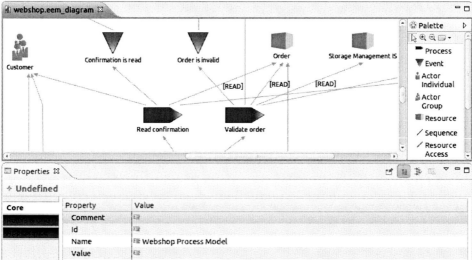

Figure 74: Model editors for the internal EEM representation of enterprise models

Part V

Reflection

13 Evaluation

When designing physical or conceptual artifacts, a chain of decisions is to be taken, to realize a concrete result out of the initial ideas which motivated the creation process. Designing in this sense means bringing ideas into existence, which is either a physical form of existence, or intersubjectively shared symbolic existence.

During this process of making ideas concrete, the design decisions taken enforce the designer to balance out between on the hand providing a most comprehensive, precise and sustainable solution, and on the other hand performing the design process efficiently and with reasonable efforts. As a consequence, this means that there are cases where it is justified to create a sub-optimal artifact, for the benefit of a more efficient development process. Scientific design processes should be completed with a methodical reflection on the created artifacts, to explicate the deficiencies that have reasonably been taken into account when the artifacts were designed [HMP04].

The description of the developed method closes with an evaluation that reflects on the degree of elaboration reached by the proposed approach. As evaluation method, an analytical evaluation is applied, by setting the created artifacts and the methodical description in relation to the requirements initially stated in Sect. 4, and analyzing their architectural structure, properties, and behavioral features with regard to their contribution to the fulfillment of the requirements. Each requirement is individually evaluated with respect to the degree of fulfillment. The results of these considerations are roughly estimated to fit into the categories "good", "medium" and "bad".

Other means of evaluation, e. g., via an observational case study, cannot reasonably be applied to the proposed development method, because the expenses and efforts to perform such an evaluation would exceed a method engineer's capacities by multiple times of the effort that is required to formulate the method itself [Fra06]. Empirical evaluation is thus to be considered external to the proposed method. It does not belong to the reflective evaluation phase at the end of the method design process, but may be carried out in a distinct research project.

To give an overview on the evaluation, Table 3 summarizes the evaluated status for each requirement. The degree of fulfillment per requirement is classified using the categories "good", "medium" and "bad", which are represented in the overview table by the symbols $\oplus$, $\bigcirc$, and $\ominus$, respectively.

Req. 1: Provide effective and efficient methodical guidance	$\oplus$
Req. 2: Support various enterprise modeling languages	$\oplus$
Req. 3: Support distributed and heterogeneous architectures	$\oplus$
Req. 4: Provide multi-user support	$\oplus$
Req. 5: Enable process awareness	$\oplus$
Req. 6: Enable information awareness	$\oplus$
Req. 7: Incorporate security aspects	$\ominus$
Req. 8: Support the use of graphical user interfaces	$\bigcirc$
Req. 9: Offer automatic processing capabilities	$\bigcirc$
Req. 10: Allow for integration of external software components	$\bigcirc$
Req. 11: Allow for integration of organization-specific functionality	$\oplus$
Req. 12: Handle the abstraction gap between enterprise models and implementation descriptions	$\oplus$
Req. 13: Support performing the ontological turn from a bird's-eye-view perspective to an inner system perspective	$\oplus$
Req. 14: Incorporate domain experts into the development process	$\bigcirc$
Req. 15: Strengthen trust among stakeholders	$\bigcirc$

Table 3: Evaluation overview on how requirements are met by the approach

The following paragraphs discuss to which degree each individual requirement is met.

Req. 1: Provide effective and efficient methodical guidance The method suggests a procedure, which, when followed according to its description, effectively leads from enterprise models as a starting point to running software applications that make up an EIS. On this coarse-grained methodical level, software architects and developers are guided by the instructions of the individual steps in the method, and by the documentation of components and artifacts they deal with.

In addition to this, an efficient software engineering process is fostered by utilizing three independent methodical means. At first, the method uses suitable abstractions both in the conceptual domain of EIS, which is covered by the use of enterprise models, as well as in the technical domains of diverse target architectures, for which EIS software is generated. Combining both sides of abstractions gives software architects and developers means at hand, which allow to describe software systems more efficiently than with other techniques that either focus on a single domain only, or aim at using generic descriptive means with a lower degree of semantics. The combination of both sides in an integrated method avoids these frictions.

The second methodical component, which increases efficiency of the development process compared to methods not specifically dedicated to software development from enterprise models, is the use of a default-guessing initialization transformation for creating new mapping models with accompanied implementation strategy model instances. The initialization transformation is introduced in Sect. 6.3.2. While the initialization transformation cannot be expected to always create reasonable default entries, using such a mechanism can unburden developers especially from repeating lowbrow work over and over again. To capture the most often occurring default cases, the initialization transformation script can also be modified to automatically grasp project-specific default cases, or to parse specific hints in the enterprise models (EMs) which control the automatic default detection.

The third introduced methodical means for supplementing an efficient application of the method is the use of validity checks after every automatic model transformation step in the method with optional subsequent manual editing activities. These checks are introduced in Sect. 6.4. On the one hand, the validity checks help to prevent mistakes in later steps of the method, by checking whether the validated model instances carry content which is complete and consistent to be used for subsequent processing. On the other hand, the result of a failed validity check delivers a list of problem locations in the models, which can be used by a wizard-style GUI tool to automatically guide software architects and developers through the set of affected model instances, until all problems are resolved.

The method provides multiple simultaneous approaches to foster development efficiency. It allows for realizing innovatively efficient development processes by separating duties and responsibilities along adequate lines of responsibility. From the point of a theoretical reflection, the methodical requirement for an increase of development efficiency by providing advanced methodical guidance is thus fulfilled, and it is theoretically justified to expect increased development efficiency in concrete engineering projects. Following these arguments, the requirement is in total evaluated as being fulfilled well, shown by the $\oplus$ symbol in the overview table.

Req. 2: Support various enterprise modeling languages An important requirement from a scientific perspective is the demand for keeping the method open to using any enterprise modeling language (EML) or family of EMLs. By keeping the method adaptable to any set of languages, it is proven that the method offers a generic solution to a class of problems, not only to a single modeling use-case constellation.

The requirement is fulfilled by the use of the EEM language, introduced in Sect. 6.2.1, and the adapter transformation, introduced in Sect. 6.3.1, which creates a model instance in the EEM language as output. The EEM instance serves as an intermediate means of expressing domain-specific semantics. This mechanism allows to decouple the entire further processing steps in the method from the original EMs, and makes any set of EMLs pluggable to the method, by developing suitable adapter transformations.

The adapter transformation also allows to use conceptual modeling languages which are not fully capable of expressing all the required enterprise model semantics, e. g., the business process modeling language Business Process Modeling Notation (BPMN), which misses an elaborate resource description perspective. The adapter transformation can enrich the transformed EEM instance with additional concepts from other auxiliary models, which, e. g., declare actors and resources referenced in the BPMN model.

Since the methodical approach fully allows to decouple the software engineering process from any concrete underlying EML, the requirement for using diverse EMLs with the method is regarded as completely fulfilled, it is thus marked with a ⊕ symbol in the overview table.

Req. 3: Support distributed and heterogeneous architectures The requirement for supporting the development of a distributed software system, with multiple participating, remotely distributed components, is met by the method through several independent means.

One aspect related to distributed system development is the ability to describe individual remote system components, and distinguish both between multiple human actors and multiple automatic processing nodes in the distributed environment. The method takes this into account by offering concepts for giving fine-grained explications of actors, resources, and accesses to resources, using the formal concepts `AbstractActorImplementation`, described in Sect. 9.2, `AbstractResourceImplementation`, explained in Sect. 9.3, and `AbstractResourceAccessImplementation`, introduced in Sect. 9.3.4.

Another relevant aspect of distributed systems is the coordination of control flow among multiple participating nodes and possibly involved human actors. The method handles this by offering the notion of sequence implementation strategies (see Sect. 9.1.5), which specifically cover the implementation view on this system aspect, and allow, e. g., to distinguish between control flow passed locally on the same front-end device, or remotely to a different system component.

The prototypical implementation realizes a basic distributed architecture by grounding on a client-server approach, as it is designed in the domain API given in Sect. 6.5.

The notion of a heterogeneous system environment, in which different hardware platforms, different operating systems, and different interaction protocols are combined together to form a comprehensive EIS, is also supported by the method. This is achieved by using individual implementation strategy models in their own architecture-specific modeling language, specified via meta-models. Sect. 6.2.3 describes this approach in detail.

Incorporating meta-modeling techniques to explicate architecture-specific and technology-dependent component types in a model-driven engineering method is an innovative approach to cope with system heterogeneity. The use of this technique is also thoroughly demonstrated by the prototypical application of the method, during which two architecture-specific meta-models and corresponding model instances are created.

Altogether, the variety of available means for dealing with distributed system engineering, and the included prototypical realization of a basic distributed system for further explanation of the method, make it appear justified to evaluate the support for distributed and heterogeneous environments as good, marked in the overview table above with the ⊕ symbol.

Req. 4: Provide multi-user support   Support for multi-user systems, which is an inherent demand towards distributed systems for organizations, is offered by the method through the integration and disambiguation of actor concepts, using the `AbstractActorImplementation` and `AbstractActorResolverImplementation` strategies, introduced in Sections 9.2 and 9.1.5.

By integrating the organization perspective of EMLs into the engineering method, the notion of a multi-user system is modeled on a highly abstract, domain-specific level, which is well suited for being consulted as the basis for engineering software components that implement multi-user support.

Due to the comprehensive set of multi-user concepts offered by the method, the overall support for developing multi-user software systems is evaluated as having reached the requirements well. This is indicated by the ⊕ symbol in the overview table.

Req. 5: Enable process awareness   The requirement for being process-aware can be explicated as the demand towards the method to efficiently make use of conceptual knowledge specified via business process models (BPMs), and to provide means to foster the development of process initiation mechanisms and process control implementations, including resource handling and user management capabilities, in distributed EIS components.

The method provides a rich set of concepts which give support for spanning the interpretational bridge from conceptual BPMs to executable software. With regard to the individual elements of a business process, which are process-steps and events, the concept of a `ProcessMemberMapping` entry in the mapping model allows to associate instances of subclasses of `AbstractProcessMemberImplementation` to declare any possible detail information about how to represent this process-member in a software system. This pattern is introduced in Sect. 6.2.2. An implementation for a process-member can make use of any functionality a software system can perform, including user interaction via a GUI on an EIS front-end, automatic computation without interaction, or invocation of external software components.

Each individual process-member is embedded in a set of specifications regarding the dynamics of a BPM. This includes the flow of control among process-members, i. e., the logical order in which process-members can occur in a concrete process realization, the flow of information objects, which may be shared among the implementations of different process-members, and, among others, the flow of responsibility, i. e., changes throughout the process with regard to human operational and managerial responsibility for carrying out the process-step. The method also provides means for explicating software technical interpretations of these relationships. The notion of control flow implementations and flows of responsibility are handled by `SequenceMapping` entries in the mapping model, which refer to three types of implementation strategies. These describe the control flow handling as subclasses of `AbstractControlFlowImplementation` and `AbstractConditionImplementation`, responsibility handling is realized by concrete subclasses of the `AbstractActorResolverImplementation` implementation strategy, which take care of assigning concrete human users as responsible actors to process-step instantiations at runtime. These concepts are introduced in Sect. 9.1.5. Implementations for data-flow handling, which is another aspect of dynamics in BPMs, are modeled via resource access implementation strategies specified as subclasses of `AbstractResourceAccessImplementation` (see Sect. 9.3.4).

With the comprehensive set of methodical concepts to cover the technical interpretation of BPMs, and the elaboration of corresponding example implementation strategies, the degree of fulfillment for this requirement can be evaluated as complete for the purposes of the method. The result is thus marked with a $\oplus$ symbol in the overview table.

Req. 6: Enable information awareness Requiring a development method to foster "information-aware" EIS implementations, as they are called in the course of the method's elaboration, demands for methodical means that explicate the implementation-level handling of information. Handling of information is one central purpose an EIS is supposed to fulfil, and also a general purpose of any software system in a broader sense.

The method provides a broad variety of concepts to lead from information conceptualizations in enterprise models to corresponding implementations in a software system. `ResourceMapping` entries in the mapping model bind conceptual resource specifications, which describe information resources, to information resource implementation strategies specified as subclasses of the abstract meta-class `AbstractInformationResourceImplementation`. These concepts are elaborated in Sect. 9.3.1. Resource implementation strategies are conceptualized as consisting of two orthogonal aspects, which are information object types, and information object storages, represented by subclasses of the meta-classes `AbstractInformationTypeImplementation` and `AbstractInformationStorageImplementation`, respectively (see Sect. 9.3.1).

The way how information objects are accessed is orthogonally modeled as subclasses of the `AbstractResourceAccessImplementation` meta-class. Example implementation strategies for this are introduced in Sect. 9.3.4.

Retrieving and storing information is modeled by the method in form of a life-cycle pattern implicitly associated with each process-member implementation. This pattern assumes that before any process-member implementation is executed, it fetches information objects either from a persistent or temporary storage, then executes the core process-member functionality, and afterwards optionally stores information objects back to persistent or temporary storages. This life-cycle model, introduced in Sect. 9.3.4, guides the software architects' and developers' declarations of how information access is implemented.

For the overall evaluation of the method's capabilities the methodical means provided by the approach appear complete to serve the method's purpose in fostering an efficient engineering process. The degree of fulfillment of this requirement is thus rated good, which is shown in the overview table by the $\oplus$ symbol.

Req. 7: Incorporate security aspects Handling security aspects may be valued with different relevance, depending on the purpose and situation of an organization. For those organizations that require a specifically high degree of security, either because they handle especially sensitive products, or they own a competitive position which makes them extraordinarily vulnerable towards security attacks, the method does not yet cover sufficient suggestions for incorporating security aspects.

Taking care for security could be realized on multiple levels in the method. At first, the EEM representation could incorporate aspects of security by introducing organizational security concepts, such as indisputability of user interaction, authenticity of electronic documents, or the two-eye principle in performing sensitive actions. In addition to realizing these organizational security issues with technical means on the implementation level, technical security properties, e. g., the use of encrypted data transmission, can be taken care of by corresponding security-aware implementation strategies.

An elaboration of how to extend the method for the development of security-aware EISs appears possible from the current state of maturity of the method, but is not included in the elaboration yet. Since its realization is unavailable, the degree of fulfillment of this requirement is considered insufficient and marked with the $\ominus$ symbol in the overview table.

Req. 8: Support the use of graphical user interfaces   The requirement for realizing front-end functionality that uses graphical user interfaces (GUIs) has been partially met by incorporating GUI conceptualizations in the method as described in Sect. 8.2.

The GUI sketches given in that section provide a rudimentary methodical basis for applying the method with an underlying user interface conceptualization. Further elaboration is not available, especially the creation of GUI functionality specific to single process-steps is not discussed during the method elaboration. The prototypical method application in the introductory example in Sect. 2, however, contains sketches for the implementation of a form-based GUI generator, which derives form entries from data type specifications associated to information resource elements in the conceptual models.

As an overall rating, the fulfillment of this requirement is rated on a medium level, which is indicated by the $\bigcirc$ symbol in the overview table.

Req. 9: Offer automatic processing capabilities   For supporting the development of automatic processing steps as part of implemented business processes some concepts are offered by the method. Among them are the notion of a process-step's life-cycle, which starts with fetching information, then performs its processing task, and in the end optionally stores information objects back to a temporary or a persistent storage. This general process life-cycle pattern, which is introduced in Sect. 9.3.4 allows to specify data-flows between different process-steps, and makes it possible to implement the conceptual notion of information objects in technical terms of data, which can be read and written from or to a persistent storage.

Other aspects of implementing automatic functionality in an EIS are not covered by the current version of the method. E. g., in a distributed environment, the design decision has to be made on which physical node automatic functionality is to be performed, i. e., which computer in a distributed network actually performs the automatic tasks. If the decision is to be taken between a local client executing functionality, and a central server component, the decision resembles a balance between a fat-client solution, where automatic processing is mostly rolled out to the client, and a thin-client solution, in which processing on the server side is preferred. The method offers no concept to explicate this design decision on an abstract level. This kind of localizing functionality in the distributed system is left to lower-level architectural decisions, e. g., using the `WebService` resource implementation strategy (see Sect. 9.3) to declare web-services running on specific nodes in the network, and invoking them from other nodes via a realization of the `WebServiceCall` process-step implementation strategy (see Sect. 9.1).

As an overall rating, the method only goes half the way of efficiently supporting the development of automatic functionality, which is why the corresponding requirement is evaluated with a medium degree of fulfillment, indicated by the ◯ symbol in the overview table.

Req. 10: Allow for integration of external software components The method proposes fundamental abstractions that prepare the use of implementation strategies for interfacing to external software components. Among these abstractions are the meta-class `AbstractSoftwareResourceImplementation` introduced in Sect. 9.3, which represents the notion of interpreting a conceptual resource specification as describing a deployed and accessible piece of software. As example implementation strategies, the meta-classes `ExternalApplication` and `WebService` (see Sect. 9.3.2) represent implementation strategies to access external application components. They are accompanied by the two process-step implementation strategies `WebServiceCall` and `ExternalApplicationAccess`, which serve to describe the invocation of external components of these kinds (see Sect. 9.1.3).

With the concepts introduced, the method provides an elaborated skeleton for describing an approach of how to implement access to external software components in the course of the engineering process. However, the available example strategies are too generic to give full insight into the potential of the approach. E. g., the `ExternalApplication` meta-class does not distinguish between different invocation methods for external applications. The notion of parameters is neither explicated by the meta-class `ExternalApplication`, nor is the notion of how to pass parameters specified with the `ExternalApplicationAccess` meta-class. These fine-grained acts of interpretation are left to the code generation templates. They may contain a list of referenced applications based on the application name, and decide how to pass parameters to the external component.

Since the overall abstract conceptualization of external software access is available, but the concepts are not further refined by the method, the degree of fulfillment of the requirement for integration of external software is evaluated to be on a medium degree. In the overview table, this is shown by the ◯ symbol.

Req. 11: Allow for integration of organization-specific functionality The requirement for allowing to integrate organization-specific software functionality into EIS is met by the engineering method's capabilities for architecture-specific enhancements. The mapping model language specification, which is presented in Sect. 6.2.2, offers a set of abstract classes that serve as explicit extension points for adding new specific implementation strategies. Organization-specific functionality can be explicated via implementation strategy meta-models and corresponding model instances, introduced in Sect. 6.2.3.

The method also comprises traditional solutions to incorporate special functionality by program code that gets developed using traditional programming skills. Examples for implementation strategies that offer this fallback solution are the process-step implementation strategy `CustomCode` (see Sect. 9.1.3), and the resource implementation strategy `CustomResource` (see Sect. 9.3.2).

The combination of implementation strategy meta-modeling, and emphasizing of extension points in the mapping meta-model, qualifies the approach to be evaluated as fully supporting the integration of organization-specific functionality. The requirement is thus marked in the overview table with a $\oplus$ symbol.

Req. 12: Handle the abstraction gap between enterprise models and implementation descriptions A central methodical means for performing the required bridging between abstract domain-specific enterprise model concepts on the one hand, and technically concrete constructs describing desired target output artifacts on the other hand, is offered by explicit language constructs in the mapping model language introduced in Sect. 6.2.2. A mapping model entry is a modeling construct, which allows to formally express how conceptual elements from the enterprise models are interpreted in technical terms. The use of such a construct as a central part of the development procedure allows for a controlled bridging between both levels of abstraction.

From an evaluation perspective, the dedicated concepts for reflecting design decisions taken to interpret the conceptual semantics of enterprise models provide an effective solution for methodically grounding a domain-specific development approach on conceptually modeled knowledge from a non-technical organizational business perspective. The good evaluation result for the fulfillment of this requirement is represented by a $\oplus$ symbol in the overview table.

Req. 13: Support performing the ontological turn from a bird's-eye-view perspective to an inner system perspective Dedicated means are offered by the method for turning the description perspective from an overall bird's-eye-view, which is the ontologic point of view taken in by enterprise models, to an inner description perspective of a technical system specified relative to an underlying technical architecture. This is achieved by introducing the notion of implementation strategies (see Sect. 6.2.2), which are conceptual means for representing technical components in models independent from the actual artifacts which realize the components. The notion of an implementation strategy allows to conceptually refer to implementation artifacts before they actually exist. Having this modeling construct at hand enables to formally express intended design decisions with respect to model elements in the conceptual enterprise models. This is the key idea which makes the ontological turn possible. Once a mapping model is completely set up with associations between enterprise model concepts and implementation strategies, subsequent steps of the development procedure can exclusively focus on realizing the included implementation strategies, without the need to know about the conceptual motivations behind the chosen strategies. This way, the mapping model structure becomes a methodical anker point, which is initially used to interlink different description perspectives by capturing design decisions, and then allows to neglect the conceptual origins, and perform a model-driven artifact generation procedure which is entirely operating in terms of implementation artifacts operating relative to a technical system architecture.

The method provides an elaborated approach for supporting the development process in performing the required ontological turn from conceptual modeling constructs to technical system descriptions. Dedicated methodical means for this are provided by notion of implementation strategies. The degree of fulfillment of this requirement is thus rated good, and displayed with a ⊕ symbol in the overview table.

Req. 14: Incorporate domain experts into the development process   The method demands that enterprise models are to be created and maintained in collaboration of multiple stakeholder groups, attended by a software architect who knows about necessary conventions that have to be considered during modeling. Besides demanding for inclusion of the software architect among the groups of stakeholders, the process of enterprise modeling by itself is not in focus of the method. Instead, it is assumed that enterprise models are existing as a starting point of the method, and that they can be edited, if this turns out to be required by the subsequent processing steps of the method.

The method provides a suitable framework for the inclusion of domain experts in the conceptual modeling work, however, it does not suggest any explicit methodical means that further foster expert integration beyond participation in enterprise modeling activities. Altogether, the degree of fulfillment of the requirement for incorporating domain experts is thus achieved on a medium level. This is shown in the overview table using the ◯ symbol.

Req. 15: Strengthen trust among stakeholders   Trust is established by an active participation of the domain stakeholders in the conceptual modeling process, and the use of the defined engineering method that bridges from the conceptual models to the software system. This way, the modeling activities of the domain's stakeholders actively shape the development process. This fosters mutual understanding, and increases efficiency when it comes to clarifying those aspects of knowledge explicated in models, which turn out to be not self-evident for all involved participants in the development process.

The described effects implicitly arise from the use of a methodical procedure in the suggested way. Besides this, the method does not introduce explicit means to additionally foster trust. The overall evaluation of the degree, with which this requirement is fulfilled, is thus rated on a medium level, indicated in the overview table by the ◯ symbol.

14   Remaining Work

The presented work has shown the conceptualization of a software engineering method, which spans the entire range from interpreting conceptual enterprise model semantics, through providing explicit means for capturing design decisions about how to technically realize enterprise information system (EIS) functionality, to incorporating a code-generation phase during which deployable artifacts are created. A number of methodical problems go together with the aim of supporting the complex bridging from domain-specific conceptual enterprise models to implemented software systems, which, to the extent evaluated in Sect. 13, have been solved by offering appropriate methodical means with prototypical tooling support.

As with any scientific work, a countless number of open research questions remain and can continue the considerations made in the present work. The suggested method primarily focuses on consulting business process models, resource models, and organization models, each as distinct perspectives on an organization. They are used for deriving formalized knowledge to support software engineering. Enterprise models, however, may contain a richer set of perspectives on organizations, e. g., they can cover strategic perspectives, which describe long term goals and high-level purposes of organizations, or they may model inter-organizational aspects, such as business relationships or physical transport routes to other organizations. It remains a topic of interest to investigate, to which extent these conceptual sources of information can fruitfully be utilized to foster software engineering activities in the field of EIS development.

Integrating the SEEM method as a concrete development procedure into a wider methodical framework with project management facilities could further be examined. This would mean to fill-in the abstract methodical perspectives and steps identified by a more general framework, with concrete methodical descriptions offered by the SEEM method. One possible framework for performing such an integration could be the Rational Unified Process (RUP) (see Sect. 5.3.2).

The requirement towards security in an EIS (see Req. 7) is not explicitly accounted for by the proposed method. Extending the methodical elements by aspects of security would open up a wide field of further research tasks, related to the question how conceptual demands for security can be expressed as part of domain-specific enterprise models, and how these concepts are appropriately mapped onto available security technology implementations. The abstract base concepts provided by the SEEM method, especially the notion of a mapping model which relates enterprise model concepts to according implementation strategies, provide an elegant mechanism to be extended for these purposes.

To increase the degree of interactive support offered by the method, it remains eligible to further elaborate the automatic validity checks suggested by the method (see Sect. 6.4) to an interactive procedure, supported by appropriate wizards to query relevant design decisions from software architects interactively. The creation of an initial mapping model would no longer rely on automatically derived defaults only, but an automatic mechanism could offer multiple variants for alternative implementation strategies to a software development expert, from which the most suitable can be chosen.

The mapping meta-model as presented in the method description (see Sect. 6.2.2) includes a number of example implementation strategies, which are assumed to be applicable on any target architecture platform. This is the reason why they have been included in the mapping model language for purposes of explaining the method. However, any concrete implementation strategy declaration should be separated from specifications of the core concepts of the mapping model. Instead, the example platform-independent implementation strategies given in the mapping meta-model should be specified in their own implementation strategy meta-model, which would include all platform-independent implementation strategy types suggested by the method. The core mapping meta-model would still provide abstract superclasses to interface to, but would be kept independent from any concrete implementation strategy declaration. Despite providing a cleaner conceptual distinction between core concepts of the mapping model language, and contingent example implementation strategies, this way of organizing model artifacts would allow for easier extension of the set of available platform-independent implementation strategies with project-specific additional strategies.

The method could be applied for creating self-reflective EISs (see Sect. 5.3.10), if non-standard target domain APIs were developed, which integrate EIS functionality and enterprise modeling environment (EME) features. The concrete EME to be integrated by the domain APIs should be the same EME as used for editing the enterprise models that serve as conceptual input to the engineering method and describe required EIS functionality. If such an integration could be achieved, a truly self-reflective EIS in the sense of [FS09] would be available. Since the proposed approach integrates EIS and EME at development time, it can be assumed that the method is suitable for the development of self-reflective EIS, once orthogonal research on the architecture of self-referential EIS has been carried out.

Appendices

When I was a very small boy
Very small boys talked to me
Now that we've grown up together
They're afraid of what they see

New Order, "True Faith" from the album "Substance", 1987

A   Example software artifacts

A.1   Source code packages of the provided examples

The software developed for exemplifying purposes as part of the SEEM method is available as open-source software, consisting of multiple source code project-folders to be imported into the workspace of a MEMOCENTERNG [GF10] environment. MEMOCENTERNG is a modeling platform, which is based on the ECLIPSE [Eclb] IDE, enhanced with both a set of pre-installed ECLIPSE features, such as the Eclipse Modeling Framework (EMF) and Graphical Modeling Framework (GMF), and with additional domain-specific modeling functionality specifically designed to provide model editors for the Multi-Perspective Enterprise Modeling (MEMO) [Fra12] family of modeling languages.

The SEEM source code projects can be downloaded from the SVN [Apaa] repository at `http://www.seem-method.info/svn/repo-seem`.

Further technical information about the installation and use of the source code projects is available in the README file `http://www.seem-method.info/svn/repo-seem/trunk/de.gulden.modeling.seem.workflow/readme.txt`.

Refer to `http://www.seem-method.info/` for any updates and further information about the provided online resources.

The project-folders in the SVN repository are briefly described in the following.

A.1.1   **Package** `de.gulden.modeling.seem.eem`

In this package, the meta-model of a the rudimentary EEM language is provided, which is used by the method as proposed interchange format for adapting different source enterprise modeling languages. The meta-model is formulated using the MML [Fra08]. Consequentially, the source code for corresponding tooling support to use the specified language, is to be generated by means of the MML editor generation functionality [GF10]. This is done by opening the file `eem.meta_diagram` after checking out the project, and invoking the "Generate Model Editor" function with the corresponding button in the menu panel.

A.1.2 Package `de.gulden.modeling.seem.generator`

This package assembles transformation declarations, scripts, and utility functions to support those parts of the SEEM method automatically, which are generic with respect to the used original enterprise modeling languages, and the chosen target generation architecture of a development project. This means, source packages of specifically configured development projects will most likely reference this project to invoke reusable generic components.

A.1.3 Package `de.gulden.modeling.seem.generator.memo`

Components specific to applying the SEEM method for use with the MEMO family of languages are assembled in this package.

A.1.4 Package `de.gulden.modeling.seem.generator.ui`

This package realizes a plug-in, which adds menu buttons to the GUI of the internally invoked second ECLIPSE instance. These buttons serve to invoke the adapter transformation, the enterprise model checking, the mapping model initialization and update transformation, also the corresponding model checking for the mapping model and associated implementation strategy models, and, finally, the code generation transformation. The GUI component may be helpful when developing transformation templates, and in development projects, which use manual development steps as parts of the overall projects. Manual development steps can benefit from easy manual invocation mechanisms for the transformation steps of the method. Essentially, the menu buttons provided in this package, invoke the respective `.mwe` scripts from package `de.gulden.modeling.seem.workflow`.

A.1.5 Package `de.gulden.modeling.seem.mapping`

The modeling language concepts of the mapping model, as introduced by the method, are formally defined by the meta-model in this package. As with the other EMF based modeling languages provided with the examples, the source code for the corresponding editor support is generated by invoking the EMF "Generate All" function on the provided `.genmodel` artifact.

A.1.6 Package `de.gulden.modeling.seem.workflow`

Transformation declarations, which are specific to the introductory example, and invocation scripts to run the automatic steps of the SEEM method, are included in this package. This also covers the code generation templates for outputting project-specific `.jsp` and `.jspf` source code files.

A.1.7 Package `de.gulden.modeling.seem.architecture.web`

This package contains the implementation strategy meta-model for a web-application target architecture. Since a JSP web-application is the chosen target architecture in the example project, this meta-model provides specific implementation strategies for describing the technical components of such an application. These concepts enhance the generic implementation strategies available with the mapping model. After checking out, the `.gen-model` file is to be opened and "Generate all" to be executed from the context menu of the model's root element. This generates all required EMF editor source code artifacts. These files will be written into the `src/` folder, and will provide the running implementation of a tree-style model editor for creating, displaying, and editing model instances conforming to the specified implementation strategy meta-model.

A.1.8 Package `de.gulden.server.xmldb`

This component realizes a simple, yet handy, XML database management system (DBMS). This provides additional runtime functionality, which will be invoked from the generated JSP code.

The following two packages contain artifacts from the comprehensive example in Sect. 10.

A.1.9 Package `org.rescueit.modeling.targetarchitecture`

Target architecture components of the comprehensive example are modeled on a type level by the implementation strategy meta-model included in this package. The meta-model provides abstractions over a distributed SOA, for which, in the example, executable code in the BPEL language is generated.

A.1.10 Package `org.rescueit.modeling.workflow`

Project-specific model transformation declarations, as well as the code generation templates to output BPEL code for the comprehensive example, are contained in this package. In its `example/` sub-folder, the domain-specific input example model in XML notation and EEM representation, the created mapping model, the implementation strategy model instance, and the resulting executable BPEL model with its accompanying WSDL interface declaration are included.

The project-folders listed next are intended to be checked-out into the workspace of a second MEMOCENTERNG instance, which is launched using "Run / Run As / Eclipse Application" from the menu. Inside the second instance, the modeling languages declared and implemented in the first instance are available with corresponding tooling support.

A.1.11 Package `de.gulden.modeling.seem.api.web`

An API, which offers runtime functionality for the generated JSP web-application code, is contained in this project-folder. This code has been development "manually" by directly specifying JAVA classes with corresponding methods.

A.1.12 Package `de.gulden.modeling.seem.example.webshop`

This project-folder contains the original enterprise models of the introductory example in the MEMO modeling languages, which serve as input to the applied method. During the transformation, the intermediary generated mapping model and implementation strategy model files will also be written into this folder.

A.1.13 Package `webshop`

This is the output folder for the created web application. Generated source code files will be written into the `WebContent/` sub-folder. After code generation, the project is to be deployed as a web application on a Tomcat [Apab] compatible web-application server.

A.2 Example artifacts overview

The upcoming subsections describe some of the example artifacts, which implement central concepts of the SEEM method, or are results of its application. To give an initial overview on the described components, the following list introduces each artifact briefly.

`memo2eem.ext`	Model-to-model transformation to convert a set of MEMO enterprise models to an EEM representation. See Appendix A.3.1.
`01-run-adaptEM.mwe`	Invocation script to run the `memo2eem.ext` transformation. See Appendix A.3.1.
`checkEM.chk`	Conditions to validate completeness and consistency of an EEM model. See Appendix A.3.1.

`checkEMConstraints.chk`	Generated additional conditions to validate completeness and consistency of an EEM model's relationships. See Appendix A.3.1.
`02-run-checkEM.mwe`	Invocation script to run `checkEM.chk`. See Appendix A.3.1.
`initMapping.ext`	Script to create an initial mapping model with default mapping entries See Appendix A.3.2.
`initMappingWeb.ext`	Script to create initial default mapping entries for a web application target application platform. See Appendix A.3.2.
`03-run-initMapping.mwe`	Invocation script to run the creation of initial default mapping entries. See Appendix A.3.2.
`03-run-updateMapping.mwe`	Script to update an existing mapping model and associated implementation strategy models. Earlier modifications are preserved. See Appendix A.3.2.
`checkMapping.chk`	Conditions to validate completeness and consistency of platform-independent entries in a mapping model. See Appendix A.3.2.
`checkMappingConstraints.chk`	Generated additional conditions to validate completeness and consistency of platform-independent entries in a mapping model. See Appendix A.3.2.
`04-run-checkMapping.mwe`	Invocation script to perform validity checks. See Appendix A.3.2.

`web/main.xpt`	Main code generation script for creating the web-application. See Appendix A.3.3.
`common.ext`	Extension functions shared by multiple components. See Appendix A.3.3.
`05-run-generator.mwe`	Invocation script to run `main.xpt`. See Appendix A.3.3.
`workflow.properties`	Global code generation configuration. See Appendix A.3.3.
`conventions.properties`	Conventions configuration for model transformations and code generation. See Appendix A.3.3.
`webshop.process`	The MEMO process model perspective model. See Appendix A.3.3.
`webshop.organisation`	The MEMO organization perspective model. See Appendix A.3.3.
`webshop.resml`	The MEMO resource perspective model. See Appendix A.3.3.
`webshop.eem`	A streamlined EEM representation of the MEMO input models for further processing. See Appendix A.3.3.
`webshop.mapping`	The mapping model used in the example project, generated by the mapping model initialization transformation. See Appendix A.3.3.
`index.jsp`	Generated main page of the web application. See Appendix A.3.4.

The following artifacts originate from the comprehensive example implementation (see Sect.10):

`scm-to-eem.xslt`	Model-to-model XSLT transformation of the comprehensive example to convert a supply chain modeler file to an EEM representation. See Appendix A.4.1.
`01-run-adaptEM.mwe`	Invocation script to run the `scm-to-eem.xslt` transformation together with the id conversion `make-ids.xslt`. See Appendix A.4.1.
`initMappingSOA.ext`	Script to create initial default mapping entries for a SOA target application platform. See Appendix A.4.2.
`03-run-initMapping.mwe`	Invocation script to run the creation of initial default mapping entries for the SOA target architecture. See Appendix A.4.2.
`04-run-checkMapping.mwe`	Invocation script to perform validity checks on a mapping model and a SOA implementation strategy model. See Appendix A.4.2.
`soa/main.xpt`	Main code generation script for BPEL code generation. See Appendix A.4.3.
`05-run-generator.mwe`	Invocation script to run `main.xpt` for BPEL code generation. See Appendix A.4.3.
`00-run-all.mwe`	Combined workflow script to invoke all individual transformation steps in one sequence. See Appendix A.4.3.
`workflow.properties`	Global code generation configuration. See Appendix A.4.3.

`conventions.properties`	Conventions configuration for model transformations and code generation. See Appendix A.4.3.
`GermanScenarioIceCream.xml`	XML data of the serialized supply chain example model. See Appendix A.4.4.
`SupplyChainProcess.bpel`	Generated executable BPEL workflow description as output of the applied model transformations. See Appendix A.4.4.
`SupplyChainProcessArtifacts.wsdl`	Generated WSDL interface declaration for the BPEL workflow model. See Appendix A.4.4.
`SupplyChainProcessSchema.xsd`	Manually edited XML schema declaration included in the generated WSDL file. See Appendix A.4.4.
`cardinalitiesToConstraints.xpt`	Code generation declaration to convert cardinality specifications from EMF meta-models to constraint expressions in the CHECK language. See Appendix A.4.4.
`run-cardinalitiesToConstraints.mwe`	Invocation script to run the higher-order `cardinalitiesToConstraints.xpt` transformation. See Appendix A.4.4.

These implementation artifacts are described in greater detail in the following sections.

A.3 Introductory example artifacts

To further demonstrate the use of the method, a selection of artifacts developed to apply the SEEM method as part of the introductory example, are now closer looked at. They are parts of the implementation of the introductory example given in Sect. 2. Source code artifacts are usually not printed in their entirety, which is indicated by a "..." mark below the last line printed. To get the source codes in full detail, refer to the artifacts as a whole from the above named SVN repository (see Appendix A.1).

A.3.1 Adaptation to the MEMO enterprise modeling languages

Model-to-model adapter transformation from MEMO enterprise models to an EEM model The `memo2eem.ext` script adapts model instances of the MEMO enterprise modeling language family to the method. The main entry function `transformation(OrganisationModel, ProcessModel, ResourceModel)` reads in a MEMO process model, as well as an interrelated MEMO organization model, and a MEMO resource model. The generated output of the horizontal model transformation is an enterprise model representation in the EEM modeling language, which will further be used in the course of the method.

The example model-to-model transformation is written in the XTEND language (see Sect. 12.5.3). It gets invoked either by running a "modeling workflow" script using EMF tooling operations (see Appendix A.3.1), or by choosing the corresponding GUI menu provided by the prototypical tooling implementation (see Sect. 12.3).

```
1   /* memo2eem.ext, model-to-model transformation from MEMO models to EEM
2      representation.
3      Written by Jens Gulden, jens.gulden@uni-due.de.
4      Licensed under a Creative Commons Attribution 3.0 Unported license. */
5
6   import ecore;
7   import notation;
8   import model;
9   import process;
10  import organisation;
11  import resml;
12  import eem;
13
14  extension common;
15
16  /*
17   * Transforms a set of a MEMO organization model, a MEMO control flow model, and a
18   * MEMO resource model to an Eem model representation.
19   *
20   * Throughout the transformation process, identity among model elements is judged on
21   * String values of name or label attributes.
22   */
23  create eem::EemModel transformation( organisation::OrganisationModel
        modelOrganisation, process::ProcessModel modelProcess, resml::ResourceModel
        modelResource ):
24      this.clear() ->
25      this.setName(modelProcess.name.clean()) ->
26      this.eMObjects.addAll( modelProcess.processes.viewReferences.view.diagram.name.
            clean().asTopLevelProcess() ) ->
27      this.eMObjects.addAll( modelOrganisation.unitsOfWork.asEemActor() ) ->
28      this.eMObjects.addAll( modelProcess.processes.asEemProcess() ) ->
29      this.eMObjects.addAll( modelProcess.events.asEemEvent() ) ->
30      this.eMObjects.addAll( modelProcess.synchronizers.asEemEvent() ) ->
31      this.eMObjects.addAll( modelProcess.sequences.asEemSequence2() ) ->
32      this.eMObjects.addAll( modelProcess.choices.asEemSequence2() ) ->
33      this.eMObjects.addAll( modelProcess.branches.asEemSequence2() ) ->
34      this.handleResources(modelResource) ->
35      this;
36
```

```
37  /*
38   * Gets the name of the diagram, in which a process element appears.
39   */
40  String view( process::AbstractProcess this ):
41      this.viewReferences.view.diagram.name;
42
43  /*
44   * Gets the name of the diagram, in which an event element appears.
45   */
46  String view( process::AbstractEvent this ):
47      this.viewReferences.view.diagram.name;
48
49  /*
50   * Gets the name of the diagram, in which a stop element appears.
```

...

de.gulden.modeling.seem.workflow/templates/memo2eem.ext: Model-to-model
transformation to convert a set of MEMO enterprise models to an EEM representation.

Workflow script to invoke the MEMO to EEM adapter transformation   The `01-`
`run-adaptEM.mwe` script invokes the model transformation engine to execute the
`memo2eem.ext` model transformation. As part of this "modeling workflow" script, the
MEMO process model, the MEMO organization model, and the MEMO resource model
are loaded into memory from their XML file representations, then the model transformation engine is spawned with these models as input parameters. After the transformation
has run, the generated in-memory representation of the EEM enterprise model is written
to an XML file, before the workflow script terminates.

The invocation script is written in the MWE language, which provides a rudimentary way
to specify linear sequences of transformation operations on models. The execution engine
for MWE is part of the EMF and associated plug-ins, which also provide corresponding
GUI menus from which a user manually can invoke the workflow script. An alternative
way to invoke the transformation is choosing the corresponding GUI menu provided by
the prototypical tooling implementation (see Sect. 12.3).

```
1   <!--
2       01-run-adaptEM.mwe, invocation script to run the adapter transformation.
3       Written by Jens Gulden, jens.gulden@uni-due.de.
4       Licensed under a Creative Commons Attribution 3.0 Unported license.
5   -->
6
7   <workflow>
8
9   <!-- Workflow script for running conceptual model adaptation. -->
10
11      <!-- Read configuration properties from file 'workflow.properties'. -->
12      <property file="./workflow.properties"/>
13
14      <!-- Derive other properties from loaded properties. -->
15      <property name="modelOrganisation" value="${projectRoot}/model/${projectPrefix}.
            organisation"/>
16      <property name="modelProcess" value="${projectRoot}/model/${projectPrefix}.
            process"/>
17      <property name="modelResource" value="${projectRoot}/model/${projectPrefix}.resml
            "/>
```

```
18      <property name="output" value="${projectRoot}/model/${projectPrefix}.eem"/>
19
20      <!-- Read MEMO organization model. -->
21      <component class="org.eclipse.xtend.typesystem.emf.XmiReader">
22          <modelFile value="${modelOrganisation}"/>
23          <outputSlot value="modelOrganisation"/>
24      </component>
25
26      <!-- Read MEMO process model. -->
27      <component class="org.eclipse.xtend.typesystem.emf.XmiReader">
28          <modelFile value="${modelProcess}"/>
29          <outputSlot value="modelProcess"/>
30      </component>
31
32      <!-- Read MEMO resource model. -->
33      <component class="org.eclipse.xtend.typesystem.emf.XmiReader">
34          <modelFile value="${modelResource}"/>
35          <outputSlot value="modelResource"/>
36      </component>
37
38      <!-- Run model transformation. -->
39      <component class="org.eclipse.xtend.XtendComponent">
40          <!--fileEncoding value="UTF-8"/-->
41          <metaModel class="org.eclipse.xtend.typesystem.emf.EmfMetaModel"><
                metaModelPackage value="org.eclipse.emf.ecore.EcorePackage"/></metaModel
                >
42          <metaModel class="org.eclipse.xtend.typesystem.emf.EmfMetaModel"><
                metaModelPackage value="org.eclipse.gmf.runtime.notation.NotationPackage
                "/></metaModel>
43          <metaModel class="org.eclipse.xtend.typesystem.emf.EmfMetaModel"><
                metaModelPackage value="org.memo.model.ModelPackage"/></metaModel>
44          <metaModel class="org.eclipse.xtend.typesystem.emf.EmfMetaModel"><
                metaModelPackage value="org.memo.orgml.organisation.OrganisationPackage
                "/></metaModel>
45          <metaModel class="org.eclipse.xtend.typesystem.emf.EmfMetaModel"><
                metaModelPackage value="org.memo.orgml.process.ProcessPackage"/></
                metaModel>
46          <metaModel class="org.eclipse.xtend.typesystem.emf.EmfMetaModel"><
                metaModelPackage value="org.memo.resml.ResmlPackage"/></metaModel>
47          <metaModel class="org.eclipse.xtend.typesystem.emf.EmfMetaModel"><
                metaModelPackage value="de.gulden.modeling.seem.eem.EemPackage"/></
                metaModel>
48          <!-- to include common.ext: -->
49          <metaModel class="org.eclipse.xtend.typesystem.emf.EmfMetaModel"><
                metaModelPackage value="de.gulden.modeling.seem.mapping.MappingPackage"/
                ></metaModel>
50          <invoke value="memo2eem::transformation(modelOrganisation, modelProcess,
                modelResource)"/>
```

. . .

de.gulden.modeling.seem.workflow/01-run-adaptEM.mwe: Invocation script to run the
`memo2eem.ext` transformation.

Validity constraints for an EEM model The `checkEM.chk` file contains validity
check constraints, which allow for checking aspects of formal semantic correctness of
an EEM model representation. The constraints are independent from the source enterprise modeling language, from which the EEM model instance has been generated. They
can thus be reused across multiple projects that use different enterprise modeling input
languages.

The script is written in the CHECK language, which uses the boolean expression syntax of the XTEND language to specify validity checking rules.

```
1   /* checkEM.chk, validity constraints for an EEM model.
2      Written by Jens Gulden, jens.gulden@uni-due.de.
3      Licensed under a Creative Commons Attribution 3.0 Unported license. */
4
5   import eem;
6
7   extension common;
8
9   /*
10   * Ensure, that all resource accesses have an access mode set.
11   */
12  context ResourceAccess
13      ERROR "Resource access mode must be specified.":
14      (this.mode != null) && (this.mode.size > 0);
15
16  /*
17   * Prevent inconsistencies between actor-to-process and actor-to-rescoureaccess
18   * associations.
19   */
20  context ResourceAccess
21      ERROR "When resources are accessed and performing actors are specified, at least
                one of these actors must also be specified as performing actor of the
                Process, which uses the ResourceAccess." :
22      this.performingActors.isEmpty || this.performingActors.exists(e|this.usingProcess
            .performedBy.contains(e));
23
24  /*
25   * Make sure all Sequences are part of a parent process.
26   */
27  context Sequence
28      ERROR "A sequence must belong to a process, the field inProcess must be set.":
29      (this.inProcess != null);
```

de.gulden.modeling.seem.generator/templates/checkEM.chk: Conditions to validate completeness and consistency of an EEM model.

Generated validity constraints for an EEM model, automatically derived from the cardinalities in the EEM meta-model. The constraints contained in the checkEM-Constraints.chk file are automatically derived from the cardinality specifications on relationships in the EEM meta-model (see Appendix A.4.4). These constraints enhance the validity checking rules provided in file checkEM.chk by those conditions implicitly stated with the meta-model.

```
1   /* Generated file, generator written by Jens Gulden, jens.gulden@uni-due.de.
2      Licensed under a Creative Commons Attribution 3.0 Unported license. */
3
4   import eem;
5
6   extension common;
7
8   //
9   // Tests for validity of cardinality constraints specified in the Ecore meta-model.
10  //
11
12  context Sequence
```

```
13      ERROR "From for " + this.name + " must be set." :
14      (this.from != null);
15  context Sequence
16      ERROR "To for " + this.name + " must be set." :
17      (this.to != null);
18  context ResourceAccess
19      ERROR "UsedResource for ResourceAccess must be set." :
20      (this.usedResource != null);
21  context ResourceAccess
22      ERROR "UsingProcess for ResourceAccess must be set." :
23      (this.usingProcess != null);
```

de.gulden.modeling.seem.generator/templates/checkEMConstraints.chk: Generated additional conditions to validate completeness and consistency of an EEM model's relationships.

Workflow script to invoke the constraint checking on an EEM model   To perform the constraint checking on an EEM model, the modeling workflow script run-checkEM.mwe configures the required meta-models, loads the EEM instance, and invokes the constraint checking engine with the checkEM.chk and checkEMConstraints.chk validity check scripts.

```
1   <!--
2   02-run-checkEM.mwe, invocation script to run the completeness check for an EEM
3   model.
4   Written by Jens Gulden, jens.gulden@uni-due.de.
5   Licensed under a Creative Commons Attribution 3.0 Unported license.
6   -->
7
8   <workflow>
9
10  <!-- Workflow script for running completeness checks. -->
11
12      <!-- Reads configuration properties from file 'workflow.properties'. -->
13      <property file="./workflow.properties"/>
14
15      <!-- Read enterprise model in eem representation. -->
16      <component class="org.eclipse.xtend.typesystem.emf.XmiReader">
17          <modelFile value="${projectRoot}/model/${projectPrefix}.eem"/>
18          <outputSlot value="model"/>
19      </component>
20
21      <!-- Run model checking. -->
22      <component class="org.eclipse.xtend.check.CheckComponent">
23          <metaModel class="org.eclipse.xtend.typesystem.emf.EmfMetaModel"><
                  metaModelPackage value="org.eclipse.emf.ecore.EcorePackage"/></metaModel
                  >
24          <metaModel class="org.eclipse.xtend.typesystem.emf.EmfMetaModel"><
                  metaModelPackage value="de.gulden.modeling.seem.mapping.MappingPackage"/
                  ></metaModel>
25          <metaModel class="org.eclipse.xtend.typesystem.emf.EmfMetaModel"><
                  metaModelPackage value="de.gulden.modeling.seem.eem.EemPackage"/></
                  metaModel>
26          <checkFile value="checkEMConstraints" />
27          <checkFile value="checkEM" />
28          <emfAllChildrenSlot value="model" />
29          <abortOnError value="true"/>
30      </component>
31
32  </workflow>
```

de.gulden.modeling.seem.workflow/02-run-checkEM.mwe: Invocation script to run `checkEM.chk`.

A.3.2 Mapping model handling

Model-to-model transformation to create an initial mapping model with default entries   The central model-to-model transformation of the method is implemented by the XTEND script `initMapping.ext` and accompanied, target architecture specific, enhancements to this script. It initializes or updates a mapping model by adding mapping entries for each relevant conceptual element in the enterprise model, and suggesting default implementation strategies where possible. The main entry functions for performing the initialization are `createMapping(EemModel)` to create a new mapping model and `updateMappingEntries(MappingModel)` to place default initialization values into that model where possible. `createMapping(EemModel)` takes an EEM model as input and generates a new mapping model. The existing model is then modified in-place by `updateMappingEntries(MappingModel)`.

The `initMapping.ext` script detects possible platform-independent default implementation strategies. Default settings for architecture-specific implementation strategies are detected by individual initialization transformations (see Appendix A.4.2).These target architecture specific mapping model initialization scripts are invoked together with `initMapping.ext` in the modeling workflow script `run-initMapping.mwe` (see below).

```
1   /* initMapping.ext, model-to-model transformation to create an initial mapping model
2      with generic entries.
3      Written by Jens Gulden, jens.gulden@uni-due.de.
4      Licensed under a Creative Commons Attribution 3.0 Unported license. */
5
6   import mapping;
7   import eem;
8
9   extension common;
10  extension org::eclipse::xtend::util::stdlib::globalvar;
11  extension org::eclipse::xtend::util::stdlib::properties;
12
13  /*
14   * Creates a new, blank mapping model. For every element in the eem model,
15   * that can be referenced via a mapping entry, a blank mapping entry with
16   * a null-reference to a yet unspecified implementation strategy is
17   * created.
18   */
19  create mapping::MappingModel createMapping( EemModel eem ):
20      let modelId = eem.name.without(" ").toLowerCase():
21      this.setName( eem.name.asId() ) ->
22      this.setModelURI( "http://"+modelId+"/1.0" ) ->
23      this.setBasePackage( modelId ) ->
24      this.setEemModel(eem) ->
25      this.clear() -> // clears internal caches
26      this;
27
28  /*
```

```
29    * Inserts mapping entries for each mapped conceptual model element into the mapping
30    * model.
31    */
32   MappingModel updateMappingEntries( MappingModel this ):
33       // create blank mapping entries for each actor, resource, process and process-
                elements that do not exist yet (equality judged on nameOfMapping -equals-
                nameOfEemObject )
34       this.actorMappings.addAll( this.eemModel.eMObjects.selectActors().select(e|this.
                actorMappings.forAll(ee|ee.name != e.name)).createActorMapping() ) ->
35       this.resourceMappings.addAll( this.eemModel.eMObjects.selectResources().select(e|
                this.resourceMappings.forAll(ee|ee.name != e.name)).createResourceMapping()
                ) ->
36       this.processMappings.addAll( this.eemModel.eMObjects.selectTopLevelProcesses().
                select(e|this.processMappings.forAll(ee|ee.name != e.name)).
                createProcessMapping() ) ->
37       this;
38
39   /*
40    * Interprets the enterprise model to find generic (platform independent,
41    * computation dependent) implementation strategies for entries in the
42    * mapping model.
43    * These strategies are added to the mapping model, if no
44    * strategy is already set (which might have been manually edited, too).
45    */
46   GenericArchitectureModel updateMapping( MappingModel this ):
47       // create blank mapping entries for each actor, resource, process and process-
                elements that do not exist yet (equality judged on nameOfMapping -equals-
                nameOfEemObject )
48       (this.genericArchitecture == null) ? (
49           this.setGenericArchitecture( new GenericArchitectureModel )
50       ) : (
```

...

de.gulden.modeling.seem.generator/templates/initMapping.ext: Script to create an initial
mapping model with default mapping entries

Model-to-model transformation to set default mapping model entries for a web application target architecture   The `initMappingWeb.ext` transformation suggests default architecture-specific implementation strategies for a web application architecture. The main transformation function, which gets invoked to perform the transformation, is `updateMapping(MappingModel)`. A function with this name should be used by convention for any newly created architecture adaptation, so it becomes possible to interface to all architecture-specific initializations using the same function.

```
1    /* initMappingWeb.ext, model-to-model transformation to set default mapping model
2       entries for a web application target architecture.
3       Written by Jens Gulden, jens.gulden@uni-due.de.
4       Licensed under a Creative Commons Attribution 3.0 Unported license. */
5
6    import ecore;
7    import mapping;
8    import eem;
9    import web;
10
11   extension common;
12   extension org::eclipse::xtend::util::stdlib::globalvar;
13   extension org::eclipse::xtend::util::stdlib::properties;
14
15   /*
```

```
16    * Interprets the enterprise model to find architecture-specific entries
17    * for a web application platform. Adds these entries to the mapping model.
18    *
19    * Throughout the transformation process, identity among model elements is
20    * judged on String values of name or label attributes.
21    */
22   WebArchitectureModel updateMapping( MappingModel this ):
23       this.targetArchitectures.typeSelect(WebArchitectureModel).has() ?
24           (this.targetArchitectures.typeSelect(WebArchitectureModel).update(this)
25           -> null) :
26           (let newArchModel = new WebArchitectureModel:
27           this.targetArchitectures.add(newArchModel.update(this)) ->
28           newArchModel
29           );
30
31   /*
32    * Updates web architecture specific mappings.
33    */
34   WebArchitectureModel update( WebArchitectureModel this, MappingModel mapping ):
35       this.setConfigurationFilename( projectPrefix() + ".properties" ) ->
36
37       // guess defaults for ProcessStep implementations
38       mapping.processMappings.processMemberMappings.select(e|e.implementations.isEmpty
           () && ((e.processMember.metaType != Process) || e.processMember.
           isTargetArchitectureWeb()) ).updateProcessMemberMapping(this) ->
39
40       // guess defaults for ProcessSequence implementations
41       mapping.processMappings.sequenceMappings.select(e|
42           e.actorResolverImplementations.select( e | ( e.eContainer.metaType ==
               WebArchitectureModel ) ).isEmpty()
43       ).updateSequenceMappingActorResolver(this) ->
44       mapping.processMappings.sequenceMappings.select(e|e.controlFlowImplementation==
           null).updateSequenceMappingControlFlowPass(this) ->
45       mapping.processMappings.sequenceMappings.select(e|e.conditionImplementation==null
           ).updateSequenceMappingCondition(this) ->
46
47       // guess defaults for Actor implementations
48       mapping.actorMappings.select(e|e.implementations.isEmpty()).updateActorMapping(
           this) ->
49
50       // guess defaults for Resource implementations
```

...

de.gulden.modeling.seem.workflow/templates/initMappingWeb.ext: Script to create
initial default mapping entries for a web application target application platform.

Workflow script to initialize the mapping model To integrate the `initMap-`
`ping.ext` and `initMappingWeb.ext` scripts to perform a complete mapping model
initialization together, the modeling workflow script `03a-run-initMapping.mwe` is
used.

`03a-run-initMapping.mwe` loads the EEM model representation into memory, and
subsequently invokes the main entries functions of `initMapping.ext` and `initMap-`
`pingWeb.ext`.

```
1   <!--
2     03-run-initMapping.mwe, invocation script to initialize the mapping model.
3     Written by Jens Gulden, jens.gulden@uni-due.de.
4     Licensed under a Creative Commons Attribution 3.0 Unported license.
```

```
5   -->
6
7   <workflow>
8
9       <!--
10          Workflow script for initializing a new mapping model from an
11          enterprise model representation.
12
13          The available target architectures are reflected here by invoking
14          architecture-specific initialization transformations.
15          In cases where multiple implementation options are available
16          for more than one target architecture, the order of invoking
17          the initialization transformation specifies the priority of
18          the target architecture to choose. (The transformation coming first
19          has a higher priority.)
20      -->
21
22      <!-- Reads configuration properties from file 'workflow.properties'. -->
23      <property file="./workflow.properties"/>
24
25      <!-- Makes property values available to Xtend's properties extension.
26          conventions.properties contains hints on how to interpret the
27          enterprise model semantics. -->
28      <component class="org.eclipse.xtend.util.stdlib.PropertiesReader">
29          <propertiesFile value="./workflow.properties"/>
30          <propertiesFile value="./conventions.properties"/>
31      </component>
32
33      <!-- Derive other properties from loaded properties. -->
34      <property name="eemModel" value="${projectRoot}/model/${projectPrefix}.eem"/>
35      <property name="outputMappingModel" value="${projectRoot}/model/${projectPrefix}.
            mapping"/>
36      <property name="outputArchitectureWebModel" value="${projectRoot}/model/${
            projectPrefix}.web"/>
37
38      <!-- Initialize issue reporter. -->
39      <component class="org.eclipse.xtend.util.stdlib.ExtIssueReporter"/>
40
41      <!-- Read enterprise model in eem representation. -->
42      <component class="org.eclipse.xtend.typesystem.emf.XmiReader">
43          <modelFile value="${eemModel}"/>
44          <outputSlot value="eemModel"/>
45      </component>
46
47      <!-- Create a new, blank mapping model. For every element in the eem model,
48          that can be referenced via a mapping entry, a blank mapping entry with
49          a null-reference to a yet unspecified implementation strategy is
```

...

de.gulden.modeling.seem.workflow/03-run-initMapping.mwe: Invocation script to run
the creation of initial default mapping entries.

Workflow script to update the mapping model When an existing mapping model is to
be updated instead of overall newly initialized, the `run-updateMapping.mwe` modeling workflow script is used. Like `run-initMapping.mwe`, it invokes the update
functions in the scripts `initMapping.ext` and `initMappingWeb.ext`, except that
the first initialization phase is skipped, in which a new mapping model is created. The
following steps are identical to the initialization transformation, including the creation of
mapping entries to elements which are not mapped yet, and selecting derived implementation strategies if none are available in a mapping entry yet.

```
1   <!--
2      03-run-updateMapping.mwe, invocation script to update the mapping model.
3      Written by Jens Gulden, jens.gulden@uni-due.de.
4      Licensed under a Creative Commons Attribution 3.0 Unported license.
5   -->
6
7   <workflow>
8
9       <!--
10          Workflow script for updating an existing mapping model.
11
12          The available target architectures are reflected here by invoking
13          architecture-specific initialization transformations.
14          In cases where multiple implementation options are available
15          for more than one target architecture, the order of invoking
16          the initialization transformation specifies the priority of
17          the target architecture to choose. (The transformation coming first
18          has a higher priority.)
19      -->
20
21      <!-- Reads configuration properties from file 'workflow.properties'. -->
22      <property file="./workflow.properties"/>
23
24      <!-- Makes property values available to Xtend's properties extension.
25          conventions.properties contains hints on how to interpret the
26          enterprise model semantics. -->
27      <component class="org.eclipse.xtend.util.stdlib.PropertiesReader">
28          <propertiesFile value="./workflow.properties"/>
29          <propertiesFile value="./conventions.properties"/>
30      </component>
31
32      <!-- Derive other properties from loaded properties. -->
33      <property name="eemModel" value="${projectRoot}/model/${projectPrefix}.eem"/>
34      <property name="outputMappingModel" value="${projectRoot}/model/${projectPrefix}.
            mapping"/>
35      <property name="outputArchitectureWebModel" value="${projectRoot}/model/${
            projectPrefix}.web"/>
36
37      <!-- Initialize issue reporter. -->
38      <component class="org.eclipse.xtend.util.stdlib.ExtIssueReporter"/>
39
40      <!-- Read enterprise model in eem representation. -->
41      <component class="org.eclipse.xtend.typesystem.emf.XmiReader">
42          <modelFile value="${eemModel}"/>
43          <outputSlot value="eemModel"/>
44      </component>
45
46      <!-- Read mapping model. -->
47      <component class="org.eclipse.xtend.typesystem.emf.XmiReader">
48          <modelFile value="${outputMappingModel}"/>
49          <outputSlot value="mappingModel"/>
50      </component>
```

...

de.gulden.modeling.seem.workflow/03-run-updateMapping.mwe: Script to update an existing mapping model and associated implementation strategy models. Earlier modifications are preserved.

Validity constraints for generic entries in the mapping model   The SEEM method intends a phase of manual revision of the mapping model and accompanied implementation strategy models after it has been initialized, because the automatic initialization does not necessarily find default values for every mapping entry, and if defaults are set, they may need manual revision to allow for choosing better implementation alternatives.

To retrieve a list of locations in the model which are yet incomplete or inconsistent, the `checkMapping.chk` CHECK script is run. Using this list, automatic methodical guidance through the process of revising the model can be provided to software architects and developers.

```
1   /* checkMapping.chk, validity constraints for generic entries in the mapping model.
2      Written by Jens Gulden, jens.gulden@uni-due.de.
3      Licensed under a Creative Commons Attribution 3.0 Unported license. */
4
5   import mapping;
6
7   extension common;
8
9   /*
10   * Make sure only information accesses can be sources to an information view process.
11   */
12  context InformationView
13      ERROR "InformationView can only have information access sources." :
14      this.resourceAccessTargets.isEmpty;
15
16  /*
17   * Force names of sequence mappings to canonical form 'sequence.from.name ->
18   * sequence.to.name'.
19   */
20  context SequenceMapping
21      ERROR "Sequence mapping must be named after the scheme 'sequence.from.name ->
                sequence.to.name'." :
22      this.name == this.sequence.mappingName();
23
24  /*
25   * Make sure control flow mode is 'Continue', when 'SameUser' is chosen as actor
26   * resolver.
27   */
28  context SequenceMapping
29      ERROR "The 'SameUser' actor resolver can only be combined with the 'Continue'
                control flow." :
30      this.actorResolverImplementations.typeSelect(SameUser).isEmpty || (this.
                controlFlowImplementation.metaType==Continuous);
31
32  /*
33   * Make sure XML accesses refer to XML resources.
34   */
35  context AbstractXMLAccess
36      ERROR "XML accesses can only refer to resources which are implemented using an
                XML type ('"+this.name+"')." :
37      resourceMapping.isEmpty() || (resourceMapping.implementations.typeSelect(
                AbstractInformationTypeImplementation).first().metaType ==
                XMLInformationType);
38
39  /*
40   * Make sure text accesses refer to text resources.
41   */
42  context TextAccess
43      ERROR "Text accesses can only refer to resources which are implemented using a
                text type ('"+this.name+"')." :
44      resourceMapping.isEmpty() || (resourceMapping.implementations.typeSelect(
                AbstractInformationTypeImplementation).first().metaType ==
                TextInformationType);
45
46  /*
```

```
47     * Make sure a send e-mail process is properly configured.
48     */
49   context SendEMail
50       ERROR "SendEMail must be provided with all required sender (From), recipient (To)
             , Subject and Text content information." :

     ...
```

de.gulden.modeling.seem.generator/templates/checkMapping.chk: Conditions to validate
completeness and consistency of platform-independent entries in a mapping model.

**Generated validity constraints for generic entries in the mapping model, de-
rived from the cardinalities in the mapping meta-model.** This script enhances the
`checkMapping.chk` CHECK script and validates, if required relationships on model elements are set. The constraints contained in the `checkMappingConstraints.chk`
file are automatically derived from the cardinality specifications on relationships in the
mapping model meta-model (see Appendix A.4.4).

```
1    /* Generated file, generator written by Jens Gulden, jens.gulden@uni-due.de.
2       Licensed under a Creative Commons Attribution 3.0 Unported license. */
3
4    import mapping;
5
6    extension common;
7
8    //
9    // Tests for validity of cardinality constraints specified in the Ecore meta-model.
10   //
11
12   context MappingModel
13       ERROR "TargetArchitectures for " + this.name + " must contain at least one
               element." :
14       (! this.targetArchitectures.isEmpty);
15   context MappingModel
16       ERROR "GenericArchitecture for " + this.name + " must be set." :
17       (this.genericArchitecture != null);
18   context MappingModel
19       ERROR "EemModel for " + this.name + " must be set." :
20       (this.eemModel != null);
21   context ProcessMapping
22       ERROR "Process for " + this.name + " must be set." :
23       (this.process != null);
24   context ManualExternalApplicationAccess
25       ERROR "ExternalApplication for " + this.name + " must be set." :
26       (this.externalApplication != null);
27   context EventResourceCRUD
28       ERROR "Resource for " + this.name + " must be set." :
29       (this.resource != null);
30   context EventResourceCRUD
31       ERROR "Modes for " + this.name + " must contain at least one element." :
32       (! this.modes.isEmpty);
33   context ResourceMapping
34       ERROR "Resource for " + this.name + " must be set." :
35       (this.resource != null);
36   context ResourceMapping
37       ERROR "Implementations for " + this.name + " must contain at least one element."
               :
38       (! this.implementations.isEmpty);
39   context ActorMapping
40       ERROR "Actor for " + this.name + " must be set." :
```

276

```
41      (this.actor != null);
42  context ActorMapping
43      ERROR "Implementations for " + this.name + " must contain at least one element."
            :
44      (! this.implementations.isEmpty);
45  context AbstractInformationStorageImplementation
46      ERROR "Type for " + this.name + " must be set." :
47      (this.type != null);
48  context AbstractComposedConditionImplementation
49      ERROR "Subconditions for " + this.name + " must contain at least 2 elements." :
```

...

de.gulden.modeling.seem.generator/templates/checkMappingConstraints.chk: Generated additional conditions to validate completeness and consistency of platform-independent entries in a mapping model.

Workflow script to invoke the validity checks for a mapping model 04-run-checkMapping.mwe is the modeling workflow script to invoke the previously introduced set of model validity check scripts, checking the mapping model and the associated implementation strategy models.

The script initially loads the mapping model with all references into memory, the subsequently invokes the model checking engine using the checkMapping.chk and checkMappingWeb.chk scripts, and the corresponding auto-generated checkMappingConstraints.chk and checkMappingWebConstraints.chk scripts.

```
1   <!--
2     04-run-checkMapping.mwe, invocation script to run the completeness check for a
3     mapping model.
4     Written by Jens Gulden, jens.gulden@uni-due.de.
5     Licensed under a Creative Commons Attribution 3.0 Unported license.
6   -->
7
8   <workflow>
9
10  <!-- Workflow script for running a completeness check on the mapping model. -->
11
12      <!-- Reads configuration properties from file 'workflow.properties'. -->
13      <property file="./workflow.properties"/>
14
15      <!-- Derive other properties from loaded properties. -->
16      <property name="model" value="${projectRoot}/model/${projectPrefix}.mapping"/>
17
18      <!-- Read mapping model (together with referenced models). -->
19      <component class="org.eclipse.xtend.typesystem.emf.XmiReader">
20          <modelFile value="${model}"/>
21          <outputSlot value="model"/>
22      </component>
23
24      <!-- Run model checking. -->
25      <component class="org.eclipse.xtend.check.CheckComponent">
26          <metaModel class="org.eclipse.xtend.typesystem.emf.EmfMetaModel"><
                  metaModelPackage value="org.eclipse.emf.ecore.EcorePackage"/></metaModel
                  >
27          <metaModel class="org.eclipse.xtend.typesystem.emf.EmfMetaModel"><
                  metaModelPackage value="de.gulden.modeling.seem.mapping.MappingPackage"/
                  ></metaModel>
```

```
28        <metaModel class="org.eclipse.xtend.typesystem.emf.EmfMetaModel"><
              metaModelPackage value="de.gulden.modeling.seem.eem.EemPackage"/></
              metaModel>
29        <metaModel class="org.eclipse.xtend.typesystem.emf.EmfMetaModel"><
              metaModelPackage value="de.gulden.modeling.seem.architecture.web.
              webPackage"/></metaModel>
30        <checkFile value="checkMappingConstraints" />
31        <checkFile value="checkMapping" />
32        <checkFile value="checkMappingWebConstraints" />
33        <checkFile value="checkMappingWeb" />
34        <emfAllChildrenSlot value="model" />
35        <abortOnError value="true"/>
36     </component>
37
38  </workflow>
```

de.gulden.modeling.seem.workflow/04-run-checkMapping.mwe: Invocation script to
perform validity checks.

A.3.3 Code generation

**Model-to-text transformation template to create executable source code for public
functionality of the web-application**   Code generation for publicly accessible parts of
the JSP web application is performed by this example model-to-text generation template,
which generates the main index.jsp page.

```
1   «REM»
2     main.xpt, code generation templates for generating JSP code
3     for a web application target architecture.
4     Written by Jens Gulden, jens.gulden@uni-due.de.
5     Licensed under a Creative Commons Attribution 3.0 Unported license.
6   «ENDREM»
7
8   «IMPORT mapping»
9   «IMPORT eem»
10  «IMPORT web»
11  «IMPORT process»
12
13  «EXTENSION org::eclipse::xtend::util::stdlib::globalvar»
14  «EXTENSION org::eclipse::xtend::util::stdlib::properties»
15  «EXTENSION common»
16
17  «REM»
18  *
19  * Generate a common file header.
20  *
21  «ENDREM»
22  «DEFINE header FOR Object-»
23  <!--
24    Generated file, generator written by Jens Gulden, jens.gulden@uni-due.de.
25    Licensed under a Creative Commons Attribution 3.0 Unported license.
26  -->
27
28  «ENDDEFINE»
29
30  «REM»
31  *
32  * Generate imports.
33  *
34  «ENDREM»
```

278

```
35   «DEFINE imports FOR Object-»
36   <%@page import="java.util.*" %>
37   <%@page import="java.util.Date" %>
38   <%@page import="java.io.*" %>
39   <%@page import="java.sql.*"%>
40   <%@page import="org.w3c.dom.*" %>
41   <%@page import="de.gulden.server.xmldb.*" %>
42   <%@page import="de.gulden.modeling.seem.api.web.*" %>
43   <%@page import="de.gulden.modeling.seem.api.web.jsp.BufferWriter" %>
44   «ENDDEFINE»
45
46   «REM»
47   *
48   * Main generation entry point.
49   * Generate index.jsp and included process implementations.
50   *
```
...

de.gulden.modeling.seem.workflow/templates/web/main.xpt: Main code generation script for creating the web-application.

Shared extension functions for model transformations and code generation The `common.ext` script specifies global functions in the XTEND language, which are used as utilities by other scripts. No function in `common.ext` is invoked as entry function from a modeling workflow script, `common.ext` is exclusively referenced as a library by other XTEND scripts.

```
1    /* common.ext, shared extension functions for model transformations and code
          generation.
2       Written by Jens Gulden, jens.gulden@uni-due.de.
3       Licensed under a Creative Commons Attribution 3.0 Unported license. */
4
5    import ecore;
6    import mapping;
7    import eem;
8
9    extension org::eclipse::xtend::util::stdlib::properties;
10   extension org::eclipse::xtend::util::stdlib::issues;
11
12   /*
13    * Gets the project prefix from external settings.
14    */
15   String projectPrefix(): GLOBALVAR projectPrefix;
16
17   /*
18    * Gets the input folder containing source models.
19    */
20   String inputPath(): GLOBALVAR inputPath;
21
22   /*
23    * Gets the output file for generation.
24    */
25   String outputFile(): GLOBALVAR outputFile;
26
27   /*
28    * Gets the output file base name for generation, suffix to be appended.
29    */
30   String outputName(): GLOBALVAR outputName;
31
32   /*
```

```
33      * Gets the output path for generation.
34      */
35   String outputPath(): GLOBALVAR outputPath;
36
37      /*
38      * Gets the temporary directory.
39      */
40   String tmpRoot(): GLOBALVAR tmpRoot;
41
42      /*
43      * True, if debug mode is active.
44      */
45   boolean isDebug():
46          (getProperty("debug") == "true");
47
48      /*
49      * Interprets ProcessSteps to find out the desired target architecture.
50      */
```

...

de.gulden.modeling.seem.generator/templates/common.ext: Extension functions shared by multiple components.

Workflow script to invoke code generation The `05-run-generator.mwe` modeling workflow script wraps around the `main.xpt` template to make it runnable from the tooling environment.

`run-generator.mwe` loads the mapping model with all references into memory, and invokes the code generation engine with the `generator` entry template in `main.xpt`.

```
1    <!--
2       05-run-generator.mwe, invocation script to run the code generation transformation.
3       Written by Jens Gulden, jens.gulden@uni-due.de.
4       Licensed under a Creative Commons Attribution 3.0 Unported license.
5    -->
6
7    <workflow>
8
9    <!-- Workflow script for running code-generation. -->
10
11      <!-- Reads configuration properties from file 'workflow.properties'. -->
12      <property file="./workflow.properties"/>
13
14      <!-- Initialize issue reporter. -->
15      <component class="org.eclipse.xtend.util.stdlib.ExtIssueReporter"/>
16
17      <!-- Makes property values available to Xtend's properties extension.
18           conventions.properties contains hints on how to interpret the
19           enterprise model semantics. -->
20      <component class="org.eclipse.xtend.util.stdlib.PropertiesReader">
21          <propertiesFile value="./workflow.properties"/>
22          <propertiesFile value="./conventions.properties"/>
23      </component>
24
25      <!-- Derive other properties from loaded properties. -->
26      <property name="inputFolder" value="${projectRoot}/model"/>
27      <property name="model" value="${inputFolder}/webshop.mapping"/>
28      <property name="outputFolder" value="${projectTarget}/WebContent"/>
29
30      <!-- Read mapping model (together with referenced models). -->
```

```
31      <component class="org.eclipse.xtend.typesystem.emf.XmiReader">
32          <modelFile value="${model}"/>
33          <outputSlot value="model"/>
34      </component>
35
36      <!-- Run code generation. -->
37      <component class="org.eclipse.xpand2.Generator">
38          <fileEncoding value="ISO-8859-1"/>
39          <metaModel class="org.eclipse.xtend.typesystem.emf.EmfMetaModel"><
                metaModelPackage value="org.eclipse.emf.ecore.EcorePackage"/></metaModel
                >
40          <metaModel class="org.eclipse.xtend.typesystem.emf.EmfMetaModel"><
                metaModelPackage value="de.gulden.modeling.seem.eem.EemPackage"/></
                metaModel>
41          <metaModel class="org.eclipse.xtend.typesystem.emf.EmfMetaModel"><
                metaModelPackage value="de.gulden.modeling.seem.mapping.MappingPackage"/
                ></metaModel>
42          <metaModel class="org.eclipse.xtend.typesystem.emf.EmfMetaModel"><
                metaModelPackage value="de.gulden.modeling.seem.architecture.web.
                webPackage"/></metaModel>
43          <outlet path="${outputFolder}"/>
44          <expand value="web::main::generator FOR model"/>
45          <globalVarDef name="projectPrefix" value="'${projectPrefix}'"/>
46          <globalVarDef name="inputPath" value="'${inputFolder}'"/>
47          <globalVarDef name="outputPath" value="'${outputFolder}'"/>
48          <globalVarDef name="tmpRoot" value="'${tmpRoot}'"/>
49      </component>
```

...

de.gulden.modeling.seem.workflow/05-run-generator.mwe: Invocation script to run
`main.xpt`.

Global configuration file for the code generation process In `work-flow.properties`, global settings are specified to configure the code generation process. These settings include the path to the project root directory `projectRoot`, where the model files used throughout the method are stored, and the prefix of filenames used for storing the models, `projectPrefix`.

```
1   # workflow.properties, global configuration for the code generation process.
2   # Written by Jens Gulden, jens.gulden@uni-due.de.
3   # Licensed under a Creative Commons Attribution 3.0 Unported license.
4
5   # -- projectRoot
6   # Specifies the source project root folder where source models and generated models
7   # are located.
8   projectRoot=/home/user/runtime-mml/de.gulden.modeling.seem.example.webshop
9
10  # -- projectTarget
11  # Specifies the target project root folder where generated source code and other
12  # artifacts are written to.
13  projectTarget=/home/user/runtime-mml/webshop
14
15  # -- databaseRoot
16  # Specifies the XML database root directory where generated XML data and schema files
17  # are written to.
18  databaseRoot=/home/user/runtime-mml/webshop/xmldb
19
20  # -- projectPrefix
21  # Specifies a short name for the project, that can be used as name prefix in several
22  # cases.
```

```
23  projectPrefix=webshop
24
25  # -- tmpRoot
26  # Specifies a temporary directory.
27  tmpRoot=/tmp
28
29  # -- debug
30  # Sets the debug mode.
31  debug=true
```

de.gulden.modeling.seem.workflow/templates/workflow.properties: Global code generation configuration.

Conventions configuration for model transformations and code generation To store external configuration options for conventions about hints that are used in model transformations and code generation steps throughout the method, the file `conventions.properties` is used. It declares, e. g., string fragments of identifier names, which are used to detected element types, or which are to match tagged values that are queried throughout transformations.

```
1   # conventions.properties, conventions configuration for model transformations
2   # and code generation.
3   # Written by Jens Gulden, jens.gulden@uni-due.de.
4   # Licensed under a Creative Commons Attribution 3.0 Unported license.
5
6   # Hint to detect superuser role for actors.
7   HINT_ACTOR_ADMINISTRATOR = Administrator, Admin, Root
8
9   # Hint to detect anonymous role for actors.
10  HINT_ACTOR_ANONYMOUS = Anonymous, Public, Customer
11
12  # Hint to detect automatic e-mail sending processes.
13  HINT_PROCESS_EMAIL = E-mail
14
15  # Hint to detect account administration processes.
16  HINT_PROCESS_ADMIN_ACCOUNTS = Administrate accounts, Accounts administrieren
17
18  # Hint to detect account configuration by user processes.
19  HINT_PROCESS_EDIT_MY_ACCOUNT = Edit my account, Mein Konto
20
21  # Hint to detect visit website processes.
22  HINT_PROCESS_WEBSITE = Website
23
24  # Hint to detect selection processes.
25  HINT_PROCESS_SELECT = Select, Auswahl
26
27  # Hint to detect multi-instance mode on resource access.
28  HINT_RESOURCE_INFORMATION_MULTI = List, Catalog, Set, Liste, Katalog, Menge
29
30  # Hint to detect message resources.
31  HINT_RESOURCE_INFORMATION_TEXT = Text, Message, E-Mail, Nachricht
32
33  # Hint to detect structured data resources.
34  HINT_RESOURCE_INFORMATION_XML = XML
35
36  # Hint to detect document resources.
37  HINT_RESOURCE_DOCUMENT = Document, Dokument
38
39  # Hint to detect software resources.
40  HINT_RESOURCE_SOFTWARE = Software, Service, Web-Service, Application, Applikation
```

```
41
42   # Hint to detect software service resources.
43   HINT_RESOURCE_SOFTWARE_SERVICE = Service
44
45   # Hint to detect custom software resources.
46   HINT_RESOURCE_SOFTWARE_CUSTOM = Custom
47
48   # Hint to detect ok options.
49   HINT_OK = Ok, Accept, Valid, Yes

     ...
```

de.gulden.modeling.seem.workflow/templates/conventions.properties: Conventions configuration for model transformations and code generation.

MEMO process model perspective   As one part of the MEMO input models to the method, the business process model perspective is stored in the `webshop.process` file. This file holds an XML Metadata Interchange (XMI) model conforming to the MEMO language specification. It contains references to elements in other MEMO perspective models.

```
1   <?xml version="1.0" encoding="UTF-8"?>
2   <Process:ProcessModel xmi:version="2.0" xmlns:xmi="http://www.omg.org/XMI"
        xmlns:Process="orgml.memo.org/process" xmlns:model="orgml.memo.org/model"
        xmlns:notation="http://www.eclipse.org/gmf/runtime/1.0.2/notation"
        xmlns:organisation="orgml.memo.org/organisation" xmlns:resmlAllocation="resml.
        memo.org/allocation" xmi:id="_uDRN4TcDEeCX95JTy-Rt3A" name="Webshop Process
        Model">
3     <processes xmi:type="Process:ProcessBody" xmi:id="_5TEuMDcDEeCX95JTy-Rt3A" name="
        Select products&#xA;from catalog" orgUnit="Customer" baseQualifier="Partly
        Automated">
4       <viewReferences xmi:type="model:ViewReference" xmi:id="_5V9DEDcDEeCX95JTy-Rt3A"
          key="Process Control Flow">
5         <view xmi:type="notation:Diagram" href="webshop.cflow_diagram#
            _uGp5EDcDEeCX95JTy-Rt3A"/>
6       </viewReferences>
7       <responsibleUnit xmi:type="organisation:Role" href="webshop.organisation#
          _AQZcEDp6EeCZc8qoBsE3Uw"/>
8       <resourceAllocations xmi:type="resmlAllocation:ResourceAllocation" href="webshop.
          resml#_FgqxEDj0EeCP_MqEXhOUJw"/>
9       <resourceAllocations xmi:type="resmlAllocation:ResourceAllocation" href="webshop.
          resml#_3abZsDj0EeCP_MqEXhOUJw"/>
10    </processes>
11    <processes xmi:type="Process:ProcessBody" xmi:id="_Lvls0DcEEeCX95JTy-Rt3A" name="
        Fill-in order form&#xA;or cancel" orgUnit="Customer" baseQualifier="Partly
        Automated">
12      <viewReferences xmi:type="model:ViewReference" xmi:id="_LwcocDcEEeCX95JTy-Rt3A"
          key="Process Control Flow">
13        <view xmi:type="notation:Diagram" href="webshop.cflow_diagram#
            _uGp5EDcDEeCX95JTy-Rt3A"/>
14      </viewReferences>
15      <responsibleUnit xmi:type="organisation:Role" href="webshop.organisation#
          _AQZcEDp6EeCZc8qoBsE3Uw"/>
16      <alternativeSplit xmi:type="Process:AlternativeSplit" xmi:id="_qztsMDcEEeCX95JTy-
          Rt3A" processName="Fill-in order form&#xA;or cancel"/>
17      <resourceAllocations xmi:type="resmlAllocation:ResourceAllocation" href="webshop.
          resml#_IaEAEDj0EeCP_MqEXhOUJw"/>
18      <resourceAllocations xmi:type="resmlAllocation:ResourceAllocation" href="webshop.
          resml#_4yFJIDj0EeCP_MqEXhOUJw"/>
19    </processes>
```

```
20    <processes xmi:type="Process:ProcessBody" xmi:id="_IUxdMDhAEeCRoIVBgr3r6Q" name="
          Read confirmation" orgUnit="Customer" baseQualifier="Partly Automated">
21      <viewReferences xmi:type="model:ViewReference" xmi:id="_IVDKADhAEeCRoIVBgr3r6Q"
            key="Process Control Flow">
22        <view xmi:type="notation:Diagram" href="webshop.cflow_diagram#
              _uGp5EDcDEeCX95JTy-Rt3A"/>
23      </viewReferences>
24      <responsibleUnit xmi:type="organisation:Role" href="webshop.organisation#
            _AQZcEDp6EeCZc8qoBsE3Uw"/>
25      <resourceAllocations xmi:type="resmlAllocation:ResourceAllocation" href="webshop.
            resml#_UuZLoDhIEeCRoIVBgr3r6Q"/>
26      <resourceAllocations xmi:type="resmlAllocation:ResourceAllocation" href="webshop.
            resml#_fsD6wDlTEeCGA8CAiWoPnA"/>
27    </processes>
28    <processes xmi:type="Process:ProcessBody" xmi:id="_UxXZYDhDEeCRoIVBgr3r6Q" name="
          Validate order" orgUnit="ShippingEmployee" baseQualifier="Partly Automated">
29      <viewReferences xmi:type="model:ViewReference" xmi:id="_Uxn4EDhDEeCRoIVBgr3r6Q"
            key="Process Control Flow">
30        <view xmi:type="notation:Diagram" href="webshop.cflow_diagram#
              _uGp5EDcDEeCX95JTy-Rt3A"/>
31      </viewReferences>
32      <responsibleUnit xmi:type="organisation:Position" href="webshop.organisation#
            _I707IDp6EeCZc8qoBsE3Uw"/>
33      <alternativeSplit xmi:type="Process:AlternativeSplit" xmi:id="
            _Op7wwDj2EeCP_MqEXhOUJw" processName="Validate order"/>
34      <resourceAllocations xmi:type="resmlAllocation:ResourceAllocation" href="webshop.
            resml#_5tdhYDj2EeCP_MqEXhOUJw"/>
35      <resourceAllocations xmi:type="resmlAllocation:ResourceAllocation" href="webshop.
            resml#_e17W4Dj5EeCP_MqEXhOUJw"/>
36    </processes>
37    <processes xmi:type="Process:ProcessBody" xmi:id="_osWhIDhDEeCRoIVBgr3r6Q" name="
          Pick goods from storage" orgUnit="ShippingEmployee" baseQualifier="Manual">
38      <viewReferences xmi:type="model:ViewReference" xmi:id="_os0bMDhDEeCRoIVBgr3r6Q"
            key="Process Control Flow">
39        <view xmi:type="notation:Diagram" href="webshop.cflow_diagram#
              _uGp5EDcDEeCX95JTy-Rt3A"/>
40      </viewReferences>
41      <responsibleUnit xmi:type="organisation:Position" href="webshop.organisation#
            _I707IDp6EeCZc8qoBsE3Uw"/>
42    </processes>
43    <processes xmi:type="Process:ProcessBody" xmi:id="_iWf84DhEEeCRoIVBgr3r6Q" name="
          Package goods and send" orgUnit="ShippingEmployee" baseQualifier="Manual">
44      <viewReferences xmi:type="model:ViewReference" xmi:id="_iW1UEDhEEeCRoIVBgr3r6Q"
            key="Process Control Flow">
45        <view xmi:type="notation:Diagram" href="webshop.cflow_diagram#
              _uGp5EDcDEeCX95JTy-Rt3A"/>
46      </viewReferences>
47      <responsibleUnit xmi:type="organisation:Position" href="webshop.organisation#
            _I707IDp6EeCZc8qoBsE3Uw"/>
48    </processes>
49    <processes xmi:type="Process:ProcessBody" xmi:id="_WSmyUDj2EeCP_MqEXhOUJw" name="
          Send cancellation e-mail" orgUnit="" description="From: #CONFIG_EMAIL_SENDER
          #&#xA;To: #customer-email#" baseQualifier="Automated">
50      <viewReferences xmi:type="model:ViewReference" xmi:id="_WTCQIDj2EeCP_MqEXhOUJw"
            key="Process Control Flow">
```

...

de.gulden.modeling.seem.example.webshop/model/webshop.process: The MEMO
process model perspective model.

MEMO organization perspective   The MEMO organization perspective among the input enterprise models is provided by the file webshop.organisation. The model elements are cross-referenced from the webshop.process model.

```xml
1  <?xml version="1.0" encoding="UTF-8"?>
2  <organisation:OrganisationModel xmi:version="2.0" xmlns:xmi="http://www.omg.org/XMI"
       xmlns:organisation="orgml.memo.org/organisation" xmi:id="_-I3u4Dp5EeCZc8qoBsE3Uw
       ">
3    <unitsOfWork xmi:type="organisation:Role" xmi:id="_AQZcEDp6EeCZc8qoBsE3Uw" name="
       Customer"/>
4    <unitsOfWork xmi:type="organisation:AggregatedUnit" xmi:id="_BNDRkDp6EeCZc8qoBsE3Uw
       " name="Management"/>
5    <unitsOfWork xmi:type="organisation:Group" xmi:id="_C3jrkDp6EeCZc8qoBsE3Uw" name="
       ProductionDepartment"/>
6    <unitsOfWork xmi:type="organisation:Group" xmi:id="_EFYJkDp6EeCZc8qoBsE3Uw" name="
       MarketingDepartment"/>
7    <unitsOfWork xmi:type="organisation:Group" xmi:id="_FLHpoDp6EeCZc8qoBsE3Uw" name="
       ShippingDepartment"/>
8    <unitsOfWork xmi:type="organisation:Position" xmi:id="_GbnBIDp6EeCZc8qoBsE3Uw" name
       ="ProductionEmployee"/>
9    <unitsOfWork xmi:type="organisation:Position" xmi:id="_HjGNoDp6EeCZc8qoBsE3Uw" name
       ="MarketingEmployee"/>
10   <unitsOfWork xmi:type="organisation:Position" xmi:id="_I707IDp6EeCZc8qoBsE3Uw" name
       ="ShippingEmployee"/>
11   <links xmi:type="organisation:SuperiorLink" xmi:id="_Ni0UYDp6EeCZc8qoBsE3Uw" target
       ="_C3jrkDp6EeCZc8qoBsE3Uw" source="_GbnBIDp6EeCZc8qoBsE3Uw"/>
12   <links xmi:type="organisation:SuperiorLink" xmi:id="_OAzQ4Dp6EeCZc8qoBsE3Uw" target
       ="_EFYJkDp6EeCZc8qoBsE3Uw" source="_HjGNoDp6EeCZc8qoBsE3Uw"/>
13   <links xmi:type="organisation:SuperiorLink" xmi:id="_OYYDYDp6EeCZc8qoBsE3Uw" target
       ="_FLHpoDp6EeCZc8qoBsE3Uw" source="_I707IDp6EeCZc8qoBsE3Uw"/>
14   <links xmi:type="organisation:SuperiorLink" xmi:id="_Oxnp0Dp6EeCZc8qoBsE3Uw" target
       ="_BNDRkDp6EeCZc8qoBsE3Uw" source="_C3jrkDp6EeCZc8qoBsE3Uw"/>
15   <links xmi:type="organisation:SuperiorLink" xmi:id="_PQEgYDp6EeCZc8qoBsE3Uw" target
       ="_BNDRkDp6EeCZc8qoBsE3Uw" source="_EFYJkDp6EeCZc8qoBsE3Uw"/>
16   <links xmi:type="organisation:SuperiorLink" xmi:id="_Pn4jcDp6EeCZc8qoBsE3Uw" target
       ="_BNDRkDp6EeCZc8qoBsE3Uw" source="_FLHpoDp6EeCZc8qoBsE3Uw"/>
17 </organisation:OrganisationModel>
```

de.gulden.modeling.seem.example.webshop/model/webshop.organisation: The MEMO organization perspective model.

MEMO resource perspective The MEMO resource perspective is the third and last conceptual source input model used in the example application of the method. Similar to the webshop.organisation model, the elements in this model are also cross-referenced by the process model.

```xml
1  <?xml version="1.0" encoding="UTF-8"?>
2  <resml:ResourceModel xmi:version="2.0" xmlns:xmi="http://www.omg.org/XMI"
       xmlns:Process="orgml.memo.org/process" xmlns:model="orgml.memo.org/model"
       xmlns:notation="http://www.eclipse.org/gmf/runtime/1.0.2/notation" xmlns:resml="
       resml.memo.org" xmlns:resmlAllocation="resml.memo.org/allocation" xmi:id="
       _BhFpQDhIEeCRoIVBgr3r6Q">
3    <resources xmi:type="resml:FrontEndComputingDevice" xmi:id="_FEmzUDhIEeCRoIVBgr3r6Q
       " name="Web Browser" allocatedVia="_UuZLoDhIEeCRoIVBgr3r6Q
       _3abZsDj0EeCP_MqEXhOUJw _4yFJIDj0EeCP_MqEXhOUJw">
4      <viewReferences xmi:type="model:ViewReference" xmi:id="_FF2JcDhIEeCRoIVBgr3r6Q"
         key="Resml">
5        <view xmi:type="notation:Diagram" href="resources.res_diagram#
           _BhaZYDhIEeCRoIVBgr3r6Q"/>
6      </viewReferences>
7      <viewReferences xmi:type="model:ViewReference" xmi:id="_jIJfcDhIEeCRoIVBgr3r6Q"
         key="Process Control Flow">
8        <view xmi:type="notation:Diagram" href="webshop.cflow_diagram#
           _uGp5EDcDEeCX95JTy-Rt3A"/>
```

```
 9        </viewReferences>
10     </resources>
11     <resources xmi:type="resml:Information" xmi:id="_nCPfwTjzEeCP_MqEXhOUJw" name="
           Product List" allocatedVia="_FgqxEDj0EeCP_MqEXhOUJw">
12       <viewReferences xmi:type="model:ViewReference" xmi:id="_nGBMgDjzEeCP_MqEXhOUJw"
             key="Resml">
13         <view xmi:type="notation:Diagram" href="resources.res_diagram#
             _BhaZYDhIEeCRoIVBgr3r6Q"/>
14       </viewReferences>
15       <viewReferences xmi:type="model:ViewReference" xmi:id="_1AotQDjzEeCP_MqEXhOUJw"
             key="Process Control Flow">
16         <view xmi:type="notation:Diagram" href="webshop.cflow_diagram#
             _uGp5EDcDEeCX95JTy-Rt3A"/>
17       </viewReferences>
18     </resources>
19     <resources xmi:type="resml:Information" xmi:id="_puZkADjzEeCP_MqEXhOUJw" name="
           Order" allocatedVia="_IaEAEDj0EeCP_MqEXhOUJw _5tdhYDj2EeCP_MqEXhOUJw
           _fsD6wDlTEeCGA8CAiWoPnA">
20       <viewReferences xmi:type="model:ViewReference" xmi:id="_pum_YDjzEeCP_MqEXhOUJw"
             key="Resml">
21         <view xmi:type="notation:Diagram" href="resources.res_diagram#
             _BhaZYDhIEeCRoIVBgr3r6Q"/>
22       </viewReferences>
23       <viewReferences xmi:type="model:ViewReference" xmi:id="_qw-14Dj0EeCP_MqEXhOUJw"
             key="Process Control Flow">
24         <view xmi:type="notation:Diagram" href="webshop.cflow_diagram#
             _uGp5EDcDEeCX95JTy-Rt3A"/>
25       </viewReferences>
26     </resources>
27     <resources xmi:type="resml:InformationSystem" xmi:id="_SdIOMDj5EeCP_MqEXhOUJw" name
           ="Storage Management IS" allocatedVia="_e17W4Dj5EeCP_MqEXhOUJw">
28       <viewReferences xmi:type="model:ViewReference" xmi:id="_Sd8tkDj5EeCP_MqEXhOUJw"
             key="Resml">
29         <view xmi:type="notation:Diagram" href="resources.res_diagram#
             _BhaZYDhIEeCRoIVBgr3r6Q"/>
30       </viewReferences>
31       <viewReferences xmi:type="model:ViewReference" xmi:id="_ptyYADlLEeCGA8CAiWoPnA"
             key="Process Control Flow">
32         <view xmi:type="notation:Diagram" href="webshop.cflow_diagram#
             _uGp5EDcDEeCX95JTy-Rt3A"/>
33       </viewReferences>
34     </resources>
35     <resources xmi:type="resml:Information" xmi:id="_MG3UgEJhEeC7OsczeBqlOw" name="
           Confirmation Text" description="Subject: Order #order# confirmed&#xA;&#xA;Dear
           #customer_name#,&#xA;&#xA;your order #order# is confirmed. Please pay the
           amount of #price# to our bank account 1234567, bank no. 7654321.&#xA;&#xA;
           Sincerely, &#xA;The Webshop&#xA;" allocatedVia="_A5MFsEJiEeC7OsczeBqlOw">
36       <viewReferences xmi:type="model:ViewReference" xmi:id="_MId3AEJhEeC7OsczeBqlOw"
             key="Resml">
37         <view xmi:type="notation:Diagram" href="resources.res_diagram#
             _BhaZYDhIEeCRoIVBgr3r6Q"/>
38       </viewReferences>
39       <viewReferences xmi:type="model:ViewReference" xmi:id="_25zrcEJhEeC7OsczeBqlOw"
             key="Process Control Flow">
40         <view xmi:type="notation:Diagram" href="webshop.cflow_diagram#
             _uGp5EDcDEeCX95JTy-Rt3A"/>
41       </viewReferences>
42     </resources>
43     <resources xmi:type="resml:Information" xmi:id="_Nm_qgEJhEeC7OsczeBqlOw" name="
           Cancelation Text" description="Subject: Order #order# canceled&#xA;&#xA;Dear #
           customer_name#,&#xA;&#xA;your order #order# has been canceled.&#xA;&#xA;
           Sincerely, &#xA;The Webshop&#xA;" allocatedVia="_EWM_IEJiEeC7OsczeBqlOw">
44       <viewReferences xmi:type="model:ViewReference" xmi:id="_NnQwQEJhEeC7OsczeBqlOw"
             key="Resml">
45         <view xmi:type="notation:Diagram" href="resources.res_diagram#
             _BhaZYDhIEeCRoIVBgr3r6Q"/>
46       </viewReferences>
```

```
47    <viewReferences xmi:type="model:ViewReference" xmi:id="_251goEJhEeC7OsczeBqlOw"
          key="Process Control Flow">
48      <view xmi:type="notation:Diagram" href="webshop.cflow_diagram#
          _uGp5EDcDEeCX95JTy-Rt3A"/>
49    </viewReferences>
50   </resources>
```

...

de.gulden.modeling.seem.example.webshop/model/webshop.resml: The MEMO
resource perspective model.

EEM representation of the MEMO input models   After executing the adapter transformation, the EEM model is available, generated from the 3 MEMO input models above.
It represents the same conceptual elements as the input models, in a streamlined representation, which can uniformly be processed in subsequent steps of the method. The
meta-model of this model instance is shown in Fig. 16.

```
1   <?xml version="1.0" encoding="ASCII"?>
2   <eem:EemModel xmi:version="2.0" xmlns:xmi="http://www.omg.org/XMI" xmlns:xsi="http://
        www.w3.org/2001/XMLSchema-instance" xmlns:eem="http://gulden.de/modeling/emdsd/
        eem/1.0" name="Webshop Process Model">
3     <eMObjects xsi:type="eem:Process" comment="Top Level Process" name="Webshop
        Business Process" topLevel="true"/>
4     <eMObjects xsi:type="eem:ActorGroup" name="Customer" performs="//@eMObjects.9 //
        @eMObjects.10 //@eMObjects.11"/>
5     <eMObjects xsi:type="eem:ActorGroup" name="Management" subordinate="//@eMObjects.3
        //@eMObjects.4 //@eMObjects.5"/>
6     <eMObjects xsi:type="eem:ActorGroup" name="ProductionDepartment" superordinate="//
        @eMObjects.2" subordinate="//@eMObjects.6"/>
7     <eMObjects xsi:type="eem:ActorGroup" name="MarketingDepartment" superordinate="//
        @eMObjects.2" subordinate="//@eMObjects.7"/>
8     <eMObjects xsi:type="eem:ActorGroup" name="ShippingDepartment" superordinate="//
        @eMObjects.2" subordinate="//@eMObjects.8"/>
9     <eMObjects xsi:type="eem:ActorGroup" name="ProductionEmployee" superordinate="//
        @eMObjects.3"/>
10    <eMObjects xsi:type="eem:ActorGroup" name="MarketingEmployee" superordinate="//
        @eMObjects.4"/>
11    <eMObjects xsi:type="eem:ActorGroup" name="ShippingEmployee" performs="//@eMObjects
        .12 //@eMObjects.13 //@eMObjects.14" superordinate="//@eMObjects.5"/>
12    <eMObjects xsi:type="eem:Process" name="Select products from catalog" outgoing="//
        @eMObjects.34" ingoing="//@eMObjects.32" kind="SEMIAUTOMATIC" performedBy="//
        @eMObjects.1" ProcessResourceAccess="//@eMObjects.55 //@eMObjects.57"/>
13    <eMObjects xsi:type="eem:Process" name="Fill-in order form or cancel" outgoing="//
        @eMObjects.40 //@eMObjects.43" ingoing="//@eMObjects.28" kind="SEMIAUTOMATIC"
        performedBy="//@eMObjects.1" ProcessResourceAccess="//@eMObjects.56 //
        @eMObjects.58"/>
14    <eMObjects xsi:type="eem:Process" name="Read confirmation" outgoing="//@eMObjects
        .37" ingoing="//@eMObjects.45" kind="SEMIAUTOMATIC" performedBy="//@eMObjects
        .1" ProcessResourceAccess="//@eMObjects.54 //@eMObjects.61"/>
15    <eMObjects xsi:type="eem:Process" name="Validate order" outgoing="//@eMObjects.41
        //@eMObjects.42" ingoing="//@eMObjects.44" kind="SEMIAUTOMATIC" performedBy
        ="//@eMObjects.8" ProcessResourceAccess="//@eMObjects.59 //@eMObjects.60"/>
16    <eMObjects xsi:type="eem:Process" name="Pick goods from storage" outgoing="//
        @eMObjects.30" ingoing="//@eMObjects.29" kind="MANUAL" performedBy="//
        @eMObjects.8"/>
17    <eMObjects xsi:type="eem:Process" name="Package goods and send" outgoing="//
        @eMObjects.36" ingoing="//@eMObjects.33" kind="MANUAL" performedBy="//
        @eMObjects.8"/>
18    <eMObjects xsi:type="eem:Process" value="From: #CONFIG_EMAIL_SENDER#&#xA;To: #
        customer-email#" name="Send cancellation e-mail" outgoing="//@eMObjects.35"
```

```
          ingoing="//@eMObjects.31" kind="AUTOMATIC" ProcessResourceAccess="//@eMObjects
          .63"/>
19   <eMObjects xsi:type="eem:Process" value="From: #CONFIG_EMAIL_SENDER#&#xA;To: #
          customer-email#" name="Send confirmation e-mail" outgoing="//@eMObjects.39"
          ingoing="//@eMObjects.38" kind="AUTOMATIC" ProcessResourceAccess="//@eMObjects
          .62"/>
20   <eMObjects xsi:type="eem:Event" name="Webshop entered" outgoing="//@eMObjects.32"
          kind="START"/>
21   <eMObjects xsi:type="eem:Event" name="Order canceled" ingoing="//@eMObjects.35 //
          @eMObjects.43" kind="STOP"/>
22   <eMObjects xsi:type="eem:Event" name="Products  are selected" outgoing="//
          @eMObjects.28" ingoing="//@eMObjects.34"/>
23   <eMObjects xsi:type="eem:Event" name="Order is submitted" outgoingParallel="true"
          outgoing="//@eMObjects.44 //@eMObjects.45" ingoing="//@eMObjects.40"/>
24   <eMObjects xsi:type="eem:Event" name="Order is valid" outgoing="//@eMObjects.29"
          ingoing="//@eMObjects.41"/>
25   <eMObjects xsi:type="eem:Event" name="Goods are picked" outgoing="//@eMObjects.33"
          ingoing="//@eMObjects.30"/>
26   <eMObjects xsi:type="eem:Event" name="Order complete" ingoing="//@eMObjects.39"
          kind="STOP"/>
27   <eMObjects xsi:type="eem:Event" name="Order is invalid" outgoing="//@eMObjects.31"
          ingoing="//@eMObjects.42"/>
28   <eMObjects xsi:type="eem:Event" name="Confirmation is read" outgoing="//@eMObjects
          .46" ingoing="//@eMObjects.37"/>
29   <eMObjects xsi:type="eem:Event" name="Goods are packaged and sent" outgoing="//
          @eMObjects.47" ingoing="//@eMObjects.36"/>
30   <eMObjects xsi:type="eem:Event" name="Synchronizer1" ingoingParallel="true"
          outgoing="//@eMObjects.38" ingoing="//@eMObjects.46 //@eMObjects.47"/>
31   <eMObjects xsi:type="eem:Sequence" inProcess="//@eMObjects.0" from="//@eMObjects
          .19" to="//@eMObjects.10"/>
32   <eMObjects xsi:type="eem:Sequence" inProcess="//@eMObjects.0" from="//@eMObjects
          .21" to="//@eMObjects.13"/>
33   <eMObjects xsi:type="eem:Sequence" inProcess="//@eMObjects.0" from="//@eMObjects
          .13" to="//@eMObjects.22"/>
34   <eMObjects xsi:type="eem:Sequence" inProcess="//@eMObjects.0" from="//@eMObjects
          .24" to="//@eMObjects.15"/>
35   <eMObjects xsi:type="eem:Sequence" inProcess="//@eMObjects.0" from="//@eMObjects
          .17" to="//@eMObjects.9"/>
36   <eMObjects xsi:type="eem:Sequence" inProcess="//@eMObjects.0" from="//@eMObjects
          .22" to="//@eMObjects.14"/>
37   <eMObjects xsi:type="eem:Sequence" inProcess="//@eMObjects.0" from="//@eMObjects.9"
          to="//@eMObjects.19"/>
38   <eMObjects xsi:type="eem:Sequence" inProcess="//@eMObjects.0" from="//@eMObjects
          .15" to="//@eMObjects.18"/>
39   <eMObjects xsi:type="eem:Sequence" inProcess="//@eMObjects.0" from="//@eMObjects
          .14" to="//@eMObjects.26"/>
40   <eMObjects xsi:type="eem:Sequence" inProcess="//@eMObjects.0" from="//@eMObjects
          .11" to="//@eMObjects.25"/>
41   <eMObjects xsi:type="eem:Sequence" inProcess="//@eMObjects.0" from="//@eMObjects
          .27" to="//@eMObjects.16"/>
42   <eMObjects xsi:type="eem:Sequence" inProcess="//@eMObjects.0" from="//@eMObjects
          .16" to="//@eMObjects.23"/>
43   <eMObjects xsi:type="eem:Sequence" name="Submit Order" inProcess="//@eMObjects.0"
          from="//@eMObjects.10" to="//@eMObjects.20"/>
44   <eMObjects xsi:type="eem:Sequence" inProcess="//@eMObjects.0" from="//@eMObjects
          .12" to="//@eMObjects.21"/>
45   <eMObjects xsi:type="eem:Sequence" inProcess="//@eMObjects.0" from="//@eMObjects
          .12" to="//@eMObjects.24"/>
46   <eMObjects xsi:type="eem:Sequence" name="Cancel Order" inProcess="//@eMObjects.0"
          from="//@eMObjects.10" to="//@eMObjects.18"/>
47   <eMObjects xsi:type="eem:Sequence" inProcess="//@eMObjects.0" from="//@eMObjects
          .20" to="//@eMObjects.12"/>
48   <eMObjects xsi:type="eem:Sequence" inProcess="//@eMObjects.0" from="//@eMObjects
          .20" to="//@eMObjects.11"/>
49   <eMObjects xsi:type="eem:Sequence" inProcess="//@eMObjects.0" from="//@eMObjects
          .25" to="//@eMObjects.27"/>
```

```
50    <eMObjects xsi:type="eem:Sequence" inProcess="//@eMObjects.0" from="//@eMObjects
         .26" to="//@eMObjects.27"/>

...
```

de.gulden.modeling.seem.example.webshop/model/webshop.eem: A streamlined EEM
representation of the MEMO input models for further processing.

Mapping model used in the example   The file `webshop.mapping` contains the mapping model used in the example project. It has automatically been generated using the
mapping model initialization transformation (see Sect. 6.3.2) of the example project. The
mapping model is an instance of the meta-model shown in Fig. 22 and Fig. 43 to Fig. 58.

```
1    <?xml version="1.0" encoding="ASCII"?>
2    <mapping:MappingModel xmi:version="2.0" xmlns:xmi="http://www.omg.org/XMI" xmlns:xsi
        ="http://www.w3.org/2001/XMLSchema-instance" xmlns:eem="http://gulden.de/
        modeling/emdsd/eem/1.0" xmlns:mapping="http://gulden.de/modeling/emdsd/mapping
        /1.0" xmlns:web="http://gulden.de/modeling/emdsd/architecture/web/1.0" name="
        webshop-process-model" basePackage="webshopprocessmodel" modelURI="http://
        webshopprocessmodel/1.0">
3      <processMappings name="Webshop Business Process">
4        <process href="file:/home/user/runtime-mml/de.gulden.modeling.seem.example.
            webshop/model/webshop.eem#//@eMObjects.0"/>
5        <sequenceMappings name="Webshop entered &#x2192; Select products from catalog"
            controlFlowImplementation="//@genericArchitecture/@implementations.47">
6          <sequence href="file:/home/user/runtime-mml/de.gulden.modeling.seem.example.
              webshop/model/webshop.eem#//@eMObjects.32"/>
7          <actorResolverImplementations xsi:type="web:WebSessionUser" href="webshop.web
              #//@implementations.0"/>
8        </sequenceMappings>
9        <sequenceMappings name="Select products from catalog &#x2192; Products  are
            selected" controlFlowImplementation="//@genericArchitecture/@implementations
            .47" actorResolverImplementations="//@genericArchitecture/@implementations
            .46">
10         <sequence href="file:/home/user/runtime-mml/de.gulden.modeling.seem.example.
              webshop/model/webshop.eem#//@eMObjects.34"/>
11       </sequenceMappings>
12       <sequenceMappings name="Products  are selected &#x2192; Fill-in order form or
            cancel" controlFlowImplementation="//@genericArchitecture/@implementations
            .47">
13         <sequence href="file:/home/user/runtime-mml/de.gulden.modeling.seem.example.
              webshop/model/webshop.eem#//@eMObjects.28"/>
14         <actorResolverImplementations xsi:type="web:WebSessionUser" href="webshop.web
              #//@implementations.0"/>
15       </sequenceMappings>
16       <sequenceMappings name="Fill-in order form or cancel &#x2192; Order is submitted"
            controlFlowImplementation="//@genericArchitecture/@implementations.47"
            actorResolverImplementations="//@genericArchitecture/@implementations.46">
17         <sequence href="file:/home/user/runtime-mml/de.gulden.modeling.seem.example.
              webshop/model/webshop.eem#//@eMObjects.40"/>
18       </sequenceMappings>
19       <sequenceMappings name="Fill-in order form or cancel &#x2192; Order canceled"
            conditionImplementation="//@genericArchitecture/@implementations.50"
            controlFlowImplementation="//@genericArchitecture/@implementations.47"
            actorResolverImplementations="//@genericArchitecture/@implementations.46">
20         <sequence href="file:/home/user/runtime-mml/de.gulden.modeling.seem.example.
              webshop/model/webshop.eem#//@eMObjects.43"/>
21       </sequenceMappings>
22       <sequenceMappings name="Order is submitted &#x2192; Validate order"
            controlFlowImplementation="//@genericArchitecture/@implementations.48"
            actorResolverImplementations="//@genericArchitecture/@implementations.49">
```

```
23        <sequence href="file:/home/user/runtime-mml/de.gulden.modeling.seem.example.
              webshop/model/webshop.eem#//@eMObjects.44"/>
24      </sequenceMappings>
25      <sequenceMappings name="Order is submitted &#x2192; Read confirmation"
              controlFlowImplementation="//@genericArchitecture/@implementations.47">
26        <sequence href="file:/home/user/runtime-mml/de.gulden.modeling.seem.example.
              webshop/model/webshop.eem#//@eMObjects.45"/>
27        <actorResolverImplementations xsi:type="web:WebSessionUser" href="webshop.web
              #//@implementations.0"/>
28      </sequenceMappings>
29      <sequenceMappings name="Validate order &#x2192; Order is valid"
              controlFlowImplementation="//@genericArchitecture/@implementations.47"
              actorResolverImplementations="//@genericArchitecture/@implementations.46">
30        <sequence href="file:/home/user/runtime-mml/de.gulden.modeling.seem.example.
              webshop/model/webshop.eem#//@eMObjects.41"/>
31      </sequenceMappings>
32      <sequenceMappings name="Validate order &#x2192; Order is invalid"
              controlFlowImplementation="//@genericArchitecture/@implementations.47"
              actorResolverImplementations="//@genericArchitecture/@implementations.46">
33        <sequence href="file:/home/user/runtime-mml/de.gulden.modeling.seem.example.
              webshop/model/webshop.eem#//@eMObjects.42"/>
34      </sequenceMappings>
35      <sequenceMappings name="Order is valid &#x2192; Pick goods from storage"
              controlFlowImplementation="//@genericArchitecture/@implementations.47"
              actorResolverImplementations="//@genericArchitecture/@implementations.49">
36        <sequence href="file:/home/user/runtime-mml/de.gulden.modeling.seem.example.
              webshop/model/webshop.eem#//@eMObjects.29"/>
37      </sequenceMappings>
38      <sequenceMappings name="Pick goods from storage &#x2192; Goods are picked"
              controlFlowImplementation="//@genericArchitecture/@implementations.47"
              actorResolverImplementations="//@genericArchitecture/@implementations.46">
39        <sequence href="file:/home/user/runtime-mml/de.gulden.modeling.seem.example.
              webshop/model/webshop.eem#//@eMObjects.30"/>
40      </sequenceMappings>
41      <sequenceMappings name="Goods are picked &#x2192; Package goods and send"
              controlFlowImplementation="//@genericArchitecture/@implementations.47"
              actorResolverImplementations="//@genericArchitecture/@implementations.49">
42        <sequence href="file:/home/user/runtime-mml/de.gulden.modeling.seem.example.
              webshop/model/webshop.eem#//@eMObjects.33"/>
43      </sequenceMappings>
44      <sequenceMappings name="Package goods and send &#x2192; Goods are packaged and
              sent" controlFlowImplementation="//@genericArchitecture/@implementations.47"
               actorResolverImplementations="//@genericArchitecture/@implementations.46">
45        <sequence href="file:/home/user/runtime-mml/de.gulden.modeling.seem.example.
              webshop/model/webshop.eem#//@eMObjects.36"/>
46      </sequenceMappings>
47      <sequenceMappings name="Goods are packaged and sent &#x2192; Synchronizer1"
              controlFlowImplementation="//@genericArchitecture/@implementations.47"
              actorResolverImplementations="//@genericArchitecture/@implementations.46">
48        <sequence href="file:/home/user/runtime-mml/de.gulden.modeling.seem.example.
              webshop/model/webshop.eem#//@eMObjects.47"/>
49      </sequenceMappings>
50      <sequenceMappings name="Synchronizer1 &#x2192; Send confirmation e-mail"
              controlFlowImplementation="//@genericArchitecture/@implementations.47"
              actorResolverImplementations="//@genericArchitecture/@implementations.46">
```

...

de.gulden.modeling.seem.example.webshop/model/webshop.mapping: The mapping
model used in the example project, generated by the mapping model initialization
transformation.

A.3.4   Generated example artifact

Generated main page of the web application This artifact is part of the example web-shop implementation. It is the main entry point for a user from the internet to enter the web application. The dynamic web page is generated by the code generation transformation of the introductory example (see Appendix A.3.3), and can be deployed on a JSP capable web server.

```
1   <?xml version="1.0" ?>
2   <!--
3     Generated file, generator written by Jens Gulden, jens.gulden@uni-due.de.
4     Licensed under a Creative Commons Attribution 3.0 Unported license.
5   -->
6
7   <%@page import="java.util.*" %>
8   <%@page import="java.util.Date" %>
9   <%@page import="java.io.*" %>
10  <%@page import="java.sql.*"%>
11  <%@page import="org.w3c.dom.*" %>
12  <%@page import="de.gulden.server.xmldb.*" %>
13  <%@page import="de.gulden.modeling.seem.api.web.*" %>
14  <%@page import="de.gulden.modeling.seem.api.web.jsp.BufferWriter" %>
15
16  <%@page contentType="application/xhtml+xml" %>
17  <!DOCTYPE html PUBLIC "-//W3C//DTD XHTML 1.0 Transitional//EN" "http://www.w3.org/TR/
        xhtml1/DTD/xhtml1-transitional.dtd">
18  <html xmlns="http://www.w3.org/1999/xhtml" xmlns:xf="http://www.w3.org/2002/xforms">
19
20  <%
21  Date startTime = new Date();
22
23  Context context = new Context(null, this.getServletContext(), request, response);
24
25  String processIdStr = request.getParameter("id");
26  int processId;
27  String step = request.getParameter("step");
28  String oldstep = request.getParameter("oldstep");
29  String prevOldstep = null;
30  String nextstep = request.getParameter("nextstep");
31
32  if ((processIdStr == null) || (processIdStr.trim().length() == 0)) {
33      processId = (int) ( System.currentTimeMillis() & 0x7fffffff ); // use int for db
            storage
34  } else {
35      processId = Integer.parseInt(processIdStr);
36  }
37
38  JspWriter pageOut = out;
39  JspWriter headOut = new BufferWriter();
40  JspWriter bodyOut = new BufferWriter();
41
42  XMLDBConnection con = XMLDBManager.createConnection(context.getRequired("
        CONFIG_XMLDB_URL"));
43  Class.forName(context.getRequired("CONFIG_DB_DRIVER")).newInstance();
44  Connection sql =  DriverManager.getConnection(context.getRequired("CONFIG_DB_URL"),
        context.getRequired("CONFIG_DB_USER"), context.get("CONFIG_DB_PASSWORD"));
45
46  ProcessFolder processFolder = new ProcessFolder(sql, processId);
47  context.setProcessFolder(processFolder);
48  UserManager userManager = new UserManager(con, sql, processId);
49  ToDoList todoList = new ToDoList(sql);
```

...

webshop/WebContent/index.jsp: Generated main page of the web application.

A.3.5 Modeling conventions to incorporate additional semantics into the enterprise models

The example projects each use a set of modeling conventions, to specify additional hints about intended semantics in the conceptual enterprise models. This allows to interpret the conceptual models in a more fine-grained way than possible with the conceptual modeling language elements, and retrieve all required information for realizing a 100% code generation approach.

Hints are typically given as parts of element names, or via a description text-field attached to conceptual model elements. They can also refer to specific constellations or patterns of model elements, which are interpreted in a previously acknowledged way.

The following table lists the conventions used in the introductory example. The rules are stated in an easy to understand natural language, to allow any of the involved stakeholders to understand the conventions.

Resource modeling conventions

- An information resource name ending with "List" indicates a multi-value access to a resource type or instance.

- Resource allocations should be named "read", "modify", "create", or "delete", to indicate how the resource is accessed. (Names of selected resource allocations are shown in the properties-tab below the diagram.)

- Information resources, which contain the words "Message" or "Text" in their names, are considered to be notifications displayed to the user, or other human-readable text documents.

- Software resources containing the word "Browser" in their name can be modeled to be accessed by a process-step. This denotes that the process-step is to be executed via a web-browser by an anonymous public web user (see below the according convention on process modeling).

- Other software resources are assumed to be external applications, which are locally invoked at the user's device.

Process modeling conventions

- A semi-automatic process containing the word "select" in its name, will be implemented by a form, in which the user can select from the resources accessed by this process in "read" mode.

- A semi-automatic process, which accesses a software resource with the word "Browser" in its name, will be implemented by a web-application publicly

---

accessible from the internet (see above the according convention on resource modeling).

- A semi-automatic process accessing a text resource in read mode, will be implemented by displaying the text to the user.

- A semi-automatic process accessing an information resource in create or modify mode, will be implemented by displaying an editable form to the user.

- The phrase "cancel" in the name of a sequence (a connection between two processes) after an alternative split, will cause a cancel-option to be presented in the user-interface of the process implementation.

- A branch of multiple alternative options in the process control flow after a semi-automatic process (except "cancel" branches, which are treated as described above), will present a menu to the user where the next process-step is selected.

- A branch of multiple alternative options in the process control flow after an automatic process, will compare the process result value with the branch labels, and pick the one with equal value as the outgoing sequence to be followed. If no equal value can be found, the first branch is used by default.

- An automatic process containing the word "e-mail" in its name, will be implemented by an automatic e-mail sending procedure, which picks values for mail recipient, subject and text body from an accessed text resource. The description text of the text resource model element should start with the line "Subject: ..." to set a mail subject text, then a blank line must follow, then by any number of following text lines will be used as the mail body. Text-fragments enclosed in "#" characters will be replaced by the respective runtime values from the process folder.

Actor modeling conventions

- An actor named "Anonymous", "Public", or "Customer", will be treated as unauthenticated anonymous user from the internet.

Technical artifacts, which contain concrete lists of sub-strings for use in the examples applications, are shown in Appendix A.3.3 (for the introductory example), and in Appendix A.4.3 (for the comprehensive example).

A.4 Artifacts of the comprehensive example

The artifacts presented in the following, result from a publicly funded project about security in the food industry domain (see Sect. 10.1). They show an example application of the SEEM method for creating software for a distributed SOA environment, by generating executable BPEL workflow process models.

A.4.1 Adaptation to a domain-specific supply chain modeling language

Model-to-model adapter transformation from supply chain modeler files to an EEM model The `scm-to-eem.xslt` transformation converts a file in an XML data representation that serializes a model instance from the supply chain modeler (see Sect. 10.2) to an EMF-compatible representation in the EEM format.

Unlike the previous adapter transformation in Appendix A.3.1, this transformation is not a horizontal transformation. It does not preserve the level of abstraction by performing only a syntactic restructuring and renaming of concepts, but it converts from a higher level of abstraction in the domain-specific supply chain model, to a lower, yet still conceptual and non-technical, level of generic enterprise modeling concepts in the EEM representation. I. e., concepts in the source model, which specifically refer to domain-specific properties of a supply-chain, e. g., a fixed order of operations in a supply chain (such as placing an order, dispatching an ordered good, then transporting it), or fixed actor roles (such as the involved retailer, producer and logistician), need to be reflected by the general enterprise model concepts of process-steps, actors, resources, etc. To achieve this shift in the level of abstraction, the transformation performs some interpretation operations on the input model, and represents the results in the EEM output instance.

The transformation script can be invoked by any Extensible Stylesheet Language Transformations (XSLT) interpreter integrated in a development environment, e. g., in the ECLIPSE IDE, or by a batch XSLT interpreter. For the prototypical method application, a wrapper for executing XSLT within MWE workflows has been written, which allows to invoke the transformation from an individual MWE script, and as part of a combined overall MWE workflow. See below for the MWE invocation script.

```
1   <!--
2     scm-to-eem.xslt, adapter transformation to convert a supply chain model to
3     an EEM representation.
4     Written by Jens Gulden, gulden@wiwi.uni-siegen.de.
5     Licensed under a Creative Commons Attribution 3.0 Unported license.
6   -->
7
8   <xsl:transform version="1.0"
9   xmlns:xsl="http://www.w3.org/1999/XSL/Transform"
10  xmlns:xmi="http://www.omg.org/XMI"
11  xmlns:xsi="http://www.w3.org/2001/XMLSchema-instance"
12  xmlns:eem="http://gulden.de/modeling/emdsd/eem/1.0" >
13
14  <!-- xmlns:fn="http://www.w3.org/2005/xpath-functions" -->
15
16  <xsl:strip-space elements="*" />
17  <xsl:output method="xml" indent="yes" />
```

```
18
19   <!--
20   The transformation is done in two steps:
21   1) main transformation to convert model structure
22   2) id transformation converting pseudo ids to expected xmi-locator expressions,
23   and creating back-references of bidirectional associations
24
25   This template collection performs the first step.
26   -->
27
28   <!-- - - - Main transformation - - - -->
29   <xsl:template match="/">
30       <eem:EemModel name="Supply Chain" xmi:version="2.0">
31           <eMObjects id="topLevelProcess" xsi:type="eem:Process" name="Supply Chain
                   Process" topLevel="true"/>
32           <xsl:apply-templates select="SupplyChain"/>
33       </eem:EemModel>
34   </xsl:template>
35
36   <!-- Transform all required elements. -->
37   <xsl:template match="SupplyChain">
38           <!-- actors -->
39           <xsl:apply-templates select="Participants/Participant"/>
40           <!-- resources -->
41           <xsl:apply-templates select="Assets/Asset"/>
42           <!-- entry point for process-steps -->
43           <xsl:apply-templates select="Processes/InternalProcess"/>
44           <!-- resource accesses -->
45           <xsl:apply-templates select="//CommunicationActivity/Interface/*"/>
46           <!-- Sequences -->
47           <xsl:apply-templates select="Connectors/Connector"/>
48           <!-- Locations -->
49           <xsl:apply-templates select="Locations/Location"/>
50   </xsl:template>
```

. . .

org.rescueit.modeling.workflow/xslt/scm-to-eem.xslt: Model-to-model
XSLT transformation of the comprehensive example to convert a supply chain modeler
file to an EEM representation.

Workflow script to invoke the supply chain model to EEM adapter transformation
This invocation script provides a way of invoking the adapting XSLT transformation,
which converts a supply chain model file to an EEM model instance (see above). The
script makes use of a custom-made extension to the MWE workflow mechanism, providing an executable component that runs an XSLT transformation.

The invocation script also runs a second phase transformation on the generated output of
this script, which adapts the unique element ids generated by scm-to-eem.xslt to a
format required by the EMF's XMI format.

```
1   <!--
2     01-run-adaptEM.mwe, invocation script to run the adapter transformation.
3     Written by Jens Gulden, gulden@wiwi.uni-siegen.de.
4     Licensed under a Creative Commons Attribution 3.0 Unported license.
5   -->
6
7   <workflow>
8
```

```
9    <!-- Workflow script for running conceptual model adaptation. -->
10
11       <!-- Read configuration properties from file 'workflow.properties'. -->
12       <property file="./workflow.properties"/>
13       <property name="eemModel" value="${projectRoot}/model/${projectPrefix}.eem"/>
14       <property name="eemModel1" value="/tmp/${projectPrefix}1.eem"/>
15
16       <!-- Main conversion. -->
17       <xslt in="${projectRoot}/model/${projectPrefix}.xml"
18             style="xslt/scm-to-eem.xslt"
19             out="./tmp/${projectPrefix}.eem_tmp"
20             force="true"
21             class="de.gulden.modeling.seem.generator.util.XSLTTransformation" />
22
23       <!-- Id conversion. -->
24       <xslt in="./tmp/${projectPrefix}.eem_tmp"
25             out="${eemModel1}"
26             style="xslt/make-ids.xslt"
27             force="true"
28             class="de.gulden.modeling.seem.generator.util.XSLTTransformation" />
29
30       <!-- Delete temporary file. -->
31       <!--
32       <delete filename="./tmp/${projectPrefix}.eem_tmp" class="de.gulden.modeling.seem.
            generator.util.DeleteFile"/>
33       -->
34
35       <!-- Read supply chain model in eem representation. -->
36       <component class="org.eclipse.emf.mwe.utils.Reader">
37           <uri value="${eemModel1}"/>
38           <modelSlot value="eemModel1"/>
39       </component>
40
41       <!-- Transform. -->
42       <component class="org.eclipse.xtend.XtendComponent">
43           <!--fileEncoding value="UTF-8"/-->
44           <metaModel class="org.eclipse.xtend.typesystem.emf.EmfMetaModel"><
                metaModelPackage value="de.gulden.modeling.seem.eem.EemPackage"/></
                metaModel>
45           <invoke value="eemDeferredSteps::transform(eemModel1)"/>
46           <outputSlot value="eemModel"/>
47       </component>
48
49       <!-- Write out the model. -->
50       <component class="org.eclipse.emf.mwe.utils.Writer">
51           <modelSlot value="eemModel"/>
52           <uri value="${eemModel}"/>
53       </component>
54
55  </workflow>
```

org.rescueit.modeling.workflow/01-run-adaptEM.mwe: Invocation script to run the `scm-to-eem.xslt` transformation together with the id conversion `make-ids.xslt`.

A.4.2 Mapping model handling

Model-to-model transformation to set default mapping model entries for generating code for a SOA target architecture   This target architecture specific initialization transformation creates the default entries describing a SOA environment, for which a BPEL process and accompanying files are generated as executable components. The domain-specific language of the target architecture has been described in further detail in Sect. 10.4.

```
1   /* initMappingBPEL.ext, model-to-model transformation to enrich a mapping model with
2      architecture-specific entries, and storing the referenced entries in an individual
3      architecture model.
4      Written by Jens Gulden, gulden@www.uni-siegen.de.
5      Licensed under a Creative Commons Attribution 3.0 Unported license. */
6
7   import soa;
8   import ecore;
9   import mapping;
10  import eem;
11  import reactionprocess;
12
13  extension common;
14  extension rescueit;
15  extension org::eclipse::xtend::util::stdlib::globalvar;
16  extension org::eclipse::xtend::util::stdlib::properties;
17
18  /*
19   * Interprets the conceptual model to find architecture specific for a BPEL/SOA
20   * applicaiton platform. Adds these entries to the mapping model.
21   */
22  SOAArchitectureModel updateMapping(MappingModel this):
23      this.targetArchitectures.typeSelect(SOAArchitectureModel).has() ? (
24          this.targetArchitectures.typeSelect(SOAArchitectureModel).update(this) ->
25          null // indicate that no new architecture model had to be created
26      ) : (
27          let newArchModel = new SOAArchitectureModel:
28          let genericArchModel = new GenericArchitectureModel:
29          newArchModel.implementations.add( createProcessService() ) ->
30          newArchModel.implementations.add( createMailService() ) ->
31          newArchModel.implementations.add( createConfigService() ) ->
32          newArchModel.implementations.add( createLogService() ) ->
33          newArchModel.implementations.add( createSecureLoggingService() ) ->
34          newArchModel.implementations.add( createUtilService() ) ->
35          newArchModel.implementations.add( createObservationService() ) -> // CEP
36          newArchModel.implementations.add( createSignatureService() ) ->
37          newArchModel.implementations.add( createSignatureValidateService() ) ->
38          newArchModel.implementations.add( createModelExtractionService() ) ->
39          newArchModel.implementations.add( createSecureTrackingService() ) ->
40          newArchModel.implementations.add( createBenchmarkService() ) ->
41          newArchModel.implementations.add( createContainerTrackingStatusService() ) ->
42          newArchModel.implementations.add( createContainerTrackingAlertService() ) ->
43          newArchModel.implementations.add( createIdemixProverService() ) ->
44          newArchModel.implementations.add( createIdemixVerifierService() ) ->
45          newArchModel.implementations.add( createReactionProcessService() ) ->
46          newArchModel.implementations.add( createCepService() ) -> // JMS message
                  queue
47          getProperty("reactionProcessModels").splitString().
                  createReactionProcessReference(newArchModel) ->
48          this.targetArchitectures.add( newArchModel.update(this) ) ->
49          this.setGenericArchitecture(genericArchModel) -> // unused, add for
                  completeness
50          newArchModel
```

. . .

org.rescueit.modeling.workflow/templates/initMappingSOA.ext: Script to create initial default mapping entries for a SOA target application platform.

Workflow script to initialize the mapping model with a SOA implementation strategy model In parallel to the previously introduced `run-initMapping` script, this script combines the generic initialization of the mapping model with the example SOA implementation strategy model.

```
1   <!--
2     03-run-initMapping.mwe, invocation script to initialize the mapping model.
3     Written by Jens Gulden, gulden@wiwi.uni-siegen.de.
4     Licensed under a Creative Commons Attribution 3.0 Unported license.
5   -->
6
7   <workflow>
8
9   <!-- Workflow script for initializing a new mapping model from an enterprise
10        model representation of a supply chain model. -->
11
12       <!-- Read configuration properties from file 'workflow.properties'. -->
13       <property file="./workflow.properties"/>
14
15       <!-- Make property values available to Xtend's properties extension.
16            conventions.properties contains hints on how to interpret the enterprise
17            model semantics. -->
18       <component class="org.eclipse.xtend.util.stdlib.PropertiesReader">
19           <propertiesFile value="./workflow.properties"/>
20           <propertiesFile value="./conventions.properties"/>
21       </component>
22
23       <!-- Derive other properties from loaded properties. -->
24       <property name="eemModel" value="${projectRoot}/model/${projectPrefix}.eem"/>
25       <property name="outputMappingModel" value="${projectRoot}/model/${projectPrefix}.
               mapping"/>
26       <property name="outputArchitectureSOAModel" value="${projectRoot}/model/${
               projectPrefix}.soa"/>
27
28       <!-- Initialize issue reporter. -->
29       <component class="org.eclipse.xtend.util.stdlib.ExtIssueReporter"/>
30
31       <!-- Read supply chain model in eem representation. -->
32       <component class="org.eclipse.emf.mwe.utils.Reader">
33           <uri value="${eemModel}"/>
34           <modelSlot value="eemModel"/>
35       </component>
36
37       <!-- Create a new, blank mapping model. For every element in the eem model, that
38            can be referenced via a mapping entry, a blank mapping entry with a null-
39            reference to a yet unspecified implementation strategy is created. -->
40       <component class="org.eclipse.xtend.XtendComponent">
41           <!--fileEncoding value="UTF-8"/-->
42           <metaModel class="org.eclipse.xtend.typesystem.emf.EmfMetaModel"><
                   metaModelPackage value="org.eclipse.emf.ecore.EcorePackage"/></metaModel
                   >
43           <metaModel class="org.eclipse.xtend.typesystem.emf.EmfMetaModel"><
                   metaModelPackage value="de.gulden.modeling.seem.eem.EemPackage"/></
                   metaModel>
44           <metaModel class="org.eclipse.xtend.typesystem.emf.EmfMetaModel"><
                   metaModelPackage value="de.gulden.modeling.seem.mapping.MappingPackage"/
                   ></metaModel>
45           <invoke value="initMapping::createMapping(eemModel)"/>
46           <outputSlot value="mappingModel"/>
47       </component>
48
49       <!-- Determine default implementation strategies for existing mapping entries. --
               >
```

```
        <component class="org.eclipse.xtend.XtendComponent">
```

...

org.rescueit.modeling.workflow/03-run-initMapping.mwe: Invocation script to run the creation of initial default mapping entries for the SOA target architecture.

Workflow script to invoke the validity checks for a mapping model and an associated SOA implementation strategy model   This workflow modeling script is used to invoke the mapping model and the SOA implementation strategy model validity checks.

```
1   <!--
2       04-run-checkMapping.mwe, invocation script to run the completeness check for a
3       mapping model.
4       Written by Jens Gulden, gulden@wiwi.uni-siegen.de.
5       Licensed under a Creative Commons Attribution 3.0 Unported license.
6   -->
7
8   <workflow>
9
10  <!-- Workflow script for running a completeness check on the mapping model. -->
11
12      <!-- Read configuration properties from file 'workflow.properties'. -->
13      <property file="./workflow.properties"/>
14
15      <!-- Derive other properties from loaded properties. -->
16      <property name="model" value="${projectRoot}/model/${projectPrefix}.mapping"/>
17      <property name="soaModel" value="${projectRoot}/model/${projectPrefix}.soa"/>
18
19      <!-- - - - Check mapping model. - - - -->
20
21      <!-- Read supply chain model in eem representation. -->
22      <component class="org.eclipse.emf.mwe.utils.Reader">
23          <uri value="${model}"/>
24          <modelSlot value="model"/>
25      </component>
26
27      <!-- Apply checkMapping.chk and checkMappingConstraints.chk. -->
28      <component class="org.eclipse.xtend.check.CheckComponent">
29          <metaModel class="org.eclipse.xtend.typesystem.emf.EmfMetaModel"><
                metaModelPackage value="org.eclipse.emf.ecore.EcorePackage"/></metaModel
                >
30          <metaModel class="org.eclipse.xtend.typesystem.emf.EmfMetaModel"><
                metaModelPackage value="de.gulden.modeling.seem.mapping.MappingPackage"/
                ></metaModel>
31          <metaModel class="org.eclipse.xtend.typesystem.emf.EmfMetaModel"><
                metaModelPackage value="de.gulden.modeling.seem.eem.EemPackage"/></
                metaModel>
32          <checkFile value="checkMappingConstraints" />
33          <checkFile value="checkMapping" />
34          <emfAllChildrenSlot value="model" />
35          <abortOnError value="true"/>
36      </component>
37
38      <!-- - - - Check soa model. - - - -->
39
40      <!-- Read soa model. -->
41      <component class="org.eclipse.emf.mwe.utils.Reader">
42          <uri value="${soaModel}"/>
43          <modelSlot value="model"/>
44      </component>
45
```

```
46    <!-- Apply checkMappingSOA.chk and checkMappingSOAConstraints.chk. -->
47    <component class="org.eclipse.xtend.check.CheckComponent">
48        <metaModel class="org.eclipse.xtend.typesystem.emf.EmfMetaModel"><
              metaModelPackage value="org.eclipse.emf.ecore.EcorePackage"/></metaModel
              >
49        <metaModel class="org.eclipse.xtend.typesystem.emf.EmfMetaModel"><
              metaModelPackage value="de.gulden.modeling.seem.mapping.MappingPackage"/
              ></metaModel>
50        <metaModel class="org.eclipse.xtend.typesystem.emf.EmfMetaModel"><
              metaModelPackage value="de.gulden.modeling.seem.eem.EemPackage"/></
              metaModel>
...
```

org.rescueit.modeling.workflow/04-run-checkMapping.mwe: Invocation script to
perform validity checks on a mapping model and a SOA implementation strategy model.

A.4.3   Code generation

**Model-to-text transformation template to create executable BPEL code for a SOA
target architecture**   This file defines the generation logic, which finally binds together
the conceptual enterprise model, the implementation strategy model (or multiple implementation strategy models), and the interceding mapping model, to output deployable
BPEL artifacts.

```
1    «IMPORT soa»
2    «IMPORT eem»
3    «IMPORT mapping»
4
5    «EXTENSION org::eclipse::xtend::util::stdlib::globalvar»
6    «EXTENSION org::eclipse::xtend::util::stdlib::properties»
7    «EXTENSION common»
8    «EXTENSION rescueit»
9
10   «REM»
11   ******************************************************************************
12   *
13   * Project ReSCUe-IT
14   *
15   * Model-to-model transformation to textually generate a BPEL workflow model
16   * from a supply chain model in enterprise model representation, the ReSCUE-IT
17   * target architecture model, and an intermediating mapping model. The
18   * enterprise model rerpesenting the supply chain is derived with annotations
19   * from the supply chain modeler instance, using a separate transformation
20   * which gets executed prior to executing this one.
21   *
22   * The BPEL workflow model uses a different meta-meta-model than the input
23   * models, this is why a model-to-text approach is used for implementing
24   * the transformation.
25   *
26   * Written by Jens Gulden, 2011-2013, Chair for IT Security Management,
27   * University of Siegen, gulden@wiwi.uni-siegen.de
28   *
29   ******************************************************************************
30   «ENDREM»
31
32   «REM»**
33   *
34   * generate(MappingModel this)
35   *
```

```
36   * Entry template invoked from MWE script.
37   *
38   **«ENDREM»
39   «DEFINE generate FOR MappingModel»
40       «EXPAND generateBPEL»
41       «EXPAND generateWSDL»
42       «EXPAND generateDeploy»
43   «ENDDEFINE»
44
45   «DEFINE generateBPEL FOR MappingModel»
46       «FILE outputName()+".bpel"»«EXPAND process»«ENDFILE»
47   «ENDDEFINE»
48
49   «DEFINE generateWSDL FOR MappingModel»
50       «FILE outputName()+"Artifacts.wsdl"»«EXPAND wsdl»«ENDFILE»
```
...

org.rescueit.modeling.workflow/templates/soa/main.xpt: Main code generation script for
BPEL code generation.

Invocation script to run BPEL code generation With the `05-run-generator.mwe` modeling workflow script, the `main.xpt` template is invoked from the tooling environment to generate BPEL code.

`run-generator.mwe` loads the mapping model with all references into memory, and invokes the code generation engine with the `generator` entry template in `main.xpt`.

```
1    <!--
2       05-run-generator.mwe, invocation script to run the code generation transformation.
3       Written by Jens Gulden, gulden@wiwi.uni-siegen.de.
4       Licensed under a Creative Commons Attribution 3.0 Unported license.
5    -->
6
7    <workflow>
8
9        <!-- Workflow script for running BPEL code-generation. -->
10
11       <!-- Output base name. -->
12       <property name="outputName" value="RescueitSupplyChainProcess"/>
13
14       <!-- Read configuration properties from file 'workflow.properties'. -->
15       <property file="./workflow.properties"/>
16
17       <!-- Output directory. -->
18       <property name="outputPath" value="${projectRoot}/bpelContent"/>
19
20       <!-- Input file mapping model. -->
21       <property name="model" value="${projectRoot}/model/${projectPrefix}.mapping"/>
22
23       <!-- Initialize issue reporter. -->
24       <component class="org.eclipse.xtend.util.stdlib.ExtIssueReporter"/>
25
26       <!-- Make property values available to Xtend's properties extension.
27            conventions.properties contains hints on how to interpret the enterprise
28            model semantics. -->
29       <component class="org.eclipse.xtend.util.stdlib.PropertiesReader">
30           <propertiesFile value="./workflow.properties"/>
31           <propertiesFile value="./conventions.properties"/>
32           <propertiesFile value="/etc/rescueit.properties"/>
33       </component>
```

```
34
35      <!-- Read mapping model. -->
36      <component class="org.eclipse.emf.mwe.utils.Reader">
37          <uri value="${model}"/>
38          <modelSlot value="model"/>
39      </component>
40
41      <!-- Run code generation for BPEL, WSDL, and associated files. -->
42      <component class="org.eclipse.xpand2.Generator">
43          <fileEncoding value="ISO-8859-1"/>
44          <metaModel class="org.eclipse.xtend.typesystem.emf.EmfMetaModel"><
                metaModelPackage value="org.eclipse.emf.ecore.EcorePackage"/></metaModel
                >
45          <metaModel class="org.eclipse.xtend.typesystem.emf.EmfMetaModel"><
                metaModelPackage value="de.gulden.modeling.seem.mapping.MappingPackage"/
                ></metaModel>
46          <metaModel class="org.eclipse.xtend.typesystem.emf.EmfMetaModel"><
                metaModelPackage value="de.gulden.modeling.seem.eem.EemPackage"/></
                metaModel>
47          <metaModel class="org.eclipse.xtend.typesystem.emf.EmfMetaModel"><
                metaModelPackage value="org.rescueit.modeling.targetarchitecture.soa.
                SoaPackage"/></metaModel>
48          <outlet path="${outputPath}"/>
49          <globalVarDef name="outputName" value="'${outputName}'"/>
50          <expand value="soa::main::generate FOR model"/>
```

...

org.rescueit.modeling.workflow/05-run-generator.mwe: Invocation   script   to   run
`main.xpt` for BPEL code generation.

Combined workflow script to invoke all individual transformation steps   The `00-`
`run-all.mwe` modeling workflow script invokes all previously described individual invocation steps in one combined sequence. This is useful for projects which realize a zero-
coding approach, as it allows to run a fully automated artifact generation process without
developer interaction at generation time. (The leading "00-" part of the script name is used
to sort the file above other scripts in file-system views.)

```
1   <!--
2       00-run-all.mwe, invocation script to run all steps in sequence.
3       Written by Jens Gulden, gulden@wiwi.uni-siegen.de.
4       Licensed under a Creative Commons Attribution 3.0 Unported license.
5   -->
6
7   <workflow>
8
9   <!--
10      Workflow script for running all transformations, model checks, and code-
11      generation steps in sequence.
12  -->
13
14  <component file="01-run-adaptEM.mwe"/> <!-- inheritAll="true" -->
15  <component file="02-run-checkEM.mwe"/>
16  <component file="03-run-initMapping.mwe"/>
17  <component file="04-run-checkMapping.mwe"/>
18  <component file="05-run-generator.mwe"/>
19
20  </workflow>
```

org.rescueit.modeling.workflow/00-run-all.mwe: Combined workflow script to invoke all individual transformation steps in one sequence.

Global configuration file for the code generation process In `work-flow.properties`, global settings are specified to control the configuration of the code generation process. Among others, these settings include the path to the project root directory `projectRoot`, where the model files used throughout the method are stored, and the prefix of filenames used for storing the models, `projectPrefix`.

```
1   # workflow.properties, global configuration for the code generation process.
2   # Written by Jens Gulden, gulden@wiwi.uni-siegen.de.
3   # Licensed under a Creative Commons Attribution 3.0 Unported license.
4
5   # -- projectRoot
6   # Specifies the source project root folder where source models and generated models
7   # are located.
8   projectRoot=/home/user/runtime-rescueit/org.rescueit.server.platform.process
9
10  # -- projectTarget
11  # Specifies the target project root folder where generated source code and other
12  # artifacts are written to.
13  projectTarget=/home/user/runtime-rescueit/org.rescueit.server.platform.process/tmp
14
15  # -- projectPrefix
16  # Specifies a short name for the project, that can be used as name prefix in several
17  # cases.
18  #projectPrefix=icecream
19  #projectPrefix=tiramisu
20
21  #projectPrefix=GermanScenarioIceCream
22  projectPrefix=GermanScenarioIceCream
23  #projectPrefix=FrenchScenarioChemical3
24
25  # -- databaseRoot
26  # Specifies the XML database root directory where generated XML data and schema files
27  # are written to.
28  databaseRoot=/home/user/runtime-rescueit/org.rescueit.server.platform.process/xml
29
30  # -- reactionProcessModels
31  # Reaction process models referenced for the supply chain implementation.
32  reactionProcessModels=\
33  /home/user/runtime-rescueit/org.rescueit.server.platform.reactionProcess/model/
        foodIntoxication.reactionprocess,\
34  /home/user/runtime-rescueit/org.rescueit.server.platform.reactionProcess/model/
        icecreamContamination.reactionprocess
35
36  # -- projectStepNavigatorRoot
37  # Specifies the root folder of the Step Navigator web application project.
38  projectStepNavigatorRoot=/home/user/runtime-rescueit/org.rescueit.server.application.
        stepNavigator
39
40  # -- cepConfigurationPath
41  cepConfigurationPath=/home/user/runtime-rescueit/org.rescueit.server.cep.service/conf
        /etc/rescueit/cep
42
43  # -- esbConfigurationPath
44  esbConfigurationPath=/home/user/runtime-rescueit/org.rescueit.server.platform.commons
        /src/test/resources
45
```

```
46  # -- partnerConfigurationPath
47  partnerConfigurationPath=/home/user/runtime-rescueit/org.rescueit.server.partner.
        services/WebContent
```

org.rescueit.modeling.workflow/workflow.properties: Global code generation configuration.

Conventions configuration for model transformations and code generation To store external configuration options for conventions about hints that are used in model transformations and code generation steps throughout the method, the file `conventions.properties` is used. It declares, e. g., string fragments of identifier names, which are used to detect element types, or which are to match tagged values that are queried during the transformations.

```
 1  # conventions.properties, conventions configuration for model transformations
 2  # and code generation.
 3  # Written by Jens Gulden, gulden@wiwi.uni-siegen.de.
 4  # Licensed under a Creative Commons Attribution 3.0 Unported license.
 5
 6  # Hint to detect retailer role for actors.
 7  HINT_ACTOR_RETAILER = REWE, Casino
 8
 9  # Hint to detect producer role for actors.
10  HINT_ACTOR_PRODUCER = EisBaer, Distributor, Producer, Manufacturer
11
12  # Hint to detect distributor role for actors.
13  HINT_ACTOR_DISTRIBUTOR = Baam, BaaM, KuhneNagel, FreightForwarder, FreightForwarder1,
        FreightForwarder2
14
15  # Hint to detect distributor role for actors.
16  HINT_ACTOR_LAB = Lab, Laboratory, Robert Koch Institut
17
18  # Hint to detect an order process step.
19  HINT_PROCESS_ORDER = Order
20
21  # Hint to detect a dispatch process step.
22  HINT_PROCESS_DISPATCH = Dispatch, Send Good
23
24  # Hint to detect a transport process step.
25  HINT_PROCESS_TRANSPORT = Transport, Delivery
26
27  # Hint to detect an order-receive process step.
28  HINT_PROCESS_RECEIVE = Receive
29
30  # Hint to detect a cancel option.
31  HINT_CANCEL = Cancel
32
33  # French constellation
34  # The technical capabilities of each partner's system are modeled as web-services.
35  # They get configured with parameters of the form <name>_<param>, <name> being an
36  # actor's name in the model.
37
38  # Partner service's XML namespace prefix.
39  Casino_prefix = retail
40  # Partner service's XML namespace uri.
41  #Casino_namespace = http://rescueit.org/partner/ReweRetailerService/
42  # Partner service's WSDL file.
43  #Casino_wsdlFile = ReweRetailerService.wsdl
44  # Partner service's port type name.
45  Casino_name = ReweRetailerService
```

304

```
46   # Partner service's default port name.
47   #Casino_port = ReweRetailerServiceSOAP
48   # Partner service's ESB endpoint address.
49   Casino_esbEndpointAddress = 127.0.0.10
```

...

org.rescueit.modeling.workflow/conventions.properties: Conventions configuration for
model transformations and code generation.

A.4.4   Input model and generated example artifacts

XML data of the serialized supply chain example model   The XML data of the serialized supply chain example model is stored according to a schema that reflects the conceptual elements of the domain-specific supply chain modeling language. The example file
has been contributed to the RESCUEIT project by the project partner SAP AG.

The scm-to-eem.xslt transformation (see Appendix A.4.1) converts this representation to a model in the EEM language, which is further processed in the subsequent method
steps. Fig. 59 shows an excerpt of the visual representation of the supply chain model.

```
1    <?xml version="1.0"?>
2    <SupplyChain>
3      <Assets>
4        <Asset id="Asset_0" name="PurchaseOrder" type="Logical" />
5        <Asset id="Asset_1" name="IceCream" type="Physical" />
6        <Asset id="Asset_2" name="IceCreamSample" type="Physical" />
7        <Asset id="Asset_3" name="LetterOfConfirmation" type="Logical" />
8        <Asset id="Asset_4" name="DeliveryContract" type="Logical" />
9        <Asset id="Asset_5" name="LabReport" type="Logical" />
10       <Asset id="Asset_6" name="WayBill" type="Logical" />
11     </Assets>
12     <Locations>
13       <Location Name="EisBaer" ID="location_1" Latitude="53,4340705871582" Longitude
            ="9,61501979827881">
14         <Country>Germany</Country>
15         <City>
16         </City>
17         <PostCode>
18         </PostCode>
19         <Street>
20         </Street>
21         <House>
22         </House>
23       </Location>
24       <Location Name="REWE" ID="location_2" Latitude="49,0107917785645" Longitude
            ="8,40865039825439">
25         <Country>Germany</Country>
26         <City>
27         </City>
28         <PostCode>
29         </PostCode>
30         <Street>
31         </Street>
32         <House>
33         </House>
34       </Location>
35     </Locations>
36     <Participants>
```

```
37    <Participant Name="REWE" EMail="" />
38    <Participant Name="EisBaer" EMail="" />
39    <Participant Name="BaaM" EMail="" />
40    <Participant Name="Lab" EMail="" />
41   </Participants>
42   <Processes>
43    <InternalProcess Name="Sequence" Owner="REWE">
44     <Sequence Name="Sequence">
45      <Sequence Name="Sequence">
46       <CommunicationActivity Name="Communication Activity">
47        <Interface>
48         <Output id="Argument_0" Asset="PurchaseOrder" />
49        </Interface>
50        <Controls>
```

...

org.rescueit.modeling.workflow/example/GermanScenarioIceCream.xml: XML data of
the serialized supply chain example model.

Generated executable BPEL workflow model   The BPEL workflow model is generated
as an executable artifact by the example application of the method. When deployed with
a BPEL interpreter engine, the BPEL interpreter will read the XML-encoded workflow
process description, and will execute the described process.

```
1    <!--
2      ReSCUe-IT Secure Supply Chain BPEL Process
3      Generated from supply chain model.
4      Author: Jens Gulden
5      Date: Thu Dec 20 16:55:53 CET 2012
6    -->
7
8    <bpel:process name="RescueitSupplyChainProcess"
9        targetNamespace="http://rescueit.org/platform/RescueitSupplyChainProcess"
10       suppressJoinFailure="yes"
11       xmlns:bpel="http://docs.oasis-open.org/wsbpel/2.0/process/executable"
12       xmlns:xsd="http://www.w3.org/2001/XMLSchema"
13       xmlns:tns="http://rescueit.org/platform/RescueitSupplyChainProcess"
14       xmlns:mail="http://mail.service.platform.server.rescueit.org"
15       xmlns:conf="http://config.service.platform.server.rescueit.org"
16       xmlns:log="http://log.service.platform.server.rescueit.org"
17       xmlns:util="http://util.service.platform.server.rescueit.org"
18       xmlns:obs="http://service.cep.server.rescueit.org"
19       xmlns:sign="http://signatureController.sichere-warenketten.de"
20       xmlns:verify="http://genericVerify.sichere-warenketten.de"
21       xmlns:mes="http://modelextractionagent.rwip.research.sap.com/"
22       xmlns:strack="http://securetrackeragent.rwip.research.sap.com/"
23       xmlns:bench="http://tempuri.org/"
24       xmlns:cts="http://statut.services.demsta.soget.com/"
25       xmlns:cta="http://alert.services.demsta.soget.com/"
26       xmlns:idemixProver="http://service.model.client.idews.itsec.unisiegen.de/"
27       xmlns:idemixVerify="http://verifier.services.verifier.idews.itsec.unisiegen.de/"
28       xmlns:rewe="http://rescueit.org/partner/ReweRetailerService"
29       xmlns:eisb="http://rescueit.org/partner/EisbaerProduceService"
30       xmlns:baam="http://rescueit.org/partner/BaamTransportService"
31       xmlns:lab="http://rescueit.org/partner/LabAnalysisService"
32       xmlns:orders="http://smooks.org/UNEDI/D09BUN/ORDERS"
33       xmlns:ordrsp="http://smooks.org/UNEDI/D09BUN/ORDRSP"
34       xmlns:iftmin="http://smooks.org/UNEDI/D09BUN/IFTMIN"
35       xmlns:medrpt="http://smooks.org/UNEDI/D09BUN/MEDRPT"
36       xmlns:desadv="http://smooks.org/UNEDI/D09BUN/DESADV"
```

```
37   >
38
39       <!-- import WSDLs -->
40
41       <bpel:import namespace="http://rescueit.org/platform/RescueitSupplyChainProcess"
42           location="RescueitSupplyChainProcessArtifacts.wsdl"
43           importType="http://schemas.xmlsoap.org/wsdl/" />
44       <bpel:import namespace="http://mail.service.platform.server.rescueit.org"
45           location="wsdl/MailService.wsdl"
46           importType="http://schemas.xmlsoap.org/wsdl/" />
47       <bpel:import namespace="http://config.service.platform.server.rescueit.org"
48           location="wsdl/ConfigService.wsdl"
49           importType="http://schemas.xmlsoap.org/wsdl/" />
50       <bpel:import namespace="http://log.service.platform.server.rescueit.org"
```

...

org.rescueit.modeling.workflow/example/SupplyChainProcess.bpel: Generated executable BPEL workflow description as output of the applied model transformations.

Generated WSDL interface declaration for the BPEL workflow model The corresponding interface declaration for the generated BPEL workflow model is given as a WSDL file. Like the BPEL model, it is generated via the code generation mechanism of the method based on information derived from the conceptual input models, and associated implementation strategy models. The generated file references a manually edited XML Schema Definition (XSD) part, included from a static file (see next paragraph).

```
1    <?xml version="1.0" encoding="UTF-8" standalone="no"?>
2    <!--
3      ReSCUe-IT Secure Supply Chain WSDL Interface
4      Generated from supply chain model.
5      Author: Jens Gulden
6      Date: Thu Dec 20 16:55:56 CET 2012
7    -->
8
9    <definitions xmlns="http://schemas.xmlsoap.org/wsdl/" name="
         RescueitSupplyChainProcess" targetNamespace="http://rescueit.org/platform/
         RescueitSupplyChainProcess"
10     xmlns:varprop="http://docs.oasis-open.org/wsbpel/2.0/varprop"
11     xmlns:xsd="http://www.w3.org/2001/XMLSchema"
12     xmlns:plnk="http://docs.oasis-open.org/wsbpel/2.0/plnktype"
13     xmlns:soap="http://schemas.xmlsoap.org/wsdl/soap/"
14     xmlns:http="http://schemas.xmlsoap.org/wsdl/http/"
15     xmlns:mime="http://schemas.xmlsoap.org/wsdl/mime/"
16     xmlns:tns="http://rescueit.org/platform/RescueitSupplyChainProcess"
17     xmlns:mail="http://mail.service.platform.server.rescueit.org"
18     xmlns:conf="http://config.service.platform.server.rescueit.org"
19     xmlns:log="http://log.service.platform.server.rescueit.org"
20     xmlns:util="http://util.service.platform.server.rescueit.org"
21     xmlns:obs="http://service.cep.server.rescueit.org"
22     xmlns:sign="http://signatureController.sichere-warenketten.de"
23     xmlns:verify="http://genericVerify.sichere-warenketten.de"
24     xmlns:mes="http://modelextractionagent.rwip.research.sap.com/"
25     xmlns:strack="http://securetrackeragent.rwip.research.sap.com/"
26     xmlns:bench="http://tempuri.org/"
27     xmlns:cts="http://statut.services.demsta.soget.com/"
28     xmlns:cta="http://alert.services.demsta.soget.com/"
29     xmlns:idemixProver="http://service.model.client.idews.itsec.unisiegen.de/"
30     xmlns:idemixVerify="http://verifier.services.verifier.idews.itsec.unisiegen.de/"
```

```
31      xmlns:rewe="http://rescueit.org/partner/ReweRetailerService"
32      xmlns:eisb="http://rescueit.org/partner/EisbaerProduceService"
33      xmlns:baam="http://rescueit.org/partner/BaamTransportService"
34      xmlns:lab="http://rescueit.org/partner/LabAnalysisService"
35      xmlns:orders="http://smooks.org/UNEDI/D09BUN/ORDERS"
36      xmlns:ordrsp="http://smooks.org/UNEDI/D09BUN/ORDRSP"
37      xmlns:iftmin="http://smooks.org/UNEDI/D09BUN/IFTMIN"
38      xmlns:medrpt="http://smooks.org/UNEDI/D09BUN/MEDRPT"
39      xmlns:desadv="http://smooks.org/UNEDI/D09BUN/DESADV"
40  >
41
42      <plnk:partnerLinkType name="RescueitSupplyChainProcess_PLT">
43          <plnk:role name="RescueitSupplyChainProcessRole" portType="
                tns:RescueitSupplyChainProcess_PortType"/>
44      </plnk:partnerLinkType>
45      <plnk:partnerLinkType name="MailService_PLT">
46          <plnk:role name="MailServiceRole" portType="mail:MailServicePortType"/>
47      </plnk:partnerLinkType>
48      <plnk:partnerLinkType name="ConfigService_PLT">
49          <plnk:role name="ConfigServiceRole" portType="conf:ConfigServicePortType"/>
50      </plnk:partnerLinkType>
```

...

org.rescueit.modeling.workflow/example/SupplyChainProcessArtifacts.wsdl: Generated
WSDL interface declaration for the BPEL workflow model.

XML schema declaration included in the generated WSDL file   This XSD gets included into the generated WSDL file. The type specifications given here are manually
edited.

```
1   <?xml version="1.0" encoding="UTF-8"?>
2   <!--
3     ReSCUe-IT Secure Supply Chain WSDL Interface Type Schema
4     Included by the generated file SupplyChainProcessArtifacts.wsdl.
5     Author: Jens Gulden
6   -->
7
8   <schema xmlns="http://www.w3.org/2001/XMLSchema"
9       attributeFormDefault="unqualified" elementFormDefault="qualified"
10      targetNamespace="http://rescueit.org/platform/RescueitSupplyChainProcess">
11
12      <element name="RescueitAlert">
13          <complexType>
14              <sequence>
15                  <element name="goodID" type="string"/>
16                  <element name="timestamp" type="long"/>
17                  <element name="type" type="string"/>
18                  <element name="value" type="string"/>
19                  <element name="message" type="string"/>
20                  <element name="configuration" type="string"/>
21              </sequence>
22          </complexType>
23      </element>
24
25      <element name="physicalStepReached">
26          <complexType>
27              <sequence>
28                  <element name="goodID" type="string" />
29                  <element name="stepID" type="string" />
30                  <element name="fluxnb" type="string" />
31                  <element name="statusCode" type="string" />
```

```
32          <element name="statusDescription" type="string" />
33          <element name="location" type="string" />
34          <element name="latitude" type="double" />
35          <element name="longitude" type="double" />
36        </sequence>
37      </complexType>
38    </element>
39    <element name="physicalStepHasBeenReachedResponse">
40      <complexType>
41        <sequence>
42          <element name="out" type="string" />
43        </sequence>
44      </complexType>
45    </element>
46
47    <element name="secureTrackingAlert">
48      <complexType>
49        <sequence>
50          <element name="goodID" type="string" />
```
...

org.rescueit.modeling.workflow/example/SupplyChainProcessSchema.xsd: Manually
edited XML schema declaration included in the generated WSDL file.

**Convert cardinality specifications from EMF meta-models to constraint expressions
in the Check language**   Using the `cardinalitiesToConstraints.xpt` transformation, the automatically derived CHECK scripts `checkEMConstraints.chk` (see
Appendix A.3.1), `checkMappingConstraints.chk` (see Appendix A.3.2), and
scripts for architecture-specific implementation strategy models are generated. The specified transformation converts cardinality specifications from EMF meta-models to a set of
constraint expressions in the CHECK language. Since expressions of the CHECK language
are executed by the underlying modeling transformation mechanism, one may speak of the
`cardinalitiesToConstraints.xpt` transformation as a higher-order transformation, which outputs another yet to be executed model transformation/validity check script
for performing model checks.

```
1    «REM»
2      cardinalitiesToConstraints.xpt, code generation templates for generating constraint
3      expressions in the Check language from cardinality specifications in EMF meta-
4      models.
5      Written by Jens Gulden, jens.gulden@uni-due.de.
6      Licensed under a Creative Commons Attribution 3.0 Unported license.
7    «ENDREM»
8
9    «IMPORT ecore»
10
11   «EXTENSION common»
12
13   «REM»
14   *
15   * Generate file header.
16   *
17   «ENDREM»
18   «DEFINE header FOR Object-»
19   /* Generated file, generator written by Jens Gulden, jens.gulden@uni-due.de.
20      Licensed under a Creative Commons Attribution 3.0 Unported license. */
21   «ENDDEFINE»
```

```
22
23   «REM»
24   *
25   * Generate check script from eem meta model.
26   *
27   «ENDREM»
28   «DEFINE transformEem FOR EPackage»
29   «FILE "checkEMConstraints.chk"-»
30   «EXPAND header»
31
32   import eem;
33   «EXPAND transform»
34   «ENDFILE»
35   «ENDDEFINE»
36
37   «REM»
38   *
39   * Generate check script from mapping meta model.
40   *
41   «ENDREM»
42   «DEFINE transformMapping FOR EPackage»
43   «FILE "checkMappingConstraints.chk"-»
44   «EXPAND header»
45
46   import mapping;
47   «EXPAND transform»
48   «ENDFILE»
49   «ENDDEFINE»
```

...

de.gulden.modeling.seem.generator/templates/cardinalitiesToConstraints.xpt: Code generation declaration to convert cardinality specifications from EMF meta-models to constraint expressions in the CHECK language.

Invocation script to run the `cardinalitiesToConstraints.xpt` transformation This MWE script executes the `cardinalitiesToConstraints.xpt` from within the tooling environment.

```
1    <!--
2      run-cardinalitiesToConstraints.mwe, invocation script to run the
3      cardinalitiesToConstraints.xpt transformation.
4      Written by Jens Gulden, jens.gulden@uni-due.de.
5      Licensed under a Creative Commons Attribution 3.0 Unported license.
6    -->
7
8    <workflow>
9
10   <!--
11       Workflow script for running the cardinalities-to-constraints transformation,
12       which converts cardinality information in Ecore meta-models to model constraints
13       in the Check language (related to the Xtend language).
14     -->
15
16       <!-- Base directory. -->
17       <property name="home" value="/home/user"/>
18
19       <!-- Templates directory. -->
20       <property name="templates" value="${home}/runtime-memocenter/de.gulden.modeling.
                 seem.generator/templates"/>
21
```

```
22    <!-- Eem meta-model. -->
23    <property name="metamodelEem" value="${home}/runtime-memocenter/de.gulden.
          modeling.seem.eem/model/eem.ecore"/>
24
25    <!-- Mapping meta-model. -->
26    <property name="metamodelMapping" value="${home}/runtime-memocenter/de.gulden.
          modeling.seem.mapping/model/mapping.ecore"/>
27
28    <!-- Web architecture meta-model. -->
29    <property name="metamodelWeb" value="${home}/runtime-memocenter/de.gulden.
          modeling.seem.architecture.web/model/web.ecore"/>
30
31    <!-- BPEL architecture meta-model. -->
32    <property name="metamodelBPEL" value="${home}/runtime-memocenter/org.rescueit.
          modeling.targetarchitecture/model/bpelProcess.ecore"/>
33
34    <!-- SOA architecture meta-model. -->
35    <property name="metamodelSOA" value="${home}/runtime-memocenter/org.rescueit.
          modeling.targetarchitecture/model/soa.ecore"/>
36
37    <!-- Read the Eem meta-model. -->
38    <component class="org.eclipse.xtend.typesystem.emf.XmiReader">
39        <modelFile value="${metamodelEem}"/>
40        <outputSlot value="model"/>
41    </component>
42
43    <!-- Run transformation for the Eem meta-model. -->
44    <component class="org.eclipse.xpand2.Generator">
45        <fileEncoding value="ISO-8859-1"/>
46        <metaModel class="org.eclipse.xtend.typesystem.emf.EmfMetaModel">
47            <metaModelPackage value="org.eclipse.emf.ecore.EcorePackage"/>
48        </metaModel>
49        <outlet path="${templates}"/>
```

...

de.gulden.modeling.seem.generator/templates/run-cardinalitiesToConstraints.mwe:
Invocation script to run the higher-order `cardinalitiesToConstraints.xpt`
transformation.

Glossary

Application programming interface (API) A set of functions to be called by software components. APIs are either provided by infrastructural components such as the operation system, or by applications as a basis to interface to and extend existing functionality. An abstract API, which does not provide concrete functionality to use, but declares concepts such as abstract classes and interfaces to build software upon, may also be offered by theoretical work such as the description of an engineering method. 19, 34, 72, 93, 161, 231

Binary large object (BLOB) Binary large objects represent the most general notion of a data object with unspecified semantics. To work with BLOBs means for a software component to handle any kind of data, without being capable to interpret it, i. e., it can merely store and retrieve that data. 19, 198

Business Process Execution Language (BPEL) A modeling language for expressing automatized business processes. BPEL has primarily been developed to provide a common standard for input data to configure workflow execution engines, and to decouple the workflow engine configuration mechanism from a modeling perspective. 19, 37, 53, 79, 114, 163, 214

Business process model (BPM) Business process models are graphical or textual language artifacts, which represent some aspects of dynamic behavior in an organization. They are domain-specific models with specific semantics for conceptually expressing knowledge about organizational scenarios. Business process models usually integrate multiple perspectives on an organization, by allowing to interlink multiple model perspectives about involved actors, used resources, related strategic goals, performance indicators, etc. Due to this interlinking function, BPMs form the central modeling perspective in domain-specific organization modeling. 19, 37, 53, 64, 110, 162, 247

Business process modeling language (BPML) A domain-specific modeling language for expressing the behavior of multiple actors and resources during the execution of a business process instance. Typical concepts offered by BPMLs are process-steps, events, parallel execution branches and synchronizers, and alternative decision branches and joins. To be suited for enterprise modeling, a BPML should be capable of referencing actor concepts and resource descriptions, to provide sufficient semantics. When a BPML is capable of interlinking to actor concepts and resource concepts from other domain-specific modeling language perspectives, it can be part of a set of interrelated multi-perspective EMLs. 19, 70, 110

Business Process Modeling Notation (BPMN) A graphical language for visually expressing BPMs. The current version 2.0 of the language offers a rich set of modeling elements with technical detail semantics, which allow to express implementation-near design decisions about automatic execution of the modeled processes. In this sense, the BPMN is not solely a conceptual business process modeling language, but mixes elements for describing implementation details into the language. Discussions about using BPEL as underlying formal semantic representation for BPMN underline the close relationship of BPMN to implementation concepts. . 19, 54, 79, 245

Commercial off-the-shelf (COTS) The class of commercial off-the-shelf software applications denotes software packages with a generic purpose and a broad range of applicability, such as word processors, e-mail clients, or web-browsers. Because these tools serve generic purposes without the need to be adapted to specific contextual conditions of their use, they can be produced by a small number of major vendors, and be mass-distributed to a large number of users. 19, 32

Common Objects Request Broker Architecture (CORBA) A conceptualization of a central management system for distributed environments, which makes multiple distributed and heterogeneous clients interoperable through an adaptable mechanism of a common data type system, and a common way to invoke remote functionality. 19, 146

Computation independent model (CIM) A model that expresses incidents without relation to representation in a computer system, or operation by an automatic processing technology. Domain-specific organization models are computation independent models (CIMs).

(*Also:* Computer Integrated Manufacturing, which denotes production processes of physical goods, in which software is used to control production machines.) . 19, 31, 74, 311

Computer numerical control (CNC) Traditional term for software-programmable production machines for physical goods. Typical machines of this type are automatized drilling or sawing devices, forming raw material according to programmed procedures. 19, 83

Data definition language (DDL) A formal language to specify data types and structures to be stored in a database. Typically, relational databases use language components of Structured Query Language (SQL) as DDL, which basically are the `CREATE DATABASE` and `CREATE TABLE` statements, together with corresponding statements for modifying existing data definitions, and for deleting them. 19, 319

Database management system (DBMS) A software component either run locally on a client platform for local data storage purposes, or run centrally on a server accessed by multiple client with potentially concurrent accesses. The DBMS receives SQL statements and interprets and executes them. Besides correctly interpreting SQL, DBMSs typically are designed to perform highly efficient data storage and access, and allow for synchronizing concurrent accesses from multiple clients in a distributed environment to operate concurrently without semantic defects (e. g., phantoms, orphans) due to parallel accesses to data. 19, 257

Domain-specific modeling (DSM)   Creating models about incidents in specific domains with a modeling language that is especially suited for this domain. Since the modeling language and the incident to be modeled are closely related to each other, creating a new modeling language with suitable language constructs is often part of DSM projects. 19, 77, 109, 312

Domain-specific modeling language (DSML)   A modeling language, which has especially been created to create models that describe specific incidents of a domain. To do so efficiently, the language is made up of language constructs, which provide a formal reconstruction of the natural language elements used by human experts to describe the domain. Traditional domain-specific modeling (DSM) methods suggest to create a new DSML for each domain-specific development, to be able to reach a maximum of problem-adequate representation in domain-specific models. Together with the development of a DSML, typically code generation templates, or other artifact generation mechanisms, are developed, which allow for transformation content in domain-specific model instances to technical artifact representations. . 19, 34, 73, 312

Domain-specific software engineering (DSSE)   Software engineering projects, which apply DSM techniques, including the development of a domain-specific modeling language (DSML), creation of domain-specific models, and corresponding artifacts generation mechanisms. 19, 34, 73, 76, 97, 231

Eclipse Modeling Framework (EMF)   A technology framework that extends the ECLIPSE platform by a set of software components and accompanied APIs for handling models. The EMF contains the ECORE modeling language to build meta-models that describe modeling languages. These meta-models can subsequently be used as the basis to derive model editors for the specified modeling language via code generation features, which are integrated into EMF. Besides the core EMF features, additional components are available to further extend the platform, e. g., the GMF (see there). Both frameworks are sometimes subsumed under the general term EMF in the course of this work, where a detailed distinctions of the individual components is not required. 19, 51, 101, 216, 235, 255

Enhanced Backus-Naur Form (EBNF)   Wide-spread grammar for specifying formal textual languages. Combining terminal and non-terminal symbols, the EBNF provides a recursive description scheme, which, e. g., is frequently used to describe the syntax of programming language constructs. 19, 120

Enterprise architecture (EA)   Conceptualization of the relationships between involved actors, resource and processes in an organization. An EA can be specified in an formal modeling language, e. g. EMLs, or using informal textual description means. 19, 27, 79

Enterprise information system (EIS)   A software system to support collaborative tasks in an organization. An EIS provides internal functionality, and integrates external components, to form an organization-specific integrated information system. Business companies, non-profit organizations or governmental institutions are organizations using EISs.

The identical acronym sometimes is used to refer to the term "executive information system". While an executive information system may be an integrated component in an overall enterprise information system, the term "enterprise information system" denotes a broader notion of EIS, as it is used throughout this work.1, 19, 29, 60, 93, 161, 230, 253

Enterprise model (EM) Domain-specific models, which express knowledge about the processes performed in an organization, the actors and resources involved, organizational and operational responsibility, as well as strategic aspects of an organization. EM may be purely CIMs, if they restrain to expressing conceptual statements about the organization, or may integrate references to technical concepts to bridge between conceptual organization descriptions and implementation approaches. As informal means of communication, EM foster a common understanding among multiple human modelers about the same objects of interest with regard to the modeled organization. Extending these informal semantics, EM can also be the basis for a enterprise model-driven software engineering (EMDSE) process to develop software applications for the organization.................1, 19, 27, 67, 79, 87, 97, 98, 245

Enterprise model-driven software engineering (EMDSE) A class of software engineering approaches, in which EMs are the starting point for a software development process. The method then makes proposition about how to interpret the EMs to derive technical artifacts from them. This interpretation process may be supported with automatic means, or may solely be described by the method on an abstract level. The SEEM method, which is elaborated throughout this work, is an EMDSE method with a high degree of automation. 19, 34, 118, 313

Enterprise modeling environment (EME) A software application, or combination of multiple applications, which supports in creating, editing, and managing enterprise model instances. An EME typically comes with a set of model editors, and functionality for managing persisted model artifacts, and possibly interchange them with other users...19, 87, 254

Enterprise modeling language (EML) A domain-specific language, or a family of interrelated languages, used to describe incidents in an organization. To allow for efficiently describing these incidents, an EML at least incorporates language element types for involved actors, resources, process-steps and events, and rules of the dynamic behavior of an organizations. These conceptualizations may be enriched by, e. g., strategic description elements or coarse-grained value-chain categorizations. EMLs sometimes are defined as a set of interrelated perspectives, specified by multiple interrelated modeling languages. For this reason, in the course of this work, the singular and the plural form of the term can be used interchangeably in most parts describing the method. 19, 26, 27, 61, 92, 245

Enterprise service bus (ESB) A component in a SOA, which bundles multiple services from possible heterogeneous sources to reflect them by a standardized interface, and make them available at a single entry point at the ESB. An ESB typically does not provide business functionality by its own, but combines a set of tooling services that allow to interface to existing services, allow to expose their functionality via standardized interfaces, and allow access control and secure communication techniques to be set up in front of the exposed service functionalities. 20, 214

Event-driven process chain (EPC) A widely used business process modeling language consisting primarily of the concepts of events and actions. The languages enforces a strictly alternating order between events and actions, meaning that no process models are allowed, which would result in runtime instances with two actions following each other consecutively, or two events, which follow each other directly. The EPC language has been introduced with the ARIS method [Sch02b], and corresponding tooling support is available with the software packages supporting this method. . 19, 82

Extensible Markup Language (XML) A class of formal languages, the members of which are composed according to a common meta-meta-model consisting of the meta-types element, attribute and nesting relationships. Syntactically, XML instances are expressed as textual documents, in which element instances and their attributes appear as tags of the form `<element-name attribute-name-1=attribute-value-1 attribute-name-2=attribute-value-2 ...>` `...</element-name>`. Nested child elements appear in between the starting tag `<element-name ...>` and the closing tag `</element-name>`. 21, 42, 47, 85, 218

Extensible Stylesheet Language Transformations (XSLT) A language for describing a transformation type that transforms an XML document instance into another. The XSLT language itself also is formulated in an XML syntax. 21, 292

Extracted enterprise model (EEM) A model type introduced for the developed engineering method, which contains all relevant concepts of a set of original enterprise models required for further augmentation with architectural design decisions and implementation details. It can automatically be derived from original enterprise models using a horizontal model-to-model adapter transformation. . 19, 43, 92, 119, 131, 189, 223

General purpose modeling language (GPML) A modeling language that aims at providing language constructs, which are abstract enough to not be bound to a specific context of a modeled domain. Yet, the constructs are intended to be useful for any modeling project in any context. The abstractions offered by such languages mostly resemble basic ontological concepts, such as classes, attributes, relationship, etc. The best known representative of GPMLs is the Unified Modeling Language (UML). 20, 73, 74, 235

Graphical Modeling Framework (GMF) A technology framework that extends the EMF framework on top of the ECLIPSE platform by a set of software components and accompanied APIs for describing graphical diagram languages and corresponding model editors. In parallel to the EMF, the GMF also provides code generation facilities to generatively create diagram editors that get integrated on the ECLIPSE platform. 20, 255

Graphical user interface (GUI) A set of graphical accessibility components ("widgets"), implemented as part of a software application, for a human user to interact with the software system. 20, 39, 60, 114, 161, 165, 213, 249

Hyper-Text Transfer Protocol (HTTP) Communication protocol for data communication on the application level, which is typically used for data transfer between web-browser clients and web-application servers in a distributed client-server web application architecture. In its basic functionality, HTTP allows a web-browser to identify electronic resources on a server and to issue requests for getting them. As corresponding responses from a web-server, the identified resources are returned. By convention, parameters can be attached to requests, which can dynamically be evaluated by the web-server, resulting in a returned resource which has specifically been generated as a response to the parametrized request. Using this mechanisms, interactive software applications can be created, which get used through a web-browser. 20, 226

Information systems science (ISS) An area of science which deals with questions about effective and efficient development and use of computers and software for specific purposes. ISS creates and reflects about artifacts of IT. 20, 315

Information technology (IT) Computer and software artifacts which realize concepts of information systems science (ISS). 20, 30, 54, 73, 214

Integrated development environment (IDE) A software application for end-users, typically with a rich set of GUI functionality, for supporting software development related tasks. Typical target end-users of IDEs are software architects and developers. 20, 84, 235

Internet Protocol (IP) The standard for routing data through the internet. A central conceptual introduction by IP is the use of 32 bit encoded node addresses (IP addresses notated in the form aa.bb.cc.dd) in version 4 of IP, and 128 bit wide addresses in version 6. . . . . 20, 214

Java Server Pages (JSP) A technology to build and deploy web applications using the JAVA programming language. 20, 37, 140, 226

MEMO Meta-Modeling Language (MML) The meta-modeling language, which is part of the MEMO enterprise modeling method. Using the MML, domain-specific modeling languages can be defined, and corresponding model editors can be generated, which allow to create and edit model instances in these languages. . . . 20, 100, 241

Model-Driven Architecture (MDA) A methodical approach authored by the Object Management Group (OMG) to develop software with the help of general purpose modeling languages. Central to the approach is the distinction between CIMs, platform independent models (PIMs) and platform specific models (PSMs). The method describes a methodical procedure which guides developers from creating CIMs over creating PIMs to creating PSMs. When all required levels of abstraction are described with models, code generation techniques are applied to generate deployable software artifacts from the models 20, 34, 74

Model-driven development (MDD) Synonym to model-driven software engineering (MDSE). The term MDD is had been used a method trademark by the OMG until 2004, but today generically references a class of software development procedures, which make use of modeling techniques to derive software in a defined transformation procedure. 20, 73, 317

Model-driven software engineering (MDSE) A term denoting the class of engineering methods which make use of modeling techniques to describe features of the software system to be developed, as well as of code generation approaches to formally define a projection from models into deployable software artifacts. 20, 49, 73, 316

Modeling Workflow Engine (MWE) An interpreter mechanism which can be freely configured to execute sequences of automatic operations on models. Possible operations are, e. g., model-to-model transformations, validity checks or code generation steps. The MWE is part of supplementary modeling technology packages for the EMF. 20, 225

Multi-Perspective Enterprise Modeling (MEMO) An enterprise modeling method developed by Prof. ULRICH FRANK [Fra94, Fra02, Fra11d, Fra12], which incorporates a semantically interlinked set of modeling languages. Model instances in these languages provide a multi-perspective view on the socio-technical action systems of organizations. 20, 27, 52, 80, 137, 255

Object Management Group (OMG) A standardization organization, which, among others, is responsible for issuing modeling-related development standards, e. g., BPMN, UML, XML. 20, 74, 316

Object request broker (ORB) A central coordinating software component in a distributed, heterogeneous environment, which serves to translate between syntactically incomaptible interfaces of heterogeneous components that are to be semantically integrated. 20, 62

Open Services Gateway initiative (OSGi) The OSGi Alliance, formerly Open Services Gateway initiative, has specified an architectural approach for building software applications as a set of loosely coupled components, which are loaded into a common hub platform to form a common software application. A famous example representative of a software application build on top of such an OSGi platform is the ECLIPSE platform, with its mostly used application as IDE. 20, 235

Peer-to-peer (P2P)   General type of a distributed system architecture with multiple involved clients, which autonomously communicate among each other to achieve the goals of common system functionality. A P2P system is characterized by not using a centralized communication hub for interacting among client nodes. However, parts of common system functionality may be centralized, e. g., client authentication and authorization mechanisms. 20, 164

Platform independent model (PIM)   A model which describes a software system's architectural design, without referencing details about the technical implementation of deployable artifacts. These details can be specified independently using PSMs. As a consequence, a PIM can be the basis for multiple different technical realizations on different target architecture platforms. 20, 74, 316

Platform specific model (PSM)   A software model which incorporates fine grained technological details about the implementation of a deployable artifact. As part of a model-driven development (MDD) approach, PSMs, together with PIMs and CIMs, contain all information required to apply code generation techniques which transform the models to deployable software artifacts. 20, 74, 316

Process-aware information system (PAIS)   An information system, which focuses on global processes combining individual tasks, rather than offering functionality for executing individual tasks. More fine-grained functionality for executing individual steps is expected to be available via external application or by imported components. By describing software systems in terms of there processes, their declaration gets aligned to descriptions of contextual real-world circumstances of the organizations for which PAISs are to be developed. 20, 84

Process-centered software engineering environment (PCSEE)   A software development tool or a set of tools which make use of process descriptions to create executable software artifacts. Typically, such an environment operates with process models, either by interpreting them or transforming them, to associate modeled business functionality in process models, with executable software functionality. 20, 84

Production planning and control (PPC)   Software systems, which are categorized as PPC applications, provide integrated functionality for administrative planning of production processes, as well as machine control to perform physical production processes. 20, 83

Rational Unified Process (RUP)   A method for software development, which is combined from multiple individual pieces of methodical approaches. The RUP aims at unifying these individual origins into one comprehensive method, which covers all phases in the software development life-cycle. The efforts for creating RUP originate in the same motivation as creating the UML, and have been carried out by the same key authors. In this sense, RUP complements the static set of languages suggested by the UML with a procedural framework of how the languages in the UML are to be applied. 21, 75, 253

Role-based access control (RBAC)   An authorization mechanism in multi-user software systems, which makes use of the central notion of roles to control access to resources. By both associating user accounts with roles, and specifying allowed roles for accessing resources, the concept of a role forms a suitable abstraction to formulate complex constellations of access-rights. 21, 83

Service oriented architecture (SOA)   An approach for building possibly distributed software system, which focuses primarily on a clean an generally applicable definition of interfaces and communication patterns between multiple software components. The primary abstraction for describing an outer view on a software component's functionality is the service concept, which gets further dub-divided into interfaces and operations, and corresponding type descriptions for input and output data of operations. SOA describes a general notion of how to build large-scaled software systems, the application of SOA development methods can lead to diverse methodical procedures and created artifacts in the result. To formally describe the services and interfaces in a SOA, the WSDL is typically used.21, 36, 140, 165, 214

Simple Object Access Protocol (SOAP)   A technology for remotely passing data between software components. 21, 53, 64

Software Engineering with Enterprise Models (SEEM)   The methodical software engineering procedure developed in this work, which makes use of EMs as domain description means, and applies enhanced DSSE techniques to guide the creation of software from enterprise models. 2, 21, 28, 50, 67, 94, 165, 211

Strategic Alignment Model (SAM)   A technique for conceptualizing relationships between long-term business strategies, and corresponding strategic management of IT. Mutual influences of either kinds of strategic decision making on each other are taken into account by the approach. For practical application, the model can be used as a managerial tool to support elaborating possible long-term orientated strategies. 21, 84

Structured Query Language (SQL)   A formal language for describing extraction of data from a relation database, or insertion of data into such a database. A database is understood as a collection of tables with named columns and typically uniquely identifiable row entries in each table. SQL contains language constructs both for managing the structure of databases and the tables they contain (this subset of the language is called data definition language (DDL), see there), as well as constructs for filling, querying and deleting content from the tables. The statements formulated in SQL are interpreted and executed by a DBMS, which typically receives SQL commands via network from potentially multiple concurrent clients. 21, 311

Unified Modeling Language (UML) A set of GPMLs that are intended to offer comprehensive semantic means to express all aspects of a software system required to apply MDD techniques. The UML contains languages to model static system structures, which are the commonly known class diagram language, and the package diagram language as well as the component diagram language. Dynamic aspects of behavior can be modeled either with the activity diagram language, sequence diagrams or state machine models, and a static decomposition of a system's functions can be expressed by interaction diagrams and use-case models. Newer versions of the UML contain further languages...................21, 28, 52, 67, 141, 170, 314

Uniform resource identifier (URI) A string value, which uniquely identifies an electronic resource, to make it distinguishable and accessible among other electronic resources. URIs start with a scheme identifier, which denotes how a following string encodes information about the resource. URIs may be structured hierarchically, with "/" characters separating levels of hierarchy in the resource identification. Depending on the scheme used, the information encoded in the URI may be consulted to actually retrieve the denote resource, e. g., when URIs make use of the `http://`-scheme to denote resource that can be downloaded via the internet........ 21, 146, 200

Web Services Description Language (WSDL) A formal language to describe services, interfaces, operations and their parameters of participating software components in a SOA..21, 218

Workflow management system (WfMS) A software system for coordinating process executions, usually involving multiple human and technical actors.... 21, 114, 134, 170

Workflow model (WfM) A formal description of procedural steps in a process, which can be parsed and executed by a workflow engine. A workflow model contains technical detail information about how to invoke software functionality in each workflow step, and how to continue with the workflow after a workflow step has finished. 21, 53

World Wide Web (WWW) A client-server application infrastructure in the internet for ubiquitous, multi-purpose data exchange................................21, 315

XML Metadata Interchange (XMI) An XML dialect for serializing model instances, conforming to specified meta-models...................................21, 281

XML Process Definition Language (XPDL) A workflow description language for describing executable process types. Using a corresponding workflow engine as an interpreter, process descriptions given in XPDL can be executed like any program in a programming language. Recent versions of the XPDL standard provide the entire semantics as it is introduced by the visual BPMN modeling standard, which makes XPDL the primary semantic underpinning for BPMN...............21, 80

XML Schema Definition (XSD) An XML dialect for specifying XML document types. XSD comes with a large set of built-in base types, and provides sophisticated mechanism to specify complex XML document types based on this type system. Having an XSD at hand, an XML document instance can be validated against it, to test whether it conforms to the syntax by the schema. XSD is an XML dialect itself, which means the language could be recursively applied to describe its own declaration syntax.

References

[Act]   Activiti Development Team. Activiti BPM Platform. http://www.activiti.org/.

[AG08]   João Paulo A. Almeida and Giancarlo Guizzardi. A Semantic Foundation for Role-Related Concepts in Enterprise Modelling. In V. Tosic, K. M. Goeshka, A. van Moorsel, and R. Wong, editors, *Enterprise Distributed Object Computing Conference, 2008. EDOC '08. 12th International IEEE*, 2008.

[ANT]   ANTLR Project. ANTLR Parser Generator. http://www.antlr.org/.

[Apaa]   Apache Software Foundation. Apache Subversion. Open source version control system. http://subversion.apache.org/.

[Apab]   Apache Software Foundation. Apache Tomcat. Open source implementation of the Java Servlet and JavaServer Pages technologies. http://tomcat.apache.org/.

[BAPC08]   Salah Baïna1, Pierre-Yves Ansias, Michaël Petit, and Annick Castiaux. Strategic Business/IT Alignment using Goal Models. In *Proceedings of the Third International Workshop on Business/IT Alignment and Interoperability (BUSITAL'08)*, 2008.

[Bau99]   Phillipe Baumard. *Tacit Knowledge in Organizations*. Sage Publications, London, 1999.

[BBR11]   Stephan Buchwald, Thomas Bauer, and Manfred Reichert. *Bridging the Gap Between Business Process Models and Service Composition Specifications*, pages 124–153. IGI Global, Hershey, 2011.

[BD09]   Paul Beynon-Davies. *Business Information Systems*. Palgrave, Basingstoke, 2009.

[BD10]   Bernd Bruegge and Allen H. Dutoit. *Object-oriented software engineering: using UML, patterns, and Java*. Prentice Hall, Upper Saddle River, 2010.

[BDG+00]   Michael Brundage, Patrick Dengler, Jeff Gabriel, Andy Hoskinson, Michael Kay, Thomas Maxwell, Marcelo Ochoa, Johnny Papa, and Mohan Vanmane. *Professional XML Databases*. Wrox Press, Indianapolis, 2000.

[Ber94]   John Berge. *The EDIFACT Standards*. Blackwell, Oxford, 2nd edition, 1994.

[Ber03]   Hans Bergsten. *Java Server Pages*. O'Reilly, Sebastopol, CA, 3rd edition, 2003.

[BFV+11]   Thomas Barth, Thomas Fielenbach, Pedro G. Villanueva, Mohamed Bourimi, and Dogan Kesdogan. Supporting Distributed Decision Making Using Secure Distributed User Interfaces. In *Proceedings of Distributed User Interfaces CHI Workshop*, 2011.

[BJR99]   Grady Booch, Ivar Jacobson, and James Rumbaugh. *The Unified Modeling Language Reference Manual*. Addison-Wesley, Reading, MA, 1999.

[BLW96]   Sjaak Brinkkemper, Kalle Lyytinen, and Richard J. Welke. Method engineering: principles of method construction and tool support. In *Proceedings of the IFIP TC8, WG8.1/8.2 Working Conference on Method Engineering*, Berlin, 1996. Springer.

[Bon]   BonitaSoft. Bonita Open Solution – Open Source Business Process Management and Workflow Software. http://www.bonitasoft.com/.

[CE00]   Krysztof Czarnecki and Ulrich W. Eisenecker. *Generative Programming*. Addison-Wesley, Reading, MA, 2000.

[cL]   casewise Ltd.   Corporate Modeler Suite.   `http://www.casewise.com/Products/CorporateModelerSuite/`.

[CR08]   Eric Clayberg and Dan Rubel. *Eclipse: Building Commercial-Quality Plug-ins*. Addison-Wesley Longman, Amsterdam, 2008.

[CSW08]   Tony Clark, Paul Sammut, and James Willans. *Applied Metamodelling: A Foundation For Language Driven Development*. Ceteva, 2nd edition, 2008.

[Daf09]   Richard L. Daft. *Organization Theory and Design*. South-Western College Publishing, Cincinatti, Ohio, 10th edition, 2009.

[DBLV09]   Pete Deemer, Gabrielle Benefield, Craig Larman, and Bas Vodde. The Scrum Primer, 2009. `http://scrumfoundation.com/library`.

[DDnHS99]   Weimin Du, Jim Davis, Yan nong Huang, and Ming-Chien Shan. Enterprise Workflow Resource Management. Technical Report HPL-1999-8, Software Technology Laboratory HP Laboratories, Palo Alto, 1999.

[Dia10]   Michel Diaz, editor. *Petri Nets: Fundamental Models, Verification and Applications*. John Wiley & Sons, Hoboken (NJ), 2010.

[Dub03]   Micah Dubinko. *XForms Essentials*. O'Reilly, Sebastopol, CA, 2003.

[DvdA04]   Juliane Dehnert and Wil M. P. van der Aalst. Bridging the gap between business models and workflow specifications. *International Journal of Cooperative Information Systems*, 13(3):289–323, 2004.

[DvdAtH05] Marlon Dumas, Wil M. P. van der Aalst, and Arthur H. ter Hofstede. *Process-Aware Information Systems: Bridging People and Software Through Process Technology*. Wiley, Hoboken, NJ, 2005.

[Ecla]   Eclipse Foundation.   Eclipse Modeling Framework (EMF).   `http://www.eclipse.org/modeling/emf/`.

[Eclb]   Eclipse Foundation. Eclipse Platform. `http://www.eclipse.org/`.

[Eclc]   Eclipse Foundation. Xpand – statically typed template language. `http://www.eclipse.org/modeling/m2t/?project=xpand`.

[Ecld]   Eclipse Foundation. Xtext - Language Development Framework. `http://www.eclipse.org/Xtext/`.

[Erl06]   Thomas Erl. *Service-oriented Architecture: Concepts, Technology, and Desing*. Pearson Education, Upper Saddle River, NJ, 2006.

[FC08]   Joaquim Filipe and José Cordiero, editors.   *Enterprise Information Systems*, Berlin/Heidelberg, 2008. Springer.   10th International Conference ICEIS 2008, Barcelona, Spain, June 2008.

[FFK⁺11]   Dirk Fahland, Cédric Favre, Jana Koehler, Niels Lohmann, Hagen Völzer, and Karsten Wolf. Analysis on Demand: Instantaneous Soundness Checking of Industrial Business Process Models. *Data & Knowledge Engineering*, 70(5):448–466, 2011.

[FHK+09]   Ulrich Frank, David Heise, Heiko Kattenstroth, Donald Ferguson, Ethan Hadar, and
            Marvin Waschke. ITML: A Domain-Specific Modeling Language for Supporting
            Business Driven IT Management. In Juha-Pekka Tolvanen, Matti Rossi, J. Gray, and
            J. Sprinkle, editors, *Proceedings of the 9th OOPSLA workshop on domain-specific
            modeling (DSM)*, Helsinki, 2009.

[FKC07]   D. F. Ferraiolo, D. R. Kuhn, and R. Chandramouli. *Role Based Access Control*.
            Artech House, London, Boston, 2nd edition, 2007.

[Fra94]   Ulrich Frank. MEMO: A Tool Supported Methodology for Analyzing and
            (Re-)Designing Business Information Systems. In R. Ege, M. Singh, and B. Meyer,
            editors, *Technology of Object-Oriented Languages and Systems*, pages 367–380, Up-
            per Saddle River, 1994. Prentice Hall.

[Fra02]   Ulrich Frank. Multi-Perspective Enterprise Modeling (MEMO) – Conceptual Frame-
            work and Modeling Languages. In *Proceedings of the Hawaii International Confer-
            ence on System Sciences (HICSS-35)*, page 72, Honolulu, 2002.

[Fra06]   Ulrich Frank. Towards a Pluralistic Conception of Research Methods in Informa-
            tion Systems Research. Technical Report 7, ICB Institute for Computer Science
            and Business Information Systems, University of Duisburg-Essen, Essen, December
            2006.

[Fra08]   Ulrich Frank. The MEMO Meta Modelling Language. Technical Report 24, ICB
            Institute for Computer Science and Business Information Systems, University of
            Duisburg-Essen, Essen, 2008.

[Fra10]   Ulrich Frank. Outline of a Method for Designing Domain-Specific Modelling Lan-
            guages. Technical Report 39, ICB Institute for Computer Science and Business In-
            formation Systems, University of Duisburg-Essen, Essen, May 2010.

[Fra11a]   Ulrich Frank. MEMO Organisation Modelling Language 1: Focus on Organisational
            Structure. Technical Report 48, ICB Institute for Computer Science and Business
            Information Systems, University of Duisburg-Essen, Essen, December 2011.

[Fra11b]   Ulrich Frank. MEMO Organisation Modelling Language 2: Focus on Business Pro-
            cesses. Technical Report 49, ICB Institute for Computer Science and Business In-
            formation Systems, University of Duisburg-Essen, Essen, December 2011.

[Fra11c]   Ulrich Frank. MEMO Organisation Modelling Language $OrgML$ Requirements
            and Core Diagram Types. Technical Report 47, ICB Institute for Computer Science
            and Business Information Systems, University of Duisburg-Essen, Essen, December
            2011.

[Fra11d]   Ulrich Frank. Multi-Perspective Enterprise Modelling: Background and Terminolog-
            ical Foundation. Technical Report 46, ICB Institute for Computer Science and Busi-
            ness Information Systems, University of Duisburg-Essen, Essen, December 2011.

[Fra12]   Ulrich Frank. Multi-perspective enterprise modeling: foundational concepts,
            prospects and future research challenges. *Software and Systems Modeling*, August
            2012.

[FS09]   Ulrich Frank and Stefan Strecker. Beyond ERP Systems: An Outline of Self-
            Referential Enterprise Systems. Technical Report 31, ICB Institute for Computer
            Science and Business Information Systems, University of Duisburg-Essen, Essen,
            April 2009.

[GBKK12]   Jens Gulden, Thomas Barth, Dogan Kesdogan, and Fatih Karatas.   Erhöhung der Sicherheit von Lebensmittelwarenketten durch Modell-getriebene Prozess-Implementierung.   In Dirk Christian Mattfeld and Susanne Robra-Bissantz, editors, *Tagungsband der Multikonferenz Wirtschaftsinformatik 2012*, pages 2061–2072, Berlin, 2012. GITO Verlag.

[GF10]   Jens Gulden and Ulrich Frank. MEMOCenterNG – A full-featured modeling environment for organisation modeling and model-driven software development. In Pnina Soffer and Erik Proper, editors, *Proceedings of the CAiSE Forum 2010 Hammamet, Tunisia, June 9-11, 2010*, volume 592 of *CEUR Workshop Proceedings*, pages 76–83. CEUR, 2010. ISSN 1613-0073.

[GH09]   Wim Van Grembergen and Steven De Haes. *Enterprise Governance of IT: Achieving Strategic Alignment and Value*. Springer, New York, 2009.

[GHJV94]   Erich Gamma, Richard Helm, Ralph Johnson, and John Vlissides. *Design Patterns. Elements of Reusable Object-Oriented Software*. Addison-Wesley Longman, Amsterdam, 1994.

[GL06]   Volker Gruhn and Ralf Laue.   Complexity Metrics for Business Process Models. In *9th International Conference on Business Information Systems (BIS 2006)*, volume 85 of *Lecture Notes in Informatics (LNI)*, pages 1–12, 2006.

[GPZ11]   Constantinos Giannoulis, Michaël Petit, and Jelena Zdravkovic.   Modeling Competition-Driven Business Strategy for Business IT Alignment. In Camille Salinesi and Oscar Pastor, editors, *Advanced Information Systems Engineering Workshops*, pages 16–28, Berlin Heidelberg, 2011. Springer.

[Gro04]   The Open Group. TOGAF – The Open Group Architecture Framework. Version 8.1 "Enterprise Edition", 2004.

[Gro09a]   Richard C. Gronback. *Eclipse Modeling Project: A Domain-Specific Language (DSL) Toolkit*. Addison-Wesley Longman, Amsterdam, 2009.

[Gro09b]   The Open Group. SOA Reference Architecture, 2009.

[Gru02]   Volker Gruhn. Process-centered software engineering environments. A brief history and future challenges. *Annals of Software Engineering*, 14(1–4):363–382, 2002.

[Gul09]   Jens Gulden. Minimal invasive generative Entwicklung von Modellierungswerkzeugen. In S. Fischer, E. Maehle, and R. Reischuk, editors, *Tagungsband der Konferenz INFORMATIK 2009, Lübeck, 28.9.2009 - 2.10.2009*, 2009.

[HC06]   Mary Jo Hatch and Ann L. Cunliffe. *Organization Theory: Modern, Symbolic, and Postmodern Perspectives*. Oxford University Press, Oxford, 2nd edition, 2006.

[HMP04]   Alan R. Hevner, Salvatore T. March, and Jinsoo Park. Design Science in Information Systems Research. *MIS Quarterly*, 28(1):75–105, March 2004.

[Hum48]   David Hume. *An Enquiry Concerning Human Understanding*. A. Millar, London, 1748.

[HV93]   John C. Henderson and N. Venkatraman. Strategic Alignment: Leveraging Information Technology for Transforming Organizations. *IBM Systems Journal*, 32(1):4–16, 1993.

[Ini11]   Business Process Management Initiative. Business Process Modeling Notation 2.0 (BPMN 2.0), 2011.

[JBo11]   JBoss Community team. jBPM – Business Process Management (BPM) Suite, 2011. `http://www.jboss.org/jbpm`.

[JC04]   Jinyoung Jang and Yongsun Choi. Web Service Based Universal Management of Workflow Resources. In *Proceedings of the Fourth International Conference on Electronic Business (ICEB2004), Beijing*, 2004.

[JJM09]   Manfred A. Jeusfeld, Matthias Jarke, and John Mylopoulos, editors. *Metamodeling for Method Engineering*. MIT Press, Cambridge, 2009.

[Jun04]   Jürgen Jung. Mapping of Business Process Models to Workflow Schemata – an Example using MEMO-OrgML and XPDL. Technical Report 47, Universität Koblenz-Landau, Koblenz, April 2004.

[Jun07]   Jürgen Jung. *Entwurf einer Sprache für die Modellierung von Ressourcen im Kontext der Geschäftsprozessmodellierung*. PhD thesis, Universität Duisburg-Essen, Berlin, 2007.

[Kle08]   A. Kleppe. *Software Language Engineering: Creating Domain-Specific Languages Using Metamodels*. Addison-Wesley Professional, Reading, 2008.

[Köh12]   Christian Alexander Köhling. *Entwurf einer konzeptuellen Modellierungsmethode zur Unterstützung rationaler Zielplanungsprozesse in Unternehmen*. PhD thesis, Universität Duisburg-Essen, Essen, 2012.

[Kro07]   John Krogstie. *Modelling of the People, by the People, for the People*, pages 305–318. Springer, Berlin Heidelberg, 2007.

[Kru03]   Philippe Kruchten. *The Rational Unified Process: An Introduction*. Addison-Wesley, Upper Saddle River, 3rd edition, 2003.

[KT08]   Steven Kelly and Juha-Pekka Tolvanen. *Domain Specific Modeling: enabling full code-generation*. Wiley, 2008.

[Lan09]   Marc Lankhorst. *Enterprise Architecture at Work - Modelling, Communication and Analysis*. Springer, Berlin Heidelberg, 2009.

[LHM90]   James R. Lewis, Suzanne C. Henry, and Robert L. Mack. Integrated Office Software Benchmarks: A Case Study. In D. Diaper et al., editors, *INTERACT '90 – Proceedings of the IFIP TC13 Third Interational Conference on Human-Computer Interaction*, Amsterdam, 1990. Elsevier Science Publishers B.V.

[LKT04]   Janne Luoma, Steven Kelly, and Juha-Pekka Tolvanen. Defining Domain-Specific Modeling Languages: Collected Experiences. In *Proceedings of the 4th OOPSLA Workshop on Domain-Specific Modeling (DSM04)*, 2004.

[LPW$^+$09] Martin Op't Land, Erik Proper, Maarten Waage, Jeroen Cloo, and Claudia Steghuis. *Enterprise Architecture*. Springer, Berlin Heidelberg, 2009.

[Mar00]   Chris Marshall. *Enterprise Modeling With UML: Designing Successful Software Through Business Analysis*. Addison-Wesley Professional, Boston, 2000.

[Men06]   Jan Mendling. Business Process Execution Language for Web Service (BPEL). *EMISA Forum*, 26(2):5–8, 2006.

[MLZ08]   Jan Mendling, Kristian Bisgaard Lassen, and Uwe Zdun. On the Transformation of Control Flow between Block-Oriented and Graph-Oriented Process Modeling Languages. *International Journal of Business Process Integration and Management (IJBPIM). Special Issue on Model-Driven Engineering of Executable Business Process Models*, 3(2):96–108, 2008.

[MS11]   Ganna Monakova and Andreas Schaad. Visualizing security in business processes. In *SACMAT '11 Proceedings of the 16th ACM symposium on Access control models and technologies*, pages 147–148, New York, 2011. ACM.

[MVM10]   Frederic P. Miller, Agnes F. Vandome, and John McBrewster, editors. *Extended Backus-Naur Form*. Alphascript Publishing, Beau Bassin, 2010.

[NS73]   I. Nassi and B. Shneiderman. Flowchart Techniques for Structured Programming. *ACM SIGPLAN Notices*, 8:12–26, August 1973.

[NS07]   Kioumars Namiri and Nenad Stojanovic. Using Control Patterns in Business Processes Compliance. *4832*, pages 178–190, 2007.

[OAS07]   OASIS Web Services Business Process Execution Language (WSBPEL) Technical Committee. Web Services Business Process Execution Language Version 2.0, 2007. http://docs.oasis-open.org/wsbpel/2.0/OS/wsbpel-v2.0-OS.html.

[Obj03]   Object Management Group. MDA Guide Version 1.0.1, 2003. http://www.omg.org/mda.

[Obj08]   Object Management Group. Meta Object Facility (MOF) 2.0 Query/View/Transformation Specification, 2008. http://www.omg.org/spec/QVT/1.0/PDF.

[ODvdA⁺09]   Chung Ouyang, Marlon Dumas, Wil M. P. van der Aalst, Arthur H. ter Hofstede, and Jan Mendling. From Business Process Models to Process-oriented Software Systems. *ACM Transactions on Software Engineering and Methodology (TOSEM)*, 19(1):1–37, 2009.

[Org10a]   Organization for the Advancement of Structured Information Standards (OASIS). Web Services – Human Task (WS-HumanTask) Specification Version 1.1, 2010. http://docs.oasis-open.org/bpel4people/ws-humantask-1.1.html.

[Org10b]   Organization for the Advancement of Structured Information Standards (OASIS). WS-BPEL Extension for People (BPEL4People) Specification Version 1.1, 2010. http://docs.oasis-open.org/bpel4people/bpel4people-1.1-spec-cs-01.pdf.

[PHB06]   Alexander Pretschner, Manuel Hilty, and David Basin. Distributed usage control. *Communications of the ACM - Privacy and security in highly dynamic systems*, 49, 2006.

[Put88]   Hilary Putnam. *Representation and Reality*. MIT Press, Cambridge, Mass., 1988.

[PW09]   Neil Pollock and Robin Williams. *Software and Organisations: The Biography of the Enterprise-wide System Or How Sap Conquered the World*. Taylor & Francis, Florence, Kentucky, 2009.

[Ras97]   Lars Rasmusson. Decentralized Coordination for Open Distributed Systems. Technical report, SICS Intelligent Systems Laboratory, 1997.

[Rat01]   Rational Software. Rational Unified Process Best Practices for Software Development Teams, 2001.

[RDB⁺08]   Julian Reichwald, Tim Dörnemann, Thomas Barth, Manfred Grauer, and Bernd Freisleben. Model-Driven Process Development Incorporating Human Tasks in Service-Oriented Grid Environments. In Martin Bichler, Thomas Hess, Helmut Krcmar, Ulrike Lechner, Florian Matthes, Arnold Picot, Benjamin Speitkamp, and Petra Wolf, editors, *Multikonferenz Wirtschaftsinformatik 2008*, pages 79–90, Berlin, 2008. GITO-Verlag.

[Res]   Research Group for Information Systems and Enterprise Modeling, Prof. Dr. Ulrich Frank. MEMOCenterNG. http://www.wi-inf.uni-duisburg-essen.de/FGFrank/index.php?lang=de&&groupId=1&&contentType=Project&&projId=19.

[RG03]   Raghu Ramakrishnan and Johannes Gehrke. *Database Management Systems*. Mcgraw-Hill Professional, New York, 3rd edition, 2003.

[Rit07]   Peter Rittgen. *Enterprise Modeling And Computing With UML*. Idea Group Inc. (IGI), Hershey, PA, 2007.

[RM06]   Jan Recker and Jan Mendling. On the Translation between BPMN and BPEL: Conceptual Mismatch between Process Modeling Languages. In Thibaud Latour and Michael Petit, editors, *CAiSE 2006 Workshop Proceedings - Eleventh International Workshop on Exploring Modeling Methods in Systems Analysis and Design (EMMSAD 2006)*, pages 521–532, 2006.

[RMB01]   William A. Ruh, Francis X. Maginnis, and William J. Brown. *Enterprise Application Integration*. Wiley, Hoboken, NJ, 2001.

[RMvdAR06]   Jan Recker, Jan Mendling, Wil M. P. van der Aalst, and Michael Rosemann. Model-Driven Enterprise Systems Configuration. In E. Dubois and K. Pohl, editors, *Proceedings of the 18th Conference on Advanced Information Systems Engineering (CAiSE 2006)*, number 4001 in Lecture Notes in Computer Science Volume, pages 369–383, Luxembourg, 2006. Springer.

[Rol00]   Asbjørn Rolstadås. *Enterprise Modeling: Improving Global Industrial Competitiveness*. Kluwer Academic Publishers, Dordrecht, 2000.

[Rüc11]   Bernd Rücker. Activiti 5 Open Source BPM, 2011. Invited talk on 2011-10-07 at Technical University Berlin, as part of the conference INFORMATIK 2011.

[RvdA07]   Nick Russell and Wil M.P. van der Aalst. Evaluation of the BPEL4People and WS-HumanTask Extensions to WS-BPEL 2.0 using the Workflow Resource Patterns. Technical Report BPM-07-11, BPMcenter.org, 2007.

[RvL11]   Tijs Rademakers and Ron van Liempd. *Activiti in Action*. Manning, Greenwich, 2011.

[SAP07]   SAP. *SAP Standardized Technical Architecture Modeling (SAP-TAM)*, 2007.

[SBPM09]   Dave Steinberg, Frank Budinsky, Marcelo Paternostro, and Ed Merks. *Eclipse Modeling Framework*. Addison Wesley, Amsterdam, 2nd edition, 2009.

[Sch02a]   Stephen R. Schach. *Object-oriented and classical software engineering*. McGraw-Hill, New York, 2002.

[Sch02b]   August Wilhelm Scheer. *ARIS – Vom Geschäftsprozess zum Anwendungssystem.* Springer, Berlin, 4th edition, 2002.

[SFHK11]   Stefan Strecker, Ulrich Frank, David Heise, and Heiko Kattenstroth. MetricM: A modeling method in support of the reflective design and use of performance measurement systems. *Information Systems and e-Business Management*, 2011.

[SFK00]   Ravi Sandhu, David Ferraiolo, and Richard Kuhn. The NIST Model for Role-Based Access Control: Towards A Unified Standard. In *Proceedings of the 5th ACM Workshop on Role Based Access Control, July 26-27, 2000, Berlin*, pages 47–63, 2000.

[SK08]   Ahmad K. Shuja and Jochen Krebs. *IBM Rational Unified Process Reference and Certification Guide.* IBM Press, Upper Saddle River, 2008.

[SM06]   Carlo Simon and Jan Mendling. Verification of Forbidden Behavior in EPCs. In Heinrich C. Mayr and Ruth Brey, editors, *Modellierung 2006*, volume P-82 of *Lecture Notes in Informatics (LNI)*, pages 233–242, 2006.

[SN00]   August-Wilhelm Scheer and Markus Nüttgens. *ARIS Architecture and Reference Models for Business Process Management.* Lecture Notes in Computer Science. Springer, Berlin, Heidelberg, 2000.

[Sof]   Software AG. Aris Toolset. `http://aris.softwareag.com/`.

[SS05]   August-Wilhelm Scheer and Kristof Schneider. ARIS – Architecture of Integrated Information Systems. In Peter Bernus, Kai Mertins, and Günter Schmidt, editors, *Handbook on Architectures of Information Systems*, pages 605–623. Springer, Berlin, Heidelberg, 2005.

[SSMB11]   Sigrid Schefer, Mark Strembeck, Jan Mendling, and Anne Baumgrass. Detecting and Resolving Conflicts of Mutual-Exclusion and Binding Constraints in a Business Process Context. In *19th International Conference on Cooperative Information Systems (CoopIS 2011)*, Crete, Greece, 2011.

[STH10]   Lambert M. Surhone, Mariam T. Tennoe, and Susan F. Henssonow, editors. *Bonita Open Solution.* Betascript Publishing, 2010.

[Tha00]   Bernhard Thalheim. *Entity-Relationship Modeling: Foundations of Database Technology.* Springer, Berlin Heidelberg, 2000.

[Tid01]   Doug Tidwell. *XSLT.* O'Reilly Media, Sebastopol, 2001.

[TvS03]   Andrew S. Tanenbaum and Maarten van Steen. *Distributed Systems. Principles and Paradigms.* Prentice Hall, Upper Saddle River, 2003.

[vdAvH04]   Wil M. P. van der Aalst and Kees Max van Hee. *Workflow Management: Models, Methods, and Systems.* MIT Press, Cambridge (MA), 2004.

[vDMvdA06]   B. F. van Dongen, Jan Mendling, and Wil M. P. van der Aalst. Structural Patterns for Soundness of Business Process Models. In *Proceedings of the Tenth IEEE International Enterprise Computing Conference (EDOC 2006), October, 16-20, Hong Kong, China*, pages 116–128, Washington, D.C., 2006. IEEE Computer Society.

[vdV02]   Eric van der Vlist. *XML Schema.* O'Reilly, Cambridge, 2002.

[Ver96]   F. Vernadat. *Enterprise Modeling and Integration: Principles and Applications.* Chapman & Hall, London, 1996.

[Wal92]   Jean-Baptiste Waldner. *Principles of Computer-Integrated Manufacturing.* Wiley, Hoboken, NJ, 1992.

[Wes07]   Mathias Weske. *Business Process Management: Concepts, Languages, Architectures.* Springer, Berlin Heidelberg, 2007.

[WHM08a]   Ingo Weber, Jörg Hoffmann, and Jan Mendling. Beyond soundness: On the semantic consistency of executable process models. In *ECOWS'08: Proceedings of the 6th IEEE European Conference on Web Services*, pages 102–111, 2008.

[WHM08b]   Ingo Weber, Jörg Hoffmann, and Jan Mendling. Beyond Soundness: On the Verification of Semantic Business Process Models. *Distributed and Parallel Databases (DAPD)*, 27(3):271–343, 2008.

[WHMN07]   Ingo Weber, Jörg Hoffmann, Jan Mendling, and Jörg Nitzsche. Towards a Methodology for Semantic Business Process Modeling and Configuration. In *Proc. of the 2nd International SeMSoC Workshop on Business Oriented Aspects concerning Semantics and Methodologies in Service-oriented Computing (SeMSoC 2007) at the 5th International Conference on Service Oriented Computing (ICSOC 2007)*, Vienna, 2007.

[Win02]   Robert Winter. Business Strategy Modelling in the Information Age. In *Proceedings of the 3rd international web conference*, Perth, 2002.

[WMB$^+$03]   Rolf T. Wigand, Peter Mertens, Freimut Bodendorf, Wolfgang König, Arnold Picot, and Matthias Schumann. *Introduction to Business Information Systems.* Springer, Berlin, 2003.

[XSS$^+$04]   Steven Xia, David Sun, Chengzheng Sun, David Chen, and Haifeng Shen. Leveraging single-user applications for multi-user collaboration. In *CSCW '04 Proceedings of the 2004 ACM conference on Computer supported cooperative work*, New York, 2004. ACM.

[Zac87]   J. A. Zachman. A framework for information systems architecture. *IBM Systems Journal*, 26(3):277–293, 1987.

[Zie10]   Jörg Ziemann. *Architecture of Interoperable Information Systems.* Logos, Berlin, 2010.

[zM99]   Michael zur Mühlen. Resource Modeling in Workflow Applications. In Jörg Becker, Michael zur Mühlen, and Michael Rosemann, editors, *Proceedings of the 1999 Workflow Management Conference (WFM99)*, pages 137–153, Münster, 1999.

[ZSZ11]   Iyad Zikra, Janis Stirna, and Jelena Zdravkovic. Bringing Enterprise Modeling Closer to Model-Driven Development. In *The Practice of Enterprise Modeling, 4th IFIP WG 8.1 Working Conference, PoEM 2011 Oslo, Norway, November 2-3, 2011 Proceedings*, volume 92 of *Lecture Notes in Business Information Processing*, pages 268–282. Springer, 2011.

Visit `http://www.seem-method.info/` to access updates and software resources provided with this book.